Rock Inscriptions and Graffiti Project

SOCIETY OF BIBLICAL LITERATURE
Resources for Biblical Study

Edited by
Marvin A. Sweeney

Number 29
Rock Inscriptions and Graffiti Project
Volume 2

Edited by
Michael E. Stone

ROCK INSCRIPTIONS AND GRAFFITI PROJECT

Catalogue of Inscriptions

Volume 2

Inscriptions 3001-6000

Edited by
Michael E. Stone

Editorial Assistant
Leslie Avital Kobayashi

Scholars Press
Atlanta, Georgia

Rock Inscriptions and Graffiti Project

Library of Congress Cataloging-in-Publication Data
Rock inscriptions and graffiti project: catalogue of inscriptions/
compiled and edited by Michael E. Stone; editorial assistant,
Leslie Avital Kobayashi.
p. cm. — (Resources for biblical study; no. 28-<29 >)
Includes bibliographical references and index.
Contents: v. 1. Inscriptions 1-3000 — v. 2. Inscriptions 3001-6000.
ISBN 1-55540-790-0 (v. 1) (alk. paper). — ISBN 1-55540-791-9 (v. 1) (pbk.: alk. paper). — ISBN 1-55540-792-7 (v. 2) (alk. paper). -- ISBN 1-55540-793-5 (v. 2) (pbk.: alk. paper)
1. Inscriptions—Palestine—Catalogs. 2. Inscriptions—Egypt--Sinai—Catalogs. 3. Bible—Antiquities—Catalogs. 4. Graffiti--Palestine—Antiquities—Catalogs. 7. Sinai (Egypt)—Antiquities-Catalogs. I. Stone, Michael E., 1938- . II. Series.
CN753.P19R6 1992
933—dc20
92-33418
CIP

Printed in the United States of America
on acid-free paper

Alphabetic List of Special Abbreviations

CIS indicates *Corpus Inscriptionum Semiticarum*. In **Corpus** it is cited by volume, part, page and inscription number.

Euting refers to Julius Euting, *Sinaïtische Inscriften* (Berlin: Georg Reimer, 1891). It is cited in **Access** by section number and in **Corpus** by plate and inscription number.

TABLE OF CONTENTS

CATALOGUE OF INSCRIPTIONS

Inscription **3001**
Site Jebel Sirbal, Wadi Ajaleh, #188
Condition good
Content Nabatean inscription
šlm ʾʿlʾ
br ʿmyw
Access II.2a.37 (printed, CIS)
Corpus CIS 1784

Inscription **3002**
Site Jebel Sirbal, Wadi Ajaleh, #188
Condition good
Content Nabatean inscription
šlm hʾnṭl[w br]
pṣy
bṭb
Access II.2a.37 (printed, CIS)
Corpus CIS 1785

Inscription **3003**
Site Jebel Sirbal, Wadi Ajaleh, #188
Condition good
Content Nabatean inscription
šlm ʾlktyw br ʿbdʾlbʿly
Access II.2a.37 (printed, CIS)
Corpus CIS 1786

Inscription **3004**
Site Jebel Sirbal, Wadi Ajaleh, #188
Condition poor
Content Nabatean inscription
šlm [ḥn]ʾ[w br n]šnky[h]
Comment *reconstruction doubtful*
Access II.2a.37 (printed, CIS)
Corpus CIS 1787

Inscription **3005**
Site Jebel Sirbal, Wadi Ajaleh, #188
Condition good
Content Nabatean inscription
šlm ʿmmw br
ʿbdʾlbʿly br wʾl[w]
Access II.2a.37 (printed, CIS)
Corpus CIS 1788

Inscription **3006**
Site Jebel Sirbal, Wadi Ajaleh, #188
Condition good
Content Nabatean inscription
šlm
ʿbdʾlbʿly
br wkylw bṭb
Access II.2a.37 (printed, CIS)
Corpus CIS 1789

Inscription **3007**
Site Jebel Sirbal, Wadi Ajaleh, #188
Condition good
Content Nabatean inscription
šlm ʿbdʾlhy
br ʿmyw
Access II.2a.37 (printed, CIS)
Corpus CIS 1790

Inscription **3008**
Site Jebel Sirbal, Wadi Ajaleh, #188
Condition good
Content Nabatean inscription
šlm
ḥryšw br
ʿbdʾlbʿly br [wdw]
ḥryš[w]
Access II.2a.37 (printed, CIS)
Corpus CIS 1791

Inscription **3009**
Site Jebel Sirbal, Wadi Ajaleh, #188
Condition good
Content Nabatean inscription
šlm šmrḥ
br kʿmh
Access II.2a.37 (printed, CIS)
Corpus CIS 1792

Inscription **3010**
Site Jebel Sirbal, Wadi Ajaleh, #188
Condition good
Content Nabatean inscription
šlm šmrḥ
br ʿmnw
Access II.2a.38 (printed, CIS)
Corpus CIS 1793

Inscription **3011**
Site Jebel Sirbal, Wadi Ajaleh, #188
Condition fair
Content Nabatean inscription
šlm ʿbydw br ....
Access II.2a.38 (printed, CIS)
Corpus CIS 1794

Inscription **3012**
Site Jebel Sirbal, Wadi Ajaleh, #188
Condition good
Content Nabatean inscription
šlm ʾwšw
br ʿbydw
Access II.2a.38 (printed, CIS)
Corpus CIS 1795

Inscription 3013
Site Jebel Sirbal, Wadi Ajaleh, #188
Condition fair
Content Nabatean inscription
šlm ʿbdʾlbʿly
[br wk]ylw bṭb
Access II.2a.38 (printed, CIS)
Corpus CIS 1796

Inscription 3014
Site Jebel Sirbal, Wadi Ajaleh, #188
Condition good
Content Nabatean inscription
šlm ʿmrw
br ḥnṭlw
Access II.2a.39 (printed, CIS)
Corpus CIS 1797

Inscription 3015
Site Jebel Sirbal, Wadi Ajaleh, #188
Condition good
Content Nabatean inscription
šlm ʿbdʾlbʿly br ḥryšw
Access II.2a.39 (printed, CIS)
Corpus CIS 1798

Inscription 3016
Site Jebel Sirbal, Wadi Ajaleh, #188
Condition good
Content Nabatean inscription
šlm mʿnw br
hnʾw
Access II.2a.39 (printed, CIS)
Corpus CIS 1799

Inscription 3017
Site Jebel Sirbal, Wadi Ajaleh, #188
Condition fair
Content Nabatean inscription
šlm ʾwšw
br pʾrn
....
Access II.2a.39 (printed, CIS)
Corpus CIS 1800

Inscription 3018
Site Jebel Sirbal, Wadi Ajaleh, #188
Condition fair
Content Nabatean inscription
.... ḥryšw bṭb
šlm ḥnṭlw br gʾ[ny]w
Access II.2a.39 (printed, CIS)
Corpus CIS 1801

Inscription 3019
Site Jebel Sirbal, Wadi Ajaleh, #188
Condition fair
Content Nabatean inscription
šlm ʿbdʾlbʿl[y]
šlm ʾwš[w] br wʾlw
Access II.2a.39 (printed, CIS)
Corpus CIS 1802

Inscription 3020
Site Jebel Sirbal, Wadi Ajaleh, #188
Condition good
Content Nabatean inscription
šlm ḥnṭlw br nšygw
Access II.2a.39 (printed, CIS)
Corpus CIS 1803

Inscription 3021
Site Jebel Sirbal, Wadi Ajaleh, #188
Condition fair
Content Nabatean inscription
šlm šmrḥ ....
Access II.2a.39 (printed, CIS)
Corpus CIS 1804

Inscription 3022
Site Jebel Sirbal, Wadi Ajaleh, #188
Condition good
Content Nabatean inscription
šlm ʾlktyw br ʿb[d]ʾlbʿly
Access II.2a.39 (printed, CIS)
Corpus CIS 1805

Inscription 3023
Site Jebel Sirbal, Wadi Ajaleh, #188
Condition good
Content Nabatean inscription
šlm ʾwšw br bṭšw
Access II.2a.40 (printed, CIS)
Corpus CIS 1806

Inscription 3024
Site Jebel Sirbal, Wadi Ajaleh, #188
Condition good
Content Nabatean inscription
šlm ʾwš[w] br ḥryšw
Access II.2a.40 (printed, CIS)
Corpus CIS 1807

Inscription 3025
Site Jebel Sirbal, Wadi Ajaleh, #188
Condition fair
Content Nabatean inscription
šlm wʾlw
br ʾlmbqrw
...w [w]ḥlṣt brh
Access II.2a.40 (printed, CIS)
Corpus CIS 1808

Inscription 3026
Site Jebel Sirbal, Wadi Ajaleh, #188
Condition good
Content Nabatean inscription
šlm pṣy br ḥryšw
Access II.2a.40 (printed, CIS)
Corpus CIS 1809

Inscription 3027
Site Jebel Sirbal, Wadi Ajaleh, #188
Condition fair
Content Nabatean inscription
šlm ʾḥyw br grmʾl[bʿly]
dʾbw br ʿwdw
Access II.2a.40 (printed, CIS)
Corpus CIS 1810

Inscription 3028
Site Jebel Sirbal, Wadi Ajaleh, #188
Condition good
Content Nabatean inscription
šlm ḥnṭlw
br ʿmyw
Access II.2a.40 (printed, CIS)
Corpus CIS 1811

Inscription 3029
Site Jebel Sirbal, Wadi Ajaleh, #188
Condition good
Content Nabatean inscription
šlm bryʾw
br wʾlw
Access II.2a.40 (printed, CIS)
Corpus CIS 1812

Inscription 3030
Site Jebel Sirbal, Wadi Ajaleh, #188
Condition good
Content Nabatean inscription
šlm ḥryšw
br šdʿʾlhy
Access II.2a.40 (printed, CIS)
Corpus CIS 1813

Inscription 3031
Site Jebel Sirbal, Wadi Ajaleh, #188
Condition good
Content Nabatean inscription
šlm ʿbdʾlbʿly br ʿmyw bytyʾ bṭb
Access II.2a.40 (printed, CIS)
Corpus CIS 1814

Inscription 3032
Site Jebel Sirbal, Wadi Ajaleh, #188
Condition good
Content Nabatean inscription
šlm tymw br ḥl[ṣt]
Access II.2a.40 (printed, CIS)
Corpus CIS 1815

Inscription 3033
Site Jebel Sirbal, Wadi Ajaleh, #188
Condition good
Content Nabatean inscription
šlm ʾwšw br klbw
Access II.2a.41 (printed, CIS)
Corpus CIS 1816

Inscription 3034
Site Jebel Sirbal, Wadi Ajaleh, #188
Condition poor
Content Nabatean inscription
[ʾ]lmbqrw br ʿwdw
... kl[bw] dʾbw br
...ʾlbʿly
Access II.2a.41 (printed, CIS)
Corpus CIS 1817

Inscription 3035
Site Jebel Sirbal, Wadi Ajaleh, #188
Condition fair
Content Nabatean inscription
š[l]m ʿbdʾlbʿly br ....
Access II.2a.41 (printed, CIS)
Corpus CIS 1818

Inscription 3036
Site Jebel Sirbal, Wadi Ajaleh, #188
Condition good
Content Nabatean inscription
ʿbdʾlbʿly br wkylw
Access II.2a.41 (printed, CIS)
Corpus CIS 1819

Inscription 3037
Site Jebel Sirbal, Wadi Ajaleh, #188
Condition good
Content Nabatean inscription
šlm ʿmrw br
ḥnṭlw
Access II.2a.41 (printed, CIS)
Corpus CIS 1820

Inscription 3038
Site Jebel Sirbal, Wadi Ajaleh, #188
Condition good
Content Nabatean inscription
šlm zydw br
wʾlw
Access II.2a.41 (printed, CIS)
Corpus CIS 1821

Inscription 3039
Site Jebel Sirbal, Wadi Ajaleh, #188
Condition good
Content Nabatean inscription
šlm ʿwdw br
bṭšw bṭ[b]
Access II.2a.41 (printed, CIS)
Corpus CIS 1822

Inscription 3040
Site Jebel Sirbal, Wadi Ajaleh, #188
Condition poor
Content Nabatean inscription
šlm ....
Access II.2a.41 (printed, CIS)
Corpus CIS 1823

Inscription 3041
Site Jebel Sirbal, Wadi Ajaleh, #188
Condition good
Content Nabatean inscription
šlm ʿyṣw br wʾlw
Access II.2a.41 (printed, CIS)
Corpus CIS 1824

Inscription 3042
Site Jebel Sirbal, Wadi Ajaleh, #188
Condition good
Content Nabatean inscription
šlm ḥryšw br grymw
Access II.2a.41 (printed, CIS)
Corpus CIS 1825

Inscription 3043
Site Jebel Sirbal, Wadi Ajaleh, #188
Condition fair
Content Nabatean inscription
šlm ḥryšw
br wʾlw
šlm ....
tym...
Access II.2a.42 (printed, CIS)
Corpus CIS 1826

Inscription 3044
Site Jebel Sirbal, Wadi Ajaleh, #188
Condition poor
Content Nabatean inscription
šlm ʾwšw br ....
ḥryšw br [ʿbd]ʾl[b]ʿl[y]
Access II.2a.42 (printed, CIS)
Corpus CIS 1827

Inscription 3045
Site Jebel Sirbal, Wadi Ajaleh, #188
Condition good
Content Nabatean inscription
šlm ʿmyw
br zydw
br ʿmyw bṭb
Access II.2a.42 (printed, CIS)
Corpus CIS 1828

Inscription 3046
Site Jebel Sirbal, Wadi Ajaleh, #188
Condition fair
Content Nabatean inscription
šlm [ʾlk]tyw br ʿbdʾlbʿl[y] bṭb wšlm
Access II.2a.42 (printed, CIS)
Corpus CIS 1829

Inscription 3047
Site Jebel Sirbal, Wadi Ajaleh, #188
Condition good
Content Nabatean inscription
šlm ʿlyw br
ʿbdʾlbʿly
Access II.2a.42 (printed, CIS)
Corpus CIS 1830

Inscription 3048
Site Jebel Sirbal, Wadi Ajaleh, #188
Condition good
Content Nabatean inscription
šlm ʿlyw br ʿbdʾlbʿly
Access II.2a.42 (printed, CIS)
Corpus CIS 1831

Inscription 3049
Site Jebel Sirbal, Wadi Ajaleh, #188
Condition good
Content Nabatean inscription
šlm ʿlht br pṣy bṭb
Access II.2a.42 (printed, CIS)
Corpus CIS 1832

Inscription 3050
Site Jebel Sirbal, Wadi Ajaleh, #188
Condition good
Content Nabatean inscription
šlm wdw br
ʿbdʾlbʿly
Access II.2a.42 (printed, CIS)
Corpus CIS 1833

Inscription 3051
Site Jebel Sirbal, Wadi Ajaleh, #188
Condition good
Content Nabatean inscription
šlm kʿmh
br ṣwbw
šlm
Access II.2a.42 (printed, CIS)
Corpus CIS 1834

Inscription 3052
Site Jebel Sirbal, Wadi Ajaleh, #188
Condition poor
Content Nabatean inscription
šlm wʾlw ....
Access II.2a.43 (printed, CIS)
Corpus CIS 1835

Inscription 3053
Site Jebel Sirbal, Wadi Ajaleh, #188
Condition poor
Content Nabatean inscription
[nšy]gw br ....
mḥmyw
Access II.2a.43 (printed, CIS)
Corpus CIS 1836

Inscription 3054
Site Jebel Sirbal, Wadi Ajaleh, #188
Condition fair
Content Nabatean inscription
šlm ʿwdw br ....
Access II.2a.43 (printed, CIS)
Corpus CIS 1837

Inscription 3055
Site Jebel Sirbal, Wadi Ajaleh, #188
Condition good
Content Nabatean inscription
šlm nšygw br mḥmyw [bṭb]
Access II.2a.43 (printed, CIS)
Corpus CIS 1838

Inscription 3056
Site Jebel Sirbal, Wadi Ajaleh, #188
Condition fair
Content Nabatean inscription
šlm klbw br ....
Access II.2a.43 (printed, CIS)
Corpus CIS 1839

Inscription 3057
Site Jebel Sirbal, Wadi Ajaleh, #188
Condition good
Content Nabatean inscription
šlm ʿwdw br wʾlw
Access II.2a.43 (printed, CIS)
Corpus CIS 1840

Inscription 3058
Site Jebel Sirbal, Wadi Ajaleh, #188
Condition good
Content Nabatean inscription
dkyr ṭb lʿlm ʿlmn ʾwšʾlbʿly br ʿydw bṭb wšlm
Access II.2a.43 (printed, CIS)
Corpus CIS 1841

Inscription 3059
Site Jebel Sirbal, Wadi Ajaleh, #188
Condition fair
Content Nabatean inscription
šlm ḥgw
[br g]rymw
Access II.2a.43 (printed, CIS)
Corpus CIS 1842

Inscription 3060
Site Jebel Sirbal, Wadi Ajaleh, #188
Condition poor
Content Nabatean inscription
šlm ʾ...
br ḥršw
ʾl....
šlm br ....
...qw....
Access II.2a.43 (printed, CIS)
Corpus CIS 1843

Inscription 3061
Site Jebel Sirbal, Wadi Ajaleh, #188
Condition fair
Content Nabatean inscription
šlm ʿyd[w]
Access II.2a.44 (printed, CIS)
Corpus CIS 1844

Inscription 3062
Site Jebel Sirbal, Wadi Ajaleh, #188
Condition good
Content Nabatean inscription
šlm ṣwbw br whbʾlh
Access II.2a.44 (printed, CIS)
Corpus CIS 1845

Inscription 3063
Site Jebel Sirbal, Wadi Ajaleh, #188
Condition fair
Content Nabatean inscription
šlm zydw br ʾ...
Access II.2a.44 (printed, CIS)
Corpus CIS 1846

Inscription 3064
Site Jebel Sirbal, Wadi Ajaleh, #188
Condition poor
Content Nabatean inscription
ʿbydw...
Access II.2a.44 (printed, CIS)
Corpus CIS 1847

Inscription 3065
Site Jebel Sirbal, Wadi Ajaleh, #188
Condition fair
Content Nabatean inscription
šlm p...
šlm ʾwšw
bny pṣyw
Access II.2a.44 (printed, CIS)
Corpus CIS 1848

Inscription 3066
Site Jebel Sirbal, Wadi Ajaleh, #188
Condition good
Content Nabatean inscription
šlm gblw
br ʾwšw
Access II.2a.44 (printed, CIS)
Corpus CIS 1849

Inscription 3067
Site Jebel Sirbal, Wadi Ajaleh, #188
Condition fair
Content Nabatean inscription
šlm ʾwšw br ʾbn ʾlqyn
[br] grmʾlbʿly .....
Access II.2a.44 (printed, CIS)
Corpus CIS 1850

Inscription 3068
Site Jebel Sirbal, Wadi Ajaleh, #188
Condition fair
Content Nabatean inscription
[šl]m grmʾlb[ʿly]
br ʿmyw
Access II.2a.44 (printed, CIS)
Corpus CIS 1851

Inscription 3069
Site Jebel Sirbal, Wadi Ajaleh, #188
Condition fair
Content Nabatean inscription
šlm ʿdmw
br ....
Access II.2a.44 (printed, CIS)
Corpus CIS 1852

Inscription 3070
Site Jebel Sirbal, Wadi Ajaleh, #188
Condition fair
Content Nabatean inscription
šlm [ḥr]šw br ʾwšw
Access II.2a.44 (printed, CIS)
Corpus CIS 1853

Inscription 3071
Site Jebel Sirbal, Wadi Ajaleh, #188
Condition poor
Content Nabatean inscription
šlm ʿmyw br ...yw bṭb
Access II.2a.44 (printed, CIS)
Corpus CIS 1854

Inscription 3072
Site Jebel Sirbal, Wadi Ajaleh, #188
Condition good
Content Nabatean inscription
šlm gdyw br bryʾw
bṭb
Access II.2a.45 (printed, CIS)
Corpus CIS 1855

Inscription 3073
Site Jebel Sirbal, Wadi Ajaleh, #188
Condition good
Content Nabatean inscription
šlm ḥlṣt br
wʾlw
Access II.2a.45 (printed, CIS)
Corpus CIS 1856

Inscription 3074
Site Jebel Sirbal, Wadi Ajaleh, #188
Condition good
Content Nabatean inscription
šlm grmʾlhy br ʿbydw
Access II.2a.45 (printed, CIS)
Corpus CIS 1857

Inscription 3075
Site Jebel Sirbal, Wadi Ajaleh, #188
Condition good
Content Nabatean inscription
šlm zydw br tymdwšrʾ b[ṭb]
Access II.2a.45 (printed, CIS)
Corpus CIS 1858

Inscription 3076
Site Jebel Sirbal, Wadi Ajaleh, #188
Condition good
Content Nabatean inscription
šlm wʾlw br
ʿwdw bṭb
Access II.2a.45 (printed, CIS)
Corpus CIS 1859

Inscription 3077
Site Jebel Sirbal, Wadi Ajaleh, #188
Condition fair
Content Nabatean inscription
šlm ʿmyw br ....
Access II.2a.45 (printed, CIS)
Corpus CIS 1860

Inscription 3078
Site Jebel Sirbal, Wadi Ajaleh, #188
Condition good
Content Nabatean inscription
šlm wʾlw br [ʿ]wdw
Access II.2a.45 (printed, CIS)
Corpus CIS 1861

Inscription 3079
Site Jebel Sirbal, Wadi Ajaleh, #188
Condition fair
Content Nabatean inscription
šlm pʾrn br
šlm ʿmrw br nšygw
klb[w br ʿ]bdl[hy] šlm.w
Access II.2a.45 (printed, CIS)
Corpus CIS 1862

Inscription 3080
Site Jebel Sirbal, Wadi Ajaleh, #188
Condition good
Content Nabatean inscription
šlm ḥwrw br
tymʾlhy
Access II.2a.45 (printed, CIS)
Corpus CIS 1863

Inscription 3081
Site Jebel Sirbal, Wadi Ajaleh, #188
Condition fair
Content Nabatean inscription
šlm
ʿbdʾlb[ʿly br]
bḥ[gh]
Access II.2a.45 (printed, CIS)
Corpus CIS 1864

Inscription 3082
Site Jebel Sirbal, Wadi Ajaleh, #188
Condition good
Content Nabatean inscription
šlm mʿnw br
hnʾw
Access II.2a.46 (printed, CIS)
Corpus CIS 1865

Inscription 3083
Site Jebel Sirbal, Wadi Ajaleh, #188
Condition good
Content Nabatean inscription
šlm ʿnmw br
šlmw
Access II.2a.46 (printed, CIS)
Corpus CIS 1866

Inscription 3084
Site Jebel Sirbal, Wadi Ajaleh, #188
Condition good
Content Nabatean inscription
šlm ʿbdʾlbʿly
br pʾrn
Access II.2a.46 (printed, CIS)
Corpus CIS 1867

Inscription 3085
Site Jebel Sirbal, Wadi Ajaleh, #188
Condition fair
Content Nabatean inscription
šlm ʾlkty[w br] ʿbdʾlbʿly
Access II.2a.46 (printed, CIS)
Corpus CIS 1868

Inscription 3086
Site Jebel Sirbal, Wadi Ajaleh, #188
Condition fair
Content Nabatean inscription
klbw br ʾlmbq[rw]
Access II.2a.46 (printed, CIS)
Corpus CIS 1869

Inscription 3087
Site Jebel Sirbal, Wadi Ajaleh, #188
Condition good
Content Nabatean inscription
šlm ʾbnqwm br ḥlṣt
Access II.2a.46 (printed, CIS)
Corpus CIS 1870

Inscription 3088
Site Jebel Sirbal, Wadi Ajaleh, #188
Condition good
Content Nabatean inscription
šlm ḥlṣt
br ḥryšw
Access II.2a.46 (printed, CIS)
Corpus CIS 1871

Inscription 3089
Site Jebel Sirbal, Wadi Ajaleh, #188
Condition poor
Content Nabatean inscription
šlm ʿbdʾl[bʿly] br [klbw]
[šlm] wʾlw br mš[k]w...
Access II.2a.47 (printed, CIS)
Corpus CIS 1872

Inscription 3090
Site Jebel Sirbal, Wadi Ajaleh, #188
Condition good
Content Nabatean inscription
šlm ʿbdw klbw bṭb
Access II.2a.47 (printed, CIS)
Corpus CIS 1873

Inscription 3091
Site Jebel Sirbal, Wadi Ajaleh, #188
Condition good
Content Nabatean inscription
šlm gdyw br
wʾlw
Access II.2a.47 (printed, CIS)
Corpus CIS 1874

Inscription 3092
Site Jebel Sirbal, Wadi Ajaleh, #188
Condition good
Content Nabatean inscription
šlm mʿnw br
hnʾw bṭb
Access II.2a.47 (printed, CIS)
Corpus CIS 1875

Inscription 3093
Site Jebel Sirbal, Wadi Ajaleh, #188
Condition good
Content Nabatean inscription
šlm zydw br klbw bṭb
Access II.2a.47 (printed, CIS)
Corpus CIS 1876

Inscription 3094
Site Jebel Sirbal, Wadi Ajaleh, #188
Condition fair
Content Nabatean inscription
šlm gršw br
...w...
Access II.2a.47 (printed, CIS)
Corpus CIS 1877

Inscription 3095
Site Jebel Sirbal, Wadi Ajaleh, #188
Condition good
Content Nabatean inscription
šlm ʾlkhnw br
nšygw
Access II.2a.47 (printed, CIS)
Corpus CIS 1878

Inscription 3096
Site Jebel Sirbal, Wadi Ajaleh, #188
Condition good
Content Nabatean inscription
šlm ḥlṣt br wʾlw
Access II.2a.47 (printed, CIS)
Corpus CIS 1879

Inscription 3097
Site Jebel Sirbal, Wadi Ajaleh, #188
Condition fair
Content Nabatean inscription
šlm ḥnṭlw br t....
Access II.2a.47 (printed, CIS)
Corpus CIS 1880

Inscription 3098
Site Jebel Sirbal, Wadi Ajaleh, #188
Condition good
Content Nabatean inscription
šlm ʿbdʾlbʿly
br rgbw
Access II.2a.47 (printed, CIS)
Corpus CIS 1881

Inscription 3099
Site Jebel Sirbal, Wadi Ajaleh, #188
Condition good
Content Nabatean inscription
šlm ʿwdw br klbw
Access II.2a.48 (printed, CIS)
Corpus CIS 1882

Inscription 3100
Site Jebel Sirbal, Wadi Ajaleh, #188
Condition good
Content Nabatean inscription
šlm klbw br ʿwdw
Access II.2a.48 (printed, CIS)
Corpus CIS 1883

Inscription 3101
Site Jebel Sirbal, Wadi Ajaleh, #188
Condition good
Content Nabatean inscription
šmrḥ br klbw
Access II.2a.48 (printed, CIS)
Corpus CIS 1884

Inscription 3102
Site Jebel Sirbal, Wadi Ajaleh, #188
Condition fair
Content Nabatean inscription
šmrḥ br ʿm[yw]
khn tʾ
Access II.2a.48 (printed, CIS)
Corpus CIS 1885

Inscription 3103
Site Jebel Sirbal, Wadi Ajaleh, #188
Condition fair
Content Nabatean inscription
[dky]r šʿdʾlhy
br ʿlyw bṭb
Access II.2a.48 (printed, CIS)
Corpus CIS 1886

Inscription 3104
Site Jebel Sirbal, Wadi Ajaleh, #188
Condition good
Content Nabatean inscription
šlm zydw br
klbw bṭb
Access II.2a.48 (printed, CIS)
Corpus CIS 1887

Inscription 3105
Site Jebel Sirbal, Wadi Ajaleh, #188
Condition good
Content Nabatean inscription
šlm ʾ
wšw br kl
bw
Access II.2a.48 (printed, CIS)
Corpus CIS 1888

Inscription 3106
Site Jebel Sirbal, Wadi Ajaleh, #188
Condition fair
Content Nabatean inscription
šlm ʾklw[šw]
br ʾṣlḥw bṭb
Access II.2a.48 (printed, CIS)
Corpus CIS 1889

Inscription 3107
Site Jebel Sirbal, Wadi Ajaleh, #188
Condition fair
Content Nabatean inscription
šlm ḥryšw br ....
Access II.2a.48 (printed, CIS)
Corpus CIS 1890

Inscription 3108
Site Jebel Sirbal, Wadi Ajaleh, #188
Condition fair
Content Nabatean inscription
šlm pʾrn [br]
...h...
Access II.2a.48 (printed, CIS)
Corpus CIS 1891

Inscription 3109
Site Jebel Sirbal, Wadi Ajaleh, #188
Condition good
Content Nabatean inscription
šlm wlw br zydw
Access II.2a.49 (printed, CIS)
Corpus CIS 1892

Inscription 3110
Site Jebel Sirbal, Wadi Ajaleh, #188
Condition good
Content Nabatean inscription
šlm ʾlḥšpw br ʿmyw
Access II.2a.49 (printed, CIS)
Corpus CIS 1893

Inscription 3111
Site Jebel Sirbal, Wadi Ajaleh, #188
Condition good
Content Nabatean inscription
ʿwdw br ʿtšw
Access II.2a.49 (printed, CIS)
Corpus CIS 1894

Inscription 3112
Site Jebel Sirbal, Wadi Ajaleh, #188
Condition fair
Content Nabatean inscription
[d]ky[r] ʿwdw br bṭšw
Access II.2a.49 (printed, CIS)
Corpus CIS 1895

Inscription 3113
Site Jebel Sirbal, Wadi Ajaleh, #188
Condition good
Content Nabatean inscription
šlm mʿnw br hnʾw
Access II.2a.49 (printed, CIS)
Corpus CIS 1896

Inscription 3114
Site Jebel Sirbal, Wadi Ajaleh, #188
Condition good
Content Nabatean inscription
bryʾw
br klbw
Access II.2a.49 (printed, CIS)
Corpus CIS 1897

Inscription 3115
Site Jebel Sirbal, Wadi Ajaleh, #188
Condition fair
Content Nabatean inscription
šlm
bryʾ[w]
Access II.2a.49 (printed, CIS)
Corpus CIS 1898

Inscription 3116
Site Jebel Sirbal, Wadi Ajaleh, #188
Condition fair
Content Nabatean inscription
šlm [wdw] br ʿbdʾlbʿly
Access II.2a.49 (printed, CIS)
Corpus CIS 1899

Inscription 3117
Site Jebel Sirbal, Wadi Ajaleh, #188
Condition poor
Content Nabatean inscription
šlm ʿm[r]w [br] ʾ[w]š[ʾlbʿ]ly
Access II.2a.49 (printed, CIS)
Corpus CIS 1900

Inscription 3118
Site Jebel Sirbal, Wadi Ajaleh, #188
Condition good
Content Nabatean inscription
šlm dʾbw br
ʿmyw
Access II.2a.49 (printed, CIS)
Corpus CIS 1901

Inscription 3119
Site Jebel Sirbal, Wadi Ajaleh, #188
Condition good
Content Nabatean inscription
šlm grmʾlbʿly
br zydw
Access II.2a.49 (printed, CIS)
Corpus CIS 1902

Inscription 3120
Site Jebel Sirbal, Wadi Ajaleh, #188
Condition good
Content Nabatean inscription
šlm ḥwrw br ʿmrw
Access II.2a.50 (printed, CIS)
Corpus CIS 1903

Inscription 3121
Site Jebel Sirbal, Wadi Ajaleh, #188
Condition good
Content Nabatean inscription
šlm šlm dʾybw br
ḥnṭlw
Access II.2a.50 (printed, CIS)
Corpus CIS 1904

Inscription 3122
Site Jebel Sirbal, Wadi Ajaleh, #188
Condition good
Content Nabatean inscription
šlm klybw br
pṣyw
Access II.2a.50 (printed, CIS)
Corpus CIS 1905

Inscription 3123
Site Jebel Sirbal, Wadi Ajaleh, #188
Condition fair
Content Nabatean inscription
šlm šlm [g]mlw br ....
Access II.2a.50 (printed, CIS)
Corpus CIS 1906

Inscription 3124
Site Jebel Sirbal, Wadi Ajaleh, #188
Condition poor
Content Nabatean inscription
šlm ....lh br ....
Access II.2a.50 (printed, CIS)
Corpus CIS 1907

Inscription 3125
Site Jebel Sirbal, Wadi Ajaleh, #188
Condition fair
Content Nabatean inscription
šlm ʾwšw br p...
Access II.2a.50 (printed, CIS)
Corpus CIS 1908

Inscription 3126
Site Jebel Sirbal, Wadi Ajaleh, #188
Condition fair
Content Nabatean inscription
šlm wʾlw br
ʾlmb[qr]w
Access II.2a.50 (printed, CIS)
Corpus CIS 1909

Inscription 3127
Site Jebel Sirbal, Wadi Ajaleh, #188
Condition good
Content Nabatean inscription
šlm tymlhy
br nšygw
Access II.2a.50 (printed, CIS)
Corpus CIS 1910

Inscription 3128
Site Jebel Sirbal, Wadi Ajaleh, #188
Condition good
Content Nabatean inscription
šlm mʿnw br hnʾw bṭb
Access II.2a.50 (printed, CIS)
Corpus CIS 1911

Inscription 3129
Site Jebel Sirbal, Wadi Ajaleh, #188
Condition good
Content Nabatean inscription
šlm wʾlw br mškw
Access II.2a.50 (printed, CIS)
Corpus CIS 1912

Inscription 3130
Site Jebel Sirbal, Wadi Ajaleh, #188
Condition fair
Content Nabatean inscription
šlm šmrḥ [br] ...ʾl
Access II.2a.50 (printed, CIS)
Corpus CIS 1913

Inscription 3131
Site Jebel Sirbal, Wadi Ajaleh, #188
Condition good
Content Nabatean inscription
šlm tymʾlhy br yʿly bṭb
Access II.2a.51 (printed, CIS)
Corpus CIS 1914

Inscription 3132
Site Jebel Sirbal, Wadi Ajaleh, #188
Condition good
Content Nabatean inscription
šlm grmlbʿly br ʿmyw
Access II.2a.51 (printed, CIS)
Corpus CIS 1915

Inscription 3133
Site Jebel Sirbal, Wadi Ajaleh, #188
Condition good
Content Nabatean inscription
šlm ʿbdʾlbʿly br ʿmmw
Access II.2a.51 (printed, CIS)
Corpus CIS 1916

Inscription 3134
Site Jebel Sirbal, Wadi Ajaleh, #188
Condition good
Content Nabatean inscription
šlm wʾlw br ḥlṣt
Access II.2a.51 (printed, CIS)
Corpus CIS 1917

Inscription 3135
Site Jebel Sirbal, Wadi Ajaleh, #188
Condition fair
Content Nabatean inscription
šlm ʾwšw br q[ynw]
Access II.2a.51 (printed, CIS)
Corpus CIS 1918

Inscription 3136
Site Jebel Sirbal, Wadi Ajaleh, #188
Condition poor
Content Nabatean inscription
šlm ḥry...
Access II.2a.51 (printed, CIS)
Corpus CIS 1919

Inscription 3137
Site Jebel Sirbal, Wadi Ajaleh, #188
Condition fair
Content Nabatean inscription
šlm yʿly br ....
Access II.2a.51 (printed, CIS)
Corpus CIS 1920

Inscription 3138
Site Jebel Sirbal, Wadi Ajaleh, #188
Condition good
Content Nabatean inscription
šlm bṭšw
br zydw
Access II.2a.51 (printed, CIS)
Corpus CIS 1921

Inscription 3139
Site Jebel Sirbal, Wadi Ajaleh, #188
Condition good
Content Nabatean inscription
šlm ʾwšʾlbʿly
Access II.2a.51 (printed, CIS)
Corpus CIS 1922

Inscription 3140
Site Jebel Sirbal, Wadi Ajaleh, #188
Condition good
Content Nabatean inscription
šlm ʿmyw br ʾlmbqrw
Access II.2a.51 (printed, CIS)
Corpus CIS 1923

Inscription 3141
Site Jebel Sirbal, Wadi Ajaleh, #188
Condition good
Content Nabatean inscription
šlm kʿmh br
ṣwbw
Access II.2a.51 (printed, CIS)
Corpus CIS 1924

Inscription 3142
Site Jebel Sirbal, Wadi Ajaleh, #188
Condition poor
Content Nabatean inscription
šlm pʾr[n]
[br] ʿmyw
Access II.2a.52 (printed, CIS)
Corpus CIS 1925

Inscription 3143
Site Jebel Sirbal, Wadi Ajaleh, #188
Condition good
Content Nabatean inscription
šlm kʿmh
br ṣwbw
Access II.2a.52 (printed, CIS)
Corpus CIS 1926

Inscription 3144
Site Jebel Sirbal, Wadi Ajaleh, #188
Condition good
Content Nabatean inscription
šlm ʿmyw
br ʿbydw bṭb
Access II.2a.52 (printed, CIS)
Corpus CIS 1927

Inscription 3145
Site Jebel Sirbal, Wadi Ajaleh, #188
Condition good
Content Nabatean inscription
dkyr yʿly br
tymʾlhy
Access II.2a.52 (printed, CIS)
Corpus CIS 1928

Inscription 3146
Site Jebel Sirbal, Wadi Ajaleh, #188
Condition fair
Content Nabatean inscription
šlm ʿbdʾlbʿ[ly br]
šʿdt
Access II.2a.52 (printed, CIS)
Corpus CIS 1929

Inscription 3147
Site Jebel Sirbal, Wadi Ajaleh, #188
Condition good
Content Nabatean inscription
šlm gdyw br
ḥryšw
Access II.2a.52 (printed, CIS)
Corpus CIS 1930

Inscription 3148
Site Jebel Sirbal, Wadi Ajaleh, #188
Condition fair
Content Nabatean inscription
[šl]m bry'w
[br] ḥryšw
Access II.2a.52 (printed, CIS)
Corpus CIS 1931

Inscription 3149
Site Jebel Sirbal, Wadi Ajaleh, #188
Condition good
Content Nabatean inscription
šlm ʿwdw
br w'lw bṭb
Access II.2a.52 (printed, CIS)
Corpus CIS 1932

Inscription 3150
Site Jebel Sirbal, Wadi Ajaleh, #188
Condition good
Content Nabatean inscription
šlm 'lmbqrw br šʿd'lhy
Access II.2a.52 (printed, CIS)
Corpus CIS 1933

Inscription 3151
Site Jebel Sirbal, Wadi Ajaleh, #188
Condition good
Content Nabatean inscription
šlm grm'lbʿly br
mbršw bṭb
Access II.2a.52 (printed, CIS)
Corpus CIS 1934

Inscription 3152
Site Jebel Sirbal, Wadi Ajaleh, #188
Condition good
Content Nabatean inscription
šlm ʿmyw br
ḥryšw
Access II.2a.53 (printed, CIS)
Corpus CIS 1935

Inscription 3153
Site Jebel Sirbal, Wadi Ajaleh, #188
Condition good
Content Nabatean inscription
šlm ...w
br w'lw bṭb
Access II.2a.53 (printed, CIS)
Corpus CIS 1936

Inscription 3154
Site Jebel Sirbal, Wadi Ajaleh, #188
Condition good
Content Nabatean inscription
šlm
'ʿl' br
ṣwbw
Access II.2a.53 (printed, CIS)
Corpus CIS 1937

Inscription 3155
Site Jebel Sirbal, Wadi Ajaleh, #188
Condition fair
Content Nabatean inscription
šlm ʿbd'hyw
šlm ʿ....
Access II.2a.53 (printed, CIS)
Corpus CIS 1938

Inscription 3156
Site Jebel Sirbal, Wadi Ajaleh, #188
Condition good
Content Nabatean inscription
šlm mʿnw br h[n'w]
šlm zydw br ʿbd'lbʿly bṭb wšlm
Access II.2a.53 (printed, CIS)
Corpus CIS 1939

Inscription 3157
Site Jebel Sirbal, Wadi Ajaleh, #188
Condition good
Content Nabatean inscription
šlm 'tmw
br d'ybw
Access II.2a.53 (printed, CIS)
Corpus CIS 1940

Inscription 3158
Site Jebel Sirbal, Wadi Ajaleh, #188
Condition fair
Content Nabatean inscription
šlm [w]hb'lhy br mḥmyw
šlm ...gw...
Access II.2a.53 (printed, CIS)
Corpus CIS 1941

Inscription 3159
Site Jebel Sirbal, Wadi Ajaleh, #188
Condition good
Content Nabatean inscription
šlm gdyw šlm
[br] wʾlw bryʾw
br klbw bṭb
Access II.2a.53 (printed, CIS)
Corpus CIS 1942

Inscription 3160
Site Jebel Sirbal, Wadi Ajaleh, #188
Condition poor
Content Nabatean inscription
šlm gm...lw
šlm ʿmmw
br ʾbn ʾlqyn[y]
Access II.2a.54 (printed, CIS)
Corpus CIS 1943

Inscription 3161
Site Jebel Sirbal, Wadi Ajaleh, #188
Condition fair
Content Nabatean inscription
šlm ḥršw br ....
Access II.2a.54 (printed, CIS)
Corpus CIS 1944

Inscription 3162
Site Jebel Sirbal, Wadi Ajaleh, #188
Condition good
Content Nabatean inscription
šlm gdyw
br wʾlw
Access II.2a.54 (printed, CIS)
Corpus CIS 1945

Inscription 3163
Site Jebel Sirbal, Wadi Ajaleh, #188
Condition good
Content Nabatean inscription
šlm [s]rpyw br
ʿrbyw
Access II.2a.54 (printed, CIS)
Corpus CIS 1946

Inscription 3164
Site Jebel Sirbal, Wadi Ajaleh, #188
Condition good
Content Nabatean inscription
šlm [gd]yw br wʾlw
ʿwdw br dʾbw
Access II.2a.54 (printed, CIS)
Corpus CIS 1947

Inscription 3165
Site Jebel Sirbal, Wadi Ajaleh, #188
Condition good
Content Nabatean inscription
šlm
šlm wʾlw br
ʿwdw
bṭb
Access II.2a.54 (printed, CIS)
Corpus CIS 1948

Inscription 3166
Site Jebel Sirbal, Wadi Ajaleh, #188
Condition good
Content Nabatean inscription
dkyr y[ʿly]
dkyr ḥnṭlw br
zydw bṭb
Access II.2a.54 (printed, CIS)
Corpus CIS 1949

Inscription 3167
Site Jebel Sirbal, Wadi Ajaleh, #188
Condition poor
Content Nabatean inscription
šlm z[y]dw br
.... bṭb
Access II.2a.54 (printed, CIS)
Corpus CIS 1950

Inscription 3168
Site Jebel Sirbal, Wadi Ajaleh, #188
Condition good
Content Nabatean inscription
dkyr bṭšw br
zydw
Access II.2a.55 (printed, CIS)
Corpus CIS 1951

Inscription 3169
Site Jebel Sirbal, Wadi Ajaleh, #188
Condition good
Content Nabatean inscription
šlm ḥryšw br ʾwšw
Access II.2a.55 (printed, CIS)
Corpus CIS 1952

Inscription 3170
Site Jebel Sirbal, Wadi Ajaleh, #188
Condition fair
Content Nabatean inscription
šlm ḥnṭlw
br [zyd]w
Access II.2a.55 (printed, CIS)
Corpus CIS 1953

Inscription 3171
Site Jebel Sirbal, Wadi Ajaleh, #188
Condition good
Content Nabatean inscription
dkyr ḥwrw br
tymʾlhy
Access II.2a.55 (printed, CIS)
Corpus CIS 1954

Inscription 3172
Site Jebel Sirbal, Wadi Ajaleh, #188
Condition good
Content Nabatean inscription
šlm ʿmr[w]
br wdw bṭb [w]šlm
Access II.2a.55 (printed, CIS)
Corpus CIS 1955

Inscription 3173
Site Jebel Sirbal, Wadi Ajaleh, #188
Condition good
Content Nabatean inscription
šlm ḥryšw br
šʿdʾlhy bṭb
Access II.2a.55 (printed, CIS)
Corpus CIS 1956

Inscription 3174
Site Jebel Sirbal, Wadi Ajaleh, #188
Condition good
Content Nabatean inscription
dkyr ʿmyw br ḥršw
Access II.2a.55 (printed, CIS)
Corpus CIS 1957

Inscription 3175
Site Jebel Sirbal, Wadi Ajaleh, #188
Condition fair
Content Nabatean inscription
dkyr ʿmrw br [ḥry]šw
wḥryšw ....
Access II.2a.55 (printed, CIS)
Corpus CIS 1958

Inscription 3176
Site Jebel Sirbal, Wadi Ajaleh, #188
Condition good
Content Nabatean inscription
šlm ʿyydw
br ḥryšw
Access II.2a.55 (printed, CIS)
Corpus CIS 1959

Inscription 3177
Site Jebel Sirbal, Wadi Ajaleh, #188
Condition good
Content Nabatean inscription
dkyr ʿbdʾlbʿly
br grmʾl[hy]
Access II.2a.55 (printed, CIS)
Corpus CIS 1960

Inscription 3178
Site Jebel Sirbal, Wadi Ajaleh, #188
Condition poor
Content Nabatean inscription
šlm ʿbydw
br ṣḥbw
Access II.2a.56 (printed, CIS)
Corpus CIS 1961

Inscription 3179
Site Jebel Sirbal, Wadi Ajaleh, #188
Condition good
Content Nabatean inscription
šlm ʾtm[w]
br ʿbdʾlbʿly
Access II.2a.56 (printed, CIS)
Corpus CIS 1962

Inscription 3180
Site Jebel Sirbal, Wadi Ajaleh, #188
Condition good
Content Nabatean inscription
šlm grmʾlbʿly
br ṣ[wb]w bṭb
Access II.2a.56 (printed, CIS)
Corpus CIS 1963

Inscription 3181
Site Jebel Sirbal, Wadi Ajaleh, #188
Condition fair
Content Nabatean inscription
šlm wʾlw br [ḥlṣ]t
Access II.2a.56 (printed, CIS)
Corpus CIS 1964

Inscription 3182
Site Jebel Sirbal, Wadi Ajaleh, #188
Condition good
Content Nabatean inscription
šlm bḥgh
Access II.2a.56 (printed, CIS)
Corpus CIS 1965

Inscription 3183
Site Jebel Sirbal, Wadi Ajaleh, #188
Condition poor
Content Nabatean inscription
šlm w... [br] ʿb[d]ʿbdt
Access II.2a.56 (printed, CIS)
Corpus CIS 1966

Inscription 3184
Site Jebel Sirbal, Wadi Ajaleh, #188
Condition poor
Content Nabatean inscription
šlm [ʾ]lkh[n]w
br nṣygw bṭ[b]
Access II.2a.56 (printed, CIS)
Corpus CIS 1967

Inscription 3185
Site Jebel Sirbal, Wadi Ajaleh, #188
Condition good
Content Nabatean inscription
šlm klbw br pʾrn
Access II.2a.57 (printed, CIS)
Corpus CIS 1968

Inscription 3186
Site Jebel Sirbal, Wadi Ajaleh, #188
Condition good
Content Nabatean inscription
ʿbdʾlbʿly [br] ʿmyw bytyʾ
šlm šlm mʿnw
Access II.2a.57 (printed, CIS)
Corpus CIS 1969

Inscription 3187
Site Jebel Sirbal, Hajjer Ulumbardi, #194
Condition good
Content Nabatean inscription
šlm ʿbdʾlbʿly
br ḥlṣ[t]
Access II.2a.57 (printed, CIS)
Corpus CIS 1970

Inscription 3188
Site Jebel Sirbal, Hajjer Ulumbardi, #194
Condition poor
Content Nabatean inscription
...ʿly br ʿwdw
Access II.2a.57 (printed, CIS)
Corpus CIS 1971

Inscription 3189
Site Jebel Sirbal, Hajjer Ulumbardi, #194
Condition good
Content Nabatean inscription
šlm wdw br nšygw
bṭb
Access II.2a.57 (printed, CIS)
Corpus CIS 1972

Inscription 3190
Site Jebel Sirbal, Hajjer Ulumbardi, #194
Condition poor
Content Nabatean inscription
ʿbydw br ....
Access II.2a.58 (printed, CIS)
Corpus CIS 1973

Inscription 3191
Site Jebel Sirbal, Hajjer Ulumbardi, #194
Condition poor
Content Nabatean inscription
ʿmrw
Access II.2a.58 (printed, CIS)
Corpus CIS 1974

Inscription 3192
Site Jebel Sirbal, Hajjer Ulumbardi, #194
Condition poor
Content Nabatean inscription
Access II.2a.58 (printed, CIS)
Corpus CIS 1975

Inscription 3193
Site Jebel Sirbal, Hajjer Ulumbardi, #194
Condition poor
Content Nabatean inscription
...ʿbdʿly
Access II.2a.58 (printed, CIS)
Corpus CIS 1976

Inscription 3194
Site Jebel Sirbal, Wadi Qseib, #222
Condition fair
Content Nabatean inscription
d[ky]r tymʾlhy br yʿly
Access II.2a.58 (printed, CIS)
Corpus CIS 1977

Inscription 3195
Site Jebel Sirbal, Wadi Qseib, #222
Condition poor
Content Nabatean inscription
šlm dʾbw br
....
Access II.2a.58 (printed, CIS)
Corpus CIS 1978

Inscription 3196
Site Jebel Sirbal, Wadi Qseib, #222
Condition good
Content Nabatean inscription
šlm ḥršw br ʾwšʾlhy bṭb
Access II.2a.58 (printed, CIS)
Corpus CIS 1979

Inscription 3197
Site Jebel Sirbal, Wadi Qseib, #222
Condition poor
Content Nabatean inscription
...yw
Access II.2a.58 (printed, CIS)
Corpus CIS 1980

Inscription 3198
Site Jebel Sirbal, Wadi Qseib, #222
Condition good
Content Nabatean inscription
šlm tymʾlhy br yʿly
Access II.2a.58 (printed, CIS)
Corpus CIS 1981

Inscription 3199
Site Jebel Sirbal, Wadi Qseib, #222
Condition good
Content Nabatean inscription
šlm wʾlw br nšygw
bṭb wšlm
Access II.2a.58 (printed, CIS)
Corpus CIS 1982

Inscription 3200
Site Jebel Sirbal, Wadi Qseib, #222
Condition good
Content Nabatean inscription
šlm ḥryšw br mʿyrw
Access II.2a.59 (printed, CIS)
Corpus CIS 1983

Inscription 3201
Site Jebel Sirbal, Wadi Qseib, #222
Condition good
Content Nabatean inscription
šlm bḥgh
br grmʾlbʿly
bṭb
Access II.2a.59 (printed, CIS)
Corpus CIS 1984

Inscription 3202
Site Jebel Sirbal, Wadi Qseib, #222
Condition fair
Content Nabatean inscription
ʿbdʾlbʿly [bytyʾ] br
ʿmyw
Access II.2a.59 (printed, CIS)
Corpus CIS 1985

Inscription 3203
Site Jebel Sirbal, Wadi Qseib, #222
Condition good
Content Nabatean inscription
šlm pʾrn br
grmʾlbʿly
Access II.2a.59 (printed, CIS)
Corpus CIS 1986

Inscription 3204
Site Jebel Sirbal, Wadi Qseib, #222
Condition good
Content Nabatean inscription
šlm dʾbw br grmʾlbʿly
Access II.2a.59 (printed, CIS)
Corpus CIS 1987

Inscription 3205
Site Jebel Sirbal, Wadi Qseib, #222
Condition good
Content Nabatean inscription
šlm wʾlw br ʿmyw bṭb
Access II.2a.59 (printed, CIS)
Corpus CIS 1988

Inscription 3206
Site Jebel Sirbal, Wadi Qseib, #222
Condition good
Content Nabatean inscription
šlm ʾwšw
br klbw
Access II.2a.59 (printed, CIS)
Corpus CIS 1989

Inscription 3207
Site Jebel Sirbal, Wadi Qseib, #222
Condition poor
Content Nabatean inscription
... ḥršw ....
Access II.2a.59 (printed, CIS)
Corpus CIS 1990

Inscription 3208
Site Jebel Sirbal, Wadi Qseib, #222
Condition fair
Content Nabatean inscription
šlm ʿbdʾlbʿly
Access II.2a.59 (printed, CIS)
Corpus CIS 1991

Inscription 3209
Site Jebel Sirbal, Wadi Qseib, #222
Condition good
Content Nabatean inscription
šlm ʾwšʾlbʿly br zydw
Access II.2a.59 (printed, CIS)
Corpus CIS 1992

Inscription 3210
Site Jebel Sirbal, Wadi Qseib, #222
Condition poor
Content Nabatean inscription
šlm p[ṣ]y br šʿdʾl[h]
Access II.2a.59 (printed, CIS)
Corpus CIS 1993

Inscription 3211
Site Jebel Sirbal, Wadi Qseib, #222
Condition good
Content Nabatean inscription
šlm klbw br hnʾw
Access II.2a.59 (printed, CIS)
Corpus CIS 1994

Inscription **3212**
Site Jebel Sirbal, Wadi Qseib, #222
Condition fair
Content Nabatean inscription
šlm ʾw[šw]
br ʿmnw
Access II.2a.60 (printed, CIS)
Corpus CIS 1995

Inscription **3213**
Site Jebel Sirbal, Wadi Qseib, #222
Condition good
Content Nabatean inscription
šlm wʾlw br ʿwdw
Access II.2a.60 (printed, CIS)
Corpus CIS 1996

Inscription **3214**
Site Jebel Sirbal, Wadi Qseib, #222
Condition fair
Content Nabatean inscription
šlm bḥgh br ....
Access II.2a.60 (printed, CIS)
Corpus CIS 1997

Inscription **3215**
Site Jebel Sirbal, Wadi Qseib, #222
Condition good
Content Nabatean inscription
šlm mqmʾl br wʾlw
Access II.2a.60 (printed, CIS)
Corpus CIS 1998

Inscription **3216**
Site Jebel Sirbal, Wadi Qseib, #222
Condition fair
Content Nabatean inscription
šlm ḥryšw br ʿmy[w bṭb]
Access II.2a.60 (printed, CIS)
Corpus CIS 1999

Inscription **3217**
Site Jebel Sirbal, Wadi Qseib, #222
Condition good
Content Nabatean inscription
šlm ʿmrw br grmʾlbʿly
Access II.2a.60 (printed, CIS)
Corpus CIS 2000

Inscription **3218**
Site Jebel Sirbal, Wadi Qseib, #222
Condition good
Content Nabatean inscription
šlm ʿbdʾlbʿly br ʿmmw
Access II.2a.60 (printed, CIS)
Corpus CIS 2001

Inscription **3219**
Site Jebel Sirbal, Wadi Qseib, #222
Condition fair
Content Nabatean inscription
šlm ...lw br grmʾlbʿly bṭb wšlm
Access II.2a.60 (printed, CIS)
Corpus CIS 2002

Inscription **3220**
Site Jebel Sirbal, Wadi Qseib, #222
Condition good
Content Nabatean inscription
šlm ḥlṣt br šʿwdt bṭb
Access II.2a.60 (printed, CIS)
Corpus CIS 2003

Inscription **3221**
Site Jebel Sirbal, Wadi Qseib, #222
Condition good
Content Nabatean inscription
šlm ḥrglw br ʿbydw
Access II.2a.60 (printed, CIS)
Corpus CIS 2004

Inscription **3222**
Site Jebel Sirbal, Wadi Qseib, #222
Condition good
Content Nabatean inscription
šlm pʾrn br ʿmyw
Access II.2a.60 (printed, CIS)
Corpus CIS 2005

Inscription **3223**
Site Jebel Sirbal, Wadi Qseib, #222
Condition fair
Content Nabatean inscription
šlm ʿwdw br
ʿmyw... bṭb
Access II.2a.61 (printed, CIS)
Corpus CIS 2006

Inscription **3224**
Site Jebel Sirbal, Wadi Qseib, #222
Condition good
Content Nabatean inscription
šlm ʿmyw br
[z]ydw br ʿmyw
bṭb
Access II.2a.61 (printed, CIS)
Corpus CIS 2007

Inscription **3225**
Site Jebel Sirbal, Wadi Qseib, #222
Condition poor
Content Nabatean inscription
.... br ʿwdw bṭb
Access II.2a.61 (printed, CIS)
Corpus CIS 2008

Inscription 3226
Site Jebel Sirbal, Wadi Qseib, #222
Condition good
Content Nabatean inscription
šlm ʿmyw br ʿbdʾ[hy]w
Access II.2a.61 (printed, CIS)
Corpus CIS 2009

Inscription 3227
Site Jebel Sirbal, Wadi Qseib, #222
Condition fair
Content Nabatean inscription
šlm ʾwšw br
ʿw[d]w [b]ṭ[b]
Access II.2a.61 (printed, CIS)
Corpus CIS 2010

Inscription 3228
Site Jebel Sirbal, Wadi Qseib, #222
Condition good
Content Nabatean inscription
dkyr ʾwšw br
bṭšw
Access II.2a.61 (printed, CIS)
Corpus CIS 2011

Inscription 3229
Site Jebel Sirbal, Wadi Qseib, #222
Condition good
Content Nabatean inscription
šlm ḥwrw br
mḥmyw
Access II.2a.61 (printed, CIS)
Corpus CIS 2012

Inscription 3230
Site Jebel Sirbal, Wadi Qseib, #222
Condition fair
Content Nabatean inscription
šlm ḥwrw
br [t]y[m]ʾlhy
Access II.2a.61 (printed, CIS)
Corpus CIS 2013

Inscription 3231
Site Jebel Sirbal, Wadi Qseib, #222
Condition good
Content Nabatean inscription
šlm whbʾlhy br ʿmmw
Access II.2a.62 (printed, CIS)
Corpus CIS 2014

Inscription 3232
Site Jebel Sirbal, Wadi Qseib, #222
Condition fair
Content Nabatean inscription
šlm šlm ḥry[š]w
Access II.2a.62 (printed, CIS)
Corpus CIS 2015

Inscription 3233
Site Jebel Sirbal, Wadi Alayat, #187
Condition poor
Content Nabatean inscription
šlm ʾwšw br
[šl]m w...m.
Access II.2a.62 (printed, CIS)
Corpus CIS 2016

Inscription 3234
Site Jebel Sirbal, Wadi Alayat, #187
Condition poor
Content Nabatean inscription
šlm pzʾʾt...
Access II.2a.62 (printed, CIS)
Corpus CIS 2017

Inscription 3235
Site Jebel Sirbal, Wadi Alayat, #187
Condition good
Content Nabatean inscription
šlm mʿnʾlh br hnʾw
Access II.2a.62 (printed, CIS)
Corpus CIS 2018

Inscription 3236
Site Jebel Sirbal, Wadi Alayat, #187
Condition fair
Content Nabatean inscription
šlm šʿdʾlhy br
wʾlw šlm ʾ...
Access II.2a.62 (printed, CIS)
Corpus CIS 2019

Inscription 3237
Site Jebel Sirbal, Wadi Alayat, #187
Condition poor
Content Nabatean inscription
šlm wʾ[lw br]
...w
šlm ʾwšw br
[ʾ]wšw
Access II.2a.62 (printed, CIS)
Corpus CIS 2020

Inscription 3238
Site Jebel Sirbal, Wadi Alayat, #187
Condition poor
Content Nabatean inscription
šlm ʿmyw
br ....
Access II.2a.63 (printed, CIS)
Corpus CIS 2021

Inscription 3239
Site Jebel Sirbal, Wadi Alayat, #187
Condition poor
Content Nabatean inscription
šlm [gd]yw br
[bḥg]h bṭb
Access II.2a.63 (printed, CIS)
Corpus CIS 2022

Inscription 3240
Site Jebel Sirbal, Wadi Alayat, #187
Condition good
Content Nabatean inscription
šlm ʿbdlbʿl[y]
br ʿmrw
Access II.2a.63 (printed, CIS)
Corpus CIS 2023

Inscription 3241
Site Jebel Sirbal, Wadi Alayat, #187
Condition poor
Content Nabatean inscription
.yʿ[ly br] tym[ʾlhy]
Access II.2a.63 (printed, CIS)
Corpus CIS 2024

Inscription 3242
Site Jebel Sirbal, Wadi Alayat, #187
Condition poor
Content Nabatean inscription
šlm ʾkbrw
Access II.2a.63 (printed, CIS)
Corpus CIS 2025

Inscription 3243
Site Jebel Sirbal, Wadi Alayat, #187
Condition fair
Content Nabatean inscription
šlm bḥgh
Access II.2a.63 (printed, CIS)
Corpus CIS 2026

Inscription 3244
Site Jebel Sirbal, Wadi Alayat, #187
Condition fair
Content Nabatean inscription
šlm klbw b[r] ....
Access II.2a.63 (printed, CIS)
Corpus CIS 2027

Inscription 3245
Site Jebel Sirbal, Wadi Alayat, #187
Condition good
Content Nabatean inscription
šlm
wʾlw
br mgdyw
Access II.2a.63 (printed, CIS)
Corpus CIS 2028

Inscription 3246
Site Jebel Sirbal, Wadi Alayat, #187
Condition fair
Content Nabatean inscription
bryʾw br ʾlmbqrw
Access II.2a.63 (printed, CIS)
Corpus CIS 2029

Inscription 3247
Site Jebel Sirbal, Wadi Alayat, #187
Condition fair
Content Nabatean inscription
dkyr ʾw[yšw]
br qynw
Access II.2a.63 (printed, CIS)
Corpus CIS 2030

Inscription 3248
Site Jebel Sirbal, Wadi Alayat, #187
Condition fair
Content Nabatean inscription
šlm grmʾlbʿl[y]
Access II.2a.63 (printed, CIS)
Corpus CIS 2031

Inscription 3249
Site Jebel Sirbal, Wadi Alayat, #187
Condition fair
Content Nabatean inscription
dkyr
ʾwšw br ...w
Access II.2a.63 (printed, CIS)
Corpus CIS 2032

Inscription 3250
Site Jebel Sirbal, Wadi Alayat, #187
Condition good
Content Nabatean inscription
šlm dʾbw br
ʿmyw
Access II.2a.64 (printed, CIS)
Corpus CIS 2033

Inscription 3251
Site Jebel Sirbal, Wadi Alayat, #187
Condition poor
Content Nabatean inscription
šlm ḥry[šw br ḥ]l[ṣt] šlm ḥlṣt
Access II.2a.64 (printed, CIS)
Corpus CIS 2034

Inscription 3252
Site Jebel Sirbal, Wadi Alayat, #187
Condition good
Content Nabatean inscription
šlm wʾlw
Access II.2a.64 (printed, CIS)
Corpus CIS 2035

Inscription 3253
Site Jebel Sirbal, Wadi Alayat, #187
Condition fair
Content Nabatean inscription
šlm ʿyydw
Access II.2a.64 (printed, CIS)
Corpus CIS 2036

Inscription 3254
Site Jebel Sirbal, Wadi Alayat, #187
Condition good
Content Nabatean inscription
šlm ʾwšw
br mgdyw
Access II.2a.64 (printed, CIS)
Corpus CIS 2037

Inscription 3255
Site Jebel Sirbal, Wadi Alayat, #187
Condition fair
Content Nabatean inscription
š]lm ʿwdw
br [d]ʾbw
Access II.2a.64 (printed, CIS)
Corpus CIS 2038

Inscription 3256
Site Jebel Sirbal, Wadi Alayat, #187
Condition fair
Content Nabatean inscription
šlm mḥ[myw]
šlm bryʾw
Access II.2a.64 (printed, CIS)
Corpus CIS 2039

Inscription 3257
Site Jebel Sirbal, Wadi Alayat, #187
Condition good
Content Nabatean inscription
ʾlktyw br ʿbdʾlbʿly
Access II.2a.64 (printed, CIS)
Corpus CIS 2040

Inscription 3258
Site Jebel Sirbal, Wadi Alayat, #187
Condition poor
Content Nabatean inscription
šlm ....
br ḥryšw br
...ʿbd.....
Access II.2a.64 (printed, CIS)
Corpus CIS 2041

Inscription 3259
Site Jebel Sirbal, Wadi Alayat, #187
Condition fair
Content Nabatean inscription
šlm ʿmmw [br]
whbʾlhy
Access II.2a.64 (printed, CIS)
Corpus CIS 2042

Inscription 3260
Site Jebel Sirbal, Wadi Alayat, #187
Condition fair
Content Nabatean inscription
šlm ʾbn ʾl[qyny br]
ḥnṭlw bṭb
Access II.2a.64 (printed, CIS)
Corpus CIS 2043

Inscription 3261
Site Jebel Sirbal, Wadi Alayat, #187
Condition poor
Content Nabatean inscription
šlm [d]ʾ[y]bw br ....
Access II.2a.65 (printed, CIS)
Corpus CIS 2044

Inscription 3262
Site Jebel Sirbal, Wadi Alayat, #187
Condition good
Content Nabatean inscription
šlm wdw
Access II.2a.65 (printed, CIS)
Corpus CIS 2045

Inscription 3263
Site Jebel Sirbal, Wadi Alayat, #187
Condition good
Content Nabatean inscription
šlm bryʾw
br wʾlw
bṭb
Access II.2a.65 (printed, CIS)
Corpus CIS 2046

Inscription 3264
Site Jebel Sirbal, Wadi Alayat, #187
Condition fair
Content Nabatean inscription
šlm ʿbdʾl[ʿly br]
grmʾlbʿly
Access II.2a.65 (printed, CIS)
Corpus CIS 2047

Inscription **3265**
Site Jebel Sirbal, Wadi Alayat, #187
Condition good
Content Nabatean inscription
ʿbdʾlbʿly
br šʿdt
Access II.2a.65 (printed, CIS)
Corpus CIS 2048

Inscription **3266**
Site Jebel Sirbal, Wadi Alayat, #187
Condition poor
Content Nabatean inscription
šlm wʾlw
d[ky]r p[ṣ]yw w
šlm ʾl...
[br ḥ]ryšw
Access II.2a.65 (printed, CIS)
Corpus CIS 2049

Inscription **3267**
Site Jebel Sirbal, Wadi Alayat, #187
Condition good
Content Nabatean inscription
šlm ʿmr[w] br
kʿmh
Access II.2a.65 (printed, CIS)
Corpus CIS 2050

Inscription **3268**
Site Jebel Sirbal, Wadi Alayat, #187
Condition good
Content Nabatean inscription
šlm bqw
btʾšw
Access II.2a.65 (printed, CIS)
Corpus CIS 2051

Inscription **3269**
Site Jebel Sirbal, Wadi Alayat, #187
Condition fair
Content Nabatean inscription
šlm wʾlw br ....
Access II.2a.65 (printed, CIS)
Corpus CIS 2052

Inscription **3270**
Site Jebel Sirbal, Wadi Alayat, #187
Condition good
Content Nabatean inscription
šlm ʿmrw br klbw
Access II.2a.65 (printed, CIS)
Corpus CIS 2053

Inscription **3271**
Site Jebel Sirbal, Wadi Alayat, #187
Condition good
Content Nabatean inscription
dkyr ʾtmw br
ʿbdʾlhy
Access II.2a.66 (printed, CIS)
Corpus CIS 2054

Inscription **3272**
Site Jebel Sirbal, Wadi Alayat, #187
Condition good
Content Nabatean inscription
šlm grmʾlbʿly br
ḥršw br zydw [bṭb]
Access II.2a.66 (printed, CIS)
Corpus CIS 2055

Inscription **3273**
Site Jebel Sirbal, Wadi Alayat, #187
Condition poor
Content Nabatean inscription
šlm zydw [br]
š....
Access II.2a.66 (printed, CIS)
Corpus CIS 2056

Inscription **3274**
Site Jebel Sirbal, Wadi Alayat, #187
Condition good
Content Nabatean inscription
šlm ʿbdʾlbʿly br wʾlw
Access II.2a.66 (printed, CIS)
Corpus CIS 2057

Inscription **3275**
Site Jebel Sirbal, Wadi Alayat, #187
Condition good
Content Nabatean inscription
šlm pṣy br ḥnṭlw bṭb
Access II.2a.66 (printed, CIS)
Corpus CIS 2058

Inscription **3276**
Site Jebel Sirbal, Wadi Alayat, #187
Condition fair
Content Nabatean inscription
šlm ḥnṭlw br ....
[dky]r ʿwymw br klbw
Access II.2a.66 (printed, CIS)
Corpus CIS 2059

Inscription **3277**
Site Jebel Sirbal, Wadi Alayat, #187
Condition good
Content Nabatean inscription
šlm ḥwrw br
wʾlw
Access II.2a.66 (printed, CIS)
Corpus CIS 2060

Inscription 3278
Site Jebel Sirbal, Wadi Alayat, #187
Condition good
Content Nabatean inscription
šlm ʾbn qwmw
wkʿmh bny ʿ[mr]w
Access II.2a.67 (printed, CIS)
Corpus CIS 2061

Inscription 3279
Site Jebel Sirbal, Wadi Alayat, #187
Condition good
Content Nabatean inscription
šlm šlmw
Access II.2a.67 (printed, CIS)
Corpus CIS 2062

Inscription 3280
Site Jebel Sirbal, Wadi Alayat, #187
Condition good
Content Nabatean inscription
šlm šʿdʾlhy br bryʾw
Access II.2a.67 (printed, CIS)
Corpus CIS 2063

Inscription 3281
Site Jebel Sirbal, Wadi Alayat, #187
Condition good
Content Nabatean inscription
šlm wʾlw br zydw bṭb
Access II.2a.67 (printed, CIS)
Corpus CIS 2064

Inscription 3282
Site Jebel Sirbal, Wadi Alayat, #187
Condition good
Content Nabatean inscription
dkyr ʿbydw
br gdyw bṭb
Access II.2a.67 (printed, CIS)
Corpus CIS 2065

Inscription 3283
Site Jebel Sirbal, Wadi Alayat, #187
Condition good
Content Nabatean inscription
šlm dʾbw
br ʿmyw bṭb
Access II.2a.67 (printed, CIS)
Corpus CIS 2066

Inscription 3284
Site Jebel Sirbal, Wadi Alayat, #187
Condition fair
Content Nabatean inscription
gdyw br
ḥryšw
Access II.2a.67 (printed, CIS)
Corpus CIS 2067

Inscription 3285
Site Jebel Sirbal, Wadi Alayat, #187
Condition good
Content Nabatean inscription
ʿbdʾlbʿly br ʿmyw br
šmrḥ bytyʾ bṭb
Access II.2a.67 (printed, CIS)
Corpus CIS 2068

Inscription 3286
Site Jebel Sirbal, Wadi Alayat, #187
Condition poor
Content Nabatean inscription
šlm ʾ..bšw br
....
Access II.2a.67 (printed, CIS)
Corpus CIS 2069

Inscription 3287
Site Jebel Sirbal, Wadi Alayat, #187
Condition good
Content Nabatean inscription
šlm ḥnṭlw br pṣy bṭb
Access II.2a.68 (printed, CIS)
Corpus CIS 2070

Inscription 3288
Site Jebel Sirbal, Wadi Alayat, #187
Condition good
Content Nabatean inscription
šlm ḥwrw br ʿmnw bṭb
Access II.2a.68 (printed, CIS)
Corpus CIS 2071

Inscription 3289
Site Jebel Sirbal, Wadi Alayat, #187
Condition good
Content Nabatean inscription
dkyr bṭb wšlm
šʿdw br
grmʾlbʿly
ʿd ʿlm
Access II.2a.68 (printed, CIS)
Corpus CIS 2072

Inscription 3290
Site Jebel Sirbal, Wadi Alayat, #187
Condition good
Content Nabatean inscription
šlm ʿbdʾlbʿly
[br] ʿmmw
Access II.2a.68 (printed, CIS)
Corpus CIS 2073

Inscription 3291
Site Jebel Sirbal, Wadi Alayat, #187
Condition good
Content Nabatean inscription
šlm ʿbdʾlbʿly br
ʿmmw wʿmmw brh
Access II.2a.68 (printed, CIS)
Corpus CIS 2074

Inscription 3292
Site Jebel Sirbal, Wadi Alayat, #187
Condition good
Content Nabatean inscription
dkyr ṭb wʾlw br ʾwšw
Access II.2a.68 (printed, CIS)
Corpus CIS 2075

Inscription 3293
Site Jebel Sirbal, Wadi Alayat, #187
Condition fair
Content Nabatean inscription
pṣy br m.ʾl
bṭb
Access II.2a.69 (printed, CIS)
Corpus CIS 2076

Inscription 3294
Site Jebel Sirbal, Wadi Alayat, #187
Condition poor
Content Nabatean inscription
šlm šmrḥ br ..w
...rw bṭb
...w wʾlw
...ʿmyw...
Access II.2a.69 (printed, CIS)
Corpus CIS 2077

Inscription 3295
Site Jebel Sirbal, Wadi Alayat, #187
Condition good
Content Nabatean inscription
šlm bkrw br
qyyzw
Access II.2a.69 (printed, CIS)
Corpus CIS 2078

Inscription 3296
Site Jebel Sirbal, Wadi Alayat, #187
Condition good
Content Nabatean inscription
šlm šrpyw br
ʿrbyw
Access II.2a.69 (printed, CIS)
Corpus CIS 2079

Inscription 3297
Site Jebel Sirbal, Wadi Alayat, #187
Condition good
Content Nabatean inscription
dkyr ʾwšw br
ʿwtw bṭb
wʿwtw brh
Access II.2a.69 (printed, CIS)
Corpus CIS 2080

Inscription 3298
Site Jebel Sirbal, Wadi Alayat, #187
Condition fair
Content Nabatean inscription
šlm ʿwdw br
ʿmyw ṭ...
Access II.2a.69 (printed, CIS)
Corpus CIS 2081

Inscription 3299
Site Jebel Sirbal, Wadi Alayat, #187
Condition good
Content Nabatean inscription
šlm ḥnṭlw
Access II.2a.70 (printed, CIS)
Corpus CIS 2082

Inscription 3300
Site Jebel Sirbal, Wadi Alayat, #187
Condition good
Content Nabatean inscription
dkyr grmʾlbʿly
br ṣʿbw bṭb
Access II.2a.70 (printed, CIS)
Corpus CIS 2083

Inscription 3301
Site Jebel Sirbal, Wadi Alayat, #187
Condition poor
Content Nabatean inscription
šlm ʾḥršw br ʾwšw
... br ḥryšw br ...
[br] mgdyw tḥʾ...
Access II.2a.70 (printed, CIS)
Corpus CIS 2084

Inscription 3302
Site Jebel Sirbal, Wadi Alayat, #187
Condition poor
Content Nabatean inscription
šlm wʾlw ...
šlm mʿnw...
zydw br grmʾlbʿ[ly]
dkyr ṣwbw ... qynw
Access II.2a.70 (printed, CIS)
Corpus CIS 2085

Inscription 3303
Site Jebel Sirbal, Wadi Alayat, #187
Condition good
Content Nabatean inscription
šlm ʿbdʾlbʿly br ʿmyw by[tyʾ]
Access II.2a.70 (printed, CIS)
Corpus CIS 2086

Inscription 3304
Site Jebel Sirbal, Wadi Alayat, #187
Condition good
Content Nabatean inscription
šʿdʾlhy br
bryʾw
Access II.2a.70 (printed, CIS)
Corpus CIS 2087

Inscription 3305
Site Jebel Sirbal, Wadi Alayat, #187
Condition fair
Content Nabatean inscription
ʿwdw [br]
šʿdʾlhy qynw br [ʾ]wyšw
br ʾwyšw
Access II.2a.71 (printed, CIS)
Corpus CIS 2088

Inscription 3306
Site Jebel Sirbal, Wadi Alayat, #187
Condition fair
Content Nabatean inscription
šlm ʾʿlʾ
[br ʿ]bydw bṭ[b]
Access II.2a.71 (printed, CIS)
Corpus CIS 2089

Inscription 3307
Site Jebel Sirbal, Wadi Alayat, #187
Condition poor
Content Nabatean inscription
nšygw br .... šlm ʿmyw br ....
dkyr b[r]yʾw
Access II.2a.71 (printed, CIS)
Corpus CIS 2090

Inscription 3308
Site Jebel Sirbal, Wadi Alayat, #187
Condition good
Content Nabatean inscription
šlm dmgw br ṭylt bṭb
Access II.2a.71 (printed, CIS)
Corpus CIS 2091

Inscription 3309
Site Jebel Sirbal, Wadi Alayat, #187
Condition fair
Content Nabatean inscription
šlm gd[y]w....
šlm ḥlṣt br ḥbrkn
Access II.2a.71 (printed, CIS)
Corpus CIS 2092

Inscription 3310
Site Jebel Sirbal, Wadi Alayat, #187
Condition good
Content Nabatean inscription
šlm šmr[ḥ]
br ʿmmw
Access II.2a.71 (printed, CIS)
Corpus CIS 2093

Inscription 3311
Site Jebel Sirbal, Wadi Alayat, #187
Condition good
Content Nabatean inscription
šlm mʿnw br hnʾ[w]
Access II.2a.71 (printed, CIS)
Corpus CIS 2094

Inscription 3312
Site Jebel Sirbal, Wadi Alayat, #187
Condition fair
Content Nabatean inscription
šlm zydw
br [gr]mʾlbʿly
šlm grmʾ[lbʿ]ly
Access II.2a.72 (printed, CIS)
Corpus CIS 2095

Inscription 3313
Site Jebel Sirbal, Wadi Alayat, #187
Condition good
Content Nabatean inscription
šlm ʿmyw br šmrḥ
Access II.2a.72 (printed, CIS)
Corpus CIS 2096

Inscription 3314
Site Jebel Sirbal, Wadi Alayat, #187
Condition good
Content Nabatean inscription
šlm ṣwbw
br klbw
Access II.2a.72 (printed, CIS)
Corpus CIS 2097

Inscription 3315
Site Jebel Sirbal, Wadi Alayat, #187
Condition poor
Content Nabatean inscription
šlm ʾwšw br
ḥnṭlw
dk[y]r ʾ[wšw br]
ḥ[n]ṭlw
bṭb
šlm ....
Access II.2a.72 (printed, CIS)
Corpus CIS 2098

Inscription 3316
Site Jebel Sirbal, Wadi Alayat, #187
Condition good
Content Nabatean inscription
šlm ḥryšw br
ʿbd[l]bʿly br yʿly
Access II.2a.72 (printed, CIS)
Corpus CIS 2099

Inscription 3317
Site Jebel Sirbal, Wadi Alayat, #187
Condition good
Content Nabatean inscription
šlm ʾwšw br
ʿwtw
Access II.2a.72 (printed, CIS)
Corpus CIS 2100

Inscription 3318
Site Jebel Sirbal, Wadi Alayat, #187
Condition good
Content Nabatean inscription
šlm wʾlw
br dʾybw
Access II.2a.72 (printed, CIS)
Corpus CIS 2101

Inscription 3319
Site Jebel Sirbal, Wadi Alayat, #187
Condition good
Content Nabatean inscription
šlm ḥryšw
br šmrḥ šlm
Access II.2a.72 (printed, CIS)
Corpus CIS 2102

Inscription 3320
Site Jebel Sirbal, Wadi Alayat, #187
Condition good
Content Nabatean inscription
šlm bḥgh br
ʿbdʾlbʿly
Access II.2a.72 (printed, CIS)
Corpus CIS 2103

Inscription 3321
Site Jebel Sirbal, #189
Condition fair
Content Nabatean inscription
šlm ḥnṭlw br nšnkyh
šlm ʾl...
Access II.2a.73 (printed, CIS)
Corpus CIS 2104 (1)

Inscription 3322
Site Jebel Sirbal, #189
Condition fair
Content Nabatean inscription
šlm ʾwšw wpṣyw [bny]
ḥryšw
.... bṭb wšlm
Access II.2a.73 (printed, CIS)
Corpus CIS 2104 (2)

Inscription 3323
Site Jebel Sirbal, #189
Condition fair
Content Nabatean inscription
šlm šlmw br m..w
Access II.2a.73 (printed, CIS)
Corpus CIS 2104 (3)

Inscription 3324
Site Jebel Sirbal, #189
Condition fair
Content Nabatean inscription
šlm ḥlṣt
br ʿbdʾlbʿly
w br šʿwdy...
Access II.2a.73 (printed, CIS)
Corpus CIS 2105

Inscription 3325
Site Jebel Sirbal, #189
Condition good
Content Nabatean inscription
šlm mgdyw br wʾlw ʿlymʾ
Access II.2a.74 (printed, CIS)
Corpus CIS 2106

Inscription 3326
Site Jebel Sirbal, #189
Condition good
Content Nabatean inscription
šlm šmrḥ br klbw bṭb
Access II.2a.74 (printed, CIS)
Corpus CIS 2107

Inscription 3327
Site Jebel Sirbal, #189
Condition poor
Content Nabatean inscription
šlm šl[m]
šlm m[ʿ]yrw
br m....
Access II.2a.74 (printed, CIS)
Corpus CIS 2108

Inscription 3328
Site Jebel Sirbal, #189
Condition good
Content Nabatean inscription
br šlmw
šlm ʾšwdw
Access II.2a.74 (printed, CIS)
Corpus CIS 2109

Inscription 3329
Site Jebel Sirbal, #189
Condition fair
Content Nabatean inscription
[d]kyr qynw
[br ʾ]wyšw
Access II.2a.74 (printed, CIS)
Corpus CIS 2110

Inscription 3330
Site Jebel Sirbal, #189
Condition good
Content Nabatean inscription
šlm mʿyrw
šlm ʿmmw br
šlmw
Access II.2a.74 (printed, CIS)
Corpus CIS 2111

Inscription 3331
Site Jebel Sirbal, Wadi Ajaleh, #188
Condition fair
Content Nabatean inscription
šlm ḥryšw br mʿyrw
Access II.2a.75 (printed, CIS)
Corpus CIS 2112

Inscription 3332
Site Jebel Sirbal, #189
Condition good
Content Nabatean inscription
klbw br
ʿwdw
Access II.2a.75 (printed, CIS)
Corpus CIS 2113

Inscription 3333
Site Jebel Sirbal, #189
Condition good
Content Nabatean inscription
šlm ʿmmw
br ʾbn ʾlqyny
Access II.2a.75 (printed, CIS)
Corpus CIS 2114

Inscription 3334
Site Jebel Sirbal, #189
Condition fair
Content Nabatean inscription
šlm ḥnṭlw [br] ʾ[w]šw
Access II.2a.75 (printed, CIS)
Corpus CIS 2115

Inscription 3335
Site Jebel Sirbal, #189
Condition good
Content Nabatean inscription
šlm ṣwbw
Access II.2a.75 (printed, CIS)
Corpus CIS 2116

Inscription 3336
Site Jebel Sirbal, #189
Condition good
Content Nabatean inscription
šlm ʾlmbqrw br
ʿwy[mw]
Access II.2a.75 (printed, CIS)
Corpus CIS 2217

Inscription 3337
Site Jebel Sirbal, #189
Condition good
Content Nabatean inscription
šlm ʿbydw
br ḥrglw mbq[rʾ]
Access II.2a.75 (printed, CIS)
Corpus CIS 2118

Inscription 3338
Site Jebel Sirbal, #189
Condition poor
Content Nabatean inscription
Access II.2a.75 (printed, CIS)
Corpus CIS 2219

Inscription 3339
Site Jebel Sirbal, #189
Condition fair
Content Nabatean inscription
šlm wʾlw br ʿw[dw]
Access II.2a.75 (printed, CIS)
Corpus CIS 2120

Inscription 3340
Site Jebel Sirbal, #189
Condition poor
Content Nabatean inscription
šlm ᵓlmbq[rw]
br ᶜwdw bṭb
....
šlm wᵓlw br tym...'
Access II.2a.76 (printed, CIS)
Corpus CIS 2121

Inscription 3341
Site Jebel Sirbal, #189
Condition good
Content Nabatean inscription
šlm ᶜmmw br šlmw
Access II.2a.76 (printed, CIS)
Corpus CIS 2122

Inscription 3342
Site Jebel Sirbal, #189
Condition fair
Content Nabatean inscription
šlm mšlmw br wᵓlw [bṭb]
....
Access II.2a.76 (printed, CIS)
Corpus CIS 2123

Inscription 3343
Site Jebel Sirbal, #189
Condition poor
Content Nabatean inscription
Access II.2a.76 (printed, CIS)
Corpus CIS 2124

Inscription 3344
Site Jebel Sirbal, #189
Condition poor
Content Nabatean inscription
Access II.2a.76 (printed, CIS)
Corpus CIS 2125

Inscription 3345
Site Jebel Sirbal, #189
Condition poor
Content Nabatean inscription
Access II.2a.76 (printed, CIS)
Corpus CIS 2126

Inscription 3346
Site Jebel Sirbal, #189
Condition poor
Content Nabatean inscription
Access II.2a.76 (printed, CIS)
Corpus CIS 2127

Inscription 3347
Site Jebel Sirbal, #189
Condition fair
Content Nabatean inscription
šlm grymw br ᵓw...
Access II.2a.76 (printed, CIS)
Corpus CIS 2128

Inscription 3348
Site Jebel Sirbal, #189
Condition good
Content Nabatean inscription
šlm ḥlṣt
[br] šᶜwdt
Access II.2a.76 (printed, CIS)
Corpus CIS 2129

Inscription 3349
Site Jebel Sirbal, #189
Condition fair
Content Nabatean inscription
šlm tymᵓlhy br [ᶜ]wdw
šlm grmᵓl[hy]
Access II.2a.77 (printed, CIS)
Corpus CIS 2130

Inscription 3350
Site Jebel Sirbal, Wadi Alayat, #187
Condition good
Content Nabatean inscription
dkyr ḥlṣt wḥbrkn
[bny] šᶜdᵓlhy
Access II.2a.77 (printed, CIS)
Corpus CIS 2131

Inscription 3351
Site Jebel Sirbal, Wadi Alayat, #187
Condition poor
Content Nabatean inscription
šlm [ḥnṭ]lw br
ᵓwšw ᵓwšw
br [ḥn]ṭ[l]w
Access II.2a.77 (printed, CIS)
Corpus CIS 2132

Inscription 3352
Site Jebel Sirbal, Wadi Alayat, #187
Condition poor
Content Nabatean inscription
šlm ḥršw
Access II.2a.77 (printed, CIS)
Corpus CIS 2133

Inscription 3353
Site Jebel Sirbal, Wadi Alayat, #187
Condition fair
Content Nabatean inscription
šlm
bṭšw
šlm w
dw
Access II.2a.77 (printed, CIS)
Corpus CIS 2134

Inscription 3354
Site Jebel Sirbal, Wadi Alayat, #187
Condition fair
Content Nabatean inscription
šlm nšygw ....
Access II.2a.78 (printed, CIS)
Corpus CIS 2135

Inscription 3355
Site Jebel Sirbal, Wadi Alayat, #187
Condition poor
Content Nabatean inscription
šlm ʾ[wš]w br [ʿ]m[m]w bṭb w[šlm]
Access II.2a.78 (printed, CIS)
Corpus CIS 2136

Inscription 3356
Site Jebel Sirbal, Wadi Alayat, #187
Condition good
Content Nabatean inscription
šlm ʿbdʾlbʿly br
pʾrn
Access II.2a.78 (printed, CIS)
Corpus CIS 2137

Inscription 3357
Site Jebel Sirbal, Wadi Alayat, #187
Condition poor
Content Nabatean inscription
šlm hnʾw
....
Access II.2a.78 (printed, CIS)
Corpus CIS 2138

Inscription 3358
Site Jebel Sirbal, Wadi Alayat, #187
Condition fair
Content Nabatean inscription
šlm pʾrn br ʾlmbq[rw]
Access II.2a.78 (printed, CIS)
Corpus CIS 2139

Inscription 3359
Site Jebel Sirbal, Wadi Alayat, #187
Condition poor
Content Nabatean inscription
šlm wʾ.ʾp.. br ʾ...
Access II.2a.78 (printed, CIS)
Corpus CIS 2140

Inscription 3360
Site Jebel Sirbal, Wadi Alayat, #187
Condition poor
Content Nabatean inscription
ḥnṭlw wʾw[šw]
Access II.2a.78 (printed, CIS)
Corpus CIS 2141

Inscription 3361
Site Jebel Sirbal, Wadi Alayat, #187
Condition good
Content Nabatean inscription
šlm ḥlṣw
Access II.2a.78 (printed, CIS)
Corpus CIS 2142

Inscription 3362
Site Jebel Sirbal, Wadi Alayat, #187
Condition good
Content Nabatean inscription
šlm ʿbydw br
gdyw bṭb
Access II.2a.78 (printed, CIS)
Corpus CIS 2143

Inscription 3363
Site Jebel Sirbal, Wadi Alayat, #187
Condition good
Content Nabatean inscription
šlm šrpyw b[r]
ʿrbyw
Access II.2a.78 (printed, CIS)
Corpus CIS 2144

Inscription 3364
Site Jebel Sirbal, Wadi Alayat, #187
Condition good
Content Nabatean inscription
šlm ʾlkhnw br nšygw bṭb wšlm
Access II.2a.78 (printed, CIS)
Corpus CIS 2145

Inscription 3365
Site Jebel Sirbal, Wadi Alayat, #187
Condition good
Content Nabatean inscription
šlm ʾlktyw br ʿbdʾlbʿly bṭb wšlm
Access II.2a.79 (printed, CIS)
Corpus CIS 2146

Inscription 3366
Site Jebel Sirbal, Wadi Alayat, #187
Condition poor
Content Nabatean inscription
šmrḥ *or* šlmw
Access II.2a.79 (printed, CIS)
Corpus CIS 2147

Inscription **3367**
Site Jebel Sirbal, Wadi Alayat, #187
Condition fair
Content Nabatean inscription
šlm ḥrwṣw br ....
Access II.2a.79 (printed, CIS)
Corpus CIS 2148

Inscription **3368**
Site Jebel Sirbal, Wadi Alayat, #187
Condition good
Content Nabatean inscription
šlm ʿbdʾ[h]yw br
ʿwdw
Access II.2a.79 (printed, CIS)
Corpus CIS 2149

Inscription **3369**
Site Jebel Sirbal, Wadi Alayat, #187
Condition good
Content Nabatean inscription
šlm ʿmyw br ʿwdw
Access II.2a.79 (printed, CIS)
Corpus CIS 2150

Inscription **3370**
Site Jebel Sirbal, Wadi Alayat, #187
Condition fair
Content Nabatean inscription
[ḥ]rwṣw
šlm gšmw
Access II.2a.79 (printed, CIS)
Corpus CIS 2151

Inscription **3371**
Site Jebel Sirbal, Wadi Alayat, #187
Condition poor
Content Nabatean inscription
šlm ʿwdw br ....
šlm ʾlmbqrw
br [ʾ]wšʾl
ʿly
Access II.2a.79 (printed, CIS)
Corpus CIS 2152

Inscription **3372**
Site Jebel Sirbal, Wadi Alayat, #187
Condition poor
Content Nabatean inscription
šlm mḥ[my]w
br ....
Access II.2a.79 (printed, CIS)
Corpus CIS 2153

Inscription **3373**
Site Jebel Sirbal, Wadi Alayat, #187
Condition good
Content Nabatean inscription
šlm ʿmyw
br ʿmyw
Access II.2a.80 (printed, CIS)
Corpus CIS 2154

Inscription **3374**
Site Jebel Sirbal, Wadi Alayat, #187
Condition fair
Content Nabatean inscription
[ʿ]bydw br ʾwšw
Access II.2a.80 (printed, CIS)
Corpus CIS 2155

Inscription **3375**
Site Jebel Sirbal, Wadi Alayat, #187
Condition poor
Content Nabatean inscription
šlm ṣwbw
br ...ʾlh...
Access II.2a.80 (printed, CIS)
Corpus CIS 2156

Inscription **3376**
Site Jebel Sirbal, Wadi Alayat, #187
Condition good
Content Nabatean inscription
šlm ḥwrw br
ʿmrw
Access II.2a.80 (printed, CIS)
Corpus CIS 2157

Inscription **3377**
Site Jebel Sirbal, Wadi Alayat, #187
Condition good
Content Nabatean inscription
šlm hnyʾw br šlmw ḥgh
Access II.2a.80 (printed, CIS)
Corpus CIS 2158

Inscription **3378**
Site Jebel Sirbal, Wadi Alayat, #187
Condition good
Content Nabatean inscription
šlm [ʿ]mrw br ʿmmw
Access II.2a.80 (printed, CIS)
Corpus CIS 2159

Inscription 3379
Site Jebel Sirbal, Wadi Alayat, #187
Condition poor
Content Nabatean inscription
dk[yr bṭb]
lʿlm ʿlm[n]
ḥryšw br
.....
Access II.2a.80 (printed, CIS)
Corpus CIS 2160

Inscription 3380
Site Jebel Sirbal, Wadi Alayat, #187
Condition good
Content Nabatean inscription
šlm ḥnṭlw br nšnkyh wʿbdbʿly brh
Access II.2a.80 (printed, CIS)
Corpus CIS 2161

Inscription 3381
Site Jebel Sirbal, Wadi Alayat, #187
Condition poor
Content Nabatean inscription
šlm wʾlw br ....
Access II.2a.80 (printed, CIS)
Corpus CIS 2162

Inscription 3382
Site Jebel Sirbal, Wadi Alayat, #187
Condition poor
Content Nabatean inscription
šlm [ʾw]šlhy br [ʿbdʾlbʿly]
wʿbdʾlbʿly brh ....
Access II.2a.81 (printed, CIS)
Corpus CIS 2163

Inscription 3383
Site Jebel Sirbal, Wadi Alayat, #187
Condition good
Content Nabatean inscription
šlm ʿbṭt
br ḥryšw bṭb
br ḥnʾw wḥryšw brh
Access II.2a.81 (printed, CIS)
Corpus CIS 2164

Inscription 3384
Site Jebel Sirbal, Wadi Alayat, #187
Condition poor
Content Nabatean inscription
šlm ḥlṣw ....
.... br ḥwrw
Access II.2a.81 (printed, CIS)
Corpus CIS 2165

Inscription 3385
Site Jebel Sirbal, Wadi Alayat, #187
Condition good
Content Nabatean inscription
šlm ʾbʾwšw
wbryʾw wʿyydw bny ḥry
šw bṭb
Access II.2a.81 (printed, CIS)
Corpus CIS 2166

Inscription 3386
Site Jebel Sirbal, Wadi Alayat, #187
Condition good
Content Nabatean inscription
šlm ʿmyw br ʿbdʾhyw
Access II.2a.81 (printed, CIS)
Corpus CIS 2167

Inscription 3387
Site Jebel Sirbal, Wadi Alayat, #187
Condition good
Content Nabatean inscription
šlm mšlmw
br ʿmyw.
Access II.2a.81 (printed, CIS)
Corpus CIS 2168

Inscription 3388
Site Jebel Sirbal, Wadi Alayat, #187
Condition fair
Content Nabatean inscription
šlm ʾwšw
br ....w
Access II.2a.81 (printed, CIS)
Corpus CIS 2169

Inscription 3389
Site Jebel Sirbal, Wadi Alayat, #187
Condition good
Content Nabatean inscription
šlm wʾlw
br hnyʾw
Access II.2a.82 (printed, CIS)
Corpus CIS 2170

Inscription 3390
Site Jebel Sirbal, Wadi Alayat, #187
Condition good
Content Nabatean inscription
šlm klbw br
šʿdʾlhy
Access II.2a.82 (printed, CIS)
Corpus CIS 2171

Inscription 3391
Site Jebel Sirbal, Wadi Alayat, #187
Condition fair
Content Nabatean inscription
šlm wʾlw br
š.....w
Access II.2a.82 (printed, CIS)
Corpus CIS 2172

Inscription 3392
Site Jebel Sirbal, Wadi Alayat, #187
Condition good
Content Nabatean inscription
šlm wʾlw
br nqybw
Access II.2a.82 (printed, CIS)
Corpus CIS 2173

Inscription 3393
Site Jebel Sirbal, Wadi Alayat, #187
Condition good
Content Nabatean inscription
šlm pṣy br ḥnṭlw
Access II.2a.82 (printed, CIS)
Corpus CIS 2174

Inscription 3394
Site Jebel Sirbal, Wadi Alayat, #187
Condition good
Content Nabatean inscription
šlm gdyw
br dʾbw
Access II.2a.82 (printed, CIS)
Corpus CIS 2175

Inscription 3395
Site Jebel Sirbal, Wadi Alayat, #187
Condition good
Content Nabatean inscription
šlm ʿmyw br
ḥnṭlw bṭ[b]
Access II.2a.82 (printed, CIS)
Corpus CIS 2176

Inscription 3396
Site Jebel Sirbal, Wadi Alayat, #187
Condition good
Content Nabatean inscription
šlm ḥnṭlw
ʾwšw .ymw
Access II.2a.82 (printed, CIS)
Corpus CIS 2177

Inscription 3397
Site Jebel Sirbal, Wadi Alayat, #187
Condition good
Content Nabatean inscription
šlm ʿbdʾl[gy]ʾ
br ʾwšw
Access II.2a.82 (printed, CIS)
Corpus CIS 2178

Inscription 3398
Site Jebel Sirbal, Wadi Alayat, #187
Condition good
Content Nabatean inscription
dkyr šrpyw
br ʿrbyw
Access II.2a.83 (printed, CIS)
Corpus CIS 2179

Inscription 3399
Site Jebel Sirbal, Wadi Alayat, #187
Condition poor
Content Nabatean inscription
...
..ʿwymw...
Access II.2a.83 (printed, CIS)
Corpus CIS 2180

Inscription 3400
Site Jebel Sirbal, Wadi Alayat, #187
Condition poor
Content Nabatean inscription
šlm grmʾl[bʿ]l[y] ....
Access II.2a.83 (printed, CIS)
Corpus CIS 2181

Inscription 3401
Site Jebel Sirbal, Wadi Alayat, #187
Condition good
Content Nabatean inscription
šlm ḥryšw
[br] šʿdʾlhy
Access II.2a.83 (printed, CIS)
Corpus CIS 2182

Inscription 3402
Site Jebel Sirbal, Wadi Alayat, #187
Condition fair
Content Nabatean inscription
šlm ʿmyw
br .....
Access II.2a.83 (printed, CIS)
Corpus CIS 2183

Inscription 3403
Site Jebel Sirbal, Wadi Alayat, #187
Condition good
Content Nabatean inscription
šlm ʿbdʾlbʿly
br ḥlṣt bṭ[b]
Access II.2a.83 (printed, CIS)
Corpus CIS 2184

Inscription 3404
Site Jebel Sirbal, Wadi Alayat, #187
Condition fair
Content Nabatean inscription
šlm klbw br
ʿw[y]mw ....
Access II.2a.83 (printed, CIS)
Corpus CIS 2185

Inscription 3405
Site Jebel Sirbal, Wadi Alayat, #187
Condition good
Content Nabatean inscription
šlm ʾwšʾlbʿly
br grmʾlbʿly
Access II.2a.83 (printed, CIS)
Corpus CIS 2186

Inscription 3406
Site Jebel Sirbal, Wadi Alayat, #187
Condition fair
Content Nabatean inscription
šlm ḥ[gr]w [br] šmw
Access II.2a.83 (printed, CIS)
Corpus CIS 2187

Inscription 3407
Site Jebel Sirbal, Wadi Alayat, #187
Condition good
Content Nabatean inscription
šlm ʿmyw ʾkplʾ
br klbw bṭb
Access II.2a.84 (printed, CIS)
Corpus CIS 2188

Inscription 3408
Site Jebel Sirbal, Wadi Alayat, #187
Condition good
Content Nabatean inscription
šlm yʿly
Access II.2a.84 (printed, CIS)
Corpus CIS 2189

Inscription 3409
Site Jebel Sirbal, Wadi Alayat, #187
Condition good
Content Nabatean inscription
šlm ʿmmw br ʿbdʾlbʿly br
wʾlw
Access II.2a.84 (printed, CIS)
Corpus CIS 2190

Inscription 3410
Site Jebel Sirbal, Wadi Alayat, #187
Condition fair
Content Nabatean inscription
šlm
...w br
grmʾlbʿly
Access II.2a.84 (printed, CIS)
Corpus CIS 2191

Inscription 3411
Site Jebel Sirbal, Wadi Alayat, #187
Condition good
Content Nabatean inscription
šlm ḥlyṣw br
ʾwšʾl[b]ʿly bṭb
Access II.2a.84 (printed, CIS)
Corpus CIS 2192

Inscription 3412
Site Jebel Sirbal, Wadi Alayat, #187
Condition poor
Content Nabatean inscription
šl[m] .....w w....
br hn[ʾw]
Access II.2a.84 (printed, CIS)
Corpus CIS 2193

Inscription 3413
Site Jebel Sirbal, Wadi Alayat, #187
Condition good
Content Nabatean inscription
šlm šmrḥ
br kʿmh
Access II.2a.84 (printed, CIS)
Corpus CIS 2194

Inscription 3414
Site Jebel Sirbal, Wadi Alayat, #187
Condition fair
Content Nabatean inscription
dkyr wʾlw br .....
dkyr wʾlw br ʿwdw
Access II.2a.84 (printed, CIS)
Corpus CIS 2195

Inscription 3415
Site Jebel Sirbal, Wadi Alayat, #187
Condition fair
Content Nabatean inscription
dkyr ʿydw
dkyr grmʾlbʿly
..... bṭb w[šlm]
Access II.2a.85 (printed, CIS)
Corpus CIS 2196

Inscription **3416**
Site Jebel Sirbal, Wadi Alayat, #187
Condition fair
Content Nabatean inscription
dkyr dʾbw br ʿmyw
dky[r ʿb]ydw br ....
Access II.2a.85 (printed, CIS)
Corpus CIS 2197

Inscription **3417**
Site Jebel Sirbal, Wadi Alayat, #187
Condition poor
Content Nabatean inscription
šlm ʾl[dʾ]bw br ʾw[šw]
šlm [ḥ]ryšw br ....
Access II.2a.85 (printed, CIS)
Corpus CIS 2198

Inscription **3418**
Site Jebel Sirbal, Wadi Alayat, #187
Condition good
Content Nabatean inscription
šlm šmrḥ b[r]
ʾwšw
Access II.2a.85 (printed, CIS)
Corpus CIS 2199

Inscription **3419**
Site Jebel Sirbal, Wadi Alayat, #187
Condition fair
Content Nabatean inscription
šlm
ʿmrw br
..wʾ..
Access II.2a.85 (printed, CIS)
Corpus CIS 2200

Inscription **3420**
Site Jebel Sirbal, Wadi Alayat, #187
Condition good
Content Nabatean inscription
šlm ḥrwṣw br
grmʾlbʿly b[ṭb]
Access II.2a.85 (printed, CIS)
Corpus CIS 2201

Inscription **3421**
Site Jebel Sirbal, Wadi Alayat, #187
Condition fair
Content Nabatean inscription
šlm bryʾw br wʾ[lw]
šlm ʾl...
Access II.2a.85 (printed, CIS)
Corpus CIS 2202

Inscription **3422**
Site Jebel Sirbal, Wadi Alayat, #187
Condition fair
Content Nabatean inscription
šlm wʾlw br ʾwš[w]
mgdyw
Access II.2a.85 (printed, CIS)
Corpus CIS 2203

Inscription **3423**
Site Jebel Sirbal, Wadi Alayat, #187
Condition good
Content Nabatean inscription
šlm ʾwšw
br bṭšw
Access II.2a.86 (printed, CIS)
Corpus CIS 2204

Inscription **3424**
Site Jebel Sirbal, Wadi Alayat, #187
Condition poor
Content Nabatean inscription
šlm ʿmyw br ....
...wṭbš.w
Access II.2a.86 (printed, CIS)
Corpus CIS 2205

Inscription **3425**
Site Jebel Sirbal, Wadi Alayat, #187
Condition good
Content Nabatean inscription
dkyr ʿydw br
ḥššw
Access II.2a.86 (printed, CIS)
Corpus CIS 2206

Inscription **3426**
Site Jebel Sirbal, Wadi Alayat, #187
Condition good
Content Nabatean inscription
šlm ḥryšw br
ʿṣyw
Access II.2a.86 (printed, CIS)
Corpus CIS 2207

Inscription **3427**
Site Jebel Sirbal, Wadi Alayat, #187
Condition fair
Content Nabatean inscription
šlm wʾlw
br ....
Access II.2a.86 (printed, CIS)
Corpus CIS 2208

Inscription 3428
Site Jebel Sirbal, Wadi Alayat, #187
Condition good
Content Nabatean inscription
šlm ʿmrw
br ʿmmw
Access II.2a.86 (printed, CIS)
Corpus CIS 2209

Inscription 3429
Site Jebel Sirbal, Wadi Alayat, #187
Condition good
Content Nabatean inscription
šlm ḥryšw
br ʿmyw
Access II.2a.86 (printed, CIS)
Corpus CIS 2210

Inscription 3430
Site Jebel Sirbal, Wadi Alayat, #187
Condition good
Content Nabatean inscription
dkyr ʿrbyw br
srpyw m
Access II.2a.86 (printed, CIS)
Corpus CIS 2211

Inscription 3431
Site Jebel Sirbal, Wadi Alayat, #187
Condition fair
Content Nabatean inscription
[d]ky[r] bṭšw w
br ʿbd...
Access II.2a.87 (printed, CIS)
Corpus CIS 2212

Inscription 3432
Site Jebel Sirbal, Wadi Alayat, #187
Condition fair
Content Nabatean inscription
dkyr mgdyw
....šlw
Access II.2a.87 (printed, CIS)
Corpus CIS 2213

Inscription 3433
Site Jebel Sirbal, Wadi Alayat, #187
Condition good
Content Nabatean inscription
šlm ʾlmbqrw br ʿmyw
Access II.2a.87 (printed, CIS)
Corpus CIS 2214

Inscription 3434
Site Jebel Sirbal, Wadi Alayat, #187
Condition fair
Content Nabatean inscription
dkyr ʿmyw br [ḥ]nṭ[lw]
šlm ʾl...
Access II.2a.87 (printed, CIS)
Corpus CIS 2215

Inscription 3435
Site Jebel Sirbal, Wadi Alayat, #187
Condition good
Content Nabatean inscription
dkyr ḥnṭlw br
ʿmyw
Access II.2a.87 (printed, CIS)
Corpus CIS 2216

Inscription 3436
Site Jebel Sirbal, Wadi Alayat, #187
Condition fair
Content Nabatean inscription
dkyr šmrḥ
br ʾbn ʾlqy[ny] bṭb
Access II.2a.87 (printed, CIS)
Corpus CIS 2217

Inscription 3437
Site Jebel Sirbal, Wadi Alayat, #187
Condition good
Content Nabatean inscription
šlm ʾʿlʾ br
šmrḥ bṭ[b]
Access II.2a.87 (printed, CIS)
Corpus CIS 2218

Inscription 3438
Site Jebel Sirbal, Wadi Alayat, #187
Condition good
Content Nabatean inscription
šlm šmrḥ
br ʿmyw
Access II.2a.87 (printed, CIS)
Corpus CIS 2219

Inscription 3439
Site Jebel Sirbal, Wadi Alayat, #187
Condition good
Content Nabatean inscription
šlm ṭylt br dmgw
Access II.2a.88 (printed, CIS)
Corpus CIS 2220

Inscription 3440
Site Jebel Sirbal, Wadi Alayat, #187
Condition poor
Content Nabatean inscription
šlm šlmw [br]
ʿbdʾl[bʿly]
Access II.2a.88 (printed, CIS)
Corpus CIS 2221

Inscription 3441
Site Jebel Sirbal, Wadi Alayat, #187
Condition poor
Content Nabatean inscription
dkyr mgdyw
...šlw
Access II.2a.88 (printed, CIS)
Corpus CIS 2222

Inscription 3442
Site Jebel Sirbal, Wadi Alayat, #187
Condition good
Content Nabatean inscription
dkyr yʿly br tymʾlhy
Access II.2a.88 (printed, CIS)
Corpus CIS 2223

Inscription 3443
Site Jebel Sirbal, Wadi Alayat, #187
Condition good
Content Nabatean inscription
šlm mʿnw br
hnʾw bṭb
Access II.2a.88 (printed, CIS)
Corpus CIS 2224 (1)

Inscription 3444
Site Jebel Sirbal, Wadi Alayat, #187
Condition poor
Content Nabatean inscription
...yw...p...
Access II.2a.88 (printed, CIS)
Corpus CIS 2224 (2)

Inscription 3445
Site Jebel Sirbal, Wadi Alayat, #187
Condition fair
Content Nabatean inscription
šlm ḥr[y]šw br w[ʾlw]
Access II.2a.88 (printed, CIS)
Corpus CIS 2225

Inscription 3446
Site Jebel Sirbal, Wadi Alayat, #187
Condition poor
Content Nabatean inscription
šlm ...y.
[by]tyʾ br ʿlyw
Access II.2a.88 (printed, CIS)
Corpus CIS 2226

Inscription 3447
Site Jebel Sirbal, Wadi Alayat, #187
Condition good
Content Nabatean inscription
šlm ḥršw
br ḥgyrw
Access II.2a.89 (printed, CIS)
Corpus CIS 2227

Inscription 3448
Site Jebel Sirbal, Wadi Alayat, #187
Condition good
Content Nabatean inscription
šlm ʿmmw br ḥgyrw
Access II.2a.89 (printed, CIS)
Corpus CIS 2228

Inscription 3449
Site Jebel Sirbal, Wadi Alayat, #187
Condition fair
Content Nabatean inscription
šlm ḥwrw br ....
Access II.2a.89 (printed, CIS)
Corpus CIS 2229

Inscription 3450
Site Jebel Sirbal, Wadi Alayat, #187
Condition good
Content Nabatean inscription
šlm pʾrn
Access II.2a.89 (printed, CIS)
Corpus CIS 2230

Inscription 3451
Site Jebel Sirbal, Wadi Alayat, #187
Condition fair
Content Nabatean inscription
šlm dʾbw br
ʿwdw
šlm ʾtmw
br ʿwdw
šl[m] ʾʿ[lʾ]
Access II.2a.89 (printed, CIS)
Corpus CIS 2231

Inscription 3452
Site Jebel Sirbal, Wadi Alayat, #187
Condition good
Content Nabatean inscription
šlm grmʾlbʿly
br ṣwbw
Access II.2a.89 (printed, CIS)
Corpus CIS 2232

Inscription 3453
Site Jebel Sirbal, Wadi Alayat, #187
Condition good
Content Nabatean inscription
šlm kʿmh br
ṣwbw bṭb
Access II.2a.89 (printed, CIS)
Corpus CIS 2233

Inscription 3454
Site Jebel Sirbal, Wadi Alayat, #187
Condition fair
Content Nabatean inscription
šlm ʾwšw ...
Access II.2a.90 (printed, CIS)
Corpus CIS 2234

Inscription 3455
Site Jebel Sirbal, Wadi Alayat, #187
Condition fair
Content Nabatean inscription
šlm ʿmrw br nšy[gw bṭb]
Access II.2a.90 (printed, CIS)
Corpus CIS 2235

Inscription 3456
Site Jebel Sirbal, Wadi Alayat, #187
Condition good
Content Nabatean inscription
šlm dʾbw br ʿmyw
Access II.2a.90 (printed, CIS)
Corpus CIS 2236

Inscription 3457
Site Jebel Sirbal, Wadi Alayat, #187
Condition fair
Content Nabatean inscription
šlm ʾwšw br .... bṭb
šlm ḥnṭlw
Access II.2a.90 (printed, CIS)
Corpus CIS 2237 (1)

Inscription 3458
Site Jebel Sirbal, Wadi Alayat, #187
Condition good
Content Nabatean inscription
šlm ʾwšw br klbw wklbw brh bṭb
Access II.2a.90 (printed, CIS)
Corpus CIS 2237 (2)

Inscription 3459
Site Jebel Sirbal, Wadi Alayat, #187
Condition good
Content Nabatean inscription
šlm ʿbydw br gdyw bṭb
Access II.2a.90 (printed, CIS)
Corpus CIS 2238

Inscription 3460
Site Jebel Sirbal, Wadi Alayat, #187
Condition poor
Content Nabatean inscription
pṣy...
Access II.2a.90 (printed, CIS)
Corpus CIS 2239

Inscription 3461
Site Jebel Sirbal, Wadi Alayat, #187
Condition good
Content Nabatean inscription
šlm gdyw br ʾwšw
Access II.2a.90 (printed, CIS)
Corpus CIS 2240

Inscription 3462
Site Jebel Sirbal, Wadi Alayat, #187
Condition good
Content Nabatean inscription
šlm ʿbydw br gdyw
Access II.2a.90 (printed, CIS)
Corpus CIS 2241

Inscription 3463
Site Jebel Sirbal, Wadi Alayat, #187
Condition poor
Content Nabatean inscription
šlm grmʾ[lbʿly]
Access II.2a.90 (printed, CIS)
Corpus CIS 2242

Inscription 3464
Site Jebel Sirbal, Wadi Alayat, #187
Condition fair
Content Nabatean inscription
šlm gdyw
br wʾlw
bṭ[b]
šlm ḥl...
Access II.2a.90 (printed, CIS)
Corpus CIS 2243

Inscription 3465
Site Jebel Sirbal, Wadi Alayat, #187
Condition fair
Content Nabatean inscription
lmdk[wr] wʾlw
br nkybw k[r]mh
bṭb
Access II.2a.91 (printed, CIS)
Corpus CIS 2244

Inscription 3466
Site Jebel Sirbal, Wadi Alayat, #187
Condition good
Content Nabatean inscription
šlm mʿnw br hnʾw
Access II.2a.91 (printed, CIS)
Corpus CIS 2245

Inscription 3467
Site Jebel Sirbal, Wadi Alayat, #187
Condition good
Content Nabatean inscription
šlm ʾlmbqrw
br klbw
Access II.2a.91 (printed, CIS)
Corpus CIS 2246

Inscription 3468
Site Jebel Sirbal, Wadi Alayat, #187
Condition good
Content Nabatean inscription
šlm gdyw
ḥlṣt br ḥlṣ[t]
Access II.2a.91 (printed, CIS)
Corpus CIS 2247

Inscription 3469
Site Jebel Sirbal, Wadi Alayat, #187
Condition good
Content Nabatean inscription
šlm ʾwšw
br ʾwšʾlbʿl[y]
Access II.2a.91 (printed, CIS)
Corpus CIS 2248

Inscription 3470
Site Jebel Sirbal, Wadi Alayat, #187
Condition good
Content Nabatean inscription
šlm mgdyw br ʿmyw
br ʾwšw
Access II.2a.91 (printed, CIS)
Corpus CIS 2249

Inscription 3471
Site Jebel Sirbal, Wadi Alayat, #187
Condition good
Content Nabatean inscription
šlm hnyʾw br
wʾlw
Access II.2a.91 (printed, CIS)
Corpus CIS 2250

Inscription 3472
Site Jebel Sirbal, Wadi Alayat, #187
Condition good
Content Nabatean inscription
dkyr ṣwbw br
nšy[gw] bṭb
Access II.2a.92 (printed, CIS)
Corpus CIS 2251

Inscription 3473
Site Jebel Sirbal, Wadi Alayat, #187
Condition good
Content Nabatean inscription
šlm qwmw
br ʿbdʾlbʿl[y] bṭb
Access II.2a.92 (printed, CIS)
Corpus CIS 2252

Inscription 3474
Site Jebel Sirbal, Wadi Alayat, #187
Condition good
Content Nabatean inscription
šlm ḥrwṣw
šlm ḥrwṣ[w]
Access II.2a.92 (printed, CIS)
Corpus CIS 2253

Inscription 3475
Site Jebel Sirbal, Wadi Alayat, #187
Condition fair
Content Nabatean inscription
šlm ʾlhyw [br] ....
Access II.2a.92 (printed, CIS)
Corpus CIS 2254

Inscription 3476
Site Jebel Sirbal, Wadi Alayat, #187
Condition good
Content Nabatean inscription
šlm grmʾlbʿ[ly]
Access II.2a.92 (printed, CIS)
Corpus CIS 2255

Inscription 3477
Site Jebel Sirbal, Wadi Alayat, #187
Condition good
Content Nabatean inscription
šlm ḥwrw br mʿyrw
Access II.2a.92 (printed, CIS)
Corpus CIS 2256

Inscription 3478
Site Jebel Sirbal, Wadi Alayat, #187
Condition good
Content Nabatean inscription
šlm ʿbdʾlbʿly br ḥryšw
Access II.2a.92 (printed, CIS)
Corpus CIS 2257

Inscription 3479
Site Jebel Sirbal, Wadi Alayat, #187
Condition good
Content Nabatean inscription
šlm bryʾ[w] br klbw bṭb
Access II.2a.92 (printed, CIS)
Corpus CIS 2258

Inscription 3480
Site Jebel Sirbal, Wadi Alayat, #187
Condition good
Content Nabatean inscription
šlm ʾʿlʾ br ḥlṣt bṭb
Access II.2a.92 (printed, CIS)
Corpus CIS 2259

Inscription 3481
Site Jebel Sirbal, Wadi Alayat, #187
Condition good
Content Nabatean inscription
šlm grmʾlbʿly
Access II.2a.93 (printed, CIS)
Corpus CIS 2260 (1)

Inscription 3482
Site Jebel Sirbal, Wadi Alayat, #187
Condition good
Content Nabatean inscription
šlm whbʾlhy
Access II.2a.93 (printed, CIS)
Corpus CIS 2260 (2)

Inscription 3483
Site Jebel Sirbal, Wadi Alayat, #187
Condition good
Content Nabatean inscription
šlm ʿmmw br ....
Access II.2a.93 (printed, CIS)
Corpus CIS 2260 (3)

Inscription 3484
Site Jebel Sirbal, Wadi Alayat, #187
Condition good
Content Nabatean inscription
šl[m]
ʿmyrt br
ʿmyw
Access II.2a.93 (printed, CIS)
Corpus CIS 2261

Inscription 3485
Site Jebel Sirbal, Wadi Alayat, #187
Condition good
Content Nabatean inscription
šlm g[d]yw
Access II.2a.93 (printed, CIS)
Corpus CIS 2262

Inscription 3486
Site Jebel Sirbal, Wadi Alayat, #187
Condition poor
Content Nabatean inscription
šlm ...
[br] ʾlmbqrw
Access II.2a.93 (printed, CIS)
Corpus CIS 2263

Inscription 3487
Site Jebel Sirbal, Wadi Alayat, #187
Condition poor
Content Nabatean inscription
šlm ...ʾlbʿly br ....
Access II.2a.93 (printed, CIS)
Corpus CIS 2264

Inscription 3488
Site Jebel Sirbal, Wadi Alayat, #187
Condition poor
Content Nabatean inscription
dkyr ʿyd[w br] ḥš[šw]
Access II.2a.94 (printed, CIS)
Corpus CIS 2265

Inscription 3489
Site Jebel Sirbal, Wadi Alayat, #187
Condition fair
Content Nabatean inscription
šlm ʿmyw br ḥnṭlw
šlm ḥnṭ[lw]
Access II.2a.94 (printed, CIS)
Corpus CIS 2266

Inscription 3490
Site Jebel Sirbal, Wadi Alayat, #187
Condition poor
Content Nabatean inscription
šlm bryʾw br ....
Access II.2a.94 (printed, CIS)
Corpus CIS 2267

Inscription 3491
Site Jebel Sirbal, Wadi Alayat, #187
Condition fair
Content Nabatean inscription
šlm wʾlw
šlm klbw [br] p[ʾrn]
Access II.2a.94 (printed, CIS)
Corpus CIS 2268

Inscription 3492
Site Jebel Sirbal, Wadi Alayat, #187
Condition good
Content Nabatean inscription
nbhw br ʾlktyw
Access II.2a.94 (printed, CIS)
Corpus CIS 2269

Inscription 3493
Site Jebel Sirbal, Wadi Alayat, #187
Condition good
Content Nabatean inscription
šmrḥ br šʿdʾlhy
Access II.2a.94 (printed, CIS)
Corpus CIS 2270

Inscription 3494
Site Jebel Sirbal, Wadi Alayat, #187
Condition good
Content Nabatean inscription
šlm ʿmrw br qrḥw
Access II.2a.95 (printed, CIS)
Corpus CIS 2271

Inscription 3495
Site Jebel Sirbal, Wadi Alayat, #187
Condition good
Content Nabatean inscription
šlm ʾʿl[ʾ] br ʾwšʾlhy bṭb
Access II.2a.95 (printed, CIS)
Corpus CIS 2272

Inscription 3496
Site Jebel Sirbal, Wadi Alayat, #187
Condition good
Content Nabatean inscription
šlm ʾlmbqrw br
mškw [b]kl ṭb
Access II.2a.95 (printed, CIS)
Corpus CIS 2273

Inscription 3497
Site Jebel Sirbal, Wadi Alayat, #187
Condition good
Content Nabatean inscription
[šl]m ʿbdw br klbw
Access II.2a.95 (printed, CIS)
Corpus CIS 2274

Inscription 3498
Site Jebel Sirbal, Wadi Alayat, #187
Condition fair
Content Nabatean inscription
šlm ʾlkhnw
[ʾʿl]ʾ br ḥlṣt
Access II.2a.95 (printed, CIS)
Corpus CIS 2275

Inscription 3499
Site Jebel Sirbal, Wadi Alayat, #187
Condition good
Content Nabatean inscription
šlm wʾlw
br grmʾlhy
Access II.2a.95 (printed, CIS)
Corpus CIS 2276

Inscription 3500
Site Jebel Sirbal, Wadi Alayat, #187
Condition good
Content Nabatean inscription
šlm ʾwšʾlhy br
ʿbdʾlbʿly
Access II.2a.95 (printed, CIS)
Corpus CIS 2277

Inscription 3501
Site Jebel Sirbal, Wadi Alayat, #187
Condition good
Content Nabatean inscription
šlm zydw br pṣyw bṭb
Access II.2a.95 (printed, CIS)
Corpus CIS 2278

Inscription 3502
Site Jebel Sirbal, Wadi Alayat, #187
Condition fair
Content Nabatean inscription
šlm ʾwšw br ....
ʾ....
Access II.2a.95 (printed, CIS)
Corpus CIS 2279

Inscription 3503
Site Jebel Sirbal, Wadi Alayat, #187
Condition poor
Content Nabatean inscription
šlm .mw br grmʾlbʿly
šlm ʾlm...
Access II.2a.96 (printed, CIS)
Corpus CIS 2280

Inscription 3504
Site Jebel Sirbal, Wadi Alayat, #187
Condition good
Content Nabatean inscription
šlm wʾlw br kʿmh bṭb
Access II.2a.96 (printed, CIS)
Corpus CIS 2281

Inscription 3505
Site Jebel Sirbal, Wadi Alayat, #187
Condition fair
Content Nabatean inscription
šlm ʿbdʾlbʿly br ....
Access II.2a.96 (printed, CIS)
Corpus CIS 2282

Inscription 3506
Site Jebel Sirbal, Wadi Alayat, #187
Condition fair
Content Nabatean inscription
šlm m[ʿ]nw [b]r pʾrn
Access II.2a.96 (printed, CIS)
Corpus CIS 2283

Inscription 3507
Site Jebel Sirbal, Wadi Alayat, #187
Condition good
Content Nabatean inscription
šlm wʾ[l]w br ʿlht bṭb
Access II.2a.96 (printed, CIS)
Corpus CIS 2284

Inscription 3508
Site Jebel Sirbal, Wadi Alayat, #187
Condition fair
Content Nabatean inscription
šlm ʾwšʾ[lhy] ....
Access II.2a.96 (printed, CIS)
Corpus CIS 2285

Inscription 3509
Site Jebel Sirbal, Wadi Alayat, #187
Condition poor
Content Nabatean inscription
dkyr ḥlṣt [br] .....rʾ
Access II.2a.96 (printed, CIS)
Corpus CIS 2286

Inscription 3510
Site Jebel Sirbal, Wadi Alayat, #187
Condition good
Content Nabatean inscription
dkyr ʾwšw
br ʿwtw
Access II.2a.96 (printed, CIS)
Corpus CIS 2287

Inscription 3511
Site Jebel Sirbal, Wadi Alayat, #187
Condition good
Content Nabatean inscription
šlm ḥryšw
[br] ʿbdʾlbʿly
Access II.2a.96 (printed, CIS)
Corpus CIS 2288

Inscription 3512
Site Jebel Sirbal, Wadi Alayat, #187
Condition good
Content Nabatean inscription
šlm ʿmmw
Access II.2a.97 (printed, CIS)
Corpus CIS 2289

Inscription 3513
Site Jebel Sirbal, Wadi Alayat, #187
Condition poor
Content Nabatean inscription
Access II.2a.97 (printed, CIS)
Corpus CIS 2290

Inscription 3514
Site Jebel Sirbal, Wadi Alayat, #187
Condition poor
Content Nabatean inscription
Access II.2a.97 (printed, CIS)
Corpus CIS 2291

Inscription 3515
Site Jebel Sirbal, Wadi Alayat, #187
Condition fair
Content Nabatean inscription
šlm [ʾ]wšw br ....
Access II.2a.97 (printed, CIS)
Corpus CIS 2292

Inscription 3516
Site Jebel Sirbal, Wadi Alayat, #187
Condition good
Content Nabatean inscription
šlm gdyw br
wʾlw bṭb
Access II.2a.97 (printed, CIS)
Corpus CIS 2293

Inscription 3517
Site Jebel Sirbal, Wadi Alayat, #187
Condition good
Content Nabatean inscription
šlm wdw br ʾšmrt
wʾlw br ʿbdʾlhy
Access II.2a.97 (printed, CIS)
Corpus CIS 2294

Inscription 3518
Site Jebel Sirbal, Wadi Alayat, #187
Condition good
Content Nabatean inscription
šlm bḥg[h]
br grm
ʾlbʿly
Access II.2a.97 (printed, CIS)
Corpus CIS 2295

Inscription 3519
Site Jebel Sirbal, Wadi Ajaleh, #188
Condition good
Content Nabatean inscription
šlm bryʾw br
klbw bkl ṭ[b]
Access II.2a.97 (printed, CIS)
Corpus CIS 2296

Inscription 3520
Site Jebel Sirbal, Wadi Alayat, #187
Condition good
Content Nabatean inscription
šlm ḥryšw [br]
tymʾlhy bṭb
Access II.2a.97 (printed, CIS)
Corpus CIS 2297

Inscription	**3521**
Site	Jebel Sirbal, Wadi Alayat, #187
Condition	poor
Content	Nabatean inscription šlm [ḫlṣ]t br bryʾw wbryʾw br[h]
Access	II.2a.97 (printed, CIS)
Corpus	CIS 2298

Inscription	**3522**
Site	Jebel Sirbal, Wadi Alayat, #187
Condition	good
Content	Nabatean inscription šlm mʿnw
Access	II.2a.98 (printed, CIS)
Corpus	CIS 2299

Inscription	**3523**
Site	Jebel Sirbal, Wadi Alayat, #187
Condition	good
Content	Nabatean inscription šlm ʿmrw br klbw
Access	II.2a.98 (printed, CIS)
Corpus	CIS 2300

Inscription	**3524**
Site	Jebel Sirbal, Wadi Alayat, #187
Condition	good
Content	Nabatean inscription dkyr ʾbn qwmw br ʿmrw
Access	II.2a.98 (printed, CIS)
Corpus	CIS 2301

Inscription	**3525**
Site	Jebel Naqus, #103
Condition	poor
Content	Greek inscription
Limitation	*Tentative decipherment only*
Access	Euting 1 (printed, J. Euting)
Corpus	Euting I.2a

Inscription	**3526**
Site	Jebel Naqus, #103
Condition	good
Content	rock drawing
Comment	*five-pointed star*
Access	Euting 1 (printed, J. Euting)
Corpus	Euting I.2a

Inscription	**3527**
Site	Jebel Naqus, #103
Condition	good
Content	Greek inscription
Limitation	*Tentative decipherment only*
Access	Euting 1 (printed, J. Euting)
Corpus	Euting I.2b

Inscription	**3528**
Site	Jebel Naqus, #103
Condition	good
Content	unidentified inscription
Access	Euting 1 (printed, J. Euting)
Corpus	Euting I.2c

Inscription	**3529**
Site	Jebel Naqus, #103
Condition	good
Content	Arabic inscription
Access	Euting 1 (printed, J. Euting)
Corpus	Euting I.2d

Inscription	**3530**
Site	Jebel Naqus, #103
Dating	1843
Condition	good
Content	Greek inscription
Limitation	*Tentative decipherment only*
Access	Euting 1 (printed, J. Euting)
Corpus	Euting I.1e

Inscription	**3531**
Site	Wadi Leja, #27
Condition	poor
Content	Greek inscription
Limitation	*Tentative decipherment only*
Access	Euting 2 (printed, J. Euting)
Corpus	Euting III.29

Inscription	**3532**
Site	Wadi Leja, #27
Condition	good
Content	Greek inscription
Limitation	*Tentative decipherment only*
Access	Euting 2 (printed, J. Euting)
Corpus	Euting III.30

Inscription	**3533**
Site	Wadi Leja, #27
Condition	good
Content	crosses with inscription
Access	Euting 3 (printed, J. Euting)
Corpus	Euting III.30

Inscription	**3534**
Site	Jebel Sirbal, Wadi Nakhleh, #221
Condition	good
Content	Nabatean inscription šlm yʿly
Access	II.2a.98 (printed, CIS)
Corpus	CIS 2302

Inscription	**3535**
Site	Jebel Sirbal, Wadi Nakhleh, #221
Condition	good
Content	Nabatean inscription šlm ʿbydw [br] mḥmyw bṭb
Access	II.2a.98 (printed, CIS)
Corpus	CIS 2303

Inscription 3536
Site Jebel Sirbal, Wadi Nakhleh, #221
Condition good
Content Nabatean inscription
šlm mʿnw
hnʾw
šlm ḥgw [br]
ʿbdʾlbʿly bṭb
Access II.2a.98 (printed, CIS)
Corpus CIS 2304

Inscription 3537
Site Jebel Sirbal, Wadi Nakhleh, #221
Condition fair
Content Nabatean inscription
šlm ḥgw
br ʿbdʾl[bʿ]l[y]
Access II.2a.98 (printed, CIS)
Corpus CIS 2305

Inscription 3538
Site Jebel Sirbal, Wadi Nakhleh, #221
Condition good
Content Nabatean inscription
šlm ʿwdw br dʾbw
Access II.2a.99 (printed, CIS)
Corpus CIS 2306

Inscription 3539
Site Jebel Sirbal, Wadi Nakhleh, #221
Condition good
Content Nabatean inscription
šlm ʿzytw br
nšygw
Access II.2a.99 (printed, CIS)
Corpus CIS 2307

Inscription 3540
Site Jebel Sirbal, Wadi Nakhleh, #221
Condition good
Content Nabatean inscription
šlm mʿnw br
hnʾw
Access II.2a.99 (printed, CIS)
Corpus CIS 2308

Inscription 3541
Site Jebel Sirbal, Wadi Nakhleh, #221
Condition good
Content Nabatean inscription
šmrḥ br klbw
Access II.2a.99 (printed, CIS)
Corpus CIS 2309

Inscription 3542
Site Jebel Sirbal, Wadi Nakhleh, #221
Condition good
Content Nabatean inscription
šlm wʾlw [br]
mgdyw
šlm
Access II.2a.99 (printed, CIS)
Corpus CIS 2310

Inscription 3543
Site Jebel Sirbal, Wadi Nakhleh, #221
Condition fair
Content Nabatean inscription
šlm ḥr
šw ʾw...w
Access II.2a.99 (printed, CIS)
Corpus CIS 2311

Inscription 3544
Site Jebel Sirbal, Wadi Nakhleh, #221
Condition good
Content Nabatean inscription
šlm ḥryšw
br ʾwšw
Access II.2a.99 (printed, CIS)
Corpus CIS 2312

Inscription 3545
Site Jebel Sirbal, Wadi Nakhleh, #221
Condition poor
Content Nabatean inscription
šlm hnyʾ[w]
[br] š[ʿd]ʾlhy b[ṭb]
Access II.2a.99 (printed, CIS)
Corpus CIS 2313

Inscription 3546
Site Jebel Sirbal, Wadi Nakhleh, #221
Condition fair
Content Nabatean inscription
šlm ʾʿlʾ br
....
Access II.2a.99 (printed, CIS)
Corpus CIS 2314

Inscription 3547
Site Jebel Sirbal, Wadi Nakhleh, #221
Condition fair
Content Nabatean inscription
šlm wʾ[l]w
Access II.2a.99 (printed, CIS)
Corpus CIS 2315

Inscription 3548
Site Wadi Leja, #27
Dating 1868
Condition good
Content Latin inscription
Limitation *Tentative decipherment only*
Access Euting 3 (printed, J. Euting)
Corpus Euting III.40

Inscription 3549
Site Nahal Avdat 2, Nahal Avdat, #158
Technique incised
Condition good
Dimensions 50 x 9 cm.
Content Old North Arabic inscription
Access GE21 (photograph, Project)

Inscription 3550
Site Wadi Leja, #27
Condition good
Content crosses with inscription
Access Euting 3 (printed, J. Euting)
Corpus Euting III.45a

Inscription 3551
Site Wadi Leja, #27
Condition good
Content Greek inscription
Limitation *Tentative decipherment only*
Access Euting 4 (printed, J. Euting)
Corpus Euting III.52

Inscription 3552
Site Wadi Leja, #27
Condition good
Content Greek inscription
Limitation *Tentative decipherment only*
Access Euting 4 (printed, J. Euting)
Corpus Euting III.54

Inscription 3553
Site Wadi Leja, #27
Condition fair
Content Greek inscription
Limitation *Tentative decipherment only*
Access Euting 4 (printed, J. Euting)
Corpus Euting III.55

Inscription 3554
Site Wadi Leja, #27
Condition fair
Content Greek inscription
Limitation *Tentative decipherment only*
Access Euting 4 (printed, J. Euting)
Corpus Euting III.56

Inscription 3555
Site Wadi Leja, #27
Condition good
Content Greek inscription
Limitation *Tentative decipherment only*
Access Euting 4 (printed, J. Euting)
Corpus Euting III.57

Inscription 3556
Site Wadi Leja, #27
Condition good
Content crosses with inscription
Access Euting 4 (printed, J. Euting)
Corpus Euting III. 57

Inscription 3557
Site Wadi Leja, #27
Condition good
Content crosses with inscription
Access Euting 4 (printed, J. Euting)
Corpus Euting III.54

Inscription 3558
Site Wadi Leja, #27
Condition fair
Content Greek inscription
Limitation *Tentative decipherment only*
Access Euting 4 (printed, J. Euting)
Corpus Euting III.59

Inscription 3559
Site Jebel Sirbal, Wadi Alayat, #187
Condition fair
Content Arabic inscription
Access Euting 10 (printed, J. Euting)
Corpus Euting VII.183

Inscription 3560
Site Jebel Sirbal, Wadi Alayat, #187
Condition good
Content Greek inscription
Limitation *Tentative decipherment only*
Access Euting 10 (printed, J. Euting)
Corpus Euting VII.183

Inscription 3561
Site Jebel Sirbal, Wadi Ajaleh, #188
Condition good
Content Greek inscription
Limitation *Tentative decipherment only*
Access Euting 13 (printed, J. Euting)
Corpus Euting VIII.229

Inscription 3562
Site Jebel Sirbal, Wadi Ajaleh, #188
Condition good
Content Greek inscription
Limitation *Tentative decipherment only*
Access Euting 13 (printed, J. Euting)
Corpus Euting VIII.253

Inscription 3563
Site Jebel Sirbal, Wadi Ajaleh, #188
Condition good
Content Greek inscription
Limitation *Tentative decipherment only*
Access Euting 15 (printed, J. Euting)
Corpus Euting VIII.259

Inscription **3564**
Site Wadi Firan, #53
Condition good
Content Greek inscription
Limitation *Tentative decipherment only*
Access Euting 18 (printed, J. Euting)
Corpus Euting XI.328

Inscription **3565**
Site Wadi Firan, #53
Condition good
Content Greek inscription
Limitation *Tentative decipherment only*
Access Euting 18 (printed, J. Euting)
Corpus Euting XI.334

Inscription **3566**
Site Wadi Firan, #53
Condition good
Content Arabic inscription
Access Euting 18 (printed, J. Euting)
Corpus Euting XI.333

Inscription **3567**
Site Wadi Firan, #53
Condition good
Content Coptic inscription
Access Euting 18 (printed, J. Euting)
Corpus Euting XI.335

Inscription **3568**
Site Wadi Firan, #53
Condition good
Content crosses with inscription
Access Euting 18 (printed, J. Euting)
Corpus Euting XI.335

Inscription **3569**
Site Wadi Firan, #53
Condition good
Content Greek inscription
Limitation *Tentative decipherment only*
Access Euting 19 (printed, J. Euting)
Corpus Euting XI.337

Inscription **3570**
Site Wadi Firan, #53
Condition good
Content Arabic inscription
Access Euting 19 (printed, J. Euting)
Corpus Euting XI.339

Inscription **3571**
Site Wadi Firan, #53
Condition good
Content crosses with inscription
Access Euting 19 (printed, J. Euting)
Corpus Euting XI.337

Inscription **3572**
Site Wadi Firan, #53
Condition good
Content Greek inscription
Limitation *Tentative decipherment only*
Access Euting 19 (printed, J. Euting)
Corpus Euting XI.342

Inscription **3573**
Site Wadi Firan, #53
Condition good
Content crosses with inscription
Access Euting 19 (printed, J. Euting)
Corpus Euting XI.342

Inscription **3574**
Site Wadi Mukatab, #64
Condition good
Content Old North Arabic inscription
Limitation *Tentative decipherment only*
Access Euting 19 (printed, J. Euting)
Corpus Euting XII.346

Inscription **3575**
Site Wadi Mukatab, #64
Condition good
Content rock drawing
Comment *ibex*
Access Euting 19 (printed, J. Euting)
Corpus Euting XII.346

Inscription **3576**
Site Wadi Mukatab, #64
Condition fair
Content Greek inscription
Limitation *Tentative decipherment only*
Access Euting 21 (printed, J. Euting)
Corpus Euting XII.380

Inscription **3577**
Site Wadi Mukatab, #64
Condition good
Content crosses with inscription
Access Euting 21 (printed, J. Euting)
Corpus Euting XII.380

Inscription **3578**
Site Wadi Mukatab, #64
Condition fair
Content rock drawing
Comment *camel*
Access Euting 21 (printed, J. Euting)
Corpus Euting XII.380

Inscription **3579**
Site Wadi Mukatab, #64
Condition good
Content Old North Arabic inscription
Limitation *Tentative decipherment only*
Access Euting 21 (printed, J. Euting)
Corpus Euting XII.384

Inscription 3580
Site Wadi Mukatab, #64
Dating 1887
Condition good
Content Latin inscription
Limitation *Tentative decipherment only*
Access Euting 21 (printed, J. Euting)
Corpus Euting XII.389

Inscription 3581
Site Jebel Sirbal, Wadi Nakhleh, #221
Condition good
Content Nabatean inscription
šlm zydw br
ʿmyw
Access II.2a.99 (printed, CIS)
Corpus CIS 2316

Inscription 3582
Site Jebel Sirbal, Wadi Nakhleh, #221
Condition good
Content Nabatean inscription
šʿdʾlhy
šlm
br bryʾw
Access II.2a.100 (printed, CIS)
Corpus CIS 2317

Inscription 3583
Site Jebel Sirbal, Wadi Nakhleh, #221
Condition good
Content Nabatean inscription
šlm ḥršw br
wʾlw
Access II.2a.100 (printed, CIS)
Corpus CIS 2318

Inscription 3584
Site Jebel Sirbal, Wadi Nakhleh, #221
Condition good
Content Nabatean inscription
šlm wʾlw br
šmrḥ
Access II.2a.100 (printed, CIS)
Corpus CIS 2319

Inscription 3585
Site Jebel Sirbal, Wadi Nakhleh, #221
Condition poor
Content Nabatean inscription
šlm ʿbdʾl[bʿly]
Access II.2a.100 (printed, CIS)
Corpus CIS 2320

Inscription 3586
Site Jebel Sirbal, Wadi Nakhleh, #221
Condition poor
Content Nabatean inscription
... ḥnṭw...
Access II.2a.100 (printed, CIS)
Corpus CIS 2321

Inscription 3587
Site Jebel Sirbal, Wadi Nakhleh, #221
Condition good
Content Nabatean inscription
šlm bryʾw
br ʿbdʾlbʿly
Access II.2a.100 (printed, CIS)
Corpus CIS 2322

Inscription 3588
Site Jebel Sirbal, Wadi Nakhleh, #221
Condition good
Content Nabatean inscription
šlm ʿbdʾlb[ʿly]
br wʾlw
Access II.2a.100 (printed, CIS)
Corpus CIS 2323

Inscription 3589
Site Jebel Sirbal, Wadi Nakhleh, #221
Condition good
Content Nabatean inscription
šlm ʿmrt br ḥnṭlw bṭb
Access II.2a.100 (printed, CIS)
Corpus CIS 2324

Inscription 3590
Site Jebel Sirbal, Wadi Nakhleh, #221
Condition good
Content Nabatean inscription
šlm ʾwšw br ḥnṭlw
Access II.2a.100 (printed, CIS)
Corpus CIS 2325

Inscription 3591
Site Jebel Sirbal, Wadi Nakhleh, #221
Condition fair
Content Nabatean inscription
šlm wʾlw br ....
Access II.2a.101 (printed, CIS)
Corpus CIS 2326

Inscription 3592
Site Jebel Sirbal, Wadi Nakhleh, #221
Condition good
Content Nabatean inscription
šlm hnyʾw
Access II.2a.101 (printed, CIS)
Corpus CIS 2327

Inscription 3593
Site Jebel Sirbal, Wadi Nakhleh, #221
Condition good
Content Nabatean inscription
šlm ḥryšw br
šmrḥ
Access II.2a.101 (printed, CIS)
Corpus CIS 2328

Inscription 3594
Site Jebel Sirbal, Wadi Nakhleh, #221
Condition excellent
Content Nabatean inscription
šlm šmrḥ br ʿmyw
zydw wwʾlw bnyh
šlm
Access II.2a.101 (printed, CIS)
Corpus CIS 2329

Inscription 3595
Site Jebel Sirbal, Wadi Nakhleh, #221
Condition good
Content Nabatean inscription
šlm ʾʿlʾ br
pṣy [bṭb]
Access II.2a.101 (printed, CIS)
Corpus CIS 2330

Inscription 3596
Site Jebel Sirbal, Wadi Nakhleh, #221
Condition poor
Content Nabatean inscription
šlm ʿ...w šʿdʾ[lhy]
Access II.2a.101 (printed, CIS)
Corpus CIS 2331

Inscription 3597
Site Jebel Sirbal, Wadi Nakhleh, #221
Condition fair
Content Nabatean inscription
šlm wʾlw
Access II.2a.101 (printed, CIS)
Corpus CIS 2332

Inscription 3598
Site Jebel Sirbal, Wadi Nakhleh, #221
Condition good
Content Nabatean inscription
šlm ʿmyw br šmrḥ
Access II.2a.101 (printed, CIS)
Corpus CIS 2333

Inscription 3599
Site Jebel Sirbal, Wadi Nakhleh, #221
Condition poor
Content Nabatean inscription
[š]l[m ḥ]ryšw br wʾlw
Access II.2a.101 (printed, CIS)
Corpus CIS 2334 (1)

Inscription 3600
Site Jebel Sirbal, Wadi Nakhleh, #221
Condition good
Content Greek inscription
ΜΝΗΣΘΗ
Access II.2a.101 (printed, CIS)
Corpus CIS 2334 (2)

Inscription 3601
Site Jebel Sirbal, Wadi Nakhleh, #221
Condition good
Content Nabatean inscription
šlm wʾlw br šmrḥ
Access II.2a.101 (printed, CIS)
Corpus CIS 2335

Inscription 3602
Site Jebel Sirbal, Wadi Nakhleh, #221
Condition fair
Content Nabatean inscription
šlm ʿnmw br ʿ....
Access II.2a.101 (printed, CIS)
Corpus CIS 2336

Inscription 3603
Site Jebel Sirbal, Wadi Nakhleh, #221
Condition good
Content Nabatean inscription
šlm šʿdʾlhy
br ḥnṭlw
Access II.2a.102 (printed, CIS)
Corpus CIS 2337

Inscription 3604
Site Jebel Sirbal, Wadi Nakhleh, #221
Condition good
Content Nabatean inscription
šlm ʾwšw
br mbršw
Access II.2a.102 (printed, CIS)
Corpus CIS 2338

Inscription 3605
Site Jebel Sirbal, Wadi Nakhleh, #221
Condition fair
Content Nabatean inscription
dkyr
wʾlw br ....
Access II.2a.102 (printed, CIS)
Corpus CIS 2339

Inscription 3606
Site Jebel Sirbal, Wadi Nakhleh, #221
Condition good
Content Nabatean inscription
šlm mʿnw [br]
hnʾw bṭb
Access II.2a.102 (printed, CIS)
Corpus CIS 2340

Inscription 3607
Site Jebel Sirbal, Wadi Nakhleh, #221
Condition good
Content Nabatean inscription
šlm ḥršw
br ʿmyw
Access II.2a.102 (printed, CIS)
Corpus CIS 2341

Inscription **3608**
Site Jebel Sirbal, Wadi Nakhleh, #221
Condition good
Content Nabatean inscription
šlm klbw
Access II.2a.102 (printed, CIS)
Corpus CIS 2342

Inscription **3609**
Site Jebel Sirbal, Wadi Nakhleh, #221
Condition good
Content Nabatean inscription
šlm grmʾlhy
Access II.2a.102 (printed, CIS)
Corpus CIS 2343

Inscription **3610**
Site Jebel Sirbal, Wadi Nakhleh, #221
Condition poor
Content Nabatean inscription
šlm ʿmy[w]
Access II.2a.102 (printed, CIS)
Corpus CIS 2344

Inscription **3611**
Site Jebel Sirbal, Wadi Nakhleh, #221
Condition good
Content Nabatean inscription
šlm šmrḥ
br wʾlw
Access II.2a.102 (printed, CIS)
Corpus CIS 2345

Inscription **3612**
Site Jebel Sirbal, Wadi Nakhleh, #221
Condition poor
Content Nabatean inscription
šlm m....
šlm bryʾw br
wʾlw ....
Access II.2a.102 (printed, CIS)
Corpus CIS 2346

Inscription **3613**
Site Jebel Sirbal, Wadi Nakhleh, #221
Condition good
Content Nabatean inscription
šlm qynw br
ʾwyšw
Access II.2a.102 (printed, CIS)
Corpus CIS 2347

Inscription **3614**
Site Jebel Sirbal, Wadi Nakhleh, #221
Condition fair
Content Nabatean inscription
šlm mʿyrw br ḥr[yšw]
Access II.2a.102 (printed, CIS)
Corpus CIS 2348

Inscription **3615**
Site Jebel Sirbal, Wadi Nakhleh, #221
Condition good
Content Nabatean inscription
šlm mʿnw br hnʾ[w] bṭb
Access II.2a.103 (printed, CIS)
Corpus CIS 2349

Inscription **3616**
Site Jebel Sirbal, Wadi Nakhleh, #221
Condition good
Content Nabatean inscription
šlm zydw br
tymdwšrʾ
Access II.2a.103 (printed, CIS)
Corpus CIS 2350

Inscription **3617**
Site Jebel Sirbal, Wadi Nakhleh, #221
Condition good
Content Nabatean inscription
šlm ḥnṭlw
br [n]šy
gw
Access II.2a.103 (printed, CIS)
Corpus CIS 2351

Inscription **3618**
Site Jebel Sirbal, Wadi Nakhleh, #221
Condition fair
Content Nabatean inscription
šlm bryʾw br
wʾlw ....
Access II.2a.103 (printed, CIS)
Corpus CIS 2352

Inscription **3619**
Site Jebel Sirbal, Wadi Nakhleh, #221
Condition good
Content Nabatean inscription
šlm wʾlw br
šmrḥ
Access II.2a.103 (printed, CIS)
Corpus CIS 2353

Inscription **3620**
Site Wadi Firan, Jebel Tahuneh, #325
Condition fair
Content Nabatean inscription
šlm ʿmmw
br w....
Access II.2a.103 (printed, CIS)
Corpus CIS 2354

Inscription 3621
Site Jebel Serabit, Wadi Thmareh, #282
Condition fair
Content Nabatean inscription
šlm .... [br]
ʿbdʾlbʿly
Access II.2a.104 (printed, CIS)
Corpus CIS 2355

Inscription 3622
Site Jebel Serabit, Wadi Thmareh, #282
Condition good
Content Nabatean inscription
šlm ʿbdʾlbʾly br
ʿmyw [b]kl ṭb
Access II.2a.104 (printed, CIS)
Corpus CIS 2356

Inscription 3623
Site Jebel Serabit, Wadi Thmareh, #282
Condition poor
Content Nabatean inscription
Access II.2a.104 (printed, CIS)
Corpus CIS 2357

Inscription 3624
Site Jebel Serabit, Wadi Thmareh, #282
Condition good
Content Nabatean inscription
šlm ʾtmw
Access II.2a.104 (printed, CIS)
Corpus CIS 2358

Inscription 3625
Site Jebel Serabit, Wadi Thmareh, #282
Condition poor
Content Nabatean inscription
Access II.2a.104 (printed, CIS)
Corpus CIS 2359

Inscription 3626
Site Jebel Serabit, Wadi Thmareh, #282
Condition good
Content Nabatean inscription
šlm dmgw br
ṭylt šlm
Access II.2a.104 (printed, CIS)
Corpus CIS 2360

Inscription 3627
Site Jebel Serabit, Wadi Thmareh, #282
Condition good
Content Nabatean inscription
šlm ʿmyw br
nšygw bṭb ....
Access II.2a.104 (printed, CIS)
Corpus CIS 2361

Inscription 3628
Site Jebel Serabit, Wadi Thmareh, #282
Condition good
Content Nabatean inscription
šlm ʿtmw
br ʾwdw
Access II.2a.104 (printed, CIS)
Corpus CIS 2362

Inscription 3629
Site Jebel Serabit, Wadi Thmareh, #282
Condition fair
Content Nabatean inscription
šlm ʿbydw
ʿbdʾ[lbʿly]
mn ḥtyt
Access II.2a.105 (printed, CIS)
Corpus CIS 2363

Inscription 3630
Site Jebel Serabit, Wadi Thmareh, #282
Condition fair
Content Nabatean inscription
šlm ʿwdw
br ...
Access II.2a.105 (printed, CIS)
Corpus CIS 2364

Inscription 3631
Site Jebel Serabit, Wadi Thmareh, #282
Condition good
Content Nabatean inscription
šlm bryʾw
Access II.2a.105 (printed, CIS)
Corpus CIS 2365

Inscription 3632
Site Jebel Serabit, Wadi Thmareh, #282
Condition good
Content Nabatean inscription
šlm ʿbdʾlʿly
šlm dm[g]w
br ṭylt
Access II.2a.105 (printed, CIS)
Corpus CIS 2366

Inscription 3633
Site Jebel Serabit, Wadi Thmareh, #282
Condition good
Content Nabatean inscription
šlm grmʾlbʿly br pʾrn
Access II.2a.105 (printed, CIS)
Corpus CIS 2367

Inscription 3634
Site Jebel Serabit, Wadi Thmareh, #282
Condition good
Content Nabatean inscription
šlm ḥrglw [br]
ʿbydw
Access II.2a.105 (printed, CIS)
Corpus CIS 2368

Inscription 3635
Site Jebel Serabit, Wadi Thmareh, #282
Condition fair
Content Nabatean inscription
dkyr kynw [br]
ʾwyšw
[ʾw]šw wpṣy bny
ḥryšw
Access II.2a.105 (printed, CIS)
Corpus CIS 2369

Inscription 3636
Site Jebel Serabit, Wadi Thmareh, #282
Condition fair
Content Nabatean inscription
šlm pṣyw [br]
šʿdʾ[lh]
Access II.2a.105 (printed, CIS)
Corpus CIS 2370

Inscription 3637
Site Jebel Serabit, Wadi Thmareh, #282
Condition good
Content Nabatean inscription
šlm ḥryšw br
ʾwyšw ...
Access II.2a.106 (printed, CIS)
Corpus CIS 2371

Inscription 3638
Site Jebel Serabit, Wadi Thmareh, #282
Condition fair
Content Nabatean inscription
[šl]m ʿbdʾlbʿly
Access II.2a.106 (printed, CIS)
Corpus CIS 2372

Inscription 3639
Site Jebel Serabit, Wadi Thmareh, #282
Condition good
Content Nabatean inscription
šlm zydw br whbʾlhy
Access II.2a.106 (printed, CIS)
Corpus CIS 2373

Inscription 3640
Site Jebel Serabit, Wadi Thmareh, #282
Condition poor
Content Nabatean inscription
šlm ʿbdʾlbʿl[y]
[br] wʾlw....
[š]l[m] ḥryšw br
...yw...
šlm ʾwšw
Access II.2a.106 (printed, CIS)
Corpus CIS 2374

Inscription 3641
Site Jebel Serabit, Wadi Thmareh, #282
Condition good
Content Nabatean inscription
šlm pʾrn br
ʿwtʾlhy
Access II.2a.106 (printed, CIS)
Corpus CIS 2375

Inscription 3642
Site Jebel Serabit, Wadi Thmareh, #282
Condition good
Content Nabatean inscription
šlm ʾwšw [br]
ʿmmw
Access II.2a.106 (printed, CIS)
Corpus CIS 2376

Inscription 3643
Site Jebel Serabit, Wadi Thmareh, #282
Condition good
Content Nabatean inscription
dkyr mgdw
Access II.2a.106 (printed, CIS)
Corpus CIS 2377

Inscription 3644
Site Jebel Serabit, Wadi Thmareh, #282
Condition good
Content Nabatean inscription
dkyr ʾwyšw
br kynw bṭb
Access II.2a.106 (printed, CIS)
Corpus CIS 2378

Inscription 3645
Site Jebel Serabit, Wadi Thmareh, #282
Condition good
Content Nabatean inscription
šlm ʿmyw br
dʾbw bṭb
Access II.2a.106 (printed, CIS)
Corpus CIS 2379

Inscription 3646
Site Jebel Serabit, Wadi Thmareh, #282
Condition good
Content Nabatean inscription
ʾwyšw
bn kynw
bṭb
Access II.2a.107 (printed, CIS)
Corpus CIS 2380

Inscription 3647
Site Jebel Serabit, Wadi Thmareh, #282
Condition good
Content Nabatean inscription
šlm zy[dw]
šlm ʾlmbqrw
br klbw bṭb
wšlm
Access II.2a.107 (printed, CIS)
Corpus CIS 2381

Inscription 3648
Site Jebel Serabit, Wadi Thmareh, #282
Condition good
Content Nabatean inscription
šlm ʿbdʾlhy br
pʾrn
šlm ʿbd...
Access II.2a.107 (printed, CIS)
Corpus CIS 2382

Inscription 3649
Site Jebel Serabit, Wadi Thmareh, #282
Condition good
Content Nabatean inscription
šlm ʾlmbqrw
br ʿmyw
Access II.2a.107 (printed, CIS)
Corpus CIS 2383

Inscription 3650
Site Jebel Serabit, Wadi Thmareh, #282
Condition good
Content Nabatean inscription
šlm ʿbdʾlbʿ[l]y
br wdw
šlm wdw
Access II.2a.107 (printed, CIS)
Corpus CIS 2384

Inscription 3651
Site Jebel Serabit, Wadi Thmareh, #282
Condition good
Content Nabatean inscription
šlm kʿmh br
grm[ʾlb]ʿly
Access II.2a.107 (printed, CIS)
Corpus CIS 2385

Inscription 3652
Site Jebel Serabit, Wadi Thmareh, #282
Condition good
Content Nabatean inscription
šlm ḥry[šw]
br ʿmyw
Access II.2a.107 (printed, CIS)
Corpus CIS 2386

Inscription 3653
Site Jebel Serabit, Wadi Thmareh, #282
Condition good
Content Nabatean inscription
šlm šlm mgdyw br [ʿm]yw šlm
Access II.2a.108 (printed, CIS)
Corpus CIS 2387

Inscription 3654
Site Jebel Serabit, Wadi Thmareh, #282
Condition good
Content Nabatean inscription
šlm mgdw
br ḥryšw
Access II.2a.108 (printed, CIS)
Corpus CIS 2388

Inscription 3655
Site Jebel Serabit, Wadi Thmareh, #282
Condition good
Content Nabatean inscription
šlm wʾlw br
ḥnṭlw bṭb
Access II.2a.108 (printed, CIS)
Corpus CIS 2389

Inscription 3656
Site Jebel Serabit, Wadi Thmareh, #282
Condition good
Content Nabatean inscription
šlm bryʾw br klbw bṭb
Access II.2a.108 (printed, CIS)
Corpus CIS 2390

Inscription 3657
Site Jebel Serabit, Wadi Thmareh, #282
Condition fair
Content Nabatean inscription
[wʾ]lw
br ʿwdw
Access II.2a.108 (printed, CIS)
Corpus CIS 2391

Inscription 3658
Site Jebel Serabit, Wadi Thmareh, #282
Condition good
Content Nabatean inscription
šlm šmrḥ [br]
ʿmnw bṭb
Access II.2a.108 (printed, CIS)
Corpus CIS 2392

Inscription 3659
Site Jebel Serabit, Wadi Thmareh, #282
Condition fair
Content Nabatean inscription
...ʿly
šlm ʿnmw br ʿbdʾlb[y]
Access II.2a.108 (printed, CIS)
Corpus CIS 2393

Inscription 3660
Site Jebel Serabit, Wadi Thmareh, #282
Condition poor
Content Nabatean inscription
ʿbdʾlbʿly br
ʾ[l]ky[nt]
Access II.2a.108 (printed, CIS)
Corpus CIS 2394

Inscription 3661
Site Jebel Serabit, Wadi Thmareh, #282
Condition good
Content Nabatean inscription
šlm
klbw br
ʿwymw
bṭb
Access II.2a.109 (printed, CIS)
Corpus CIS 2395

Inscription 3662
Site Jebel Serabit, Wadi Thmareh, #282
Condition good
Content Nabatean inscription
bryʾw br
klbw
Access II.2a.109 (printed, CIS)
Corpus CIS 2396

Inscription 3663
Site Jebel Serabit, Wadi Thmareh, #282
Condition good
Content Nabatean inscription
[ʾ]wšw br
ʿmmw
Access II.2a.109 (printed, CIS)
Corpus CIS 2397

Inscription 3664
Site Jebel Serabit, Wadi Thmareh, #282
Condition good
Content Nabatean inscription
šlm klbw br ʿbydw
Access II.2a.109 (printed, CIS)
Corpus CIS 2398

Inscription 3665
Site Jebel Serabit, Wadi Thmareh, #282
Condition fair
Content Nabatean inscription
grmlbʿl[y]
br ʾbn [ʾlkyny]
Access II.2a.109 (printed, CIS)
Corpus CIS 2399

Inscription 3666
Site Jebel Serabit, Wadi Thmareh, #282
Condition poor
Content Nabatean inscription
šlm w.l.
...lṣ...
Access II.2a.109 (printed, CIS)
Corpus CIS 2400

Inscription 3667
Site Jebel Serabit, Wadi Thmareh, #282
Condition good
Content Nabatean inscription
šlm wʾlw br
ʾwdw
Access II.2a.109 (printed, CIS)
Corpus CIS 2401

Inscription 3668
Site Jebel Serabit, Wadi Thmareh, #282
Condition poor
Content Nabatean inscription
šlm ʿmmw
[br] whbʾlhy
... brh
Access II.2a.109 (printed, CIS)
Corpus CIS 2402

Inscription 3669
Site Jebel Serabit, Wadi Thmareh, #282
Condition good
Content Nabatean inscription
šlm ʾwš[w]
br zydw
Access II.2a.109 (printed, CIS)
Corpus CIS 2403

Inscription 3670
Site Jebel Serabit, Wadi Thmareh, #282
Condition good
Content Nabatean inscription
ʾlmb[k]rw br ḥlṣt
Access II.2a.109 (printed, CIS)
Corpus CIS 2405

Inscription 3671
Site Jebel Serabit, Wadi Thmareh, #282
Condition fair
Content Nabatean inscription
[š]lm ḥršw br
zydw b[ṭb]
Access II.2a.109 (printed, CIS)
Corpus CIS 2406

Inscription 3672
Site Jebel Serabit, Wadi Thmareh, #282
Condition good
Content Nabatean inscription
šlm ʾwšʾlbʿly br
šlmw
Access II.2a.110 (printed, CIS)
Corpus CIS 2407

Inscription 3673
Site Jebel Serabit, Wadi Thmareh, #282
Condition good
Content Nabatean inscription
šlm klbw
br hnʾw
Access II.2a.110 (printed, CIS)
Corpus CIS 2408

Inscription 3674
Site Jebel Serabit, Wadi Thmareh, #282
Condition fair
Content Nabatean inscription
pʾrn ʿw[dw] .... šlm ʿmmw
br nmylw
Access II.2a.110 (printed, CIS)
Corpus CIS 2409

Inscription 3675
Site Jebel Serabit, Wadi Thmareh, #282
Condition good
Content Nabatean inscription
šlm zydw br whbʾlhy [b]ṭb
Access II.2a.110 (printed, CIS)
Corpus CIS 2410

Inscription 3676
Site Jebel Serabit, Wadi Thmareh, #282
Condition good
Content Nabatean inscription
šlm ʿbydw br
ḥlyṣw
Access II.2a.110 (printed, CIS)
Corpus CIS 2411

Inscription 3677
Site Jebel Serabit, Wadi Thmareh, #282
Condition good
Content Nabatean inscription
ʿyṣw br
ʿbdʾlbʿly
Access II.2a.110 (printed, CIS)
Corpus CIS 2412

Inscription 3678
Site Jebel Serabit, Wadi Thmareh, #282
Condition good
Content Nabatean inscription
šlm ʿbydw br ʿbdʾkwmy
yhwy .... šlm
Access II.2a.110 (printed, CIS)
Corpus CIS 2413

Inscription 3679
Site Jebel Serabit, Wadi Thmareh, #282
Condition good
Content Nabatean inscription
šlm klbw br
ʿwymw bṭb wšlm
Access II.2a.110 (printed, CIS)
Corpus CIS 2414

Inscription 3680
Site Jebel Serabit, Wadi Thmareh, #282
Condition fair
Content Nabatean inscription
[ʿ]y[ṣ]w br
ʿbdʾlbʿly bṭb
Access II.2a.110 (printed, CIS)
Corpus CIS 2415

Inscription 3681
Site Jebel Serabit, Wadi Thmareh, #282
Condition good
Content Nabatean inscription
šlm pʾrn br
whbʾlhy
Access II.2a.111 (printed, CIS)
Corpus CIS 2416

Inscription 3682
Site Jebel Serabit, Wadi Thmareh, #282
Condition good
Content Nabatean inscription
ʿmmw br
whbʾlhy
bṭb w[šlm]
Access II.2a.111 (printed, CIS)
Corpus CIS 2417

Inscription **3683**
Site Jebel Serabit, Wadi Thmareh, #282
Condition fair
Content Nabatean inscription
šlm ʾwšʾl.y br
gywʾ
Access II.2a.111 (printed, CIS)
Corpus CIS 2418

Inscription **3684**
Site Jebel Serabit, Wadi Thmareh, #282
Condition good
Content Nabatean inscription
šlm grmʾlbʿly
br šʿdʾlhy
Access II.2a.111 (printed, CIS)
Corpus CIS 2419

Inscription **3685**
Site Jebel Serabit, Wadi Thmareh, #282
Condition good
Content Nabatean inscription
šlm klbw
br pʾrn
Access II.2a.111 (printed, CIS)
Corpus CIS 2420

Inscription **3686**
Site Jebel Serabit, Wadi Thmareh, #282
Condition good
Content Nabatean inscription
ʾwšw br
ʿmmw bṭb
Access II.2a.111 (printed, CIS)
Corpus CIS 2421

Inscription **3687**
Site Jebel Serabit, Wadi Thmareh, #282
Condition good
Content Nabatean inscription
pʾrn br
whbʾlhy
Access II.2a.111 (printed, CIS)
Corpus CIS 2422

Inscription **3688**
Site Jebel Serabit, Wadi Thmareh, #282
Condition good
Content Nabatean inscription
šlm ʿbdʾlhy br pʾrn
Access II.2a.111 (printed, CIS)
Corpus CIS 2423

Inscription **3689**
Site Jebel Serabit, Wadi Thmareh, #282
Condition fair
Content Nabatean inscription
šlm ʿbydw br ....w
Access II.2a.111 (printed, CIS)
Corpus CIS 2424

Inscription **3690**
Site Jebel Serabit, Wadi Thmareh, #282
Condition good
Content Nabatean inscription
šlm wʾlw br
ʿmyw
Access II.2a.112 (printed, CIS)
Corpus CIS 2425

Inscription **3691**
Site Jebel Serabit, Wadi Thmareh, #282
Condition fair
Content Nabatean inscription
šlm ʿmrt
br ....
Access II.2a.112 (printed, CIS)
Corpus CIS 2426

Inscription **3692**
Site Jebel Serabit, Wadi Thmareh, #282
Condition good
Content Nabatean inscription
šlmw ʿbdʾlbʿl[y]
Access II.2a.112 (printed, CIS)
Corpus CIS 2427

Inscription **3693**
Site Jebel Serabit, Wadi Thmareh, #282
Condition good
Content Nabatean inscription
šlm grmʾlhy
br ʿbydw
Access II.2a.112 (printed, CIS)
Corpus CIS 2428

Inscription **3694**
Site Jebel Serabit, Wadi Thmareh, #282
Condition good
Content Nabatean inscription
šlm
ḥlṣt br
ʾʿlʾ
Access II.2a.112 (printed, CIS)
Corpus CIS 2429

Inscription **3695**
Site Jebel Serabit, Wadi Thmareh, #282
Condition fair
Content Nabatean inscription
ʿmyw br
k[lb]w
bṭb
Access II.2a.112 (printed, CIS)
Corpus CIS 2430

Inscription 3696
Site Jebel Serabit, Wadi Thmareh, #282
Condition good
Content Nabatean inscription
šlm ʿwdw
Access II.2a.112 (printed, CIS)
Corpus CIS 2431

Inscription 3697
Site Jebel Serabit, Wadi Thmareh, #282
Condition good
Content Nabatean inscription
šl[m] wʾ[l]w br mkwmw bṭb
Access II.2a.112 (printed, CIS)
Corpus CIS 2432

Inscription 3698
Site Jebel Serabit, Wadi Thmareh, #282
Condition fair
Content Nabatean inscription
šl[m] šlm šlm ʾwšw br grm[ʾlhy]
Access II.2a.112 (printed, CIS)
Corpus CIS 2433

Inscription 3699
Site Jebel Serabit, Wadi Thmareh, #282
Condition fair
Content Nabatean inscription
šlm wdw br
nšygw
....
Access II.2a.113 (printed, CIS)
Corpus CIS 2434

Inscription 3700
Site Jebel Serabit, Wadi Thmareh, #282
Condition fair
Content Nabatean inscription
ḥbrkn
br ʿw[d]w
Access II.2a.113 (printed, CIS)
Corpus CIS 2435

Inscription 3701
Site Jebel Serabit, Wadi Thmareh, #282
Condition good
Content Nabatean inscription
šlm nšygw
br grmʾlbʿly
Access II.2a.113 (printed, CIS)
Corpus CIS 2436

Inscription 3702
Site Jebel Serabit, Wadi Thmareh, #282
Condition good
Content Nabatean inscription
šlm ʿmmw
Access II.2a.113 (printed, CIS)
Corpus CIS 2437

Inscription 3703
Site Jebel Serabit, Wadi Thmareh, #282
Condition fair
Content Nabatean inscription
šlm ʾlky[n]t
Access II.2a.113 (printed, CIS)
Corpus CIS 2438

Inscription 3704
Site Jebel Serabit, Wadi Thmareh, #282
Condition fair
Content Nabatean inscription
šlm ʾlmbqrw
Access II.2a.113 (printed, CIS)
Corpus CIS 2439

Inscription 3705
Site Jebel Serabit, Wadi Thmareh, #282
Condition poor
Content Nabatean inscription
[šl]m ʿmyw
[br ʿ]wymw bṭb
Access II.2a.113 (printed, CIS)
Corpus CIS 2440

Inscription 3706
Site Jebel Serabit, Wadi Thmareh, #282
Condition good
Content Nabatean inscription
šlm ʾwšw
br nšygw
Access II.2a.113 (printed, CIS)
Corpus CIS 2441

Inscription 3707
Site Jebel Serabit, Wadi Thmareh, #282
Condition good
Content Nabatean inscription
šlm grmʾlhy
br ʿbydw
Access II.2a.113 (printed, CIS)
Corpus CIS 2442

Inscription 3708
Site Jebel Serabit, Wadi Thmareh, #282
Condition poor
Content Nabatean inscription
mgdw
Access II.2a.113 (printed, CIS)
Corpus CIS 2443

Inscription 3709
Site Jebel Serabit, Wadi Thmareh, #282
Condition fair
Content Nabatean inscription
šlm ʿmy[w]
br [m]gdyw bkl ṭb
Access II.2a.113 (printed, CIS)
Corpus CIS 2444

Inscription 3710
Site Jebel Serabit, Wadi Thmareh, #282
Condition good
Content Nabatean inscription
šlm ʾtmw
br ʿwdw
Access II.2a.113 (printed, CIS)
Corpus CIS 2445

Inscription 3711
Site Jebel Serabit, Wadi Thmareh, #282
Condition poor
Content Nabatean inscription
šlm ....
ʾlk[hnw]
br [y]ʿly
w...y.
Access II.2a.114 (printed, CIS)
Corpus CIS 2446

Inscription 3712
Site Jebel Serabit, Wadi Thmareh, #282
Condition fair
Content Nabatean inscription
šlm ....
br mgdyw
wmgdyw brh
Access II.2a.114 (printed, CIS)
Corpus CIS 2447

Inscription 3713
Site Jebel Serabit, Wadi Thmareh, #282
Condition poor
Content Nabatean inscription
šlm bryʾw [br] pṣy
šlm [ʾw]šw b[r] ....
Access II.2a.114 (printed, CIS)
Corpus CIS 2448

Inscription 3714
Site Jebel Serabit, Wadi Thmareh, #282
Condition good
Content Nabatean inscription
šlm ʾlšrk[y]w br
ʾlktyw
Access II.2a.114 (printed, CIS)
Corpus CIS 2449

Inscription 3715
Site Jebel Serabit, Wadi Thmareh, #282
Condition good
Content Nabatean inscription
šlm dʾbw br ʿwdw bṭb wšlm
Access II.2a.114 (printed, CIS)
Corpus CIS 2450

Inscription 3716
Site Jebel Serabit, Wadi Thmareh, #282
Condition fair
Content Nabatean inscription
šlm ʿbdʾl[bʿly]
br bḫgh
Access II.2a.114 (printed, CIS)
Corpus CIS 2451

Inscription 3717
Site Jebel Serabit, Wadi Thmareh, #282
Condition fair
Content Nabatean inscription
dkyr ʾbn ʾlkyny br
[šʿd]ʾlhy
Access II.2a.114 (printed, CIS)
Corpus CIS 2452

Inscription 3718
Site Jebel Serabit, Wadi Thmareh, #282
Condition good
Content Nabatean inscription
šlm grmʾlbʿly
br hnʾw
Access II.2a.114 (printed, CIS)
Corpus CIS 2453

Inscription 3719
Site Jebel Serabit, Wadi Thmareh, #282
Condition good
Content Nabatean inscription
šlm wʾlw br mkwmw
Access II.2a.115 (printed, CIS)
Corpus CIS 2454

Inscription 3720
Site Jebel Serabit, Wadi Thmareh, #282
Condition fair
Content Nabatean inscription
šlm ʿnmw
[br] ḥryšw
Access II.2a.115 (printed, CIS)
Corpus CIS 2455

Inscription 3721
Site Jebel Serabit, Wadi Thmareh, #282
Condition good
Content Nabatean inscription
šlm wdʿw br
ʾwyšw
Access II.2a.115 (printed, CIS)
Corpus CIS 2456

Inscription 3722
Site Jebel Serabit, Wadi Thmareh, #282
Condition good
Content Nabatean inscription
šlm ʾwšw br
ʿmmw bṭb
Access II.2a.115 (printed, CIS)
Corpus CIS 2457

Inscription 3723
Site Jebel Serabit, Wadi Thmareh, #282
Condition good
Content Nabatean inscription
šlm ḥršw
br wʾlw
Access II.2a.115 (printed, CIS)
Corpus CIS 2458

Inscription 3724
Site Jebel Serabit, Wadi Thmareh, #282
Condition good
Content Nabatean inscription
šlm mgdyw
Access II.2a.115 (printed, CIS)
Corpus CIS 2459

Inscription 3725
Site Jebel Serabit, Wadi Thmareh, #282
Condition good
Content Nabatean inscription
šlm ʿ[lh]t br
pṣy bṭb
Access II.2a.115 (printed, CIS)
Corpus CIS 2460

Inscription 3726
Site Jebel Serabit, Wadi Thmareh, #282
Condition good
Content Nabatean inscription
šlm ʿmmw
br whbʾlhy
Access II.2a.115 (printed, CIS)
Corpus CIS 2461

Inscription 3727
Site Jebel Serabit, Wadi Thmareh, #282
Condition good
Content Nabatean inscription
šlm ʿwdw
br šmrḥ
Access II.2a.115 (printed, CIS)
Corpus CIS 2462

Inscription 3728
Site Jebel Serabit, Wadi Thmareh, #282
Condition poor
Content Nabatean inscription
šlm ʿmrt
[br ḥn]ṭ[lw]
Access II.2a.115 (printed, CIS)
Corpus CIS 2463

Inscription 3729
Site Jebel Serabit, Wadi Thmareh, #282
Condition good
Content Nabatean inscription
dkyr ʿbdʿmr br
ʿwtʾlhy bṭb
Access II.2a.115 (printed, CIS)
Corpus CIS 2464

Inscription 3730
Site Jebel Serabit, Wadi Thmareh, #282
Condition good
Content Nabatean inscription
šlm grymw
br ḥršw bṭb
Access II.2a.116 (printed, CIS)
Corpus CIS 2465

Inscription 3731
Site Jebel Serabit, Wadi Thmareh, #282
Condition poor
Content Nabatean inscription
ḥ[brkn] br ʿwdw
Access II.2a.116 (printed, CIS)
Corpus CIS 2466

Inscription 3732
Site Wadi Firan, Wadi Khabar, #328
Condition good
Content Nabatean inscription
šlm ḥryšw br
zydw bṭb
Access II.2a.116 (printed, CIS)
Corpus CIS 2467

Inscription 3733
Site Wadi Firan, Wadi Khabar, #328
Condition poor
Content Nabatean inscription
šlm m....
br ḥ....
Access II.2a.116 (printed, CIS)
Corpus CIS 2468

Inscription 3734
Site Wadi Firan, Wadi Khabar, #328
Condition fair
Content Nabatean inscription
šlm bryʾw br ....
Access II.2a.116 (printed, CIS)
Corpus CIS 2469

Inscription 3735
Site Wadi Firan, Wadi Khabar, #328
Condition good
Content Nabatean inscription
šlm bhʾgh br ʿbydw
Access II.2a.116 (printed, CIS)
Corpus CIS 2470

Inscription 3736
Site Wadi Firan, Wadi Khabar, #328
Condition good
Content Nabatean inscription
šlm ʿmrw br ʿmyw
Access II.2a.116 (printed, CIS)
Corpus CIS 2471

Inscription 3737
Site Wadi Firan, Wadi Khabar, #328
Condition good
Content Nabatean inscription
dkyr
bryʾw
br klbw
bṭb
Access II.2a.116 (printed, CIS)
Corpus CIS 2472

Inscription 3738
Site Wadi Firan, Wadi Khabar, #328
Condition good
Content Nabatean inscription
šlm ʿbdʾlbʿly
br ʿlht...
Access II.2a.116 (printed, CIS)
Corpus CIS 2473

Inscription 3739
Site Wadi Firan, Wadi Khabar, #328
Condition fair
Content Nabatean inscription
šlm wʾlw
br krḥh...
Access II.2a.116 (printed, CIS)
Corpus CIS 2474

Inscription 3740
Site Wadi Firan, Wadi Khabar, #328
Condition poor
Content Nabatean inscription
šlm ʾlṣ...
br ʿbd...
Access II.2a.117 (printed, CIS)
Corpus CIS 2475

Inscription 3741
Site Wadi Firan, Wadi Khabar, #328
Condition good
Content Nabatean inscription
šlm mʿnw br
hnʾw bṭb
Access II.2a.117 (printed, CIS)
Corpus CIS 2476

Inscription 3742
Site Wadi Firan, Wadi Khabar, #328
Condition good
Content Nabatean inscription
šlm ḥlṣt
br ḥryšw
wḥryšw
brh b[ṭb]
Access II.2a.117 (printed, CIS)
Corpus CIS 2477

Inscription 3743
Site Wadi Firan, Wadi Khabar, #328
Condition good
Content Nabatean inscription
br šlmw
šlm ʿmmw
Access II.2a.117 (printed, CIS)
Corpus CIS 2478

Inscription 3744
Site Wadi Firan, Wadi Khabar, #328
Condition fair
Content Nabatean inscription
ʿbdʾlbʿly
br šʿd[ʾlhy]
Access II.2a.117 (printed, CIS)
Corpus CIS 2479

Inscription 3745
Site Wadi Firan, Wadi Khabar, #328
Condition good
Content Nabatean inscription
šlm ʾwyšw
br kynw bṭb
Access II.2a.117 (printed, CIS)
Corpus CIS 2480

Inscription 3746
Site Wadi Firan, Wadi Khabar, #328
Condition good
Content Nabatean inscription
šlm mʿnw br
hnʾw
Access II.2a.117 (printed, CIS)
Corpus CIS 2481

Inscription 3747
Site Wadi Firan, Wadi Khabar, #328
Condition fair
Content Nabatean inscription
šlm ...w br
ʾl[t]bqw bṭb
Access II.2a.117 (printed, CIS)
Corpus CIS 2482

Inscription 3748
Site Wadi Firan, Wadi Khabar, #328
Condition good
Content Nabatean inscription
šlm ʾlšrq
yw br
ʿmyw
Access II.2a.117 (printed, CIS)
Corpus CIS 2483

Inscription 3749
Site Wadi Firan, Wadi Khabar, #328
Condition good
Content Nabatean inscription
dkyr nšy
gw br
ʿmyw
bṭb
Access II.2a.117 (printed, CIS)
Corpus CIS 2484

Inscription 3750
Site Wadi Firan, Wadi Khabar, #328
Condition good
Content Nabatean inscription
ʿbdʾlbʿly br
ʿmyw bṭ[b]
Access II.2a.118 (printed, CIS)
Corpus CIS 2485

Inscription 3751
Site Wadi Firan, Wadi Khabar, #328
Condition fair
Content Nabatean inscription
šlm ʿmmw br ....
Access II.2a.118 (printed, CIS)
Corpus CIS 2486

Inscription 3752
Site Wadi Firan, Wadi Khabar, #328
Condition good
Content Nabatean inscription
dbyr bryʾw
br yʿly
bṭb wšlm
Access II.2a.118 (printed, CIS)
Corpus CIS 2487

Inscription 3753
Site Wadi Firan, Wadi Khabar, #328
Condition poor
Content Nabatean inscription
dkyryn
Access II.2a.118 (printed, CIS)
Corpus CIS 2488

Inscription 3754
Site Wadi Firan, Wadi Khabar, #328
Condition good
Content Nabatean inscription
šlm ʿyydw br
šʿldʾlhy bṭb
Access II.2a.118 (printed, CIS)
Corpus CIS 2489

Inscription 3755
Site Wadi Firan, Wadi Khabar, #328
Condition good
Content Nabatean inscription
šlm šlmw br
ʿbdw
Access II.2a.118 (printed, CIS)
Corpus CIS 2490

Inscription 3756
Site Wadi Firan, Wadi Khabar, #328
Condition good
Content Nabatean inscription
ʿmrw br
ḥršw kh
n tʾ
Access II.2a.118 (printed, CIS)
Corpus CIS 2491

Inscription 3757
Site Wadi Firan, Wadi Khabar, #328
Condition good
Content Nabatean inscription
šlm ʾwyšw
br qynw bṭb
Access II.2a.118 (printed, CIS)
Corpus CIS 2492

Inscription 3758
Site Wadi Firan, Wadi Khabar, #328
Condition good
Content Nabatean inscription
šlm ʾwšw
br ʿmmw
Access II.2a.118 (printed, CIS)
Corpus CIS 2493

Inscription 3759
Site Wadi Firan, Wadi Khabar, #328
Condition good
Content Nabatean inscription
šlm grmʾlbʿly
br wʾlt br ʿmyw
Access II.2a.119 (printed, CIS)
Corpus CIS 2494

Inscription 3760
Site Wadi Firan, Wadi Khabar, #328
Condition poor
Content Nabatean inscription
[šlm gr]mʾlbʿly
br ʾ.....w
Access II.2a.119 (printed, CIS)
Corpus CIS 2495

Inscription 3761
Site Wadi Firan, Wadi Khabar, #328
Condition good
Content Nabatean inscription
šlm klbw br
šʿdʾlhy
Access II.2a.119 (printed, CIS)
Corpus CIS 2496

Inscription 3762
Site Wadi Firan, Wadi Khabar, #328
Condition good
Content Nabatean inscription
šlm [kl]bw
br ʿmrw
Access II.2a.119 (printed, CIS)
Corpus CIS 2497

Inscription 3763
Site Wadi Firan, Wadi Khabar, #328
Condition poor
Content Nabatean inscription
...dw
br ʿwdw
Access II.2a.119 (printed, CIS)
Corpus CIS 2498

Inscription 3764
Site Wadi Firan, Wadi Khabar, #328
Condition good
Content Nabatean inscription
šlm ʾtmw br
ḥlyṣw
Access II.2a.119 (printed, CIS)
Corpus CIS 2499

Inscription 3765
Site Wadi Firan, Wadi Khabar, #328
Condition good
Content Nabatean inscription
šlm dʾbw
br grmʾlb[ʿly]
Access II.2a.119 (printed, CIS)
Corpus CIS 2500

Inscription 3766
Site Wadi Firan, Wadi Khabar, #328
Condition fair
Content Nabatean inscription
dkyr ʿbdʾlbʿly br ʿmyw
br š[m]r[ḥ] b[yt]yʾ
bṭb
wšlm
Access II.2a.119 (printed, CIS)
Corpus CIS 2501

Inscription 3767
Site Wadi Firan, Wadi Khabar, #328
Condition good
Content Nabatean inscription
šlm ʾwšw
br ḥnṭlw
Access II.2a.119 (printed, CIS)
Corpus CIS 2502

Inscription 3768
Site Wadi Firan, Wadi Khabar, #328
Condition poor
Content Nabatean inscription
dkyr .... [br]
tymʾlhy bṭb
Access II.2a.120 (printed, CIS)
Corpus CIS 2503

Inscription 3769
Site Wadi Firan, Wadi Khabar, #328
Condition good
Content Nabatean inscription
šlm ʿwdw
br ʾl[m]bqrw
Access II.2a.120 (printed, CIS)
Corpus CIS 2504

Inscription 3770
Site Wadi Firan, Wadi Khabar, #328
Condition good
Content Nabatean inscription
šlm ʾʿlʾ br
ḥlṣt bṭb
Access II.2a.120 (printed, CIS)
Corpus CIS 2505

Inscription 3771
Site Wadi Firan, Wadi Khabar, #328
Condition good
Content Nabatean inscription
klbw br
ʿmrw
Access II.2a.120 (printed, CIS)
Corpus CIS 2506

Inscription 3772
Site Wadi Firan, Wadi Khabar, #328
Condition fair
Content Nabatean inscription
šlm zydw br ʾ...
Access II.2a.120 (printed, CIS)
Corpus CIS 2507

Inscription 3773
Site Wadi Firan, Wadi Khabar, #328
Condition good
Content Nabatean inscription
šlm ḥryšw
br grmʾlbʿly
bṭb
Access II.2a.328 (printed, CIS)
Corpus CIS 2508

Inscription 3774
Site Wadi Firan, Wadi Khabar, #328
Condition good
Content Nabatean inscription
šlm ʿbydw
Access II.2a.120 (printed, CIS)
Corpus CIS 2509

Inscription 3775
Site Wadi Firan, Wadi Khabar, #328
Condition fair
Content Nabatean inscription
šlm
ʿwymw br .l..
Access II.2a.120 (printed, CIS)
Corpus CIS 2510

Inscription 3776
Site Wadi Firan, Wadi Khabar, #328
Condition poor
Content Nabatean inscription
.... br ʾ[l]šqry
Access II.2a.120 (printed, CIS)
Corpus CIS 2511

Inscription 3777
Site Wadi Firan, Wadi Khabar, #328
Condition good
Content Nabatean inscription
šlm ʾlkhnw br
nšygw
Access II.2a.120 (printed, CIS)
Corpus CIS 2512

Inscription 3778
Site Wadi Firan, Wadi Khabar, #328
Condition good
Content Nabatean inscription
šlm ʾwyšw br qynw
Access II.2a.120 (printed, CIS)
Corpus CIS 2513

Inscription 3779
Site Wadi Firan, Wadi Khabar, #328
Condition good
Content Nabatean inscription
ʿbdʾlbʿly br
ʿmyw bytyʾ
bṭb
Access II.2a.121 (printed, CIS)
Corpus CIS 2514

Inscription 3780
Site Jebel Serabit, Wadi Thmareh, #282
Condition fair
Content Nabatean inscription
....
ʿmmw
ʾtmw br ʿmyw
Access II.2a.142 (printed, CIS)
Corpus CIS 2687

Inscription 3781
Site Wadi Firan, Wadi Khabar, #328
Condition good
Content Nabatean inscription
dkyr šmrḥ
[br] klbw
Access II.2a.121 (printed, CIS)
Corpus CIS 2515

Inscription 3782
Site Wadi Firan, Wadi Khabar, #328
Condition fair
Content Nabatean inscription
šlm dʾbw
br ʾl[zʿb]lyw
Access II.2a.121 (printed, CIS)
Corpus CIS 2516

Inscription 3783
Site Wadi Firan, Wadi Khabar, #328
Condition good
Content Nabatean inscription
šlm ʿmyw
br wʾl[w]
bṭb
Access II.2a.121 (printed, CIS)
Corpus CIS 2517

Inscription 3784
Site Wadi Firan, Wadi Khabar, #328
Condition fair
Content Nabatean inscription
šlm ḥršw br ʿ....
Access II.2a.121 (printed, CIS)
Corpus CIS 2518

Inscription 3785
Site Wadi Firan, Wadi Khabar, #328
Condition good
Content Nabatean inscription
šlm ...w
šmrḥ br ḥry
šw bṭb
Access II.2a.121 (printed, CIS)
Corpus CIS 2519

Inscription 3786
Site Wadi Firan, Wadi Khabar, #328
Condition poor
Content Nabatean inscription
ḥ[brkn] br
ḥlṣt
Access II.2a.121 (printed, CIS)
Corpus CIS 2520

Inscription 3787
Site Wadi Firan, Wadi Khabar, #328
Condition poor
Content Nabatean inscription
Access II.2a.121 (printed, CIS)
Corpus CIS 2521

Inscription 3788
Site Wadi Firan, Wadi Khabar, #328
Condition fair
Content Nabatean inscription
šlm [ḥry]šw
br ʿbdʾlbʿly
Access II.2a.121 (printed, CIS)
Corpus CIS 2522

Inscription 3789
Site Wadi Firan, Wadi Khabar, #328
Condition good
Content Nabatean inscription
mlyḥw br
ʾšwdw
Access II.2a.121 (printed, CIS)
Corpus CIS 2523

Inscription 3790
Site Wadi Firan, Wadi Khabar, #328
Condition poor
Content Nabatean inscription
šlm bry[ʾw br]
klbw b[ṭb]
Access II.2a.121 (printed, CIS)
Corpus CIS 2524

Inscription 3791
Site Wadi Firan, Wadi Khabar, #328
Condition fair
Content Nabatean inscription
šlm ḥršw ʾl....
Access II.2a.122 (printed, CIS)
Corpus CIS 2525

Inscription 3792
Site Wadi Firan, Wadi Khabar, #328
Condition poor
Content Nabatean inscription
[šlm] hnʾw br
[ʾlm]bqrw
Access II.2a.122 (printed, CIS)
Corpus CIS 2526

Inscription 3793
Site Wadi Firan, Wadi Khabar, #328
Condition poor
Content Nabatean inscription
šlm ..ṣy br
...bʿly
Access II.2a.122 (printed, CIS)
Corpus CIS 2527

Inscription 3794
Site Wadi Firan, Wadi Khabar, #328
Condition poor
Content Nabatean inscription
Access II.2a.122 (printed, CIS)
Corpus CIS 2528

Inscription 3795
Site Wadi Firan, Wadi Khabar, #328
Condition poor
Content Nabatean inscription
Access II.2a.122 (printed, CIS)
Corpus CIS 2529

Inscription 3796
Site Wadi Firan, Wadi Khabar, #328
Condition poor
Content Nabatean inscription
Access II.2a.122 (printed, CIS)
Corpus CIS 2530

Inscription 3797
Site Wadi Firan, #53
Condition good
Content Nabatean inscription
šlm ʿrqbw
Access II.2a.122 (printed, CIS)
Corpus CIS 2531

Inscription 3798
Site Wadi Firan, #53
Condition fair
Content Nabatean inscription
šlm ʿbdʾl[bʿly]
br ḥr[yšw]
Access II.2a.122 (printed, CIS)
Corpus CIS 2532

Inscription 3799
Site Wadi Firan, #53
Condition good
Content Nabatean inscription
dkyr ʿmrw br
šʿdʾl[h]
Access II.2a.122 (printed, CIS)
Corpus CIS 2533

Inscription 3800
Site Wadi Firan, #53
Condition good
Content Nabatean inscription
šlm ʿwdw
br ʿydw
Access II.2a.123 (printed, CIS)
Corpus CIS 2534

Inscription 3801
Site Wadi Firan, #53
Condition good
Content Nabatean inscription
šlm ḥgw
br grymw
Access II.2a.123 (printed, CIS)
Corpus CIS 2535

Inscription 3802
Site Wadi Firan, #53
Condition fair
Content Nabatean inscription
šlm mšlmw br
ʿm[yw]...
Access II.2a.123 (printed, CIS)
Corpus CIS 2536

Inscription 3803
Site Wadi Firan, #53
Condition good
Content Nabatean inscription
ḥryšw
qrḥw
Access II.2a.123 (printed, CIS)
Corpus CIS 2537

Inscription 3804
Site Wadi Firan, #53
Condition good
Content Nabatean inscription
šlm ʿbdʾh[y]w
br šʿdʾlhy
Access II.2a.123 (printed, CIS)
Corpus CIS 2538

Inscription 3805
Site Wadi Firan, #53
Condition fair
Content Nabatean inscription
šlm wʾlw br
ʾl[br]yw b[ṭb]
Access II.2a.123 (printed, CIS)
Corpus CIS 2539

Inscription 3806
Site Wadi Firan, #53
Condition good
Content Nabatean inscription
šlm šʿdʾlhy
br bryʾw
Access II.2a.123 (printed, CIS)
Corpus CIS 2540

Inscription 3807
Site Wadi Firan, #53
Condition good
Content Nabatean inscription
šlm wdʿw br ʾwyšw
Access II.2a.123 (printed, CIS)
Corpus CIS 2541

Inscription 3808
Site Wadi Firan, #53
Condition good
Content Nabatean inscription
šlm ʾlm[b]qrw br wʾlw
Access II.2a.123 (printed, CIS)
Corpus CIS 2542

Inscription 3809
Site Wadi Firan, #53
Condition poor
Content Nabatean inscription
...bw bṭ[b]
[d]kyr š[ʿ]
dʾl[hy] br ....
Access II.2a.123 (printed, CIS)
Corpus CIS 2543

Inscription 3810
Site Wadi Firan, #53
Condition good
Content Nabatean inscription
dkyr ḥrw
Access II.2a.123 (printed, CIS)
Corpus CIS 2544

Inscription **3811**
Site Wadi Firan, #53
Condition good
Content Nabatean inscription
šlm wʾlw br
mḥmy[w]
Access II.2a.124 (printed, CIS)
Corpus CIS 2545

Inscription **3812**
Site Wadi Firan, #53
Condition good
Content Nabatean inscription
šlm [ʾw]šw br zydw
Access II.2a.124 (printed, CIS)
Corpus CIS 2546

Inscription **3813**
Site Wadi Firan, #53
Condition good
Content Nabatean inscription
dkyr ʿbdʾlbʿly br ḥlṣt
br bryʾw bṭb
Access II.2a.124 (printed, CIS)
Corpus CIS 2547

Inscription **3814**
Site Wadi Firan, #53
Condition good
Content Nabatean inscription
šlm šnrḥ br ʿmrw bṭb
Access II.2a.124 (printed, CIS)
Corpus CIS 2548

Inscription **3815**
Site Wadi Firan, #53
Condition good
Content Nabatean inscription
šlm zydw br wʾlw
Access II.2a.124 (printed, CIS)
Corpus CIS 2549

Inscription **3816**
Site Wadi Firan, #53
Condition good
Content Nabatean inscription
š[lm] ḥryšw br ʾwyšw
Access II.2a.124 (printed, CIS)
Corpus CIS 2550

Inscription **3817**
Site Wadi Firan, #53
Condition good
Content Nabatean inscription
šlm ʿwdw br
[q]rḥw
Access II.2a.124 (printed, CIS)
Corpus CIS 2551

Inscription **3818**
Site Wadi Firan, #53
Condition good
Content Nabatean inscription
šlm ʿmyw br
ṣwbw
Access II.2a.124 (printed, CIS)
Corpus CIS 2552

Inscription **3819**
Site Wadi Firan, #53
Condition fair
Content Nabatean inscription
šlm ʿbydw
br g[dyw]
Access II.2a.124 (printed, CIS)
Corpus CIS 2553

Inscription **3820**
Site Wadi Firan, #53
Condition good
Content Nabatean inscription
šlm šʿdw br
grmʾlbʿly
Access II.2a.124 (printed, CIS)
Corpus CIS 2554

Inscription **3821**
Site Wadi Firan, #53
Condition poor
Content Nabatean inscription
šlm] ḥ[l]ṣ[t] br bryʾw
Access II.2a.125 (printed, CIS)
Corpus CIS 2555

Inscription **3822**
Site Wadi Firan, #53
Condition good
Content Nabatean inscription
šlm qymw br
ʿwdw ḥnyʾh
šlm šlm[w]
Access II.2a.125 (printed, CIS)
Corpus CIS 2556

Inscription **3823**
Site Wadi Firan, #53
Condition good
Content Nabatean inscription
šlm ḥnṭlw
br gdyw
Access II.2a.125 (printed, CIS)
Corpus CIS 2557

Inscription 3824
Site Wadi Firan, #53
Condition poor
Content Nabatean inscription
[šl]m bryʾw
[br] pṣyw
Access II.2a.125 (printed, CIS)
Corpus CIS 2558

Inscription 3825
Site Wadi Firan, #53
Condition good
Content Nabatean inscription
šlm wʾlw br
ʾwšw
Access II.2a.125 (printed, CIS)
Corpus CIS 2559

Inscription 3826
Site Wadi Firan, #53
Condition fair
Content Nabatean inscription
šlm [ʾwy]šw
br qynw
Access II.2a.125 (printed, CIS)
Corpus CIS 2560

Inscription 3827
Site Wadi Firan, #53
Condition poor
Content Nabatean inscription
š[l]m grm[ʾlhy]
dkyr ...dyw.
Access II.2a.125 (printed, CIS)
Corpus CIS 2561

Inscription 3828
Site Wadi Firan, #53
Condition fair
Content Nabatean inscription
šlm ḥnṭlw br ....
Access II.2a.125 (printed, CIS)
Corpus CIS 2562

Inscription 3829
Site Wadi Firan, #53
Condition fair
Content Nabatean inscription
šlm ʿmyw br ʿ[b]d[ʾ]hyw
Access II.2a.125 (printed, CIS)
Corpus CIS 2563

Inscription 3830
Site Wadi Firan, #53
Condition poor
Content Nabatean inscription
šlm šmr[ḥ br] ʿm[y]w...
Access II.2a.125 (printed, CIS)
Corpus CIS 2564

Inscription 3831
Site Wadi Firan, #53
Condition fair
Content Nabatean inscription
šlm ʿmmw
ʾbn ʾl[qyny]
Access II.2a.125 (printed, CIS)
Corpus CIS 2565

Inscription 3832
Site Wadi Firan, #53
Condition fair
Content Nabatean inscription
šlm bryʾw
Access II.2a.126 (printed, CIS)
Corpus CIS 2566

Inscription 3833
Site Wadi Firan, #53
Condition good
Content Nabatean inscription
šlm ḥršw b[r]
ʿmnw
Access II.2a.126 (printed, CIS)
Corpus CIS 2567

Inscription 3834
Site Wadi Firan, #53
Condition good
Content Nabatean inscription
šlm ḥršw
br ʾ[w]šʾlhy
Access II.2a.126 (printed, CIS)
Corpus CIS 2568

Inscription 3835
Site Wadi Firan, #53
Condition good
Content Nabatean inscription
šlm ʾwšʾlbʿly br
ḥlyṣw bṭb w[šlm]
Access II.2a.126 (printed, CIS)
Corpus CIS 2569

Inscription 3836
Site Wadi Firan, #53
Condition good
Content Nabatean inscription
šlm ʿwdw br
[q]rḥw
Access II.2a.126 (printed, CIS)
Corpus CIS 2570

Inscription 3837
Site Wadi Firan, #53
Condition good
Content Nabatean inscription
šlm ytʿw br wdw br ytʿw
Access II.2a.126 (printed, CIS)
Corpus CIS 2571

Inscription 3838
Site Wadi Firan, #53
Condition poor
Content Nabatean inscription
.... br pṣy...
br grmlbʿl[y]
Access II.2a.126 (printed, CIS)
Corpus CIS 2572

Inscription 3839
Site Wadi Firan, #53
Condition fair
Content Nabatean inscription
ʿbṭt [br]
ʿmmw
Access II.2a.126 (printed, CIS)
Corpus CIS 2573

Inscription 3840
Site Wadi Firan, #53
Condition good
Content Nabatean inscription
šlm ḥyyw br
[gr]mʾlbʿly
Access II.2a.126 (printed, CIS)
Corpus CIS 2574

Inscription 3841
Site Wadi Firan, #53
Condition poor
Content Nabatean inscription
šlm ʾl[ṭ]mw wgrmlbʿly
[bny ʾbn] ʾlky[n]y b[ṭ]b
Access II.2a.127 (printed, CIS)
Corpus CIS 2575

Inscription 3842
Site Wadi Firan, #53
Condition fair
Content Nabatean inscription
[šlm] wdw br ʿbdʾlbʿly
Access II.2a.126 (printed, CIS)
Corpus CIS 2576

Inscription 3843
Site Wadi Firan, #53
Condition good
Content Nabatean inscription
šlm ʿwdw br krḥw
Access II.2a.127 (printed, CIS)
Corpus CIS 2577

Inscription 3844
Site Wadi Firan, #53
Condition poor
Content Nabatean inscription
šlm šlm[w] wmḥ[m]y[w]
[bny] grmʾlbʿly
Access II.2a.127 (printed, CIS)
Corpus CIS 2578

Inscription 3845
Site Wadi Firan, #53
Condition good
Content Nabatean inscription
šlm ʿwšw br
ʿmyw
Access II.2a.127 (printed, CIS)
Corpus CIS 2579

Inscription 3846
Site Wadi Firan, #53
Condition good
Content Nabatean inscription
šlm grmlbʿly
br ʿmm[w] br ḥršw
Access II.2a.127 (printed, CIS)
Corpus CIS 2580

Inscription 3847
Site Wadi Firan, #53
Condition good
Content Nabatean inscription
šlm nšnkyh br zydw
Access II.2a.127 (printed, CIS)
Corpus CIS 2581

Inscription 3848
Site Wadi Firan, #53
Condition fair
Content Nabatean inscription
šlm [r]šw br ʿmr[w]
Access II.2a.127 (printed, CIS)
Corpus CIS 2582

Inscription 3849
Site Wadi Firan, #53
Condition good
Content Nabatean inscription
šlm ʿmmw br wʾlw
Access II.2a.127 (printed, CIS)
Corpus CIS 2583

Inscription 3850
Site Wadi Firan, #53
Condition good
Content Nabatean inscription
šlm š[m]rḥ br ʾwšw
Access II.2a.128 (printed, CIS)
Corpus CIS 2584

Inscription 3851
Site Wadi Firan, #53
Condition fair
Content Nabatean inscription
šlm grmʾl[bʿ]ly br [w]ʾlw
Access II.2a.128 (printed, CIS)
Corpus CIS 2585

Inscription 3852
Site Wadi Firan, #53
Condition good
Content Nabatean inscription
šlm ʾʿlʾ br ʾwšw
Access II.2a.128 (printed, CIS)
Corpus CIS 2586

Inscription 3853
Site Wadi Firan, #53
Condition good
Content Nabatean inscription
šlm ḥryšw
br ʿmyw
br škmw
Access II.2a.128 (printed, CIS)
Corpus CIS 2587

Inscription 3854
Site Wadi Firan, #53
Condition good
Content Nabatean inscription
šlm ʿbydw br ḥlyṣw
Access II.2a.128 (printed, CIS)
Corpus CIS 2588

Inscription 3855
Site Wadi Firan, #53
Condition poor
Content Nabatean inscription
šlm ʿ...
Access II.2a.128 (printed, CIS)
Corpus CIS 2589

Inscription 3856
Site Wadi Firan, #53
Condition fair
Content Nabatean inscription
šlm .... br ʾwšw
Access II.2a.128 (printed, CIS)
Corpus CIS 2590

Inscription 3857
Site Wadi Firan, #53
Condition poor
Content Nabatean inscription
šlm ʾl...w
Access II.2a.128 (printed, CIS)
Corpus CIS 2591

Inscription 3858
Site Wadi Firan, #53
Condition fair
Content Nabatean inscription
šlm ḥgyrw
Access II.2a.128 (printed, CIS)
Corpus CIS 2592

Inscription 3859
Site Wadi Firan, #53
Condition good
Content Nabatean inscription
šlm ʾwšʾlhy br
[h]nyʾw mʾrʾ
Access II.2a.129 (printed, CIS)
Corpus CIS 2593

Inscription 3860
Site Wadi Firan, #53
Condition good
Content Nabatean inscription
dkyr ʾbn ʾlqyny
br ʾʿlʾ bṭb
Access II.2a.129 (printed, CIS)
Corpus CIS 2594

Inscription 3861
Site Wadi Firan, #53
Condition good
Content Nabatean inscription
šlm ʿtygw
Access II.2a.129 (printed, CIS)
Corpus CIS 2595

Inscription 3862
Site Wadi Firan, #53
Condition fair
Content Nabatean inscription
šlm wʾlw wʿw[dw]
[bn]y ʿyydw bṭb
Access II.2a.129 (printed, CIS)
Corpus CIS 2596

Inscription 3863
Site Wadi Firan, #53
Condition good
Content Nabatean inscription
šlm ʿbdʾlbʿly
br šlmw [bṭb]
Access II.2a.129 (printed, CIS)
Corpus CIS 2597

Inscription 3864
Site Wadi Firan, #53
Condition good
Content Nabatean inscription
šlm wʾlw br [ʿ]bdʾlbʿly
Access II.2a.129 (printed, CIS)
Corpus CIS 2598

Inscription 3865
Site Wadi Firan, #53
Condition good
Content Nabatean inscription
šlm wʾlw br ḥršw
Access II.2a.129 (printed, CIS)
Corpus CIS 2599

Inscription **3866**
Site Wadi Firan, #53
Condition good
Content Nabatean inscription
šlm ʿmrw
ʿwbw
Access II.2a.129 (printed, CIS)
Corpus CIS 2600

Inscription **3867**
Site Wadi Firan, #53
Condition fair
Content Nabatean inscription
šlm ʾwšw br
[ʿbd]ʾlgyʾ
Access II.2a.129 (printed, CIS)
Corpus CIS 2601

Inscription **3868**
Site Wadi Firan, #53
Condition good
Content Nabatean inscription
šlm hʾršw br ʿmnw
Access II.2a.130 (printed, CIS)
Corpus CIS 2602

Inscription **3869**
Site Wadi Firan, #53
Condition poor
Content Nabatean inscription
šl ʿlm.ry
Access II.2a.130 (printed, CIS)
Corpus CIS 2603

Inscription **3870**
Site Wadi Firan, #53
Condition good
Content Nabatean inscription
šlm klbw br ʿmrw
mn ʾl ḥttw [bṭb]
Access II.2a.130 (printed, CIS)
Corpus CIS 2604

Inscription **3871**
Site Wadi Firan, #53
Condition good
Content Nabatean inscription
šlm ʿmrw br ḥryšw
Access II.2a.130 (printed, CIS)
Corpus CIS 2605

Inscription **3872**
Site Wadi Firan, #53
Condition poor
Content Nabatean inscription
dkyr ʾbn ʾ[lq]yn[y]
br ʾʿlʾ wʾ[ʿlʾ]
wʿm[mw]
ʿ...
Access II.2a.130 (printed, CIS)
Corpus CIS 2606

Inscription **3873**
Site Wadi Firan, #53
Condition good
Content Nabatean inscription
šlm ʿmrw
Access II.2a.130 (printed, CIS)
Corpus CIS 2607

Inscription **3874**
Site Wadi Firan, #53
Condition good
Content Nabatean inscription
šlm ʾtmw br
ʿydw bṭb
Access II.2a.130 (printed, CIS)
Corpus CIS 2608

Inscription **3875**
Site Wadi Firan, #53
Condition good
Content Nabatean inscription
dkyr bryʾw
br ʾwšw br ʾ
wšʾl[h]y bṭb
Access II.2a.130 (printed, CIS)
Corpus CIS 2609

Inscription **3876**
Site Wadi Firan, #53
Condition good
Content Nabatean inscription
dkyr grmʾlhy
br ʿbydw
Access II.2a.130 (printed, CIS)
Corpus CIS 2610

Inscription **3877**
Site Wadi Firan, #53
Condition good
Content Nabatean inscription
šlm bryʾw br pṣy bṭb
wʿbdʾlbʿly ʾḥwhy
Access II.2a.130 (printed, CIS)
Corpus CIS 2611

Inscription 3878
Site Wadi Firan, #53
Condition good
Content Nabatean inscription
šlm ḥlyṣw br
ʾwšʾlbʿly
bṭb
Access II.2a.130 (printed, CIS)
Corpus CIS 2612

Inscription 3879
Site Wadi Firan, #53
Condition good
Content Nabatean inscription
šlm ʿbydw br
ʾ[t]mw
Access II.2a.130 (printed, CIS)
Corpus CIS 2613

Inscription 3880
Site Wadi Firan, #53
Condition fair
Content Nabatean inscription
šlm nšnkyh
br [ʿ]ṣ[r]w
Access II.2a.131 (printed, CIS)
Corpus CIS 2614

Inscription 3881
Site Wadi Firan, #53
Condition poor
Content Nabatean inscription
[s]l[wn]s [d]y [mt]qrʾ qyzw...
br ....drʾ bṭb
Access II.2a.131 (printed, CIS)
Corpus CIS 2615

Inscription 3882
Site Wadi Firan, #53
Condition fair
Content Nabatean inscription
dkyr bṭb [yʿly] br tymʾlhy
Access II.2a.131 (printed, CIS)
Corpus CIS 2616

Inscription 3883
Site Wadi Firan, #53
Condition fair
Content Nabatean inscription
šlm ʾlbrkw [b]r ʾwšw
b[ṭb]
Access II.2a.131 (printed, CIS)
Corpus CIS 2617

Inscription 3884
Site Wadi Firan, #53
Condition fair
Content Nabatean inscription
šlm ʾwšw br
ʾlmbqrw b[ṭb]
Access II.2a.131 (printed, CIS)
Corpus CIS 2618

Inscription 3885
Site Wadi Firan, #53
Condition good
Content Nabatean inscription
šlm ṣhmbw
br grmʾlhy
Access II.2a.131 (printed, CIS)
Corpus CIS 2619

Inscription 3886
Site Wadi Firan, #53
Condition good
Content Nabatean inscription
šlm ʾlh[g]rw
br šʿdʾlhy
Access II.2a.132 (printed, CIS)
Corpus CIS 2620

Inscription 3887
Site Wadi Firan, #53
Condition good
Content Nabatean inscription
šlm ʾwšʾlhy
br ʾlmbqrw
Access II.2a.132 (printed, CIS)
Corpus CIS 2621

Inscription 3888
Site Wadi Firan, #53
Condition good
Content Nabatean inscription
šlm ʿm[y]w br ʿwdw
Access II.2a.132 (printed, CIS)
Corpus CIS 2622

Inscription 3889
Site Wadi Firan, #53
Condition poor
Content Nabatean inscription
šlm ʾ[wy]š[w]
br wdʿ[w]
Access II.2a.132 (printed, CIS)
Corpus CIS 2623

Inscription 3890
Site Wadi Firan, #53
Condition fair
Content Nabatean inscription
šlm ʾlmbqrw
[br ʿ]wymw
Access II.2a.132 (printed, CIS)
Corpus CIS 2624

Inscription 3891
Site Jebel Serabit, Wadi Suwiq, #280
Condition good
Content Nabatean inscription
šlm ʾwšw br grmʾlhy
Access II.2a.133 (printed, CIS)
Corpus CIS 2625

Inscription 3892
Site Jebel Serabit, Wadi Suwiq, #280
Condition fair
Content Nabatean inscription
šlm grm...
br ʿnmw bṭb
Access II.2a.133 (printed, CIS)
Corpus CIS 2626

Inscription 3893
Site Jebel Serabit, Wadi Suwiq, #280
Condition good
Content Nabatean inscription
šlm ʿmyw br ṣwbw bṭb w[šlm]
Access II.2a.133 (printed, CIS)
Corpus CIS 2627

Inscription 3894
Site Jebel Serabit, Wadi Suwiq, #280
Condition good
Content Nabatean inscription
šlm ʿbdʾlbʿly br ʿmyw bṭb
wʿmyw brh mšqʾ
Access II.2a.133 (printed, CIS)
Corpus CIS 2628

Inscription 3895
Site Jebel Serabit, Wadi Suwiq, #280
Condition good
Content Nabatean inscription
šlm ʿwdw br qrḥw
Access II.2a.133 (printed, CIS)
Corpus CIS 2629

Inscription 3896
Site Jebel Serabit, Wadi Suwiq, #280
Condition poor
Content Nabatean inscription
[šl]m šlmw [br] ʾlmbqrw
Access II.2a.133 (printed, CIS)
Corpus CIS 2630

Inscription 3897
Site Jebel Serabit, Wadi Suwiq, #280
Condition good
Content Nabatean inscription
šlm hnyʾw br
wʾlw bṭb
Access II.2a.133 (printed, CIS)
Corpus CIS 2631

Inscription 3898
Site Jebel Serabit, Wadi Suwiq, #280
Condition good
Content Nabatean inscription
šlm ʿnmw
br ḥ[ry]šw
Access II.2a.133 (printed, CIS)
Corpus CIS 2632

Inscription 3899
Site Jebel Serabit, Wadi Suwiq, #280
Condition good
Content Nabatean inscription
šlm ʾʿlʾ
br ḥryšw
Access II.2a.134 (printed, CIS)
Corpus CIS 2633

Inscription 3900
Site Jebel Serabit, Wadi Suwiq, #280
Condition poor
Content Nabatean inscription
šlm šlmt
ʾ...
Access II.2a.134 (printed, CIS)
Corpus CIS 2634

Inscription 3901
Site Jebel Serabit, Wadi Suwiq, #280
Condition good
Content Nabatean inscription
šlm ʿmmw br wʾl[w]
Access II.2a.134 (printed, CIS)
Corpus CIS 2635

Inscription 3902
Site Jebel Serabit, Wadi Suwiq, #280
Condition fair
Content Nabatean inscription
.....
w šlm šlmw br ḥryšw bṭb
Access II.2a.134 (printed, CIS)
Corpus CIS 2636

Inscription 3903
Site Jebel Serabit, Wadi Suwiq, #280
Condition poor
Content Nabatean inscription
šlm šmrḥ br ʾwšw
br ..y.w
Access II.2a.134 (printed, CIS)
Corpus CIS 2637

Inscription 3904
Site Jebel Serabit, Wadi Suwiq, #280
Condition good
Content Nabatean inscription
šlm ʾwšw br
wʾlw
Access II.2a.134 (printed, CIS)
Corpus CIS 2638

Inscription 3905
Site Jebel Serabit, Wadi Suwiq, #280
Condition good
Content Nabatean inscription
šlm ʾwšʾlbʿly br
šlmw wḥlyṣw bṭb
Access II.2a.134 (printed, CIS)
Corpus CIS 2639

Inscription 3906
Site Jebel Serabit, Wadi Suwiq, #280
Condition good
Content Nabatean inscription
šlm ḥryšw br
ʾ wʾlw bṭb
Access II.2a.134 (printed, CIS)
Corpus CIS 2640

Inscription 3907
Site Jebel Serabit, Wadi Suwiq, #280
Condition poor
Content Nabatean inscription
šlm [grm]ʾ[lbʿly br]
ʾʿlʾ
Access II.2a.134 (printed, CIS)
Corpus CIS 2641

Inscription 3908
Site Jebel Serabit, Wadi Suwiq, #280
Condition good
Content Nabatean inscription
šlm ʿ
bydw br ʾwšw
šrh
Access II.2a.135 (printed, CIS)
Corpus CIS 2642

Inscription 3909
Site Jebel Serabit, Wadi Suwiq, #280
Condition poor
Content Nabatean inscription
.šw
[š]lm [g]mlw br pn[dšw]
Access II.2a.135 (printed, CIS)
Corpus CIS 2643

Inscription 3910
Site Jebel Serabit, Wadi Suwiq, #280
Condition good
Content Nabatean inscription
šlm ṭylh
br wʾlw
Access II.2a.135 (printed, CIS)
Corpus CIS 2644

Inscription 3911
Site Jebel Serabit, Wadi Suwiq, #280
Condition fair
Content Nabatean inscription
šlm ḥršw
br ʾl..w bṭb
Access II.2a.135 (printed, CIS)
Corpus CIS 2645

Inscription 3912
Site Jebel Serabit, Wadi Suwiq, #280
Condition poor
Content Nabatean inscription
šlm prq[w]
....
šlm ʾwšw br
šʿdw bṭb
Access II.2a.135 (printed, CIS)
Corpus CIS 2646

Inscription 3913
Site Jebel Serabit, Wadi Suwiq, #280
Condition good
Content Nabatean inscription
šlm ʿmrw br
ʾbn ʾlqyny [bk]l ṭb
Access II.2a.135 (printed, CIS)
Corpus CIS 2647

Inscription 3914
Site Jebel Serabit, Wadi Suwiq, #280
Condition poor
Content Nabatean inscription
dkyr ʿbdʾlbʿly br ʿ[m]yw bytyʾ
....
[šlm] ʾlhm[š]w [br hn]yʾ[w] bkl ṭb
Access II.2a.135 (printed, CIS)
Corpus CIS 2648

Inscription 3915
Site Jebel Serabit, Wadi Suwiq, #280
Condition good
Content Nabatean inscription
šlm šmrḥ br
ʿmrw
Access II.2a.135 (printed, CIS)
Corpus CIS 2649

Inscription 3916
Site Jebel Serabit, Wadi Suwiq, #280
Condition good
Content Nabatean inscription
šlm ʿbdlbʿly
br ʾwšw br ḥryšw
Access II.2a.136 (printed, CIS)
Corpus CIS 2650

Inscription 3917
Site Jebel Serabit, Wadi Suwiq, #280
Condition good
Content Nabatean inscription
šlm ḥwrw br ʿdʾ
mʿyrw
Access II.2a.136 (printed, CIS)
Corpus CIS 2651

Inscription 3918
Site Jebel Serabit, Wadi Suwiq, #280
Condition good
Content Nabatean inscription
šlm šmrḥ
[br z]ydw
Access II.2a.136 (printed, CIS)
Corpus CIS 2652

Inscription 3919
Site Jebel Serabit, Wadi Suwiq, #280
Condition good
Content Nabatean inscription
šlm lwʾ hnyʾw
Access II.2a.136 (printed, CIS)
Corpus CIS 2653

Inscription 3920
Site Jebel Serabit, Wadi Suwiq, #280
Condition good
Content Nabatean inscription
šlm ʿmmw br
wʾlw wškmw ʾḥwh
Access II.2a.136 (printed, CIS)
Corpus CIS 2654

Inscription 3921
Site Jebel Serabit, Wadi Suwiq, #280
Condition good
Content Nabatean inscription
šlm ʿbdʾlbʿly br
ʿmyw [bṭb]
Access II.2a.136 (printed, CIS)
Corpus CIS 2655

Inscription 3922
Site Jebel Serabit, Wadi Suwiq, #280
Condition poor
Content Nabatean inscription
šlm grmʾlbʿly
br ʾ.....
šl[m ʾl]hm[š]w br [hn]yʾw
Access II.2a.136 (printed, CIS)
Corpus CIS 2656

Inscription 3923
Site Jebel Serabit, Wadi Suwiq, #280
Condition good
Content Nabatean inscription
šlm ḥryšw
br ʿlyw
Access II.2a.137 (printed, CIS)
Corpus CIS 2657

Inscription 3924
Site Jebel Serabit, Wadi Suwiq, #280
Condition good
Content Nabatean inscription
šlm klbw br ʿmrw br
klbw bṭ[b]
Access II.2a.137 (printed, CIS)
Corpus CIS 2658

Inscription 3925
Site Jebel Muneijat F, #63
Condition good
Content Nabatean inscription
dkyr kʿ
mh br
ʿmrw
Access II.2a.137 (printed, CIS)
Corpus CIS 2659

Inscription 3926
Site Jebel Muneijat F, #63
Condition poor
Content Nabatean inscription
dkyr p
...ʾkplʾ
br ...w
Access II.2a.137 (printed, CIS)
Corpus CIS 2660

Inscription 3927
Site Jebel Muneijat F, #63
Condition fair
Content Nabatean inscription
šlm ʿmyw
br wʾ[lw]
pdyw
mbqrʾ
Access II.2a.138 (printed, CIS)
Corpus CIS 2661

Inscription 3928
Site Jebel Muneijat F, #63
Condition good
Content Nabatean inscription
mdkryn ʾw
šw wšmrḥ
bny ʿbydw
Access II.2a.138 (printed, CIS)
Corpus CIS 2662

Inscription 3929
Site Jebel Muneijat F, #63
Condition good
Content Nabatean inscription
šlm ʿwdw br wʾl
w wqrḥw bṭb
Access II.2a.138 (printed, CIS)
Corpus CIS 2663

Inscription 3930
Site Jebel Muneijat F, #63
Condition good
Content Nabatean inscription
ʿbydw br
ṣhbw
bṭb
Access II.2a.138 (printed, CIS)
Corpus CIS 2664

Inscription 3931
Site Jebel Muneijat F, #63
Condition poor
Content Nabatean inscription
š[lm] hnʾw [w]zydw
bny bryʾw khnʾ...
dkyr ʿbdʾlbʿl[y br] ....
Access II.2a.138 (printed, CIS)
Corpus CIS 2665

Inscription 3932
Site Jebel Muneijat F, #63
Dating 253
Condition good
Content Nabatean inscription
šlm klbw br ʿmrw
šnt 148
bṭb
Access II.2a.139 (printed, CIS)
Corpus CIS 2666

Inscription 3933
Site Jebel Muneijat F, #63
Condition good
Content Nabatean inscription
dkyr gdyw ʾkplʾ
br zydw bṭb ʿbydw
mbkrʾ br wʾlw bṭb
Access II.2a.139 (printed, CIS)
Corpus CIS 2667 (1)

Inscription 3934
Site Jebel Muneijat F, #63
Condition poor
Content Nabatean inscription
ʿbydw kt
bʾ
Access II.2a.139 (printed, CIS)
Corpus CIS 2667 (2)

Inscription 3935
Site Jebel Muneijat F, #63
Condition good
Content Nabatean inscription
dkyr ʾlmbqr
w br zydw
mbkrʾ
Access II.2a.139 (printed, CIS)
Corpus CIS 2668

Inscription 3936
Site Jebel Muneijat F, #63
Condition good
Content Nabatean inscription
ʿmrw
dkyr hnyʾw mbkrʾ
[br ʾ]wšʾlhy
bṭb
Access II.2a.140 (printed, CIS)
Corpus CIS 2669

Inscription 3937
Site Jebel Muneijat F, #63
Condition fair
Content Nabatean inscription
šlm ḥlṣw
br
...yw
Access II.2a.140 (printed, CIS)
Corpus CIS 2670

Inscription 3938
Site Jebel Muneijat F, #63
Condition fair
Content Nabatean inscription
šlm ʿmyw br z[ydw]
Access II.2a.140 (printed, CIS)
Corpus CIS 2671

Inscription 3939
Site Jebel Muneijat F, #63
Condition fair
Content Nabatean inscription
dkyr ḥryšw
ʾkplʾ [br] ʿm[y]w
bṭb
Access II.2a.140 (printed, CIS)
Corpus CIS 2672

Inscription 3940
Site Jebel Muneijat F, #63
Condition fair
Content Nabatean inscription
dkyr zydw
ʾkplʾ br bryʾw b[r]
[š]lmw bṭb
Access II.2a.140 (printed, CIS)
Corpus CIS 2673

Inscription 3941
Site Jebel Muneijat F, #63
Condition good
Content Nabatean inscription
dkyr ḥryšw ʾkplʾ
br ʿmyw bṭb wpṣyw
[wbr]yʾ[w w]zydw bnyh
Access II.2a.140 (printed, CIS)
Corpus CIS 2674

Inscription 3942
Site Jebel Muneijat F, #63
Condition good
Content Nabatean inscription
dkyr ḥlṣt br grm[w]
Access II.2a.140 (printed, CIS)
Corpus CIS 2675

Inscription 3943
Site Jebel Muneijat F, #63
Condition good
Content Nabatean inscription
šlm ʿmyw br
ʿlht
Access II.2a.140 (printed, CIS)
Corpus CIS 2676

Inscription 3944
Site Jebel Muneijat F, #63
Condition good
Content Nabatean inscription
dk[y]r bṭb grmʾlbʿly
ʾkplʾ br w[ʾ]lt
Access II.2a.140 (printed, CIS)
Corpus CIS 2677

Inscription 3945
Site Jebel Muneijat F, #63
Condition good
Content Nabatean inscription
šlm ʿmyw ʾkpl
ʾ br ʿbdʾhyw
Access II.2a.141 (printed, CIS)
Corpus CIS 2678

Inscription 3946
Site Jebel Muneijat F, #63
Condition poor
Content Nabatean inscription
....ʾ
wbrh...
Access II.2a.141 (printed, CIS)
Corpus CIS 2679

Inscription 3947
Site Wadi Sulaf, #48
Condition good
Content Nabatean inscription
šlm šʿdw br
grmʾlbʿly
ʿd ʿlm
Access II.2a.141 (printed, CIS)
Corpus CIS 2680

Inscription 3948
Site Wadi Sulaf, #48
Condition good
Content Nabatean inscription
šlm ʿmyw br
ḥnṭlw b[ṭb]
Access II.2a.141 (printed, CIS)
Corpus CIS 2681

Inscription 3949
Site Wadi Sulaf, #48
Condition fair
Content Nabatean inscription
šlm ḥlṣt br .....
Access II.2a.141 (printed, CIS)
Corpus CIS 2682

Inscription 3950
Site Wadi Sulaf, #48
Condition good
Content Nabatean inscription
šlm ʿmmw br ʾbn ʾlqyny
Access II.2a.142 (printed, CIS)
Corpus CIS 2683

Inscription 3951
Site Wadi Sulaf, #48
Condition fair
Content Nabatean inscription
šlm bḥgh
šlm ʿbdʾl[bʿly]
ʿmmw
Access II.2a.142 (printed, CIS)
Corpus CIS 2684

Inscription 3952
Site Wadi Sulaf, #48
Condition good
Content Nabatean inscription
šlm šmrḥ br ʿmrw
Access II.2a.142 (printed, CIS)
Corpus CIS 2685

Inscription 3953
Site Wadi Sulaf, #48
Condition poor
Content Nabatean inscription
šlm grmlbʿly
br ....
šlm br ....
Access II.2a.142 (printed, CIS)
Corpus CIS 2686

Inscription 3954
Site Wadi Sulaf, #48
Condition poor
Content Nabatean inscription
šlm grmʾl[b]ʿl[y]
br ʿmmw
šlm ....
Access II.2a.142 (printed, CIS)
Corpus CIS 2688

Inscription 3955
Site Wadi Sulaf, #48
Condition good
Content Nabatean inscription
šlm wʾlw br
hnyʾ[w]
Access II.2a.142 (printed, CIS)
Corpus CIS 2689

Inscription 3956
Site Wadi Sulaf, #48
Condition poor
Content Nabatean inscription
šlm wʾlw [br ʾ]lmbqrw
[šlm ḥlṣt] br ʾwšw
Access II.2a.143 (printed, CIS)
Corpus CIS 2690

Inscription 3957
Site Wadi Sulaf, #48
Condition poor
Content Nabatean inscription
Access II.2a.143 (printed, CIS)
Corpus CIS 2691

Inscription 3958
Site Wadi Sulaf, #48
Condition good
Content Nabatean inscription
šlm šʿdw br ḥnṭ[lw]
šlm ʿbdʾlbʿly
Access II.2a.143 (printed, CIS)
Corpus CIS 2692

Inscription 3959
Site Wadi Sulaf, #48
Condition poor
Content Nabatean inscription
šlm ʿl[h]t br šmrḥ b[ṭb]
Access II.2a.143 (printed, CIS)
Corpus CIS 2693

Inscription 3960
Site Wadi Sulaf, #48
Condition good
Content Nabatean inscription
šlm
ʿmyw br
mbršw
Access II.2a.143 (printed, CIS)
Corpus CIS 2694

Inscription 3961
Site Wadi Sulaf, #48
Condition good
Content Nabatean inscription
š[l]m mbršw
br bṭšw
Access II.2a.143 (printed, CIS)
Corpus CIS 2695

Inscription **3962**
Site Wadi Sulaf, #48
Condition poor
Content Nabatean inscription
ʿmmw
Access II.2a.143 (printed, CIS)
Corpus CIS 2696

Inscription **3963**
Site Wadi Sulaf, #48
Condition fair
Content Nabatean inscription
šlm ḥnṭlw br nšnkyh bṭb
.... br ʿmmw
Access II.2a.143 (printed, CIS)
Corpus CIS 2697

Inscription **3964**
Site Wadi Hibran, #51
Condition good
Content Nabatean inscription
šlm
bryʾw br
klbw bṭb
Access II.2a.144 (printed, CIS)
Corpus CIS 2698

Inscription **3965**
Site Wadi Hibran, #51
Condition poor
Content Nabatean inscription
šlm ʾl[khnw]
br nš[gy]w
bṭb
Access II.2a.144 (printed, CIS)
Corpus CIS 2699

Inscription **3966**
Site Wadi Hibran, #51
Condition fair
Content Nabatean inscription
šlm bḥgh br [grmʾl]bʿly
br ʿbdʾlbʿly
Access II.2a.144 (printed, CIS)
Corpus CIS 2700

Inscription **3967**
Site Wadi Hibran, #51
Condition poor
Content Nabatean inscription
šlm [qr]ḥw br [ḥry]
šw
Access II.2a.144 (printed, CIS)
Corpus CIS 2701

Inscription **3968**
Site Wadi Hibran, #51
Condition good
Content Nabatean inscription
šlm ʿmrw
br grm
grmbʿly
bṭb
Access II.2a.144 (printed, CIS)
Corpus CIS 2702

Inscription **3969**
Site Wadi Hibran, #51
Condition poor
Content Nabatean inscription
šlm grm[ʾ]lbʿ[ly]
[br ʿm]mw
Access II.2a.144 (printed, CIS)
Corpus CIS 2703

Inscription **3970**
Site Wadi Hibran, #51
Condition fair
Content Nabatean inscription
šlm š...
br mbršw
Access II.2a.144 (printed, CIS)
Corpus CIS 2704

Inscription **3971**
Site Wadi Hibran, #51
Condition fair
Content Nabatean inscription
šlm ...w br ʿwdw bṭb
Access II.2a.145 (printed, CIS)
Corpus CIS 2705

Inscription **3972**
Site Wadi Hibran, #51
Condition good
Content Nabatean inscription
šlm ḥnṭlw
Access II.2a.145 (printed, CIS)
Corpus CIS 2706

Inscription **3973**
Site Wadi Hibran, #51
Condition good
Content Nabatean inscription
šlm grmʾlbʿly br ʿmmw
Access II.2a.145 (printed, CIS)
Corpus CIS 2707

Inscription **3974**
Site Wadi Hibran, #51
Condition poor
Content Nabatean inscription
šlm hnʾw
br ʿb[dʾlbʿly]
Access II.2a.145 (printed, CIS)
Corpus CIS 2708

Inscription **3975**
Site Wadi Hibran, #51
Condition good
Content Nabatean inscription
šlm ḥlṣt br ʿbdʾlbʿly
Access II.2a.145 (printed, CIS)
Corpus CIS 2709

Inscription **3976**
Site Wadi Hibran, #51
Condition good
Content Nabatean inscription
šlm ʾwšw br
ʿbdlbʿly bṭ[b]
Access II.2a.145 (printed, CIS)
Corpus CIS 2710

Inscription **3977**
Site Wadi Hibran, #51
Condition fair
Content Nabatean inscription
šlm ʾlhmšw br [dbylt]
Access II.2a.145 (printed, CIS)
Corpus CIS 2711

Inscription **3978**
Site Wadi Hibran, #51
Condition good
Content Nabatean inscription
šlm [ʾ]lmbqrw br
ʿwymw
Access II.2a.145 (printed, CIS)
Corpus CIS 2712

Inscription **3979**
Site Wadi Hibran, #51
Condition poor
Content Nabatean inscription
šlm šʿdʾlhy br
.... ʾl....
Access II.2a.145 (printed, CIS)
Corpus CIS 2713

Inscription **3980**
Site Wadi Hibran, #51
Condition fair
Content Nabatean inscription
šlm grmw ʾkpl[ʾ]
br ....
Access II.2a.146 (printed, CIS)
Corpus CIS 2714

Inscription **3981**
Site Wadi Hibran, #51
Condition poor
Content Nabatean inscription
ṣʿbw
br wʾlw
Access II.2a.146 (printed, CIS)
Corpus CIS 2715

Inscription **3982**
Site Wadi Hibran, #51
Condition fair
Content Nabatean inscription
šlm hnʾw br
.... šlm
Access II.2a.146 (printed, CIS)
Corpus CIS 2716

Inscription **3983**
Site Wadi Hibran, #51
Condition good
Content Nabatean inscription
šlm ʿrqbw br
whbʾl[h]y wdkyr
Access II.2a.146 (printed, CIS)
Corpus CIS 2717

Inscription **3984**
Site Wadi Hibran, #51
Condition good
Content Nabatean inscription
šlm ʿmyw
br wʾlw
Access II.2a.146 (printed, CIS)
Corpus CIS 2718

Inscription **3985**
Site Wadi Hibran, #51
Condition fair
Content Nabatean inscription
dkyr ʾwy[š]w
br ʿbdʾlhy b[ṭb]
Access II.2a.146 (printed, CIS)
Corpus CIS 2719

Inscription **3986**
Site Wadi Hibran, #51
Condition fair
Content Nabatean inscription
dkyr wʾlw
br ʿyydw
wʿ[yydw brh]
Access II.2a.146 (printed, CIS)
Corpus CIS 2720

Inscription 3987
Site Wadi Hibran, #51
Condition poor
Content Nabatean inscription
šlm [z]ydw br ʾptḥ
...w br ṣḥbw
Access II.2a.146 (printed, CIS)
Corpus CIS 2721

Inscription 3988
Site Wadi Hibran, #51
Condition fair
Content Nabatean inscription
šlm zydw br wʾ[lw]
Access II.2a.146 (printed, CIS)
Corpus CIS 2722

Inscription 3989
Site Wadi Hibran, #51
Condition good
Content Nabatean inscription
lḥlṣt
wšlmw ʾlmbqrw
br nšnkyh
Access II.2a.147 (printed, CIS)
Corpus CIS 2723

Inscription 3990
Site Wadi Hibran, #51
Condition poor
Content Nabatean inscription
ʿwdw [br]
ḥršw šlm ....
šlm ʿwdw b[r] ʿwy[m]w
Access II.2a.147 (printed, CIS)
Corpus CIS 2724

Inscription 3991
Site Wadi Hibran, #51
Condition poor
Content Nabatean inscription
šlm ʾʿl[ʾ] br
ʾbn [ʾ]lqyny
dk[yr]
Access II.2a.147 (printed, CIS)
Corpus CIS 2725

Inscription 3992
Site Wadi Hibran, #51
Condition poor
Content Nabatean inscription
šlm w[hb]ʾl[h]
[br] ṣwbw
Access II.2a.147 (printed, CIS)
Corpus CIS 2726

Inscription 3993
Site Wadi Hibran, #51
Condition fair
Content Nabatean inscription
šlm šʿdʾlh[y]
br bryʾw
Access II.2a.147 (printed, CIS)
Corpus CIS 2727

Inscription 3994
Site Wadi Hibran, #51
Condition poor
Content Nabatean inscription
dkyr ʿbd...
Access II.2a.147 (printed, CIS)
Corpus CIS 2728

Inscription 3995
Site Wadi Hibran, #51
Condition good
Content Nabatean inscription
šlm ʿbdʾlbʿly br ʾlmbqrw
Access II.2a.147 (printed, CIS)
Corpus CIS 2729

Inscription 3996
Site Wadi Hibran, #51
Condition good
Content Nabatean inscription
šlm gšmw br
ḥrwṣw
kʿm[h] br
ḥršw br ʿlydw
Access II.2a.147 (printed, CIS)
Corpus CIS 2730

Inscription 3997
Site Wadi Hibran, #51
Condition good
Content Nabatean inscription
šlm ʾwšw br
[ʿ]wrw bṭb
Access II.2a.148 (printed, CIS)
Corpus CIS 2731

Inscription 3998
Site Wadi Hibran, #51
Condition poor
Content Nabatean inscription
grmw br ....
Access II.2a.148 (printed, CIS)
Corpus CIS 2732

Inscription 3999
Site Wadi Hibran, #51
Condition fair
Content Nabatean inscription
šlm m...
šlm ḥnṭlw
Access II.2a.148 (printed, CIS)
Corpus CIS 2733

Inscription 4000
Site Wadi Hibran, #51
Condition good
Content Nabatean inscription
šlm grmʾl
bʿl[y]
Access II.2a.148 (printed, CIS)
Corpus CIS 2734

Inscription 4001
Site Wadi Hibran, #51
Condition good
Content Nabatean inscription
grmʾlbʿly šlm
br ʿbdʾlbʿly
Access II.2a.148 (printed, CIS)
Corpus CIS 2735

Inscription 4002
Site Wadi Hibran, #51
Condition fair
Content Nabatean inscription
dkyr mgdyw br ʾ...
Access II.2a.148 (printed, CIS)
Corpus CIS 2736

Inscription 4003
Site Wadi Hibran, #51
Condition good
Content Nabatean inscription
šlm ʾwšʾlbʿly br
tymdwšrʾ
Access II.2a.148 (printed, CIS)
Corpus CIS 2737

Inscription 4004
Site Wadi Hibran, #51
Condition fair
Content Nabatean inscription
dkyr šlm bryʾw br [p]ṣyw bṭb w[šlm]
Access II.2a.148 (printed, CIS)
Corpus CIS 2738

Inscription 4005
Site Wadi Hibran, #51
Condition good
Content Nabatean inscription
ḥnṭlw br nšnkyh bṭb
y.. šlm
Access II.2a.149 (printed, CIS)
Corpus CIS 2739

Inscription 4006
Site Wadi Hibran, #51
Condition fair
Content Nabatean inscription
[dkyr nš]nkyh br grmlbʿl[y]
šlm ʿmmw br ...
Access II.2a.149 (printed, CIS)
Corpus CIS 2740

Inscription 4007
Site Wadi Hibran, #51
Condition poor
Content Nabatean inscription
Comment *illegible*
Access II.2a.149 (printed, CIS)
Corpus CIS 2741

Inscription 4008
Site Wadi Hibran, #51
Condition good
Content Nabatean inscription
A. šlm grmlbʿly br nšnkyh
br bḥgh
B. šlm ʿ[w]ymw
br ....
Access II.2a.149 (printed, CIS)
Corpus CIS 2742

Inscription 4009
Site Wadi Hibran, #51
Condition poor
Content Nabatean inscription
Comment *illegible fragments*
Access II.2a.149 (printed, CIS)
Corpus CIS 2743

Inscription 4010
Site Wadi Hibran, #51
Condition good
Content Nabatean inscription
šlm ḥryšw br
ʿbdʾlbʿly br wdw
Access II.2a.149 (printed, CIS)
Corpus CIS 2744

Inscription 4011
Site Wadi Hibran, #51
Condition poor
Content Nabatean inscription
qrḥw
Access II.2a.149 (printed, CIS)
Corpus CIS 2745

Inscription 4012
Site Wadi Hibran, #51
Condition good
Content Nabatean inscription
šlm gšmw
br ḥrwṣw
bṭb
Access II.2a.149 (printed, CIS)
Corpus CIS 2746

Inscription 4013
Site Naqb el Hawa, #44
Condition good
Content Nabatean inscription
[šl]m ṣḥbw br grmʾlhy
Access II.2a.150 (printed, CIS)
Corpus CIS 2747

Inscription 4014
Site Naqb el Hawa, #44
Condition good
Content Nabatean inscription
wdw br ytʿw
Access II.2a.150 (printed, CIS)
Corpus CIS 2748

Inscription 4015
Site Naqb el Hawa, #44
Condition good
Content Nabatean inscription
dkyr wdʿw br bṭšw bṭb
Access II.2a.150 (printed, CIS)
Corpus CIS 2749

Inscription 4016
Site Naqb el Hawa, #44
Condition good
Content Nabatean inscription
šlm ʿlht br ʾwšw bṭb
Access II.2a.151 (printed, CIS)
Corpus CIS 2750

Inscription 4017
Site Naqb el Hawa, #44
Condition fair
Content Nabatean inscription
šlm klbw br ʿmrw [bṭb]
Access II.2a.151 (printed, CIS)
Corpus CIS 2751

Inscription 4018
Site Naqb el Hawa, #44
Condition good
Content Nabatean inscription
šlm wdw br ʾwyšw
Access II.2a.151 (printed, CIS)
Corpus CIS 2752

Inscription 4019
Site Naqb el Hawa, #44
Condition fair
Content Nabatean inscription
šlm ʾtmw br ḥr[yšw]
dkyr wdw br ʾwyšw
Access II.2a.151 (printed, CIS)
Corpus CIS 2753

Inscription 4020
Site Naqb el Hawa, #44
Condition fair
Content Nabatean inscription
šlm ʾwyšw br ʿ[ydw]
Access II.2a.151 (printed, CIS)
Corpus CIS 2754

Inscription 4021
Site Naqb el Hawa, #44
Condition good
Content Nabatean inscription
šlm ʾtmw
br ḥryšw
Access II.2a.151 (printed, CIS)
Corpus CIS 2755

Inscription 4022
Site Naqb el Hawa, #44
Condition fair
Content Nabatean inscription
šlm zy[dw]
br ḥryšw
Access II.2a.151 (printed, CIS)
Corpus CIS 2756

Inscription 4023
Site Naqb el Hawa, #44
Condition poor
Content Nabatean inscription
šlm wʾlw [br] ....
Access II.2a.151 (printed, CIS)
Corpus CIS 2757

Inscription 4024
Site Jebel Musa, Wadi el Deir, #35
Condition fair
Content Nabatean inscription
dkyr bryʾw br ʿydw
šlm ʿwdw br [qrḥw]
Access II.2a.153 (printed, CIS)
Corpus CIS 2759

Inscription 4025
Site Jebel Musa, Wadi el Deir, #35
Condition poor
Content Nabatean inscription
[.... b]r ḥlṣw
Access II.2a.153 (printed, CIS)
Corpus CIS 2760

Inscription 4026
Site Jebel Musa, Wadi el Deir, #35
Condition fair
Content Nabatean inscription
šlm ʾlḥšpw
br ʿw[d]w
Access II.2a.153 (printed, CIS)
Corpus CIS 2761

Inscription 4027
Site Jebel Musa, Wadi el Deir, #35
Condition fair
Content Nabatean inscription
... br dʾbw wdʾbw [brh]
Access II.2a.153 (printed, CIS)
Corpus CIS 2762

Inscription 4028
Site Jebel Musa, Wadi el Deir, #35
Condition fair
Content Nabatean inscription
šlm t[ymʾ]lhy
br wdw
Access II.2a.153 (printed, CIS)
Corpus CIS 2763

Inscription 4029
Site Jebel Musa, Wadi el Deir, #35
Condition poor
Content Nabatean inscription
tymʾlhy
Access II.2a.153 (printed, CIS)
Corpus CIS 2764

Inscription 4030
Site Jebel Musa, Wadi el Deir, #35
Condition fair
Content Nabatean inscription
šlm ʿmnw br ....
Access II.2a.153 (printed, CIS)
Corpus CIS 2765

Inscription 4031
Site Jebel Musa, Wadi el Deir, #35
Condition poor
Content Nabatean inscription
bḥgḥ
Access II.2a.154 (printed, CIS)
Corpus CIS 2766

Inscription 4032
Site Jebel Musa, #19
Condition fair
Content Nabatean inscription
šlm ḥwrw br mʿy[rw]
Access II.2a.154 (printed, CIS)
Corpus CIS 2767

Inscription 4033
Site Jebel Musa, #19
Condition fair
Content Nabatean inscription
mdkwr wʾlw
wḥlṣw bny [nq]w[b] w
bṭb
Access II.2a.154 (printed, CIS)
Corpus CIS 2768

Inscription 4034
Site Jebel Musa, #19
Condition good
Content Nabatean inscription
šlm ʿmyw br ʿlht
Access II.2a.154 (printed, CIS)
Corpus CIS 2769

Inscription 4035
Site Jebel Musa, #19
Condition poor
Content Nabatean inscription
mʿnw
Access II.2a.154 (printed, CIS)
Corpus CIS 2770

Inscription 4036
Site Jebel Musa, #19
Condition good
Content Nabatean inscription
dkyr ʾbn qwmw
br ʿmrw bṭb
Access II.2a.155 (printed, CIS)
Corpus CIS 2771

Inscription 4037
Site Jebel Musa, #19
Condition fair
Content Nabatean inscription
šlm bryʾw br ʿmnw [w]bry[ʾw brh]
Access II.2a.155 (printed, CIS)
Corpus CIS 2772

Inscription 4038
Site Jebel Musa, #19
Condition fair
Content Nabatean inscription
šlm zydw br ʿbdʾ[lbʿly]
Access II.2a.155 (printed, CIS)
Corpus CIS 2773

Inscription 4039
Site Jebel Musa, #19
Condition good
Content Nabatean inscription
šlm klbw br ḥnʾw bṭb
Access II.2a.155 (printed, CIS)
Corpus CIS 2774

Inscription **4040**
Site Jebel Musa, #19
Condition good
Content Nabatean inscription
šlm mgdyw
br ʾwšw
Access II.2a.155 (printed, CIS)
Corpus CIS 2775

Inscription **4041**
Site Jebel Musa, #19
Condition good
Content Nabatean inscription
šlm pṣy br ʾwšw
Access II.2a.155 (printed, CIS)
Corpus CIS 2776

Inscription **4042**
Site Jebel Musa, #19
Condition good
Content Nabatean inscription
šlm šmrḥ br ʿlht
Access II.2a.155 (printed, CIS)
Corpus CIS 2777

Inscription **4043**
Site Jebel Musa, #19
Condition fair
Content Nabatean inscription
šlm nšygw
br [p]ṣyw
Access II.2a.155 (printed, CIS)
Corpus CIS 2778

Inscription **4044**
Site Jebel Musa, #19
Condition good
Content Nabatean inscription
šlm klbw br
ʿwymw bṭb
Access II.2a.156 (printed, CIS)
Corpus CIS 2779

Inscription **4045**
Site Jebel Musa, #19
Condition fair
Content Nabatean inscription
šlm ḥlṣt
Access II.2a.156 (printed, CIS)
Corpus CIS 2780

Inscription **4046**
Site Jebel Musa, #19
Condition fair
Content Nabatean inscription
šlm wʾlw br [qrḥh bkl ṭb]
Access II.2a.156 (printed, CIS)
Corpus CIS 2781

Inscription **4047**
Site Jebel Musa, #19
Condition fair
Content Nabatean inscription
šlm ʿmyw br ṣwbw
Access II.2a.156 (printed, CIS)
Corpus CIS 2782

Inscription **4048**
Site Jebel Musa, #19
Condition fair
Content Nabatean inscription
ʾwšw br mḥmyw
[b]ṭb wšlm
Access II.2a.156 (printed, CIS)
Corpus CIS 2783

Inscription **4049**
Site Jebel Musa, #19
Condition good
Content Nabatean inscription
šlm ʾwšw br ʿwdw
Access II.2a.156 (printed, CIS)
Corpus CIS 2784

Inscription **4050**
Site Jebel Musa, #19
Condition fair
Content Nabatean inscription
šlm nšnky[h] br ʾwšʾlbʿly
Access II.2a.156 (printed, CIS)
Corpus CIS 2785

Inscription **4051**
Site Jebel Musa, #19
Condition fair
Content Nabatean inscription
šlm ʾlm[bqrw]
Access II.2a.156 (printed, CIS)
Corpus CIS 2786

Inscription **4052**
Site Wadi Umm Sidra, #174
Technique incised
Condition poor
Content Greek inscription
Limitation *Tentative decipherment only*
Access FL38-38a (photograph, Project)

Inscription **4053**
Site Jebel Musa, #19
Condition poor
Content Nabatean inscription
Comment *illegible*
Access II.2a.157 (printed, CIS)
Corpus CIS 2787

Inscription 4054
Site Jebel Musa, #19
Condition good
Content Nabatean inscription
šlm ʿbydw br ʿwdw bṭb
Access II.2a.157 (printed, CIS)
Corpus CIS 2788

Inscription 4055
Site Jebel Musa, #19
Condition poor
Content Nabatean inscription
Comment *illegible*
Access II.2a.157 (printed, CIS)
Corpus CIS 2789

Inscription 4056
Site Jebel Musa, #19
Condition fair
Content Nabatean inscription
bryʾw br ʾwšw
br ʾwšʾlh[y]
wʾwšlhy brh
Access II.2a.157 (printed, CIS)
Corpus CIS 2790

Inscription 4057
Site Jebel Musa, #19
Condition good
Content Nabatean inscription
šlm klbw br grmʾlbʿly bṭb
Access II.2a.157 (printed, CIS)
Corpus CIS 2791

Inscription 4058
Site Jebel Musa, #19
Condition good
Content Nabatean inscription
šlm ʾlḥšpw
br zydw
Access II.2a.157 (printed, CIS)
Corpus CIS 2792

Inscription 4059
Site Jebel Musa, #19
Condition fair
Content Nabatean inscription
šlm ʿwymw br m.....
Access II.2a.157 (printed, CIS)
Corpus CIS 2793

Inscription 4060
Site Jebel Musa, #19
Condition poor
Content Nabatean inscription
Comment *illegible*
Access II.2a.157 (printed, CIS)
Corpus CIS 2794

Inscription 4061
Site Jebel Musa, #19
Condition poor
Content Nabatean inscription
Comment *illegible*
Access II.2a.157 (printed, CIS)
Corpus CIS 2795

Inscription 4062
Site Jebel Musa, #19
Condition poor
Content Nabatean inscription
šlm klbw br
grmʾlbʿly
Access II.2a.158 (printed, CIS)
Corpus CIS 2796

Inscription 4063
Site Jebel Musa, #19
Condition poor
Content Nabatean inscription
...ynw br
ḥnṭlw...
Access II.2a.158 (printed, CIS)
Corpus CIS 2797

Inscription 4064
Site Jebel Musa, #19
Condition good
Content Nabatean inscription
šlm ḥnṭlw br ʾwšʾlbʿly
Access II.2a.158 (printed, CIS)
Corpus CIS 2798

Inscription 4065
Site Jebel Musa, #19
Condition good
Content Nabatean inscription
šlmt br ʿytw
Access II.2a.158 (printed, CIS)
Corpus CIS 2799

Inscription 4066
Site Jebel Musa, #19
Condition good
Content Nabatean inscription
šlm dʾbw ʾ
br ʾtmw bṭb
Access II.2a.158 (printed, CIS)
Corpus CIS 2800

Inscription 4067
Site Jebel Musa, #19
Condition poor
Content Nabatean inscription
Comment *illegible*
Access II.2a.158 (printed, CIS)
Corpus CIS 2801

Inscription **4068**
Site Jebel Musa, #19
Condition good
Content Nabatean inscription
šlm gšmw br
ḥrwṣw
Access II.2a.158 (printed, CIS)
Corpus CIS 2802

Inscription **4069**
Site Jebel Musa, #19
Condition fair
Content Nabatean inscription
[šlm] ʿwdw br qrḥw
Access II.2a.158 (printed, CIS)
Corpus CIS 2803

Inscription **4070**
Site Jebel Musa, #19
Condition fair
Content Nabatean inscription
šlm ḥršw
Access II.2a.158 (printed, CIS)
Corpus CIS 2804

Inscription **4071**
Site Jebel Musa, #19
Condition poor
Content Nabatean inscription
šlm hprw
... ʿbdʾlbʿ[l]y
Access II.2a.158 (printed, CIS)
Corpus CIS 2805

Inscription **4072**
Site Jebel Musa, #19
Condition good
Content Nabatean inscription
šlm grmw br nqlw
Access II.2a.159 (printed, CIS)
Corpus CIS 2806

Inscription **4073**
Site Jebel Musa, #19
Condition fair
Content Nabatean inscription
šlm ....
ʿmyrt br zydw
Access II.2a.159 (printed, CIS)
Corpus CIS 2807

Inscription **4074**
Site Jebel Musa, #19
Condition good
Content Nabatean inscription
šlm wʾlw br ʿmyw
Access II.2a.159 (printed, CIS)
Corpus CIS 2808

Inscription **4075**
Site Jebel Musa, #19
Condition good
Content Nabatean inscription
šlm brʿtw br ḥnṭlw
Access II.2a.159 (printed, CIS)
Corpus CIS 2809

Inscription **4076**
Site Jebel Musa, #19
Condition good
Content Nabatean inscription
šlm ḥnṭlw br nšnkyh
Access II.2a.159 (printed, CIS)
Corpus CIS 2810

Inscription **4077**
Site Jebel Musa, #19
Condition fair
Content Nabatean inscription
...lm.... br ḥwbn bṭb w[šlm]
Access II.2a.159 (printed, CIS)
Corpus CIS 2811

Inscription **4078**
Site Jebel Musa, #19
Condition fair
Content Nabatean inscription
.... br ʿbdʾlbʿly
šlm zydw br ʾ....
Access II.2a.160 (printed, CIS)
Corpus CIS 2812

Inscription **4079**
Site Jebel Musa, #19
Condition poor
Content Nabatean inscription
Comment *illegible*
Access II.2a.160 (printed, CIS)
Corpus CIS 2813

Inscription **4080**
Site Jebel Musa, #19
Condition good
Content Nabatean inscription
šlm yʿly br bṭšw
ʾš[d]w br ʿlyw
Access II.2a.160 (printed, CIS)
Corpus CIS 2814

Inscription **4081**
Site Jebel Musa, #19
Condition poor
Content Nabatean inscription
Comment *illegible*
Access II.2a.160 (printed, CIS)
Corpus CIS 2815

Inscription **4082**
Site Jebel Musa, #19
Condition poor
Content Nabatean inscription
Comment *illegible*
Access II.2a.160 (printed, CIS)
Corpus CIS 2816

Inscription **4083**
Site Jebel Musa, #19
Condition poor
Content Nabatean inscription
Comment *illegible*
Access II.2a.160 (printed, CIS)
Corpus CIS 2817

Inscription **4084**
Site Jebel Musa, #19
Condition fair
Content Nabatean inscription
šlm ʾlmbqrw
br nšygw...
Access II.2a.160 (printed, CIS)
Corpus CIS 2818

Inscription **4085**
Site Jebel Musa, #19
Condition fair
Content Nabatean inscription
šlm ...wy br tyml...
Access II.2a.160 (printed, CIS)
Corpus CIS 2819

Inscription **4086**
Site Jebel Musa, #19
Condition poor
Content Nabatean inscription
Comment *illegible*
Access II.2a.160 (printed, CIS)
Corpus CIS 2820

Inscription **4087**
Site Jebel Musa, #19
Condition fair
Content Nabatean inscription
ʿbdʾlbʿly
[br] pʾ[rn]
Access II.2a.160 (printed, CIS)
Corpus CIS 2821

Inscription **4088**
Site Jebel Musa, #19
Condition fair
Content Nabatean inscription
šlm grmʾl[hy] br ʾlktyw
Access II.2a.161 (printed, CIS)
Corpus CIS 2822

Inscription **4089**
Site Jebel Musa, #19
Condition good
Content Nabatean inscription
šlm ḥgyrw br ḥršw
Access II.2a.161 (printed, CIS)
Corpus CIS 2823

Inscription **4090**
Site Jebel Musa, #19
Condition good
Content Nabatean inscription
šlm ʿmyw br ʿbdʾlbʿl[y]
Access II.2a.161 (printed, CIS)
Corpus CIS 2824

Inscription **4091**
Site Jebel Musa, #19
Condition fair
Content Nabatean inscription
šlm ḥlṣt br mš..w
Access II.2a.161 (printed, CIS)
Corpus CIS 2825

Inscription **4092**
Site Jebel Musa, #19
Condition fair
Content Nabatean inscription
šlm ʿbdʾlbʿly [br ʿbdʾ]lhy
Access II.2a.161 (printed, CIS)
Corpus CIS 2826

Inscription **4093**
Site Jebel Musa, #19
Condition fair
Content Nabatean inscription
šlm ḥryšw br
br[y]ʾ[w bṭb]
Access II.2a.161 (printed, CIS)
Corpus CIS 2827

Inscription **4094**
Site Jebel Musa, #19
Condition fair
Content Nabatean inscription
šlm ḥršw br [grm]lbʿly
Access II.2a.161 (printed, CIS)
Corpus CIS 2828

Inscription **4095**
Site Jebel Musa, #19
Condition good
Content Nabatean inscription
šlm ʿwdw
[b]r ḥryšw
Access II.2a.161 (printed, CIS)
Corpus CIS 2829

Inscription **4096**
Site Jebel Musa, #19
Condition good
Content Nabatean inscription
šlm pṣyw
br ʾwšw
Access II.2a.162 (printed, CIS)
Corpus CIS 2830

Inscription **4097**
Site Jebel Musa, #19
Condition good
Content Nabatean inscription
šlm nmyl[w] br šlmw
Access II.2a.162 (printed, CIS)
Corpus CIS 2831

Inscription **4098**
Site Jebel Musa, #19
Condition good
Content Nabatean inscription
šlm ḥnṭlw
br nšygw
Access II.2a.162 (printed, CIS)
Corpus CIS 2832

Inscription **4099**
Site Jebel Musa, #19
Condition fair
Content Nabatean inscription
šlm bṭšw [br qyn]w
šlm gdyw br ʿ[m]yw...
Access II.2a.162 (printed, CIS)
Corpus CIS 2833

Inscription **4100**
Site Jebel Musa, #19
Condition fair
Content Nabatean inscription
ṣwbw br [ʿm]yw
Access II.2a.162 (printed, CIS)
Corpus CIS 2834

Inscription **4101**
Site Jebel Musa, #19
Condition good
Content Nabatean inscription
ʿmyw br šmrḥ
Access II.2a.162 (printed, CIS)
Corpus CIS 2835

Inscription **4102**
Site Jebel Musa, #19
Condition poor
Content Nabatean inscription
[š]lm šmrḥw ʿmyw...
... šlm ...
dm.y. br ʿmnw... šlm ṣ...
Access II.2a.162 (printed, CIS)
Corpus CIS 2836

Inscription **4103**
Site Jebel Musa, #19
Condition fair
Content Nabatean inscription
šlm šmrḥw br ....
Access II.2a.163 (printed, CIS)
Corpus CIS 2837

Inscription **4104**
Site Jebel Musa, #19
Condition poor
Content Nabatean inscription
Comment *illegible*
Access II.2a.163 (printed, CIS)
Corpus CIS 2838

Inscription **4105**
Site Jebel Musa, #19
Condition fair
Content Nabatean inscription
dkyr wbryk .... šlm [t]ymw br ḥry[šw]
Access II.2a.163 (printed, CIS)
Corpus CIS 2839

Inscription **4106**
Site Jebel Musa, #19
Condition fair
Content Nabatean inscription
[ḥn]yʾw br mḥmyw
Access II.2a.163 (printed, CIS)
Corpus CIS 2840

Inscription **4107**
Site Jebel Musa, #19
Condition fair
Content Nabatean inscription
šlm ʿ[m]nw br ....
Access II.2a.163 (printed, CIS)
Corpus CIS 2841

Inscription **4108**
Site Jebel Musa, #19
Condition poor
Content Nabatean inscription
šlm ʿmrw br šlm[w]
[šl]m ....w br šlmw
Access II.2a.163 (printed, CIS)
Corpus CIS 2842

Inscription **4109**
Site Jebel Musa, #19
Condition good
Content Nabatean inscription
šlm gdyw br
wʾlw
Access II.2a.163 (printed, CIS)
Corpus CIS 2843

Inscription 4110
Site Jebel Musa, #19
Condition good
Content Nabatean inscription
šlm wʾlw br nšygw
Access II.2a.163 (printed, CIS)
Corpus CIS 2844

Inscription 4111
Site Jebel Musa, #19
Condition excellent
Content Nabatean inscription
dkyr ʿbdʾlbʿly br ʿmyw br šmrḥ b
ytyʾ bṭb
Access II.2a.163 (printed, CIS)
Corpus CIS 2845

Inscription 4112
Site Jebel Musa, #19
Condition good
Content Nabatean inscription
šlm ʿbdʾhyw br ʿwdw
Access II.2a.164 (printed, CIS)
Corpus CIS 2846

Inscription 4113
Site Jebel Musa, #19
Condition good
Content Nabatean inscription
dkyr grmʾlbʿly br wʾl[w]
Access II.2a.164 (printed, CIS)
Corpus CIS 2847

Inscription 4114
Site Jebel Musa, #19
Condition good
Content Nabatean inscription
šlm ḥryšw br ḥl[y]ṣw
Access II.2a.164 (printed, CIS)
Corpus CIS 2848

Inscription 4115
Site Jebel Musa, #19
Condition fair
Content Nabatean inscription
dk[y]r šʿ[d]w br ....
šlm yʿly br ḥryšw
Access II.2a.164 (printed, CIS)
Corpus CIS 2849

Inscription 4116
Site Jebel Musa, #19
Condition poor
Content Nabatean inscription
dky[r ḥ]lṣt br wʾlw ....
Access II.2a.164 (printed, CIS)
Corpus CIS 2850

Inscription 4117
Site Jebel Musa, #19
Condition good
Content Nabatean inscription
šlm bḥ
gh br grmʾ
lbʿly
Access II.2a.165 (printed, CIS)
Corpus CIS 2851

Inscription 4118
Site Jebel Musa, #19
Condition fair
Content Nabatean inscription
šlm ....
ʿbydw bṭb
ʿbydw
Access II.2a.165 (printed, CIS)
Corpus CIS 2852

Inscription 4119
Site Jebel Musa, #19
Condition good
Content Nabatean inscription
šlm ʿwdw [br]
qrḥw
Access II.2a.165 (printed, CIS)
Corpus CIS 2853

Inscription 4120
Site Jebel Musa, #19
Condition fair
Content Nabatean inscription
šlm ʾʿl[ʾ]
br ʿmyw
Access II.2a.165 (printed, CIS)
Corpus CIS 2854

Inscription 4121
Site Jebel Musa, #19
Condition fair
Content Nabatean inscription
šlm
[gr]mʾlbʿly
br bḥgh
Access II.2a.165 (printed, CIS)
Corpus CIS 2855

Inscription 4122
Site Jebel Musa, #19
Condition good
Content Nabatean inscription
šlm
ʿmyw br
ʿwdw
Access II.2a.165 (printed, CIS)
Corpus CIS 2856

Inscription **4123**
Site Jebel Musa, #19
Condition good
Content Nabatean inscription
šlm tydw b[r]
.wdw
Access II.2a.165 (printed, CIS)
Corpus CIS 2857

Inscription **4124**
Site Jebel Musa, #19
Condition fair
Content Nabatean inscription
šlm wʾlw br ḥnyʾw
[ḥl]ṣt br ....
Access II.2a.165 (printed, CIS)
Corpus CIS 2858

Inscription **4125**
Site Jebel Musa, #19
Condition fair
Content Nabatean inscription
šlm grmw br šmr[ḥ]
šlm lṣḥbw br ....
Access II.2a.165 (printed, CIS)
Corpus CIS 2859

Inscription **4126**
Site Jebel Musa, #19
Condition poor
Content Nabatean inscription
šlm kʿm[h br] .... dkyr šlmw br ....
Access II.2a.166 (printed, CIS)
Corpus CIS 2860

Inscription **4127**
Site Jebel Musa, #19
Condition fair
Content Nabatean inscription
dkyr ḥgrw bṭb
.... br ḥryšw
Access II.2a.166 (printed, CIS)
Corpus CIS 2861

Inscription **4128**
Site Jebel Musa, #19
Condition poor
Content Nabatean inscription
[šlm ʾ]wšw br
.... wdw
Access II.2a.166 (printed, CIS)
Corpus CIS 2862

Inscription **4129**
Site Jebel Musa, #19
Condition good
Content Nabatean inscription
šlm ʾlmbqrw
br ʿmrw
Access II.2a.166 (printed, CIS)
Corpus CIS 2863

Inscription **4130**
Site Jebel Musa, #19
Condition fair
Content Nabatean inscription
šʿdʾlh[y]
br bryʾw
Access II.2a.166 (printed, CIS)
Corpus CIS 2864

Inscription **4131**
Site Jebel Musa, #19
Condition fair
Content Nabatean inscription
[ʾ]lmbqrw
br ʿwymw
Access II.2a.166 (printed, CIS)
Corpus CIS 2865

Inscription **4132**
Site Jebel Musa, #19
Condition fair
Content Nabatean inscription
šlm ḥnṭl[w br]
ʿmyw bṭb
Access II.2a.166 (printed, CIS)
Corpus CIS 2866

Inscription **4133**
Site Jebel Musa, #19
Condition poor
Content Nabatean inscription
Comment *illegible*
Access II.2a.166 (printed, CIS)
Corpus CIS 2867

Inscription **4134**
Site Jebel Musa, #19
Condition fair
Content Nabatean inscription
šlm w....
grmʾlb[ʿly] ʿbd....
Access II.2a.166 (printed, CIS)
Corpus CIS 2868

Inscription 4135
Site Jebel Musa, #19
Condition fair
Content Nabatean inscription
šlm ʾkbrw
br ḥb[r]kn
....m ʿm
Access II.2a.167 (printed, CIS)
Corpus CIS 2869

Inscription 4136
Site Jebel Musa, #19
Condition good
Content Nabatean inscription
šlm wʾlw br ḥryšw
Access II.2a.167 (printed, CIS)
Corpus CIS 2870

Inscription 4137
Site Jebel Musa, #19
Condition good
Content Nabatean inscription
šlm [ʾw]šw br ʿlht
wʾlw br ʿwdw
Access II.2a.167 (printed, CIS)
Corpus CIS 2871

Inscription 4138
Site Jebel Musa, #19
Condition fair
Content Nabatean inscription
dkyr ʾwyšw
[br q]y[n]w
Access II.2a.167 (printed, CIS)
Corpus CIS 2872

Inscription 4139
Site Jebel Musa, #19
Condition good
Content Nabatean inscription
ʾlmbqrw
dʾybw
Access II.2a.167 (printed, CIS)
Corpus CIS 2873

Inscription 4140
Site Jebel Musa, #19
Condition excellent
Content Nabatean inscription
šlm ʿbdʾlbʿly
br ʿbṭt
Access II.2a.167 (printed, CIS)
Corpus CIS 2874

Inscription 4141
Site Jebel Musa, #19
Condition good
Content Nabatean inscription
šlm bḥgh br grmʾlbʿly
Access II.2a.167 (printed, CIS)
Corpus CIS 2876

Inscription 4142
Site Jebel Musa, #19
Condition good
Content Nabatean inscription
šlm grmʾlhy
Access II.2a.167 (printed, CIS)
Corpus CIS 2877

Inscription 4143
Site Jebel Musa, #19
Condition fair
Content Nabatean inscription
dkyr [ʿmy]w br
ḥnṭlw
Access II.2a.168 (printed, CIS)
Corpus CIS 2878

Inscription 4144
Site Jebel Musa, #19
Condition fair
Content Nabatean inscription
dkyr [ʿm]yw br
ḥnṭlw br ....
Access II.2a.168 (printed, CIS)
Corpus CIS 2879

Inscription 4145
Site Jebel Musa, #19
Condition good
Content Nabatean inscription
dkyr ʾwšw
br mbršw
Access II.2a.168 (printed, CIS)
Corpus CIS 2881

Inscription 4146
Site Jebel Musa, #19
Condition good
Content Nabatean inscription
šlm ʿbdʾhy[w] br
ʿwdw
Access II.2a.168 (printed, CIS)
Corpus CIS 2882

Inscription 4147
Site Jebel Musa, #19
Condition good
Content Nabatean inscription
šlm hnyʾw br šlmw
Access II.2a.168 (printed, CIS)
Corpus CIS 2883

Inscription 4148
Site Jebel Musa, #19
Condition good
Content Nabatean inscription
šlm ʿwymw br ʾl
mbqrw br wʾlw bṭb
Access II.2a.168 (printed, CIS)
Corpus CIS 2884

Inscription 4149
Site Jebel Musa, #19
Condition fair
Content Nabatean inscription
šlm wʾl[w]
br g[r]mʾlbʿly
Access II.2a.168 (printed, CIS)
Corpus CIS 2885

Inscription 4150
Site Jebel Musa, #19
Condition fair
Content Nabatean inscription
šlm ʾlhm
šw br
d[by]lt
Access II.2a.168 (printed, CIS)
Corpus CIS 2886

Inscription 4151
Site Jebel Musa, #19
Condition good
Content Nabatean inscription
šlm ʾwyšw
br ʿmyw
Access II.2a.169 (printed, CIS)
Corpus CIS 2887

Inscription 4152
Site Jebel Musa, #19
Condition poor
Content Nabatean inscription
...w.bryʾw br wʾlw
Access II.2a.169 (printed, CIS)
Corpus CIS 2888

Inscription 4153
Site Jebel Musa, #19
Condition fair
Content Nabatean inscription
šlm ʾwšʾlbʿly br ʾ....
Access II.2a.169 (printed, CIS)
Corpus CIS 2889

Inscription 4154
Site Jebel Musa, #19
Condition good
Content Nabatean inscription
šlm bryʾw br ḥryšw
Access II.2a.169 (printed, CIS)
Corpus CIS 2890

Inscription 4155
Site Jebel Musa, #19
Condition fair
Content Nabatean inscription
šlm ʾ...w
ʿwymw
Access II.2a.169 (printed, CIS)
Corpus CIS 2891

Inscription 4156
Site Jebel Musa, #19
Condition good
Content Nabatean inscription
šlm nšn[kyh]
br zydw bṭb
Access II.2a.169 (printed, CIS)
Corpus CIS 2892

Inscription 4157
Site Jebel Musa, #19
Condition fair
Content Nabatean inscription
šlm ....gw br qwm[w bṭb]
Access II.2a.169 (printed, CIS)
Corpus CIS 2893

Inscription 4158
Site Jebel Musa, #19
Condition good
Content Nabatean inscription
šlm wʾlw
br šmrḥ
Access II.2a.169 (printed, CIS)
Corpus CIS 2894

Inscription 4159
Site Jebel Musa, #19
Condition good
Content Nabatean inscription
šlm ṣwbw
Access II.2a.170 (printed, CIS)
Corpus CIS 2895

Inscription 4160
Site Jebel Musa, #19
Condition poor
Content Nabatean inscription
Comment *illegible*
Access II.2a.170 (printed, CIS)
Corpus CIS 2896

Inscription 4161
Site Jebel Musa, #19
Condition poor
Content Nabatean inscription
[šl]m gdyw br
[h]nyʾw
Access II.2a.170 (printed, CIS)
Corpus CIS 2897

Inscription 4162
Site Jebel Musa, #19
Condition poor
Content Nabatean inscription
[šlm] ʿmrw br ṣ[wb]w
šlm [w]ʾ[l]w br ....
Access II.2a.170 (printed, CIS)
Corpus CIS 2898

Inscription 4163
Site Jebel Musa, #19
Condition good
Content Nabatean inscription
šlm ʾwšw br zydw
Access II.2a.170 (printed, CIS)
Corpus CIS 2899

Inscription 4164
Site Jebel Musa, #19
Condition good
Content Nabatean inscription
šlm ḥlṣt br ʿbdʾlbʿly
bṭb
Access II.2a.170 (printed, CIS)
Corpus CIS 2900

Inscription 4165
Site Jebel Musa, #19
Condition good
Content Nabatean inscription
šlm ʿmmw
Access II.2a.170 (printed, CIS)
Corpus CIS 2901

Inscription 4166
Site Jebel Musa, #19
Condition good
Content Nabatean inscription
šlm ʿwdw br ʿbdʾ[lb]ʿly
Access II.2a.170 (printed, CIS)
Corpus CIS 2902

Inscription 4167
Site Jebel Musa, #19
Condition fair
Content Nabatean inscription
[ḥn]ṭlw br ʾwšw
Access II.2a.170 (printed, CIS)
Corpus CIS 2903

Inscription 4168
Site Jebel Musa, #19
Condition poor
Content Nabatean inscription
š...brdrʾ
šlm ʿ...ʿmw
šlm
Access II.2a.171 (printed, CIS)
Corpus CIS 2904

Inscription 4169
Site Jebel Musa, #19
Condition fair
Content Nabatean inscription
šlm mʿnw
šlm ʿmyw [br] wʾl[w]
Access II.2a.171 (printed, CIS)
Corpus CIS 2905

Inscription 4170
Site Jebel Musa, #19
Condition poor
Content Nabatean inscription
...yw br
.....
....wʾlw br ...
....w brh
..w
Access II.2a.171 (printed, CIS)
Corpus CIS 2906

Inscription 4171
Site Jebel Musa, #19
Condition fair
Content Nabatean inscription
[ʿ]bydw
ʿmrw
Access II.2a.171 (printed, CIS)
Corpus CIS 2907

Inscription 4172
Site Jebel Musa, #19
Condition good
Content Nabatean inscription
šlm kʿmh br ʿwdw
Access II.2a.171 (printed, CIS)
Corpus CIS 2908

Inscription 4173
Site Jebel Musa, #19
Condition good
Content Nabatean inscription
šlm ʿbdʾl[h]y br pʾrn
Access II.2a.171 (printed, CIS)
Corpus CIS 2909

Inscription 4174
Site Jebel Musa, #19
Condition poor
Content Nabatean inscription
dkyr [ʾ]lm[bqrw]
[br ʿ]nmw bṭb
[d]kyr ʿbd...
Access II.2a.171 (printed, CIS)
Corpus CIS 2910

Inscription 4175
Site Jebel Musa, #19
Condition fair
Content Nabatean inscription
šlm wʾlw br ʾl[m]bqrw
Access II.2a.171 (printed, CIS)
Corpus CIS 2911

Inscription 4176
Site Jebel Musa, #19
Condition good
Content Nabatean inscription
šlm ḥlṣ[t] br ʾwšw
bṭb
Access II.2a.171 (printed, CIS)
Corpus CIS 2912

Inscription 4177
Site Jebel Musa, #19
Condition fair
Content Nabatean inscription
šlm bryʾw
... bṭb
Access II.2a.171 (printed, CIS)
Corpus CIS 2913

Inscription 4178
Site Jebel Musa, #19
Condition good
Content Nabatean inscription
šlm ʿbdʿmrw
br ʿwtʾlhy bṭb
Access II.2a.172 (printed, CIS)
Corpus CIS 2914

Inscription 4179
Site Jebel Musa, #19
Condition good
Content Nabatean inscription
ʾlmbqrw
šlm ʾwšw
br wʾlw
Access II.2a.172 (printed, CIS)
Corpus CIS 2915

Inscription 4180
Site Jebel Musa, #19
Condition poor
Content Nabatean inscription
šlm klbw br ....
Access II.2a.172 (printed, CIS)
Corpus CIS 2916

Inscription 4181
Site Jebel Musa, #19
Condition poor
Content Nabatean inscription
šlm ʿb.ʾ..w br
[w]ʾlw
Access II.2a.172 (printed, CIS)
Corpus CIS 2917

Inscription 4182
Site Jebel Musa, #19
Condition fair
Content Nabatean inscription
[ʾ]lmbqrw br wdw
šlm grm....
Access II.2a.172 (printed, CIS)
Corpus CIS 2918

Inscription 4183
Site Jebel Musa, #19
Condition fair
Content Nabatean inscription
šlm ḥlṣt
[br] ʾʿlʾ
Access II.2a.172 (printed, CIS)
Corpus CIS 2919

Inscription 4184
Site Jebel Musa, #19
Condition good
Content Nabatean inscription
šlm ḥryšw
br wʾlw bṭb
Access II.2a.172 (printed, CIS)
Corpus CIS 2920

Inscription 4185
Site Jebel Musa, #19
Condition good
Content Nabatean inscription
šlm ʾlm[b]qrw br wʾlw
bṭb w[š]lm
Access II.2a.172 (printed, CIS)
Corpus CIS 2921

Inscription 4186
Site Jebel Musa, #19
Condition good
Content Nabatean inscription
šlm ʾlmbq[r]w
ʿmmw
Access II.2a.172 (printed, CIS)
Corpus CIS 2922

Inscription 4187
Site Wadi el Ahdar, #52
Condition good
Content Nabatean inscription
šlm ḥrš[w]
wʾlw br w
Access II.2a.173 (printed, CIS)
Corpus CIS 2923

Inscription 4188
Site Wadi el Ahdar, #52
Condition poor
Content Nabatean inscription
šlm ....
ṣwbw
Access II.2a.173 (printed, CIS)
Corpus CIS 2924

Inscription 4189
Site Wadi el Ahdar, #52
Condition excellent
Content Nabatean inscription
dkyr [n]šygw br qymw ʿwdw br qymw
ʿwdw br ʿbdʾlbʿly br wdw
Access II.2a.173 (printed, CIS)
Corpus CIS 2925

Inscription 4190
Site Wadi el Ahdar, #52
Condition fair
Content Nabatean inscription
šlm ʿbdʾlbʿly br ʾwšʾlh
.... [ʿb]dʾlbʿly br wʾ[l]w
w br grm...
Access II.2a.173 (printed, CIS)
Corpus CIS 2926

Inscription 4191
Site Wadi el Ahdar, #52
Condition good
Content Nabatean inscription
šlm gdyw br ʿbdʾlhy
šlm ʾwšw..ʿdw.
Access II.2a.173 (printed, CIS)
Corpus CIS 2927

Inscription 4192
Site Wadi el Ahdar, #52
Condition excellent
Content Nabatean inscription
šlm ʿmyw br mbršw
bṭb
Access II.2a.174 (printed, CIS)
Corpus CIS 2928

Inscription 4193
Site Wadi el Ahdar, #52
Condition good
Content Nabatean inscription
šlm dʾbw
Access II.2a.174 (printed, CIS)
Corpus CIS 2929

Inscription 4194
Site Timna, Timna 1, #279
Condition poor
Content Nabatean inscription
šlm
Access II.2a.174 (printed, CIS)
Corpus CIS 2930

Inscription 4195
Site Timna, Timna 1, #279
Condition good
Content Nabatean inscription
dkyr ʾltbqw
br qymw bṭb
Access II.2a.174 (printed, CIS)
Corpus CIS 2931

Inscription 4196
Site Timna, Timna 1, #279
Condition poor
Content Nabatean inscription
Comment *illegible*
Access II.2a.174 (printed, CIS)
Corpus CIS 2932, 2933

Inscription 4197
Site Timna, Timna 1, #279
Condition poor
Content Nabatean inscription
šlm zydw dkyr ...h br ḥwbn
gh...šyʿm.
Access II.2a.174 (printed, CIS)
Corpus CIS 2934

Inscription 4198
Site Timna, Timna 1, #279
Condition good
Content Nabatean inscription
šmrḥ
bḥgh
Access II.2a.175 (printed, CIS)
Corpus CIS 2935

Inscription 4199
Site Timna, Timna 1, #279
Condition fair
Content Nabatean inscription
šlm pṣy br ...yw
Access II.2a.175 (printed, CIS)
Corpus CIS 2936

Inscription 4200
Site Timna, Timna 1, #279
Condition good
Content Nabatean inscription
šlm
dʾbw br zydw
Access II.2a.175 (printed, CIS)
Corpus CIS 2937

Inscription 4201
Site Timna, Timna 1, #279
Condition fair
Content Nabatean inscription
šlm ....šw
br ʿw[dw]
Access II.2a.175 (printed, CIS)
Corpus CIS 2938

Inscription 4202
Site Jebel Musa, Wadi el Deir, #35
Condition fair
Content Nabatean inscription
[dkyr] ḥršw br grmlbʿly
Access II.2a.153 (printed, CIS)
Corpus CIS 2758

Inscription 4203
Site Timna, Timna 1, #279
Condition fair
Content Nabatean inscription
šlm ʾl...w
šlm [p]ṣyw
šlm
Access II.2a.175 (printed, CIS)
Corpus CIS 2939

Inscription 4204
Site Timna, Timna 1, #279
Condition poor
Content Nabatean inscription
grmʾlbʿly .... wʾlw ḥršw
Access II.2a.175 (printed, CIS)
Corpus CIS 2940

Inscription 4205
Site Timna, Timna 1, #279
Condition poor
Content Nabatean inscription
šlm ʾklw[šw]
[br ʾṣ]lḥw bṭ[b]
.... br ʿmyw
Access II.2a.175 (printed, CIS)
Corpus CIS 2941

Inscription 4206
Site Timna, Timna 1, #279
Condition good
Content Nabatean inscription
ʾwšʾlhy
šlm klbw br grmʾlbʿly
Access II.2a.175 (printed, CIS)
Corpus CIS 2942

Inscription 4207
Site Timna, Timna 1, #279
Condition fair
Content Nabatean inscription
[š]lm ʾlḥšpw
br zydw
Access II.2a.175 (printed, CIS)
Corpus CIS 2943

Inscription 4208
Site Timna, Timna 1, #279
Condition fair
Content Nabatean inscription
šlm
ʿbdʾlb[ʿ]l[y]
Access II.2a.176 (printed, CIS)
Corpus CIS 2944 (1)

Inscription 4209
Site Timna, Timna 1, #279
Condition good
Content Nabatean inscription
šlm ʾlkyw
Access II.2a.176 (printed, CIS)
Corpus CIS 2944 (2)

Inscription 4210
Site Timna, Timna 1, #279
Condition good
Content Nabatean inscription
šlm ʾlhmšw br nšnky[h]
Access II.2a.176 (printed, CIS)
Corpus CIS 2944 (3)

Inscription 4211
Site Timna, Timna 1, #279
Condition poor
Content Nabatean inscription
šlm ʿwymw [br] ....
Access II.2a.176 (printed, CIS)
Corpus CIS 2944 (4)

Inscription 4212
Site Timna, Timna 1, #279
Condition fair
Content Nabatean inscription
šlm ḥrwṣw ʾḥwz[w]...
Access II.2a.176 (printed, CIS)
Corpus CIS 2946

Inscription 4213
Site Jebel Tarbush, Wadi Teibeh, #223
Condition poor
Content Nabatean inscription
šlm ....
br ʿwdw
šlm ṣ...w br ....
...[ʾ]l[bʿ]ly br wʾlw
Access II.2a.176 (printed, CIS)
Corpus CIS 2947

Inscription 4214
Site Jebel Tarbush, Wadi Teibeh, #223
Condition fair
Content Nabatean inscription
šlm ʿmyw
Access II.2a.176 (printed, CIS)
Corpus CIS 2945

Inscription 4215
Site Jebel Tarbush, Wadi Teibeh, #223
Condition poor
Content Nabatean inscription
[šlm] wʾlw [br] ʿbdʾl[bʿly]
Access II.2a.177 (printed, CIS)
Corpus CIS 2948

Inscription 4216
Site Jebel Tarbush, Wadi Teibeh, #223
Condition poor
Content Nabatean inscription
šlm gr[m]...
šlm ḥyyw br
šlm ʾ[ʿ]lʾ br
ʿwd[w]
Access II.2a.177 (printed, CIS)
Corpus CIS 2949

Inscription 4217
Site Jebel Tarbush, Wadi Teibeh, #223
Condition poor
Content Nabatean inscription
šlm ḥyw br ....
Access II.2a.177 (printed, CIS)
Corpus CIS 2950

Inscription 4218
Site Jebel Tarbush, Wadi Teibeh, #223
Condition fair
Content Nabatean inscription
šlm [pṣy] br ḥryšw
šlm ʾwšw
br [ʿbdʾ]lbʿly
Access II.2a.177 (printed, CIS)
Corpus CIS 2951

Inscription 4219
Site Wadi Hamileh, #218
Condition poor
Content Nabatean inscription
[dk]yr ḥršw br dʾbw
[wʿ]my[w] wdʾb[w] wšʿw
...w bṭb
Access II.2a.177 (printed, CIS)
Corpus CIS 2952

Inscription 4220
Site Wadi Hamileh, #218
Condition poor
Content Nabatean inscription
šlm ʿnmw br klbw
šlm pr... br ʿ.ʾ....
šlm grm[ʾlb]ʿly br ḥyyw
Access II.2a.178 (printed, CIS)
Corpus CIS 2953

Inscription 4221
Site Wadi Hamileh, #218
Condition poor
Content Nabatean inscription
Comment *illegible*
Access II.2a.178 (printed, CIS)
Corpus CIS 2954

Inscription 4222
Site Wadi Hamileh, #218
Condition poor
Content Nabatean inscription
šlm brʾʿw br ʿbdʾl...
....ḥnṭlw
Access II.2a.178 (printed, CIS)
Corpus CIS 2955

Inscription 4223
Site Wadi Hamileh, #218
Condition fair
Content Nabatean inscription
šlm grmʾl[hy]
Access II.2a.178 (printed, CIS)
Corpus CIS 2956

Inscription 4224
Site Wadi Hamileh, #218
Condition fair
Content Nabatean inscription
šlm .... br nšyg[w]
Access II.2a.178 (printed, CIS)
Corpus CIS 2957

Inscription 4225
Site Wadi Hamileh, #218
Condition poor
Content Nabatean inscription
Comment *illegible*
Access II.2a.178 (printed, CIS)
Corpus CIS 2958

Inscription 4226
Site Wadi Hamileh, #218
Condition poor
Content Nabatean inscription
šlm ʿbdʾl[bʿly]
Access II.2a.178 (printed, CIS)
Corpus CIS 2959

Inscription 4227
Site Wadi Hamileh, #218
Condition poor
Content Nabatean inscription
šlm [mbr]šw br ʿ[wdw]
Access II.2a.178 (printed, CIS)
Corpus CIS 2960

Inscription 4228
Site Wadi Hamileh, #218
Condition poor
Content Nabatean inscription
...yrwybʿm.. d.hw
Access II.2a.178 (printed, CIS)
Corpus CIS 2961

Inscription 4229
Site Jebel Serabit, Wadi Suwiq, #280
Condition poor
Content Nabatean inscription
šlm mʿ[yr]w [br šl]mw bṭb
Access II.2a.179 (printed, CIS)
Corpus CIS 2962

Inscription 4230
Site Jebel Serabit, Wadi Suwiq, #280
Condition good
Content Nabatean inscription
šlm ḥlypw br yʾrybh
[br] ḥryšw bṭb
Access II.2a.179 (printed, CIS)
Corpus CIS 2963

Inscription 4231
Site Jebel Serabit, Wadi Suwiq, #280
Condition poor
Content Nabatean inscription
Comment *fragments*
Access II.2a.180 (printed, CIS)
Corpus CIS 2964

Inscription 4232
Site Jebel Serabit, Wadi Suwiq, #280
Condition fair
Content Nabatean inscription
br ʿmrw .... dkyr ʾbn qwmw
Access II.2a.180 (printed, CIS)
Corpus CIS 2965

Inscription 4233
Site Jebel Serabit, Wadi Suwiq, #280
Condition poor
Content Nabatean inscription
šlm ʿbydw br
...ʿ...
.....
Access II.2a.180 (printed, CIS)
Corpus CIS 2966

Inscription 4234
Site Jebel Serabit, Wadi Suwiq, #280
Condition fair
Content Nabatean inscription
dkyr kʿmh b[r] ....
br ʿmmw
Access II.2a.180 (printed, CIS)
Corpus CIS 2967

Inscription 4235
Site Jebel Serabit, Wadi Suwiq, #280
Condition poor
Content Nabatean inscription
Comment *illegible*
Access II.2a.180 (printed, CIS)
Corpus CIS 2968

Inscription 4236
Site Jebel Serabit, Wadi Suwiq, #280
Condition poor
Content Nabatean inscription
dkyr wʾlw b[r ....]
.... br ʿbdʾlhy ....
Access II.2a.180 (printed, CIS)
Corpus CIS 2969

Inscription 4237
Site Jebel Serabit, Wadi Suwiq, #280
Condition poor
Content Nabatean inscription
šlm ʾkl[wš]w br ....
Access II.2a.180 (printed, CIS)
Corpus CIS 2970

Inscription 4238
Site Jebel Serabit, Wadi Suwiq, #280
Condition poor
Content Nabatean inscription
šlm nʾšgw...
šlm bṭšw...
Access II.2a.180 (printed, CIS)
Corpus CIS 2971

Inscription 4239
Site Jebel Serabit, Wadi Suwiq, #280
Condition fair
Content Nabatean inscription
dk[yr] ʿmrw br [ḥry]šw
Access II.2a.181 (printed, CIS)
Corpus CIS 2972

Inscription **4240**
Site Jebel Serabit, Wadi Suwiq, #280
Condition fair
Content Nabatean inscription
dkyr hlypw br
ʾryb[h]...
Access II.2a.181 (printed, CIS)
Corpus CIS 2973

Inscription **4241**
Site Jebel Serabit, Wadi Suwiq, #280
Condition fair
Content Nabatean inscription
dkyr šlm
ʾwšw
br [ʾ]wšw
bṭ[b]
Access II.2a.181 (printed, CIS)
Corpus CIS 2974

Inscription **4242**
Site Jebel Serabit, Wadi Suwiq, #280
Condition poor
Content Nabatean inscription
Comment *illegible*
Access II.2a.181 (printed, CIS)
Corpus CIS 2975

Inscription **4243**
Site Jebel Serabit, Wadi Suwiq, #280
Condition fair
Content Nabatean inscription
dkyr ....
šl[m] hʾryšw
Access II.2a.181 (printed, CIS)
Corpus CIS 2976

Inscription **4244**
Site Jebel Serabit, Wadi Suwiq, #280
Condition poor
Content Nabatean inscription
Comment *illegible*
Access II.2a.181 (printed, CIS)
Corpus CIS 2977

Inscription **4245**
Site Jebel Serabit, Wadi Suwiq, #280
Condition good
Content Nabatean inscription
šlm bryʾw br ʾwšw
br ʾwšʾlhy bṭb
Access II.2a.181 (printed, CIS)
Corpus CIS 2978

Inscription **4246**
Site Jebel Serabit, Wadi Suwiq, #280
Condition good
Content Nabatean inscription
dkyr hnyʾw br ʾwšʾlhy bṭb
Access II.2a.181 (printed, CIS)
Corpus CIS 2979

Inscription **4247**
Site Jebel Serabit, Wadi Suwiq, #280
Condition good
Content Nabatean inscription
šlm ʾlktyw br wʾlw
Access II.2a.181 (printed, CIS)
Corpus CIS 2980

Inscription **4248**
Site Jebel Serabit, Wadi Suwiq, #280
Condition good
Content Nabatean inscription
šlm ʿwdw br
krḥw bṭb
Access II.2a.182 (printed, CIS)
Corpus CIS 2981

Inscription **4249**
Site Church of the Holy Sepulchre, #375
Technique chiselled
Condition excellent
Content varied crosses
Access FH30-31 (photograph, Project)

Inscription **4250**
Site Church of the Nativity, pillar B9, #256
Technique scratched
Condition poor
Content crosses alone
Access DUa32 (photograph, M. Stone)

Inscription **4251**
Site Church of the Nativity, pillar B7, #257
Dating 1666
Technique scratched
Condition excellent
Dimensions 9 x 2 cm.
Content Armenian inscription
Limitation *Tentative decipherment only*
Access DUb52 (photograph, M. Stone)

Inscription **4252**
Site Church of the Nativity, pillar B7, #257
Technique scratched
Condition poor
Content crosses with inscription
Access DUb52 (photograph, M. Stone)

Inscription **4253**
Site Church of the Nativity, pillar B7, #257
Technique scratched
Condition good
Content Armenian inscription
Limitation *Tentative decipherment only*
Access DUb54 (photograph, M. Stone); *see also* DUb56

Inscription 4254
Site Church of the Nativity, pillar B7, #257
Dating 1627
Technique scratched
Condition fair
Dimensions 9 x 2 cm.
Content Armenian inscription
Limitation *Tentative decipherment only*
Access DUb56 (photograph, M. Stone)

Inscription 4255
Site Jebel Maharun, #317
Technique scratched
Condition poor
Content Arabic inscription
Access FS04 (photograph, Project)

Inscription 4256
Site Church of the Nativity, pillar B7, #257
Dating 1628
Technique scratched
Condition good
Dimensions 9 x 4.5 cm.
Content Armenian inscription
Limitation *Tentative decipherment only*
Access DUb56 (photograph, M. Stone)

Inscription 4257
Site Church of the Nativity, pillar B7, #257
Technique scratched
Condition poor
Dimensions 4 x 1 cm.
Content Armenian inscription
Limitation *Tentative decipherment only*
Access DUb56 (photograph, M. Stone)

Inscription 4258
Site Church of the Nativity, pillar B7, #257
Technique scratched
Condition fair
Content Arabic inscription
Access DUb56 (photograph, M. Stone)

Inscription 4259
Site Church of the Nativity, pillar B7, #257
Technique scratched
Condition fair
Content crosses with inscription
Access DUb56 (photograph, M. Stone)

Inscription 4260
Site Church of the Nativity, pillar B7, #257
Technique scratched
Condition fair
Content Arabic inscription
Access DUb56 (photograph, M. Stone)

Inscription 4261
Site Church of the Nativity, pillar B7, #257
Technique scratched
Condition good
Content crosses alone
Access DUb56 (photograph, M. Stone)

Inscription 4262
Site Church of the Nativity, south door to crypt, #258
Technique scratched
Condition excellent
Content Armenian inscription
Limitation *Tentative decipherment only*
Access DUb66 (photograph, M. Stone)

Inscription 4263
Site Church of the Nativity, south door to crypt, #258
Technique scratched
Condition good
Content crosses alone
Access DUb66 (photograph, M. Stone)

Inscription 4264
Site Church of the Nativity, south door to crypt, #258
Dating 1551
Technique scratched
Condition good
Dimensions 15 x 3 cm.
Content Armenian inscription
Limitation *Tentative decipherment only*
Access DUb66 (photograph, M. Stone)

Inscription 4265
Site Church of the Nativity, south door to crypt, #258
Technique scratched
Condition good
Content crosses alone
Access DUb66 (photograph, M. Stone)

Inscription 4266
Site Church of the Nativity, south door to crypt, #258
Technique scratched
Condition poor
Content Armenian inscription
Access DUb66 (photograph, M. Stone)

Inscription 4267
Site Church of the Nativity, south door to crypt, #258
Technique scratched
Condition poor
Content unidentified inscription
Access DUb66 (photograph, M. Stone)

Inscription 4268
Site Church of the Nativity, pillar C3, #242
Dating 1664
Technique scratched
Condition excellent
Dimensions 5 x 2 cm.
Content Latin inscription
Limitation *Tentative decipherment only*
Access DVa04 (photograph, M. Stone)

Inscription 4269
Site Church of the Nativity, pillar C3, #242
Technique scratched
Condition excellent
Content Arabic inscription
Access DVa04 (photograph, M. Stone)

Inscription 4270
Site Church of the Nativity, pillar C3, #242
Technique scratched
Condition poor
Content Arabic inscription
Access DVa04 (photograph, M. Stone)

Inscription 4271
Site Church of the Nativity, pillar C3, #242
Technique scratched
Condition poor
Content Arabic inscription
Access DVa04 (photograph, M. Stone)

Inscription 4272
Site Church of the Nativity, pillar C3, #242
Technique scratched
Condition poor
Content Arabic inscription
Access DVa04 (photograph, M. Stone)

Inscription 4273
Site Church of the Nativity, pillar C3, #242
Technique scratched
Condition good
Content Russian inscription
Limitation *Tentative decipherment only*
Access DVa04 (photograph, M. Stone)

Inscription 4274
Site Church of the Nativity, pillar C3, #242
Technique scratched
Condition good
Content crosses alone
Access DVa04 (photograph, M. Stone)

Inscription 4275
Site Church of the Nativity, pillar C3, #242
Technique scratched
Condition excellent
Dimensions 11 x 1 cm.
Content Arabic inscription
Access DVa05 (photograph, M. Stone)

Inscription 4276
Site Church of the Nativity, pillar C3, #242
Technique scratched
Condition poor
Content Arabic inscription
Access DVa05 (photograph, M. Stone)

Inscription 4277
Site Church of the Nativity, pillar C3, #242
Technique scratched
Condition good
Content crosses alone
Access DVa05 (photograph, M. Stone)

Inscription 4278
Site Church of the Nativity, iron door in narthex, #251
Dating 1773
Technique incised
Condition excellent
Dimensions 14 x 9 cm.
Content Armenian inscription
Limitation *Tentative decipherment only*
Access DSb18 (photograph, M. Stone)

Inscription 4279
Site Church of the Nativity, St. James, #270
Dating 1862
Technique incised
Condition excellent
Dimensions 15 x 4 cm.
Content Armenian inscription
Limitation *Tentative decipherment only*
Access DSb20 (photograph, M. Stone)

Inscription 4280
Site Church of the Nativity, St. James, #270
Technique chiselled
Condition good
Content ornaments
Comment *square stylized floral design*
Access DSb20 (photograph, M. Stone)

Inscription 4281
Site Church of the Nativity, St. James, #270
Technique scratched
Condition poor
Content Armenian inscription
Limitation *Tentative decipherment only*
Access DSb20 (photograph, M. Stone)

Inscription 4282
Site Church of the Nativity, St. James, #270
Technique scratched
Condition poor
Content unidentified inscription
Access DSb20 (photograph, M. Stone)

Inscription 4283
Site Church of the Nativity, St. James, #270
Technique chiselled
Condition excellent
Content Armenian inscription
Limitation *Tentative decipherment only*
Access DSb21 (photograph, M. Stone)

Inscription 4284
Site Church of the Nativity, St. James, #270
Technique chiselled
Condition excellent
Content crosses with inscription
Access DSb21 (photograph, M. Stone)

Inscription 4285
Site Church of the Nativity, St. James, #270
Technique scratched
Condition poor
Content Armenian inscription
Access DSb21 (photograph, M. Stone)

Inscription **4286**
Site Bir Sueir, #172
Technique incised
Condition poor
Content Greek inscription
Limitation *Tentative decipherment only*
Access FD04 (photograph, Project)

Inscription **4287**
Site Church of the Nativity, St. James, #270
Dating 1862
Technique chiselled
Condition excellent
Dimensions 35 x 11 cm.
Content Armenian inscription
Limitation *Study only*
Access DTa15-16 (photograph, M. Stone)

Inscription **4288**
Site Church of the Nativity, St. James, #270
Technique chiselled
Condition excellent
Dimensions 35 x 14 cm.
Content crosses with inscription
Access DTa15-16 (photograph, M. Stone)

Inscription **4289**
Site Church of the Nativity, St. James, #270
Technique scratched
Condition poor
Content unidentified inscription
Access DTa15-16 (photograph, M. Stone)

Inscription **4290**
Site Church of the Nativity, St. James, #270
Technique scratched
Condition poor
Content unidentified signs
Access DTa15-16 (photograph, M. Stone)

Inscription **4291**
Site Church of the Nativity, St. James, #270
Technique scratched
Condition poor
Dimensions 35 x 11 cm.
Content unidentified inscription
Access DTa15-16 (photograph, M. Stone)

Inscription **4292**
Site Church of the Nativity, St. James, #270
Dating 1862
Technique chiselled
Condition excellent
Dimensions 40 x 60 cm.
Content Armenian inscription
Limitation *Study only*
Access DTa21-22 (photograph, M. Stone)

Inscription **4293**
Site Church of the Nativity, St. James, #270
Technique chiselled
Condition excellent
Content crosses with inscription
Access DTa21-22 (photograph, M. Stone)

Inscription **4294**
Site Wadi Leja, #27
Technique scratched
Condition good
Content rock drawing
Comment *horse with rider*
Access FF36 (photograph, Y. Tsafrir)

Inscription **4295**
Site Wadi Arade, Arade 5, #111
Technique scratched
Condition excellent
Content rock drawing
Comment *boat with passenger steering*
Access FE05 (photograph, Project); *see also* CI05

Inscription **4296**
Site Church of the Nativity, north door to crypt, #262
Technique chiselled
Condition good
Content Armenian inscription
Limitation *Study only*
Access DTa27-28 (photograph, M. Stone)

Inscription **4297**
Site Church of the Nativity, north door to crypt, #262
Technique incised
Condition good
Content Armenian inscription
Limitation *Study only*
Access DTa27-28 (photograph, M. Stone)

Inscription **4298**
Site Wadi Lethi, Wadi Lethi 1, #150
Technique scratched
Condition good
Content rock drawing
Comment *two camels facing a palm tree*
Access FD47 (photograph, Project)

Inscription **4299**
Site Church of the Nativity, north door to crypt, #262
Technique chiselled
Condition excellent
Content crosses with inscription
Access DTa27-28 (photograph, M. Stone)

Inscription **4300**
Site Wadi Haggag, #118
Technique scratched
Condition excellent
Content Arabic inscription
Access FA35 (photograph, Project); *see also* FA33, FA34

Inscription 4301
Site Wadi Haggag, #118
Technique scratched
Condition excellent
Content rock drawing
Comment *animals*
Access FA35 (photograph, Project); *see also* FA33, FA34

Inscription 4302
Site Wadi Haggag, #118
Technique scratched
Condition excellent
Content unidentified signs
Access FA35 (photograph, Project); *see also* FA33, FA34

Inscription 4303
Site Church of the Nativity, north door to crypt, #262
Dating 1656
Technique chiselled
Condition excellent
Content Armenian inscription
Access DTa29-30 (photograph, M. Stone)

Inscription 4304
Site Church of the Nativity, north door to crypt, #262
Technique chiselled
Condition excellent
Content crosses with inscription
Access DTa29-30 (photograph, M. Stone)

Inscription 4305
Site Church of the Nativity, north door to crypt, #262
Technique chiselled
Condition excellent
Content Armenian inscription
Comment *monograms*
Access DTa29-30 (photograph, M. Stone)

Inscription 4306
Site Church of the Nativity, north door to crypt, #262
Technique chiselled
Condition good
Content ornaments
Comment *Annunciation scene*
Access DTa29-30 (photograph, M. Stone)

Inscription 4307
Site Church of the Nativity, north door to crypt, #262
Dating 1606
Technique chiselled
Condition excellent
Content Armenian inscription
Limitation *Study only*
Access DTa35-36 (photograph, M. Stone)

Inscription 4308
Site Church of the Nativity, north door to crypt, #262
Technique chiselled
Condition excellent
Content crosses with inscription
Access DTa35-36 (photograph, M. Stone)

Inscription 4309
Site Wadi Haggag, #118
Technique incised
Condition excellent
Content rock drawing
Comment *animals*
Access FA36 (photograph, Project); *see also* FB06

Inscription 4310
Site Wadi Haggag, #118
Technique incised
Condition excellent
Content rock drawing
Comment *animals and human figures, palm tree*
Access FB01 (photograph, Project); *see also* FB02

Inscription 4311
Site Church of the Nativity, north door to crypt, #262
Technique chiselled
Condition fair
Content Armenian inscription
Limitation *Tentative decipherment only*
Access DTa35-36 (photograph, M. Stone)

Inscription 4312
Site Church of the Nativity, north door to crypt, #262
Technique chiselled
Condition good
Content Armenian inscription
Limitation *Study only*
Access DTa37-38 (photograph, M. Stone)

Inscription 4313
Site Church of the Nativity, north door to crypt, #262
Technique chiselled
Condition excellent
Content crosses with inscription
Access DTa37-38 (photograph, M. Stone)

Inscription 4314
Site Church of the Nativity, north door to crypt, #262
Technique chiselled
Condition fair
Content Armenian inscription
Access DTa37-38 (photograph, M. Stone)

Inscription **4315**
Site Church of the Nativity, north door to crypt, #262
Dating 1743
Technique chiselled
Condition excellent
Content Armenian inscription
Limitation *Study only*
Access DTa37-38 (photograph, M. Stone)

Inscription **4316**
Site Church of the Nativity, north door to crypt, #262
Technique chiselled
Condition good
Content crosses with inscription
Access DTa37-38 (photograph, M. Stone)

Inscription **4317**
Site Church of the Nativity, north door to crypt, #262
Technique scratched
Condition poor
Content Armenian inscription
Access DTa37-38 (photograph, M. Stone)

Inscription **4318**
Site Church of the Nativity, north door to crypt, #262
Technique chiselled
Condition poor
Content Armenian inscription
Limitation *Study only*
Access DTb51-52 (photograph, M. Stone)

Inscription **4319**
Site Church of the Nativity, north door to crypt, #262
Technique scratched
Condition poor
Content crosses with inscription
Access DTb51-52 (photograph, M. Stone)

Inscription **4320**
Site Church of the Nativity, pillar C9, #248
Technique scratched
Condition fair
Dimensions 3.5 x .5 cm.
Content Greek inscription
Limitation *Tentative decipherment only*
Access DUa05 (photograph, M. Stone)

Inscription **4321**
Site Church of the Nativity, pillar C9, #248
Technique scratched
Condition poor
Content Greek inscription
Limitation *Tentative decipherment only*
Access DUa05 (photograph, M. Stone)

Inscription **4322**
Site Church of the Nativity, pillar C9, #248
Technique scratched
Condition poor
Content Arabic inscription
Access DUa05 (photograph, M. Stone)

Inscription **4323**
Site Church of the Nativity, pillar C9, #248
Technique scratched
Condition poor
Content crosses with inscription
Access DUa05 (photograph, M. Stone)

Inscription **4324**
Site Church of the Nativity, pillar C9, #248
Technique scratched
Condition good
Content crosses with inscription
Access DUa05 (photograph, M. Stone)

Inscription **4325**
Site Church of the Nativity, pillar C9, #248
Technique scratched
Condition poor
Content Latin inscription
Limitation *Tentative decipherment only*
Access DUa05 (photograph, M. Stone)

Inscription **4326**
Site Church of the Nativity, pillar C9, #248
Technique scratched
Condition poor
Content Latin inscription
Limitation *Tentative decipherment only*
Access DUa05 (photograph, M. Stone)

Inscription **4327**
Site Church of the Nativity, pillar C9, #248
Technique scratched
Condition poor
Content unidentified signs
Access DUa05 (photograph, M. Stone)

Inscription **4328**
Site Church of the Nativity, left stairs to podium, #249
Technique chiselled
Condition fair
Dimensions 8 x 10 cm.
Content Greek inscription
Limitation *Tentative decipherment only*
Access DVb33 (photograph, M. Stone)

Inscription **4329**
Site Church of the Nativity, left stairs to podium, #249
Technique chiselled
Condition excellent
Content Greek inscription
Limitation *Tentative decipherment only*
Access DVb33 (photograph, M. Stone)

Inscription 4330
Site Church of the Nativity, pillar B4, #266
Technique scratched
Condition good
Content Arabic inscription
Access DSa00a (photograph, M. Stone)

Inscription 4331
Site Church of the Nativity, left stairs to podium, #249
Technique scratched
Condition poor
Dimensions 50 x 20 cm.
Content Arabic inscription
Access DSa00a (photograph, M. Stone)

Inscription 4332
Site Church of the Nativity, left stairs to podium, #249
Technique scratched
Condition fair
Dimensions 6 x 2 cm.
Content Arabic inscription
Access DSa00a (photograph, M. Stone)

Inscription 4333
Site Church of the Nativity, pillar B3, #268
Technique scratched
Condition poor
Dimensions 18 x 3 cm.
Content Arabic inscription
Access DSa00a (photograph, M. Stone)

Inscription 4334
Site Church of the Nativity, pillar B3, #268
Technique scratched
Condition good
Content crosses alone
Access DSa00a (photograph, M. Stone)

Inscription 4335
Site Church of the Nativity, pillar B3, #268
Technique scratched
Condition good
Content crosses alone
Access DSa00a (photograph, M. Stone)

Inscription 4336
Site Church of the Nativity, pillar B3, #268
Technique scratched
Condition poor
Content crosses alone
Access DSa00a (photograph, M. Stone)

Inscription 4337
Site Church of the Nativity, north door to crypt, #262
Technique scratched
Condition poor
Content Arabic inscription
Access DRa10 (photograph, M. Stone)

Inscription 4338
Site Church of the Nativity, north door to crypt, #262
Technique scratched
Condition good
Content crosses alone
Access DRa10 (photograph, M. Stone)

Inscription 4339
Site Church of the Nativity, pillar B3, #268
Technique scratched
Condition poor
Dimensions 11 x 1 cm.
Content Greek inscription
Limitation *Tentative decipherment only*
Access DSa11 (photograph, M. Stone)

Inscription 4340
Site Church of the Nativity, pillar B3, #268
Technique scratched
Condition poor
Dimensions 9 x 1 cm.
Content Greek inscription
Limitation *Tentative decipherment only*
Access DSa11 (photograph, M. Stone)

Inscription 4341
Site Church of the Nativity, pillar B3, #268
Technique scratched
Condition fair
Content crosses alone
Access DSa11 (photograph, M. Stone)

Inscription 4342
Site Church of the Nativity, pillar B3, #268
Technique scratched
Condition good
Content crosses alone
Access DSa11 (photograph, M. Stone)

Inscription 4343
Site Church of the Nativity, pillar B3, #268
Technique scratched
Condition fair
Content crosses alone
Access DSa11 (photograph, M. Stone)

Inscription 4344
Site Church of the Nativity, pillar B3, #268
Technique scratched
Condition poor
Content Arabic inscription
Access DSa11 (photograph, M. Stone)

Inscription 4345
Site Church of the Nativity, pillar B3, #268
Technique scratched
Condition fair
Content crosses alone
Access DSa11 (photograph, M. Stone)

Inscription 4346
Site Church of the Nativity, pillar C4, #243
Technique scratched
Condition fair
Dimensions 8 x 9 cm.
Content Arabic inscription
Access DVa07 (photograph, M. Stone)

Inscription 4347
Site Church of the Nativity, pillar C4, #243
Technique scratched
Condition poor
Dimensions 8 x 9 cm.
Content Arabic inscription
Access DVa07 (photograph, M. Stone)

Inscription 4348
Site Church of the Nativity, pillar C9, #248
Technique scratched
Condition fair
Dimensions 5 x 5 cm.
Content Arabic inscription
Access DVb28 (photograph, M. Stone)

Inscription 4349
Site Church of the Nativity, pillar C9, #248
Technique scratched
Condition poor
Content crosses alone
Access DVb28 (photograph, M. Stone)

Inscription 4350
Site Church of the Nativity, pillar B7, #257
Technique scratched
Condition fair
Content Armenian inscription
Limitation *Study only*
Access DUa38 (photograph, M. Stone); *see also* DUa36

Inscription 4351
Site Church of the Nativity, pillar B7, #257
Dating 1176
Technique scratched
Condition poor
Dimensions 30 x 30 cm.
Content Greek inscription
Limitation *Tentative decipherment only*
Access DUa38 (photograph, M. Stone)

Inscription 4352
Site Church of the Nativity, pillar B7, #257
Technique scratched
Condition poor
Content Greek inscription
Limitation *Tentative decipherment only*
Access DUa38 (photograph, M. Stone)

Inscription 4353
Site Church of the Nativity, pillar B7, #257
Technique scratched
Condition fair
Content crosses alone
Access DUa38 (photograph, M. Stone); *see also* DUa36

Inscription 4354
Site Church of the Nativity, pillar B7, #257
Technique scratched
Condition fair
Content crosses alone
Access DUa38 (photograph, M. Stone)

Inscription 4355
Site Church of the Nativity, pillar B7, #257
Technique scratched
Condition poor
Dimensions 1.5 x 1.5 cm.
Content Latin inscription
Limitation *Tentative decipherment only*
Access DUa38 (photograph, M. Stone); *see also* DUa36

Inscription 4356
Site Church of the Nativity, pillar B7, #257
Technique scratched
Condition poor
Dimensions 5 x 2.5 cm.
Content Arabic inscription
Access DUa38 (photograph, M. Stone)

Inscription 4357
Site Church of the Nativity, pillar B7, #257
Technique scratched
Condition poor
Content Arabic inscription
Access DUa38 (photograph, M. Stone)

Inscription 4358
Site Church of the Nativity, pillar B7, #257
Technique scratched
Condition poor
Content Arabic inscription
Access DUa38 (photograph, M. Stone)

Inscription 4359
Site Church of the Nativity, pillar B7, #257
Technique scratched
Condition fair
Content crosses alone
Access DUa38 (photograph, M. Stone)

Inscription 4360
Site Church of the Nativity, pillar B3, #268
Technique scratched
Condition fair
Dimensions 24 x 4 cm.
Content Arabic inscription
Access DSa07 (photograph, M. Stone)

Inscription 4361
Site Church of the Nativity, pillar B3, #268
Technique scratched
Condition poor
Content Arabic inscription
Access DSa07 (photograph, M. Stone)

Inscription **4362**
Site Church of the Nativity, pillar B3, #268
Technique scratched
Condition poor
Content Arabic inscription
Access DSa07 (photograph, M. Stone)

Inscription **4363**
Site Church of the Nativity, pillar B3, #268
Technique scratched
Condition poor
Content Arabic inscription
Access DSa07 (photograph, M. Stone)

Inscription **4364**
Site Church of the Nativity, pillar B3, #268
Technique scratched
Condition poor
Content Arabic inscription
Access DSa07 (photograph, M. Stone)

Inscription **4365**
Site Church of the Nativity, pillar B3, #268
Technique scratched
Condition fair
Content crosses alone
Access DSa07 (photograph, M. Stone)

Inscription **4366**
Site Church of the Nativity, pillar B3, #268
Technique scratched
Condition poor
Dimensions 8 x 2 cm.
Content Greek inscription
Limitation *Tentative decipherment only*
Access DSa12 (photograph, M. Stone)

Inscription **4367**
Site Church of the Nativity, pillar B3, #268
Technique scratched
Condition poor
Dimensions 7.5 x 2 cm.
Content Arabic inscription
Access DSa12 (photograph, M. Stone)

Inscription **4368**
Site Church of the Nativity, pillar B3, #268
Technique scratched
Condition fair
Content crosses alone
Access DSa12 (photograph, M. Stone)

Inscription **4369**
Site Church of the Nativity, pillar B7, #257
Technique scratched
Condition poor
Content Arabic inscription
Access DUb40 (photograph, M. Stone)

Inscription **4370**
Site Church of the Nativity, pillar B7, #257
Technique scratched
Condition poor
Dimensions 2.1 x 5 cm.
Content Greek inscription
Limitation *Tentative decipherment only*
Access DUb40 (photograph, M. Stone)

Inscription **4371**
Site Church of the Nativity, pillar B7, #257
Technique scratched
Condition excellent
Dimensions 3 x 2.5 cm.
Content Latin inscription
Limitation *Tentative decipherment only*
Access DUb40 (photograph, M. Stone)

Inscription **4372**
Site Church of the Nativity, pillar B7, #257
Technique scratched
Condition poor
Content Arabic inscription
Access DUb40 (photograph, M. Stone)

Inscription **4373**
Site Church of the Nativity, pillar B7, #257
Technique scratched
Condition poor
Content Arabic inscription
Access DUb40 (photograph, M. Stone)

Inscription **4374**
Site Church of the Nativity, pillar B7, #257
Technique scratched
Condition poor
Content Arabic inscription
Access DUb40 (photograph, M. Stone)

Inscription **4375**
Site Church of the Nativity, pillar B7, #257
Technique scratched
Condition fair
Content crosses alone
Access DUb40 (photograph, M. Stone)

Inscription **4376**
Site Church of the Nativity, pier P, #263
Technique scratched
Condition poor
Dimensions 4 x 1 cm.
Content Armenian inscription
Limitation *Tentative decipherment only*
Access DRa14 (photograph, M. Stone)

Inscription **4377**
Site Sinai, #0
Technique incised
Condition good
Content crosses with inscription
Access ECi/3 (photograph, U. Avner)

Inscription **4378**
Site Church of the Nativity, pier P, #263
Technique scratched
Condition good
Content crosses alone
Access DRa14 (photograph, M. Stone)

Inscription **4379**
Site Church of the Nativity, pillar B4, #266
Technique scratched
Condition fair
Dimensions 8 x 6 cm.
Content Arabic inscription
Access DSa03 (photograph, M. Stone); *see also* DSa01, DSa02

Inscription **4380**
Site Church of the Nativity, pillar B4, #266
Technique scratched
Condition poor
Content Arabic inscription
Access DSa03 (photograph, M. Stone); *see also* DSa02

Inscription **4381**
Site Church of the Nativity, pillar B4, #266
Technique scratched
Condition poor
Content Arabic inscription
Access DSa03 (photograph, M. Stone); *see also* DSa02

Inscription **4382**
Site Church of the Nativity, pillar B4, #266
Technique scratched
Condition poor
Content Arabic inscription
Access DSa03 (photograph, M. Stone); *see also* DSa02

Inscription **4383**
Site Church of the Nativity, pillar B4, #266
Technique scratched
Condition poor
Content Arabic inscription
Access DSa03 (photograph, M. Stone); *see also* DSa02

Inscription **4384**
Site Church of the Nativity, pillar B4, #266
Technique scratched
Condition poor
Content Arabic inscription
Access DSa03 (photograph, M. Stone); *see also* DSa02

Inscription **4385**
Site Church of the Nativity, pillar B4, #266
Technique scratched
Condition poor
Dimensions 50 x 20 cm.
Content Arabic inscription
Access DSa03 (photograph, M. Stone); *see also* DSa02

Inscription **4386**
Site Church of the Nativity, pillar B4, #266
Technique scratched
Condition poor
Content Arabic inscription
Access DSa03 (photograph, M. Stone); *see also* DSa02

Inscription **4387**
Site Church of the Nativity, pillar B4, #266
Technique scratched
Condition poor
Content Arabic inscription
Access DSa03 (photograph, M. Stone); *see also* DSa02

Inscription **4388**
Site Church of the Nativity, pillar B4, #266
Technique scratched
Condition poor
Content Arabic inscription
Access DSa03 (photograph, M. Stone); *see also* DSa02

Inscription **4389**
Site Church of the Nativity, pillar B4, #266
Technique scratched
Condition poor
Content Arabic inscription
Access DSa03 (photograph, M. Stone); *see also* DSa02

Inscription **4390**
Site Church of the Nativity, pillar B3, #268
Technique scratched
Condition poor
Content Arabic inscription
Access DSa07 (photograph, M. Stone)

Inscription **4391**
Site Church of the Nativity, pillar B4, #266
Technique scratched
Condition fair
Content Arabic inscription
Access DSa02 (photograph, M. Stone)

Inscription **4392**
Site Church of the Nativity, pillar B4, #266
Technique scratched
Condition poor
Content Arabic inscription
Access DSa02 (photograph, M. Stone)

Inscription **4393**
Site Church of the Nativity, pillar B4, #266
Technique scratched
Condition poor
Content Armenian inscription
Limitation *Tentative decipherment only*
Access DSa02 (photograph, M. Stone)

Inscription 4394
Site Church of the Nativity, pillar B4, #266
Technique scratched
Condition good
Dimensions 30 x 8 cm.
Content Latin inscription
Access DSa06 (photograph, M. Stone)

Inscription 4395
Site Church of the Nativity, pillar B4, #266
Technique scratched
Condition poor
Content Arabic inscription
Access DSa06 (photograph, M. Stone)

Inscription 4396
Site Church of the Nativity, pillar B4, #266
Technique scratched
Condition poor
Content unidentified inscription
Access DSa06 (photograph, M. Stone)

Inscription 4397
Site Church of the Nativity, pillar B4, #266
Technique scratched
Condition poor
Content Arabic inscription
Access DSa06 (photograph, M. Stone)

Inscription 4398
Site Church of the Nativity, pillar B4, #266
Technique scratched
Condition fair
Dimensions 12 x 6 cm.
Content Arabic inscription
Access DSa09 (photograph, M. Stone)

Inscription 4399
Site Church of the Nativity, pillar B4, #266
Technique scratched
Condition fair
Content Arabic inscription
Access DSa09 (photograph, M. Stone)

Inscription 4400
Site Church of the Nativity, pillar C10, #252
Technique scratched
Condition poor
Dimensions 30 x 10 cm.
Content Arabic inscription
Access DUa09 (photograph, M. Stone); *see also* DUa11

Inscription 4401
Site Church of the Nativity, pillar C10, #252
Technique scratched
Condition poor
Dimensions 30 x 12 cm.
Content Arabic inscription
Access DUa09 (photograph, M. Stone); *see also* DUa11

Inscription 4402
Site Church of the Nativity, pillar C10, #252
Technique scratched
Condition fair
Content Arabic inscription
Access DUa09 (photograph, M. Stone); *see also* DUa11

Inscription 4403
Site Church of the Nativity, pillar C10, #252
Technique scratched
Condition poor
Content Arabic inscription
Access DUa09 (photograph, M. Stone); *see also* DUa11

Inscription 4404
Site Church of the Nativity, pillar C10, #252
Technique scratched
Condition poor
Content unidentified inscription
Access DUa09 (photograph, M. Stone); *see also* DUa11

Inscription 4405
Site Church of the Nativity, pillar C10, #252
Technique scratched
Condition poor
Content Arabic inscription
Access DUa09 (photograph, M. Stone); *see also* DUa11

Inscription 4406
Site Church of the Nativity, pillar C10, #252
Technique scratched
Condition poor
Content Arabic inscription
Access DUa09 (photograph, M. Stone); *see also* DUa11

Inscription 4407
Site Church of the Nativity, pillar C10, #252
Technique scratched
Condition poor
Content Arabic inscription
Access DUa09 (photograph, M. Stone); *see also* DUa11

Inscription 4408
Site Church of the Nativity, pillar C10, #252
Technique scratched
Condition poor
Content unidentified inscription
Access DUa09 (photograph, M. Stone); *see also* DUa11

Inscription 4409
Site Church of the Nativity, pillar C10, #252
Technique scratched
Condition poor
Content Arabic inscription
Access DUa09 (photograph, M. Stone); *see also* DUa11

Inscription 4410
Site Church of the Nativity, pillar C10, #252
Technique scratched
Condition poor
Content Arabic inscription
Access DUa09 (photograph, M. Stone); *see also* DUa11

Inscription 4411
Site Church of the Nativity, pillar C10, #252
Technique scratched
Condition poor
Content Arabic inscription
Access DUa09 (photograph, M. Stone); *see also* DUa11

Inscription 4412
Site Church of the Nativity, pillar C10, #252
Technique scratched
Condition poor
Content Arabic inscription
Access DUa09 (photograph, M. Stone); *see also* DUa11

Inscription 4413
Site Church of the Nativity, pillar C10, #252
Technique scratched
Condition poor
Content crosses alone
Access DUa09 (photograph, M. Stone); *see also* DUa11

Inscription 4414
Site Bir Sueir, #172
Technique scratched
Condition excellent
Content rock drawing
Comment *ibexes, horses with riders*
Access FD02 (photograph, Project)

Inscription 4415
Site Church of the Nativity, pillar C10, #252
Technique scratched
Condition poor
Content Arabic inscription
Access DUa09 (photograph, M. Stone); *see also* DUa11

Inscription 4416
Site Church of the Nativity, pillar C10, #252
Technique scratched
Condition fair
Content Arabic inscription
Access DUa09 (photograph, M. Stone); *see also* DUa11

Inscription 4417
Site Church of the Nativity, pillar C10, #252
Technique scratched
Condition poor
Content Arabic inscription
Access DUa09 (photograph, M. Stone); *see also* DUa11

Inscription 4418
Site Church of the Nativity, pillar C10, #252
Technique scratched
Condition fair
Content Arabic inscription
Access DUa09 (photograph, M. Stone); *see also* DUa11

Inscription 4419
Site Church of the Nativity, pillar C10, #252
Technique scratched
Condition fair
Dimensions 30 x 10 cm.
Content Arabic inscription
Access DUa11 (photograph, M. Stone)

Inscription 4420
Site Church of the Nativity, pillar C10, #252
Technique painted
Condition poor
Content Arabic inscription
Access DUa11 (photograph, M. Stone)

Inscription 4421
Site Church of the Nativity, pillar C10, #252
Technique scratched
Condition poor
Content Arabic inscription
Access DUa11 (photograph, M. Stone)

Inscription 4422
Site Church of the Nativity, pillar C10, #252
Technique scratched
Condition poor
Content Arabic inscription
Access DUa11 (photograph, M. Stone)

Inscription 4423
Site Church of the Nativity, pillar C10, #252
Technique scratched
Condition poor
Content Arabic inscription
Access DUa11 (photograph, M. Stone)

Inscription 4424
Site Church of the Nativity, pillar C10, #252
Technique scratched
Condition poor
Content Arabic inscription
Access DUa11 (photograph, M. Stone)

Inscription 4425
Site Church of the Nativity, pillar C10, #252
Technique scratched
Condition fair
Content crosses alone
Access DUa11 (photograph, M. Stone)

Inscription 4426
Site Church of the Nativity, north door to crypt, #262
Dating 1551
Technique chiselled
Condition good
Content Armenian inscription
Limitation *Study only*
Access DTa31-32 (photograph, M. Stone)

Inscription 4427
Site Church of the Nativity, north door to crypt, #262
Technique scratched
Condition good
Content crosses with inscription
Access DTa31-32 (photograph, M. Stone)

Inscription 4428
Site Wadi Shellal, #90
Technique scratched
Condition fair
Content unidentified inscription
Access FE10 (photograph, Project)

Inscription 4429
Site Church of the Nativity, north door to crypt, #262
Technique scratched
Condition poor
Content Greek inscription
Limitation *Tentative decipherment only*
Access DTa31-32 (photograph, M. Stone)

Inscription 4430
Site Church of the Nativity, north door to crypt, #262
Technique scratched
Condition poor
Content Armenian inscription
Access DTa31-32 (photograph, M. Stone)

Inscription 4431
Site Church of the Nativity, north door to crypt, #262
Technique scratched
Condition poor
Content unidentified inscription
Access DTa31-32 (photograph, M. Stone)

Inscription 4432
Site Church of the Nativity, north door to crypt, #262
Technique chiselled
Condition good
Content crosses alone
Access DTa31-32 (photograph, M. Stone)

Inscription 4433
Site Wadi Tueiba, #226
Technique scratched
Condition poor
Content Arabic inscription
Access FD20 (photograph, Project)

Inscription 4434
Site Wadi Tueiba, #226
Technique scratched
Condition poor
Content Arabic inscription
Access FD20 (photograph, Project)

Inscription 4435
Site Wadi Tueiba, #226
Technique scratched
Condition poor
Content unidentified inscription
Access FD20 (photograph, Project)

Inscription 4436
Site Wadi Tueiba, #226
Technique scratched
Condition poor
Content rock drawing
Comment *animals*
Access FD20 (photograph, Project)

Inscription 4437
Site Church of the Nativity, St. James, #270
Dating 1688
Technique chiselled
Condition good
Dimensions 30 x 30 cm.
Content Armenian inscription
Limitation *Study only*
Access DSb01-02 (photograph, M. Stone)

Inscription 4438
Site Santa Katarina, #10
Technique chiselled
Condition excellent
Content crosses alone
Access FE21 (photograph, Project); *see also* AG38

Inscription 4439
Site Church of the Nativity, pillar B11(B10), #255
Technique scratched
Condition good
Dimensions 7 x 2 cm.
Content Latin inscription
Limitation *Tentative decipherment only*
Access DUa26 (photograph, M. Stone)

Inscription 4440
Site Church of the Nativity, pillar B11(B10), #255
Technique scratched
Condition poor
Content unidentified inscription
Access DUa26 (photograph, M. Stone)

Inscription 4441
Site Church of the Nativity, pillar B11(B10), #255
Technique scratched
Condition fair
Content crosses alone
Access DUa26 (photograph, M. Stone)

Inscription 4442
Site Ein Hudra, #117
Technique incised
Condition good
Dimensions 70 x 50 cm.
Content rock drawing
Comment *animal and human figures*
Access EX27 (photograph, Project)

Inscription 4443
Site Church of the Nativity, pillar B9, #256
Technique scratched
Condition fair
Dimensions 6 x 3 cm.
Content Greek inscription
Limitation *Tentative decipherment only*
Access DUa28 (photograph, M. Stone)

Inscription 4444
Site Church of the Nativity, pillar B9, #256
Technique scratched
Condition fair
Content Arabic inscription
Access DUa28 (photograph, M. Stone)

Inscription 4445
Site Church of the Nativity, pillar B9, #256
Technique scratched
Condition poor
Content Arabic inscription
Access DUa28 (photograph, M. Stone)

Inscription 4446
Site Church of the Nativity, pillar B9, #256
Technique scratched
Condition poor
Content Arabic inscription
Access DUa28 (photograph, M. Stone)

Inscription 4447
Site Church of the Nativity, pillar B9, #256
Technique scratched
Condition poor
Content Arabic inscription
Access DUa28 (photograph, M. Stone)

Inscription 4448
Site Church of the Nativity, pillar B9, #256
Technique scratched
Condition poor
Content crosses with inscription
Access DUa28 (photograph, M. Stone)

Inscription 4449
Site Church of the Nativity, pillar B9, #256
Technique scratched
Condition poor
Content unidentified inscription
Access DUa28 (photograph, M. Stone)

Inscription 4450
Site Church of the Nativity, pillar B9, #256
Technique scratched
Condition poor
Content Arabic inscription
Access DUa28 (photograph, M. Stone)

Inscription 4451
Site Church of the Nativity, pillar B9, #256
Technique scratched
Condition poor
Content unidentified inscription
Access DUa28 (photograph, M. Stone)

Inscription 4452
Site Church of the Nativity, pillar B9, #256
Technique scratched
Condition good
Content crosses alone
Access DUa28 (photograph, M. Stone)

Inscription 4453
Site Church of the Nativity, pillar B9, #256
Technique scratched
Condition fair
Content crosses alone
Access DUa28 (photograph, M. Stone)

Inscription 4454
Site Church of the Nativity, pillar B9, #256
Technique scratched
Condition poor
Content unidentified inscription
Access DUa28 (photograph, M. Stone)

Inscription 4455
Site Church of the Nativity, pillar B9, #256
Technique scratched
Condition poor
Content Latin inscription
Access DUa28 (photograph, M. Stone)

Inscription 4456
Site Church of the Nativity, pillar C5, #244
Technique incised
Condition excellent
Dimensions 2 x 3 cm.
Content Latin inscription
Limitation *Tentative decipherment only*
Access DVa10 (photograph, M. Stone)

Inscription 4457
Site Church of the Nativity, pillar C5, #244
Dating 1541
Technique incised
Condition good
Content Latin inscription
Limitation *Tentative decipherment only*
Access DVa10 (photograph, M. Stone)

Inscription 4458
Site Church of the Nativity, pillar C8, #247
Technique scratched
Condition fair
Content crosses with inscription
Access DVa10 (photograph, M. Stone); *see also* DVb25

Inscription 4459
Site Church of the Nativity, pillar C5, #244
Technique scratched
Condition good
Content crosses alone
Access DVa10 (photograph, M. Stone)

Inscription 4460
Site Church of the Nativity, pillar C5, #244
Technique scratched
Condition good
Content crosses alone
Access DVa10 (photograph, M. Stone)

Inscription 4461
Site Church of the Nativity, pillar C5, #244
Technique scratched
Condition good
Content Latin inscription
Limitation *Tentative decipherment only*
Access DVa10 (photograph, M. Stone)

Inscription 4462
Site Church of the Nativity, pillar C8, #247
Technique scratched
Condition poor
Dimensions 6 x 5 cm.
Content Arabic inscription
Access DVb24 (photograph, M. Stone)

Inscription 4463
Site Church of the Nativity, pillar C8, #247
Technique scratched
Condition poor
Content crosses alone
Access DVb24 (photograph, M. Stone)

Inscription 4464
Site Church of the Nativity, pillar C8, #247
Technique scratched
Condition poor
Content Arabic inscription
Access DVb24 (photograph, M. Stone)

Inscription 4465
Site Church of the Nativity, pillar C8, #247
Technique scratched
Condition poor
Content Arabic inscription
Access DVb24 (photograph, M. Stone)

Inscription 4466
Site Church of the Nativity, pillar C8, #247
Technique scratched
Condition poor
Content Arabic inscription
Access DVb24 (photograph, M. Stone)

Inscription 4467
Site Church of the Nativity, pillar C8, #247
Technique scratched
Condition poor
Content Arabic inscription
Access DVb24 (photograph, M. Stone)

Inscription 4468
Site Church of the Nativity, pillar C8, #247
Technique scratched
Condition poor
Content Arabic inscription
Access DVb24 (photograph, M. Stone)

Inscription 4469
Site Church of the Nativity, pillar C8, #247
Technique scratched
Condition poor
Content Arabic inscription
Access DVb24 (photograph, M. Stone)

Inscription 4470
Site Church of the Nativity, pillar C8, #247
Technique scratched
Condition fair
Dimensions 10 x 10 cm.
Content Arabic inscription
Access DVb25 (photograph, M. Stone)

Inscription 4471
Site Church of the Nativity, pillar C8, #247
Technique scratched
Condition poor
Content Arabic inscription
Access DVb25 (photograph, M. Stone); *see also* DVb26, DVb27

Inscription 4472
Site Church of the Nativity, pillar C8, #247
Technique scratched
Condition poor
Content Arabic inscription
Access DVb25 (photograph, M. Stone)

Inscription 4473
Site Church of the Nativity, pillar C8, #247
Technique scratched
Condition poor
Content Arabic inscription
Access DVb25 (photograph, M. Stone)

Inscription 4474
Site Church of the Nativity, pillar C8, #247
Technique scratched
Condition poor
Content Arabic inscription
Access DVb25 (photograph, M. Stone)

Inscription 4475
Site Church of the Nativity, pillar C8, #247
Technique scratched
Condition poor
Content Arabic inscription
Access DVb25 (photograph, M. Stone)

Inscription **4476**
Site Church of the Nativity, pillar C8, #247
Technique scratched
Condition poor
Content Arabic inscription
Access DVb25 (photograph, M. Stone)

Inscription **4477**
Site Church of the Nativity, pillar C8, #247
Technique scratched
Condition poor
Content unidentified signs
Access DVb25 (photograph, M. Stone)

Inscription **4478**
Site Church of the Nativity, pillar C8, #247
Technique scratched
Condition fair
Dimensions 13 x 3 cm.
Content Arabic inscription
Access DVb26 (photograph, M. Stone); *see also* DVb27

Inscription **4479**
Site Church of the Nativity, pillar C8, #247
Technique scratched
Condition poor
Content Arabic inscription
Access DVb26 (photograph, M. Stone); *see also* DVb27

Inscription **4480**
Site Church of the Nativity, pillar C8, #247
Technique scratched
Condition poor
Content Arabic inscription
Access DVb26 (photograph, M. Stone); *see also* DVb27

Inscription **4481**
Site Church of the Nativity, pillar C8, #247
Technique scratched
Condition poor
Content Arabic inscription
Access DVb26 (photograph, M. Stone); *see also* DVb27

Inscription **4482**
Site Church of the Nativity, pillar C8, #247
Technique scratched
Condition poor
Content Arabic inscription
Access DVb26 (photograph, M. Stone)

Inscription **4483**
Site Church of the Holy Sepulchre, #375
Technique incised
Condition good
Content Latin inscription
Limitation *Tentative decipherment only*
Access FI09 (photograph, Project)

Inscription **4484**
Site Church of the Nativity, pillar C8, #247
Technique scratched
Condition poor
Content unidentified inscription
Access DVb26 (photograph, M. Stone)

Inscription **4485**
Site Church of the Nativity, pillar C8, #247
Technique scratched
Condition poor
Content Arabic inscription
Access DVb26 (photograph, M. Stone)

Inscription **4486**
Site Church of the Nativity, pillar C8, #247
Technique scratched
Condition poor
Content Arabic inscription
Access DVb26 (photograph, M. Stone)

Inscription **4487**
Site Church of the Nativity, pillar C8, #247
Technique scratched
Condition poor
Dimensions 13 x 3 cm.
Content unidentified inscription
Access DVb26 (photograph, M. Stone)

Inscription **4488**
Site Church of the Nativity, pillar C8, #247
Technique scratched
Condition poor
Content Arabic inscription
Access DVb26 (photograph, M. Stone)

Inscription **4489**
Site Church of the Nativity, pillar C8, #247
Technique scratched
Condition poor
Dimensions 30 x 4 cm.
Content Latin inscription
Access DVb27 (photograph, M. Stone)

Inscription **4490**
Site Church of the Nativity, pillar C8, #247
Technique scratched
Condition poor
Content Arabic inscription
Access DVb27 (photograph, M. Stone)

Inscription **4491**
Site Church of the Nativity, pillar C8, #247
Technique scratched
Condition poor
Content Arabic inscription
Access DVb27 (photograph, M. Stone)

Inscription **4492**
Site Church of the Nativity, pillar C8, #247
Technique scratched
Condition poor
Content Latin inscription
Access DVb27 (photograph, M. Stone)

Inscription **4493**
Site Church of the Nativity, pillar C9, #248
Technique scratched
Condition poor
Content Arabic inscription
Access DVb29 (photograph, M. Stone)

Inscription **4494**
Site Church of the Nativity, pillar C9, #248
Technique scratched
Condition poor
Content Arabic inscription
Access DVb29 (photograph, M. Stone); *see also* DVb30

Inscription **4495**
Site Church of the Nativity, pillar C9, #248
Technique scratched
Condition poor
Content Arabic inscription
Access DVb29 (photograph, M. Stone); *see also* DVb30

Inscription **4496**
Site Church of the Nativity, pillar C9, #248
Technique scratched
Condition poor
Content Arabic inscription
Access DVb29 (photograph, M. Stone); *see also* DVb30

Inscription **4497**
Site Church of the Nativity, pillar C9, #248
Technique scratched
Condition poor
Content Arabic inscription
Access DVb29 (photograph, M. Stone)

Inscription **4498**
Site Church of the Nativity, pillar C9, #248
Technique scratched
Condition poor
Content Greek inscription
Limitation *Tentative decipherment only*
Access DVb29 (photograph, M. Stone)

Inscription **4499**
Site Church of the Nativity, pillar C9, #248
Technique scratched
Condition poor
Content crosses with inscription
Access DVb29 (photograph, M. Stone)

Inscription **4500**
Site Church of the Nativity, pillar C9, #248
Technique scratched
Condition poor
Content Greek inscription
Limitation *Tentative decipherment only*
Access DVb29 (photograph, M. Stone)

Inscription **4501**
Site Church of the Nativity, pillar C9, #248
Technique scratched
Condition poor
Content crosses with inscription
Access DVb29 (photograph, M. Stone)

Inscription **4502**
Site Church of the Nativity, pillar C9, #248
Technique scratched
Condition poor
Content Greek inscription
Limitation *Tentative decipherment only*
Access DVb29 (photograph, M. Stone)

Inscription **4503**
Site Church of the Nativity, pillar C9, #248
Technique scratched
Condition fair
Content crosses with inscription
Access DVb29 (photograph, M. Stone)

Inscription **4504**
Site Church of the Nativity, pillar C9, #248
Technique scratched
Condition fair
Content Latin inscription
Limitation *Tentative decipherment only*
Access DVb29 (photograph, M. Stone)

Inscription **4505**
Site Church of the Nativity, pillar C9, #248
Technique scratched
Condition poor
Content crosses with inscription
Access DVb29 (photograph, M. Stone)

Inscription **4506**
Site Church of the Nativity, pillar C9, #248
Technique scratched
Condition poor
Content Latin inscription
Limitation *Tentative decipherment only*
Access DVb29 (photograph, M. Stone)

Inscription **4507**
Site Church of the Nativity, pillar C9, #248
Technique scratched
Condition poor
Content crosses with inscription
Access DVb29 (photograph, M. Stone)

Inscription **4508**
Site Church of the Nativity, pillar C9, #248
Technique scratched
Condition poor
Content crosses alone
Access DVb29 (photograph, M. Stone)

Inscription 4509
Site Church of the Nativity, pillar C9, #248
Technique scratched
Condition poor
Dimensions 10 x 6 cm.
Content Arabic inscription
Access DVb30 (photograph, M. Stone)

Inscription 4510
Site Church of the Nativity, pillar C9, #248
Technique scratched
Condition poor
Content Arabic inscription
Access DVb30 (photograph, M. Stone)

Inscription 4511
Site Church of the Nativity, pillar C9, #248
Technique scratched
Condition poor
Content Arabic inscription
Access DVb30 (photograph, M. Stone)

Inscription 4512
Site Church of the Nativity, pillar C9, #248
Technique scratched
Condition poor
Content Arabic inscription
Access DVb30 (photograph, M. Stone)

Inscription 4513
Site Church of the Nativity, pillar C9, #248
Technique scratched
Condition poor
Content Arabic inscription
Access DVb30 (photograph, M. Stone)

Inscription 4514
Site Church of the Nativity, pillar C9, #248
Technique scratched
Condition poor
Content unidentified inscription
Access DVb30 (photograph, M. Stone)

Inscription 4515
Site Church of the Nativity, pillar C9, #248
Technique scratched
Condition poor
Content crosses alone
Access DVb30 (photograph, M. Stone)

Inscription 4516
Site Church of the Nativity, pillar C9, #248
Technique scratched
Condition poor
Content crosses alone
Access DVb31 (photograph, M. Stone)

Inscription 4517
Site Church of the Nativity, pillar C9, #248
Technique scratched
Condition poor
Dimensions 5 x 2 cm.
Content Arabic inscription
Access DVb31 (photograph, M. Stone); *see also* DVb32

Inscription 4518
Site Church of the Nativity, pillar C9, #248
Technique scratched
Condition poor
Content Arabic inscription
Access DVb31 (photograph, M. Stone)

Inscription 4519
Site Church of the Nativity, pillar C9, #248
Technique scratched
Condition poor
Content Arabic inscription
Access DVb31 (photograph, M. Stone)

Inscription 4520
Site Church of the Nativity, pillar C9, #248
Technique scratched
Condition poor
Content crosses alone
Access DVb31 (photograph, M. Stone); *see also* DVb32

Inscription 4521
Site Church of the Nativity, pillar C9, #248
Technique scratched
Condition poor
Dimensions 5 x 2 cm.
Content crosses alone
Access DVb31 (photograph, M. Stone)

Inscription 4522
Site Church of the Nativity, pillar C9, #248
Technique scratched
Condition poor
Content Arabic inscription
Access DVb31 (photograph, M. Stone); *see also* DVb32

Inscription 4523
Site Church of the Nativity, pillar C9, #248
Technique scratched
Condition poor
Content Arabic inscription
Access DVb31 (photograph, M. Stone); *see also* DVb32

Inscription 4524
Site Church of the Nativity, pillar C9, #248
Technique scratched
Condition poor
Content Arabic inscription
Access DVb31 (photograph, M. Stone); *see also* DVb32

Inscription 4525
Site Church of the Nativity, pillar C9, #248
Technique scratched
Condition poor
Content Arabic inscription
Access DVb31 (photograph, M. Stone)

Inscription 4526
Site Church of the Nativity, pillar C9, #248
Technique scratched
Condition poor
Content Arabic inscription
Access DVb31 (photograph, M. Stone); *see also* DVb32

Inscription 4527
Site Church of the Nativity, pillar C9, #248
Technique scratched
Condition poor
Content crosses alone
Access DVb31 (photograph, M. Stone); *see also* DVb32

Inscription 4528
Site Church of the Nativity, pillar C9, #248
Technique scratched
Condition excellent
Content rock drawing
Comment *rectangles*
Access DVb31 (photograph, M. Stone); *see also* DVb32

Inscription 4529
Site Church of the Nativity, pillar C9, #248
Technique scratched
Condition poor
Content Arabic inscription
Access DVb31 (photograph, M. Stone); *see also* DVb32

Inscription 4530
Site Church of the Nativity, pillar C9, #248
Technique scratched
Condition poor
Content Arabic inscription
Access DVb31 (photograph, M. Stone); *see also* DVb32

Inscription 4531
Site Church of the Nativity, pillar C9, #248
Technique scratched
Condition poor
Content crosses alone
Access DVb31 (photograph, M. Stone); *see also* DVb32

Inscription 4532
Site Church of the Nativity, pillar C9, #248
Technique scratched
Condition good
Dimensions 5 x 5 cm.
Content crosses with inscription
Access DVb32 (photograph, M. Stone)

Inscription 4533
Site Church of the Nativity, pillar C9, #248
Technique scratched
Condition excellent
Dimensions 20 x 10 cm.
Content Greek inscription
Limitation *Tentative decipherment only*
Access DVb32 (photograph, M. Stone)

Inscription 4534
Site Bir Sueir, #172
Technique scratched
Condition fair
Content rock drawing
Comment *camels and horses with riders*
Access FD09 (photograph, Project)

Inscription 4535
Site Church of the Nativity, pillar C9, #248
Technique scratched
Condition good
Dimensions 5 x 5 cm.
Content crosses alone
Access DVb32 (photograph, M. Stone)

Inscription 4536
Site Church of the Nativity, pillar C9, #248
Technique scratched
Condition good
Dimensions 26 x 10 cm.
Content Arabic inscription
Access DVb32 (photograph, M. Stone)

Inscription 4537
Site Church of the Nativity, pillar C9, #248
Technique scratched
Condition poor
Content Arabic inscription
Access DVb32 (photograph, M. Stone)

Inscription 4538
Site Church of the Nativity, pillar C9, #248
Technique scratched
Condition poor
Content Arabic inscription
Access DVb32 (photograph, M. Stone)

Inscription 4539
Site Church of the Nativity, pillar C9, #248
Technique scratched
Condition good
Dimensions 5 x 5 cm.
Content crosses alone
Access DVb32 (photograph, M. Stone)

Inscription 4540
Site Church of the Nativity, left stairs to podium, #249
Technique scratched
Condition poor
Dimensions 27 x 7 cm.
Content Arabic inscription
Access DVb34 (photograph, M. Stone)

Inscription 4541
Site Church of the Nativity, left stairs to podium, #249
Technique scratched
Condition poor
Content Arabic inscription
Access DVb34 (photograph, M. Stone)

Inscription	**4542**
Site	Naqb el Hawa, #44
Technique	incised
Condition	fair
Content	unidentified inscription
Access	FE23 (photograph, Project)

Inscription	**4543**
Site	Church of the Nativity, left stairs to podium, #249
Technique	scratched
Condition	poor
Content	Arabic inscription
Access	DVb34 (photograph, M. Stone)

Inscription	**4544**
Site	Church of the Nativity, left stairs to podium, #249
Technique	scratched
Condition	poor
Content	Arabic inscription
Access	DVb34 (photograph, M. Stone)

Inscription	**4545**
Site	Church of the Nativity, left stairs to podium, #249
Technique	scratched
Condition	poor
Content	Arabic inscription
Access	DVb34 (photograph, M. Stone)

Inscription	**4546**
Site	Sinai, #0
Technique	incised
Condition	poor
Content	Greek inscription
Limitation	*Tentative decipherment only*
Access	ECi/3 (photograph, U. Avner)

Inscription	**4547**
Site	Church of the Nativity, left stairs to podium, #249
Technique	scratched
Condition	poor
Content	Arabic inscription
Access	DVb35 (photograph, M. Stone)

Inscription	**4548**
Site	Church of the Nativity, left stairs to podium, #249
Technique	scratched
Condition	poor
Content	Arabic inscription
Access	DVb35 (photograph, M. Stone)

Inscription	**4549**
Site	Church of the Nativity, left stairs to podium, #249
Technique	scratched
Condition	poor
Content	Arabic inscription
Access	DVb35 (photograph, M. Stone)

Inscription	**4550**
Site	Church of the Nativity, left stairs to podium, #249
Technique	scratched
Condition	poor
Content	Arabic inscription
Access	DVb35 (photograph, M. Stone)

Inscription	**4551**
Site	Church of the Nativity, pillar C5, #244
Dating	1611
Technique	scratched
Condition	fair
Dimensions	6 x .5 cm.
Content	Greek inscription
Limitation	*Tentative decipherment only*
Access	DVa11 (photograph, M. Stone)

Inscription	**4552**
Site	Church of the Nativity, pillar C5, #244
Technique	scratched
Condition	poor
Content	Arabic inscription
Access	DVa11 (photograph, M. Stone)

Inscription	**4553**
Site	Church of the Nativity, pillar C5, #244
Technique	scratched
Condition	poor
Content	Arabic inscription
Access	DVa11 (photograph, M. Stone)

Inscription	**4554**
Site	Church of the Nativity, pillar C5, #244
Technique	scratched
Condition	poor
Content	Greek inscription
Limitation	*Tentative decipherment only*
Access	DVa11 (photograph, M. Stone)

Inscription	**4555**
Site	Church of the Nativity, pillar C5, #244
Technique	scratched
Condition	poor
Dimensions	6 x .5 cm.
Content	Arabic inscription
Access	DVa11 (photograph, M. Stone)

Inscription	**4556**
Site	Church of the Nativity, pillar C5, #244
Technique	scratched
Condition	fair
Content	crosses alone
Access	DVa11 (photograph, M. Stone)

Inscription	**4557**
Site	Church of the Nativity, pillar C2, #241
Technique	scratched
Condition	fair
Dimensions	8 x 1 cm.
Content	Arabic inscription
Access	DVa03 (photograph, M. Stone)

Inscription **4558**
Site Church of the Nativity, pillar C2, #241
Technique scratched
Condition good
Content crosses alone
Access DVa03 (photograph, M. Stone)

Inscription **4559**
Site Church of the Nativity, pillar C2, #241
Technique scratched
Condition poor
Content Arabic inscription
Access DVa03 (photograph, M. Stone)

Inscription **4560**
Site Church of the Nativity, pillar C3, #242
Technique scratched
Condition excellent
Dimensions 2 x 1 cm.
Content Latin inscription
Limitation *Tentative decipherment only*
Access DVa06 (photograph, M. Stone)

Inscription **4561**
Site Church of the Nativity, pillar C3, #242
Technique scratched
Condition fair
Content unidentified signs
Access DVa06 (photograph, M. Stone)

Inscription **4562**
Site Church of the Nativity, pillar C3, #242
Technique scratched
Condition fair
Content unidentified signs
Access DVa06 (photograph, M. Stone)

Inscription **4563**
Site Church of the Nativity, pillar C3, #242
Technique scratched
Condition fair
Content crosses alone
Access DVa06 (photograph, M. Stone)

Inscription **4564**
Site Church of the Nativity, pillar C3, #242
Technique scratched
Condition poor
Content unidentified inscription
Access DVa06 (photograph, M. Stone)

Inscription **4565**
Site Wadi Abu Ghadhayyat, Ghadhayyat 1, #36
Technique scratched
Condition excellent
Content crosses alone
Access FE04 (photograph, Project)

Inscription **4566**
Site Wadi Abu Ghadhayyat, Ghadhayyat 1, #36
Technique scratched
Condition excellent
Content crosses alone
Access FE04 (photograph, Project)

Inscription **4567**
Site Wadi Abu Ghadhayyat, Ghadhayyat 1, #36
Technique scratched
Condition good
Content crosses alone
Access FE04 (photograph, Project)

Inscription **4568**
Site Wadi Abu Ghadhayyat, Ghadhayyat 1, #36
Technique scratched
Condition good
Content rock drawing
Comment *animals*
Access FE04 (photograph, Project)

Inscription **4569**
Site Church of the Nativity, pillar C4, #243
Technique scratched
Condition poor
Dimensions 4 x 3 cm.
Content Armenian inscription
Limitation *Tentative decipherment only*
Access DVa08 (photograph, M. Stone)

Inscription **4570**
Site Church of the Nativity, pillar C4, #243
Technique scratched
Condition fair
Content crosses alone
Access DVa08 (photograph, M. Stone)

Inscription **4571**
Site Church of the Nativity, pillar C5, #244
Technique scratched
Condition fair
Dimensions 14 x 1 cm.
Content Arabic inscription
Access DVa15 (photograph, M. Stone)

Inscription **4572**
Site Church of the Nativity, pillar C5, #244
Technique scratched
Condition fair
Content crosses alone
Access DVa15 (photograph, M. Stone)

Inscription **4573**
Site Wadi Tueiba, #226
Technique scratched
Condition excellent
Content rock drawing
Comment *boat*
Access FD25 (photograph, Project)

Inscription **4574**
Site Church of the Nativity, pillar C5, #244
Technique scratched
Condition fair
Dimensions 4 x 3 cm.
Content Arabic inscription
Access DVa16 (photograph, M. Stone); *see also* DVa17

Inscription **4575**
Site Church of the Nativity, pillar C5, #244
Technique scratched
Condition fair
Content crosses alone
Access DVa16 (photograph, M. Stone); *see also* DVa17

Inscription **4576**
Site Church of the Nativity, pillar C5, #244
Technique scratched
Condition fair
Dimensions 4 x 3 cm.
Content Greek inscription
Limitation *Tentative decipherment only*
Access DVa16 (photograph, M. Stone); *see also* DVa17

Inscription **4577**
Site Church of the Nativity, pillar C5, #244
Technique scratched
Condition fair
Content unidentified signs
Access DVa16 (photograph, M. Stone)

Inscription **4578**
Site Church of the Nativity, pillar C5, #244
Technique scratched
Condition fair
Content crosses alone
Access DVa17 (photograph, M. Stone)

Inscription **4579**
Site Church of the Nativity, pillar C5, #244
Technique scratched
Condition fair
Content unidentified signs
Access DVa17 (photograph, M. Stone)

Inscription **4580**
Site Wadi Haggag, #118
Technique scratched
Condition excellent
Content rock drawing
Comment *two humans leading camels*
Access FA05 (photograph, Project); *see also* FA06

Inscription **4581**
Site Church of the Nativity, pillar C7, #246
Technique scratched
Condition fair
Dimensions 25 x 3 cm.
Content Greek inscription
Limitation *Tentative decipherment only*
Access DVb21 (photograph, M. Stone)

Inscription **4582**
Site Church of the Nativity, pillar C7, #246
Technique scratched
Condition fair
Content crosses alone
Access DVb21 (photograph, M. Stone)

Inscription **4583**
Site Church of the Nativity, pillar C7, #246
Condition fair
Dimensions 3 x 5 cm.
Content Greek inscription
Limitation *Tentative decipherment only*
Access DVb22 (photograph, M. Stone); *see also* DVb23

Inscription **4584**
Site Church of the Nativity, pillar C7, #246
Technique scratched
Condition fair
Content varied crosses
Access DVb22 (photograph, M. Stone); *see also* DVb23

Inscription **4585**
Site Church of the Nativity, pillar C7, #246
Technique scratched
Condition fair
Content crosses with inscription
Access DVb22 (photograph, M. Stone); *see also* DVb23

Inscription **4586**
Site Church of the Nativity, pillar C7, #246
Technique scratched
Condition poor
Content unidentified signs
Access DVb22 (photograph, M. Stone); *see also* DVb23

Inscription **4587**
Site Church of the Nativity, pillar C7, #246
Technique scratched
Condition fair
Dimensions 11 x 6 cm.
Content Greek inscription
Limitation *Tentative decipherment only*
Access DVb23 (photograph, M. Stone)

Inscription **4588**
Site Church of the Nativity, pillar C7, #246
Technique scratched
Condition fair
Content crosses with inscription
Access DVb23 (photograph, M. Stone)

Inscription **4589**
Site Church of the Nativity, pillar C7, #246
Technique scratched
Condition fair
Dimensions 11 x 6 cm.
Content Greek inscription
Limitation *Tentative decipherment only*
Access DVb23 (photograph, M. Stone)

Inscription **4590**
Site Church of the Nativity, pillar C7, #246
Technique scratched
Condition fair
Content crosses with inscription
Access DVb23 (photograph, M. Stone)

Inscription 4591
Site Church of the Nativity, pillar C7, #246
Technique scratched
Condition fair
Content crosses alone
Access DVb23 (photograph, M. Stone)

Inscription 4592
Site Church of the Nativity, pillar C7, #246
Technique scratched
Condition poor
Content Arabic inscription
Access DVb23 (photograph, M. Stone)

Inscription 4593
Site Church of the Nativity, pillar C5, #244
Technique scratched
Condition poor
Dimensions 6 x .5 cm.
Content Georgian inscription
Limitation *Tentative decipherment only*
Access DVa12 (photograph, M. Stone); *see also* DVa13

Inscription 4594
Site Wadi Haggag, #118
Technique incised
Condition fair
Dimensions 135 x 125 cm.
Content rock drawing
Comment *animals*
Access FA01 (photograph, Project)

Inscription 4595
Site Church of the Nativity, pillar C5, #244
Technique scratched
Condition excellent
Content crosses alone
Access DVa12 (photograph, M. Stone); *see also* DVa13

Inscription 4596
Site Church of the Nativity, pillar C5, #244
Technique scratched
Condition poor
Content Arabic inscription
Access DVa12 (photograph, M. Stone); *see also* DVa13

Inscription 4597
Site Church of the Nativity, pillar C5, #244
Technique scratched
Condition poor
Content unidentified inscription
Access DVa12 (photograph, M. Stone); *see also* DVa13

Inscription 4598
Site Church of the Nativity, pillar C5, #244
Technique scratched
Condition fair
Content Arabic inscription
Access DVa12 (photograph, M. Stone); *see also* DVa13

Inscription 4599
Site Wadi Sidri, #77
Technique scratched
Condition excellent
Content rock drawing
Comment *two camels, bird*
Access FF20 (photograph, Y. Tsafrir)

Inscription 4600
Site Wadi Sidri, #77
Technique scratched
Condition poor
Content unidentified inscription
Access FF20 (photograph, Project)

Inscription 4601
Site Wadi Sidri, #77
Technique scratched
Condition poor
Content unidentified inscription
Access FF20 (photograph, Project)

Inscription 4602
Site Church of the Nativity, pillar C5, #244
Technique scratched
Condition poor
Content unidentified inscription
Access DVa13 (photograph, M. Stone)

Inscription 4603
Site Church of the Nativity, pillar C5, #244
Technique scratched
Condition poor
Content unidentified signs
Access DVa13 (photograph, M. Stone)

Inscription 4604
Site Wadi Tueiba, #226
Technique scratched
Condition good
Content rock drawing
Comment *nine-flame candelabrum with single horizontal arm*
Access FD26 (photograph, Project)

Inscription 4605
Site Church of the Nativity, pillar C5, #244
Technique scratched
Condition fair
Content rock drawing
Comment *circle*
Access DVa13 (photograph, M. Stone)

Inscription 4606
Site Church of the Nativity, pillar C7, #246
Technique scratched
Condition poor
Dimensions 6 x 1 cm.
Content Arabic inscription
Access DVa19 (photograph, M. Stone)

Inscription **4607**
Site Church of the Nativity, pillar C7, #246
Technique scratched
Condition fair
Content Greek inscription
Limitation *Tentative decipherment only*
Access DVa19 (photograph, M. Stone)

Inscription **4608**
Site Church of the Nativity, pillar C7, #246
Technique scratched
Condition poor
Content Arabic inscription
Access DVa19 (photograph, M. Stone)

Inscription **4609**
Site Church of the Nativity, pillar C7, #246
Technique scratched
Condition poor
Content Arabic inscription
Access DVa19 (photograph, M. Stone)

Inscription **4610**
Site Church of the Nativity, pillar C7, #246
Technique scratched
Condition fair
Content crosses alone
Access DVa19 (photograph, M. Stone)

Inscription **4611**
Site Church of the Nativity, pillar C7, #246
Technique scratched
Condition poor
Content Arabic inscription
Access DVa19 (photograph, M. Stone)

Inscription **4612**
Site Church of the Nativity, pillar B11, #254
Technique scratched
Condition fair
Content Armenian inscription
Limitation *Tentative decipherment only*
Access DUa21 (photograph, M. Stone)

Inscription **4613**
Site Church of the Nativity, pillar B11, #254
Technique scratched
Condition fair
Content Greek inscription
Limitation *Tentative decipherment only*
Access DUa21 (photograph, M. Stone); *see also* DUa24

Inscription **4614**
Site Wadi Tueiba, #226
Technique scratched
Condition fair
Content rock drawing
Comment *animals*
Access FD27 (photograph, Project)

Inscription **4615**
Site Church of the Nativity, pillar B11, #254
Technique scratched
Condition poor
Content Greek inscription
Access DUa21 (photograph, M. Stone); *see also* DUa24

Inscription **4616**
Site Church of the Nativity, pillar B11, #254
Technique scratched
Condition good
Content crosses alone
Access DUa21 (photograph, M. Stone)

Inscription **4617**
Site Church of the Nativity, pillar B11, #254
Technique scratched
Condition fair
Content Georgian inscription
Access DUa21 (photograph, M. Stone); *see also* DUa24

Inscription **4618**
Site Wadi Tueiba, #226
Technique scratched
Condition excellent
Content rock drawing
Comment *animals and human figures*
Access FD29 (photograph, project); *see also* FD28

Inscription **4619**
Site Church of the Nativity, pillar B11, #254
Technique scratched
Condition fair
Dimensions 25 x 3 cm.
Content Latin inscription
Limitation *Tentative decipherment only*
Comment *inside cross*
Access DUa21 (photograph, M. Stone); *see also* DUa24

Inscription **4620**
Site Bir Sueir, #172
Technique scratched
Condition good
Content crosses alone
Access FD05 (photograph, Project)

Inscription **4621**
Site Bir Sueir, #172
Technique scratched
Condition good
Content rock drawing
Comment *humans and camels*
Access FD05 (photograph, Project)

Inscription **4622**
Site Church of the Nativity, pillar B11, #254
Technique scratched
Condition poor
Content Arabic inscription
Access DUa21 (photograph, M. Stone)

Inscription **4623**
Site Wadi Tueiba, #226
Technique incised
Condition fair
Content Nabatean inscription
Limitation *Tentative decipherment only*
Access FD17 (photograph, Project)

Inscription **4624**
Site Wadi Tueiba, #226
Technique scratched
Condition fair
Content Arabic inscription
Access FD17 (photograph, Project)

Inscription **4625**
Site Wadi Tueiba, #226
Technique scratched
Condition fair
Content Greek inscription
Limitation *Tentative decipherment only*
Comment *Nabatean name*
Access FD17 (photograph, Project)

Inscription **4626**
Site Wadi Tueiba, #226
Technique scratched
Condition poor
Content Latin inscription
Limitation *Tentative decipherment only*
Access FD17 (photograph, Project)

Inscription **4627**
Site Wadi Tueiba, #226
Technique scratched
Condition good
Content rock drawing
Comment *camels with riders*
Access FD17 (photograph, Project)

Inscription **4628**
Site Church of the Nativity, pillar B11, #254
Technique scratched
Condition good
Dimensions 5 x 1 cm.
Content Arabic inscription
Access DUa24 (photograph, M. Stone)

Inscription **4629**
Site Church of the Nativity, pillar B11, #254
Technique scratched
Condition excellent
Content Arabic inscription
Access DUa24 (photograph, M. Stone)

Inscription **4630**
Site Church of the Nativity, pillar B11, #254
Technique scratched
Condition poor
Content Greek inscription
Limitation *Tentative decipherment only*
Access DUa24 (photograph, M. Stone)

Inscription **4631**
Site Church of the Nativity, pillar B11, #254
Technique scratched
Condition fair
Content Russian inscription
Limitation *Tentative decipherment only*
Access DUa24 (photograph, M. Stone)

Inscription **4632**
Site Church of the Nativity, pillar B11, #254
Technique scratched
Condition excellent
Content crosses alone
Access DUa24 (photograph, M. Stone)

Inscription **4633**
Site Church of the Nativity, pillar B11, #254
Technique scratched
Condition fair
Content Georgian inscription
Access DUa24 (photograph, M. Stone)

Inscription **4634**
Site Church of the Nativity, pillar B11, #254
Technique scratched
Condition good
Content unidentified signs
Access DUa24 (photograph, M. Stone)

Inscription **4635**
Site Church of the Nativity, iron door in narthex, #251
Technique scratched
Condition fair
Dimensions 3 x 2 cm.
Content Russian inscription
Limitation *Tentative decipherment only*
Access DUa03 (photograph, M. Stone)

Inscription **4636**
Site A-Tor, Bir Abu Sueira, #191
Technique scratched
Condition fair
Content Greek inscription
Limitation *Tentative decipherment only*
Access DX04 (photograph, A. Goren); *see also* DX02

Inscription **4637**
Site A-Tor, Bir Abu Sueira, #191
Technique scratched
Condition poor
Content Arabic inscription
Access DX04 (photograph, A. Goren); *see also* DX02

Inscription **4638**
Site A-Tor, Bir Abu Sueira, #191
Technique scratched
Condition fair
Content Coptic inscription
Limitation *Tentative decipherment only*
Access DX04 (photograph, A. Goren); *see also* DX02

Inscription **4639**
Site A-Tor, Bir Abu Sueira, #191
Technique scratched
Condition poor
Content Latin inscription
Limitation *Tentative decipherment only*
Access DX04 (photograph, A. Goren); *see also* DX02

Inscription **4640**
Site A-Tor, Bir Abu Sueira, #191
Technique scratched
Condition fair
Content Greek inscription
Limitation *Tentative decipherment only*
Access DX04 (photograph, A. Goren); *see also* DX02

Inscription **4641**
Site A-Tor, Bir Abu Sueira, #191
Technique scratched
Condition poor
Content English inscription
Limitation *Tentative decipherment only*
Access DX04 (photograph, A. Goren); *see also* DX02

Inscription **4642**
Site A-Tor, Bir Abu Sueira, #191
Technique scratched
Condition poor
Content Greek inscription
Limitation *Tentative decipherment only*
Access DX04 (photograph, A. Goren); *see also* DX02

Inscription **4643**
Site A-Tor, Bir Abu Sueira, #191
Technique scratched
Condition fair
Content Polish inscription
Limitation *Tentative decipherment only*
Access DX04 (photograph, A. Goren); *see also* DX02

Inscription **4644**
Site A-Tor, Bir Abu Sueira, #191
Technique scratched
Condition poor
Content Greek inscription
Limitation *Tentative decipherment only*
Access DX04 (photograph, A. Goren); *see also* DX02

Inscription **4645**
Site A-Tor, Bir Abu Sueira, #191
Technique scratched
Condition poor
Content Greek inscription
Access DX04 (photograph, A. Goren); *see also* DX02

Inscription **4646**
Site A-Tor, Bir Abu Sueira, #191
Technique scratched
Condition poor
Content Greek inscription
Limitation *Tentative decipherment only*
Access DX04 (photograph, A. Goren); *see also* DX02

Inscription **4647**
Site A-Tor, Bir Abu Sueira, #191
Technique scratched
Condition poor
Content Greek inscription
Limitation *Tentative decipherment only*
Access DX04 (photograph, A. Goren); *see also* DX02

Inscription **4648**
Site A-Tor, Bir Abu Sueira, #191
Technique scratched
Condition poor
Content Greek inscription
Limitation *Tentative decipherment only*
Access DX04 (photograph, A. Goren); *see also* DX02

Inscription **4649**
Site A-Tor, Bir Abu Sueira, #191
Technique scratched
Condition poor
Content Greek inscription
Limitation *Tentative decipherment only*
Access DX04 (photograph, A. Goren); *see also* DX02

Inscription **4650**
Site A-Tor, Bir Abu Sueira, #191
Technique scratched
Condition poor
Content Greek inscription
Access DX04 (photograph, A. Goren); *see also* DX02

Inscription **4651**
Site A-Tor, Bir Abu Sueira, #191
Technique scratched
Condition poor
Content unidentified inscription
Access DX04 (photograph, A. Goren); *see also* DX02

Inscription **4652**
Site A-Tor, Bir Abu Sueira, #191
Technique scratched
Condition excellent
Content Greek inscription
Limitation *Tentative decipherment only*
Access DX04 (photograph, A. Goren); *see also* DX02

Inscription **4653**
Site A-Tor, Bir Abu Sueira, #191
Technique scratched
Condition poor
Content Arabic inscription
Access DX02 (photograph, A. Goren)

Inscription **4654**
Site A-Tor, Bir Abu Sueira, #191
Technique scratched
Condition excellent
Content crosses alone
Access DX02 (photograph, A. Goren)

Inscription **4655**
Site A-Tor, Bir Abu Sueira, #191
Technique scratched
Condition good
Content unidentified signs
Access DX02 (photograph, A. Goren)

Inscription **4656**
Site A-Tor, Bir Abu Sueira, #191
Technique scratched
Condition poor
Content unidentified signs
Access DX02 (photograph, A. Goren)

Inscription **4657**
Site A-Tor, Bir Abu Sueira, #191
Technique scratched
Condition poor
Content Russian inscription
Limitation *Tentative decipherment only*
Access DX02 (photograph, A. Goren)

Inscription **4658**
Site A-Tor, Bir Abu Sueira, #191
Technique scratched
Condition poor
Content Greek inscription
Limitation *Tentative decipherment only*
Access DX02 (photograph, A. Goren)

Inscription **4659**
Site A-Tor, Bir Abu Sueira, #191
Technique scratched
Condition poor
Content unidentified inscription
Access DX02 (photograph, A. Goren)

Inscription **4660**
Site A-Tor, Bir Abu Sueira, #191
Technique scratched
Condition fair
Content Greek inscription
Limitation *Tentative decipherment only*
Access DX02 (photograph, A. Goren)

Inscription **4661**
Site Wadi Tueiba, #226
Technique scratched
Condition poor
Content unidentified inscription
Access FD17 (photograph, Project)

Inscription **4662**
Site Wadi Tueiba, #226
Technique scratched
Condition poor
Content Arabic inscription
Access FD17 (photograph, Project)

Inscription **4663**
Site A-Tor, Bir Abu Sueira, #191
Technique scratched
Condition excellent
Content Greek inscription
Limitation *Tentative decipherment only*
Access DX05 (photograph, A. Goren)

Inscription **4664**
Site A-Tor, Bir Abu Sueira, #191
Technique scratched
Condition excellent
Content English inscription
Limitation *Tentative decipherment only*
Access DX05 (photograph, A. Goren)

Inscription **4665**
Site A-Tor, Bir Abu Sueira, #191
Technique incised
Condition excellent
Content Latin inscription
Limitation *Tentative decipherment only*
Access DX05 (photograph, A. Goren)

Inscription **4666**
Site A-Tor, Bir Abu Sueira, #191
Technique scratched
Condition poor
Content Latin inscription
Limitation *Tentative decipherment only*
Access DX05 (photograph, A. Goren)

Inscription **4667**
Site A-Tor, Bir Abu Sueira, #191
Technique scratched
Condition poor
Content Greek inscription
Limitation *Tentative decipherment only*
Access DX05 (photograph, A. Goren)

Inscription **4668**
Site A-Tor, Bir Abu Sueira, #191
Dating 1888
Technique scratched
Condition excellent
Content English inscription
Limitation *Tentative decipherment only*
Access DX05 (photograph, A. Goren)

Inscription **4669**
Site A-Tor, Bir Abu Sueira, #191
Dating 1898
Technique scratched
Condition poor
Content English inscription
Limitation *Tentative decipherment only*
Access DX05 (photograph, A. Goren)

Inscription **4670**
Site A-Tor, Bir Abu Sueira, #191
Dating 1698
Technique scratched
Condition fair
Content Greek inscription
Limitation *Tentative decipherment only*
Access DX05 (photograph, A. Goren)

Inscription **4671**
Site A-Tor, Bir Abu Sueira, #191
Technique scratched
Condition fair
Content Greek inscription
Limitation *Tentative decipherment only*
Access DX05 (photograph, A. Goren)

Inscription **4672**
Site A-Tor, Bir Abu Sueira, #191
Technique scratched
Condition poor
Content unidentified signs
Access DX05 (photograph, A. Goren)

Inscription **4673**
Site A-Tor, Bir Abu Sueira, #191
Technique scratched
Condition poor
Content Greek inscription
Limitation *Tentative decipherment only*
Access DX05 (photograph, A. Goren)

Inscription **4674**
Site A-Tor, Bir Abu Sueira, #191
Dating 1687
Technique scratched
Condition good
Content Arabic inscription
Access DX05 (photograph, A. Goren)

Inscription **4675**
Site A-Tor, Bir Abu Sueira, #191
Technique scratched
Condition fair
Content Greek inscription
Limitation *Tentative decipherment only*
Access DX05 (photograph, A. Goren)

Inscription **4676**
Site A-Tor, Bir Abu Sueira, #191
Technique scratched
Condition poor
Content Greek inscription
Limitation *Tentative decipherment only*
Access DX05 (photograph, A. Goren)

Inscription **4677**
Site A-Tor, Bir Abu Sueira, #191
Technique scratched
Condition fair
Content Latin inscription
Access DX05 (photograph, A. Goren)

Inscription **4678**
Site A-Tor, Bir Abu Sueira, #191
Technique scratched
Condition poor
Content Arabic inscription
Access DX05 (photograph, A. Goren)

Inscription **4679**
Site A-Tor, Bir Abu Sueira, #191
Technique scratched
Condition excellent
Content English inscription
Limitation *Tentative decipherment only*
Access DX05 (photograph, A. Goren)

Inscription **4680**
Site A-Tor, Bir Abu Sueira, #191
Technique incised
Condition excellent
Content rock drawing
Comment *three rectangles*
Access DX05 (photograph, A. Goren)

Inscription **4681**
Site A-Tor, Bir Abu Sueira, #191
Technique scratched
Condition poor
Content Arabic inscription
Access DX05 (photograph, A. Goren)

Inscription **4682**
Site A-Tor, Bir Abu Sueira, #191
Technique scratched
Condition poor
Content unidentified inscription
Access DX05 (photograph, A. Goren)

Inscription **4683**
Site A-Tor, Bir Abu Sueira, #191
Technique scratched
Condition poor
Content Arabic inscription
Access DX05 (photograph, A. Goren)

Inscription **4684**
Site A-Tor, Bir Abu Sueira, #191
Technique scratched
Condition poor
Content Arabic inscription
Access DX05 (photograph, A. Goren)

Inscription **4685**
Site A-Tor, Bir Abu Sueira, #191
Technique scratched
Condition fair
Content Latin inscription
Limitation *Tentative decipherment only*
Access DX05 (photograph, A. Goren)

Inscription 4686
Site A-Tor, Bir Abu Sueira, #191
Technique scratched
Condition poor
Content Greek inscription
Limitation *Tentative decipherment only*
Access DX05 (photograph, A. Goren)

Inscription 4687
Site A-Tor, Bir Abu Sueira, #191
Technique scratched
Condition poor
Content Greek inscription
Access DX05 (photograph, A. Goren)

Inscription 4688
Site A-Tor, Bir Abu Sueira, #191
Technique scratched
Condition fair
Content rock drawing
Comment *two squares*
Access DX05 (photograph, A. Goren)

Inscription 4689
Site A-Tor, Bir Abu Sueira, #191
Technique scratched
Condition poor
Content Greek inscription
Limitation *Tentative decipherment only*
Access DX05 (photograph, A. Goren)

Inscription 4690
Site A-Tor, Bir Abu Sueira, #191
Technique scratched
Condition poor
Content Greek inscription
Access DX05 (photograph, A. Goren)

Inscription 4691
Site Sinai, #0
Technique incised
Condition poor
Content unidentified inscription
Access ECi/3 (photograph, U. Avner)

Inscription 4692
Site Church of the Nativity, pillar C9, #248
Technique scratched
Condition poor
Dimensions 12 x 3 cm.
Content Arabic inscription
Access DUa07 (photograph, M. Stone)

Inscription 4693
Site Church of the Nativity, pillar B7, #257
Technique scratched
Condition good
Dimensions 3 x 2 cm.
Content Armenian inscription
Limitation *Study only*
Access DUa34 (photograph, M. Stone)

Inscription 4694
Site Church of the Nativity, pillar B7, #257
Technique scratched
Condition good
Content crosses alone
Access DUa34 (photograph, M. Stone)

Inscription 4695
Site Church of the Nativity, pillar B7, #257
Dating 1666
Technique scratched
Condition excellent
Content English inscription
Limitation *Tentative decipherment only*
Access DUa34 (photograph, M. Stone)

Inscription 4696
Site Church of the Nativity, pillar B7, #257
Technique scratched
Condition poor
Content Greek Inscription
Limitation *Tentative decipherment only*
Access FD14 (photograph, Project)

Inscription 4697
Site Church of the Nativity, pillar B7, #257
Technique scratched
Condition fair
Content Greek inscription
Limitation *Tentative decipherment only*
Access DUa34 (photograph, M. Stone)

Inscription 4698
Site Church of the Nativity, pillar B7, #257
Technique scratched
Condition fair
Content Greek inscription
Limitation *Tentative decipherment only*
Access DUa34 (photograph, M. Stone)

Inscription 4699
Site Church of the Nativity, pillar B7, #257
Technique scratched
Condition fair
Content Armenian inscription
Limitation *Study only*
Access DUa34 (photograph, M. Stone); *see also* DUa36

Inscription 4700
Site Church of the Nativity, pillar B7, #257
Technique scratched
Condition fair
Content Greek inscription
Limitation *Tentative decipherment only*
Access DUa34 (photograph, M. Stone); *see also* DUa36

Inscription 4701
Site Church of the Nativity, pillar B7, #257
Technique scratched
Condition good
Content crosses with inscription
Access DUa34 (photograph, M. Stone)

Inscription **4702**
Site Church of the Nativity, pillar B7, #257
Technique scratched
Condition fair
Content Greek inscription
Limitation *Tentative decipherment only*
Access DUa34 (photograph, M. Stone); *see also* DUa36

Inscription **4703**
Site Wadi Tueiba, #226
Technique scratched
Condition good
Content rock drawing
Comment *animals and humans*
Access FD16 (photograph, Project)

Inscription **4704**
Site Wadi Tueiba, #226
Technique scratched
Condition poor
Content unidentified inscription
Access FD16 (photograph, Project)

Inscription **4705**
Site Church of the Nativity, pillar B7, #257
Technique scratched
Condition poor
Content Greek inscription
Limitation *Tentative decipherment only*
Access DUa34 (photograph, M. Stone); *see also* DUa36

Inscription **4706**
Site Church of the Nativity, pillar B7, #257
Technique scratched
Condition poor
Content Greek inscription
Access DUa34 (photograph, M. Stone)

Inscription **4707**
Site Church of the Nativity, pillar B7, #257
Technique scratched
Condition poor
Content Greek inscription
Limitation *Tentative decipherment only*
Access DUa34 (photograph, M. Stone)

Inscription **4708**
Site Church of the Nativity, pillar B7, #257
Technique scratched
Condition poor
Content Greek inscription
Limitation *Tentative decipherment only*
Access DUa34 (photograph, M. Stone); *see also* DUa36

Inscription **4709**
Site Church of the Nativity, pillar B7, #257
Technique scratched
Condition poor
Content Arabic inscription
Access DUa34 (photograph, M. Stone); *see also* DUa37

Inscription **4710**
Site Church of the Nativity, pillar B7, #257
Technique scratched
Condition poor
Content Arabic inscription
Access DUa34 (photograph, M. Stone)

Inscription **4711**
Site Church of the Nativity, pillar B7, #257
Technique scratched
Condition good
Content crosses alone
Access DUa34 (photograph, M. Stone); *see also* DUa36

Inscription **4712**
Site Church of the Nativity, pillar B7, #257
Technique scratched
Condition poor
Content crosses alone
Access DUa34 (photograph, M. Stone)

Inscription **4713**
Site Church of the Nativity, pillar B7, #257
Technique scratched
Condition poor
Content crosses alone
Access DUa36 (photograph, M. Stone)

Inscription **4714**
Site Church of the Nativity, pillar B7, #257
Technique scratched
Condition good
Content crosses alone
Access DUa36 (photograph, M. Stone)

Inscription **4715**
Site Church of the Nativity, pillar B7, #257
Dating 1516
Technique scratched
Condition good
Dimensions 20 x 7 cm.
Content Armenian inscription
Limitation *Study only*
Access DUb50 (photograph, M. Stone)

Inscription **4716**
Site Church of the Nativity, pillar B7, #257
Technique scratched
Condition good
Content crosses with inscription
Access DUb50 (photograph, M. Stone)

Inscription **4717**
Site Church of the Nativity, pillar B7, #257
Technique scratched
Condition good
Content Armenian inscription
Limitation *Tentative decipherment only*
Access DUb50 (photograph, M. Stone)

Inscription 4718
Site Church of the Nativity, pillar B7, #257
Technique scratched
Condition good
Content crosses alone
Access DUb50 (photograph, M. Stone)

Inscription 4719
Site Church of the Nativity, pillar B7, #257
Technique scratched
Condition poor
Content Arabic inscription
Access DUb50 (photograph, M. Stone)

Inscription 4720
Site Church of the Nativity, pillar B7, #257
Technique scratched
Condition fair
Content Armenian inscription
Access DUb50 (photograph, M. Stone)

Inscription 4721
Site Church of the Nativity, pillar B7, #257
Technique scratched
Condition poor
Content Arabic inscription
Access DUb50 (photograph, M. Stone)

Inscription 4722
Site Church of the Nativity, south door to crypt, #258
Technique scratched
Condition poor
Content Arabic inscription
Access DUb62 (photograph, M. Stone)

Inscription 4723
Site Church of the Nativity, south door to crypt, #258
Technique scratched
Condition excellent
Content crosses alone
Access DUb62 (photograph, M. Stone)

Inscription 4724
Site Church of the Nativity, south door to crypt, #258
Technique scratched
Condition poor
Content Greek inscription
Limitation *Tentative decipherment only*
Access DUb62 (photograph, M. Stone)

Inscription 4725
Site Church of the Nativity, south door to crypt, #258
Technique scratched
Condition poor
Content unidentified inscription
Access DUb62 (photograph, M. Stone)

Inscription 4726
Site Church of the Nativity, south door to crypt, #258
Technique scratched
Condition good
Content crosses with inscription
Access DUb62 (photograph, M. Stone)

Inscription 4727
Site Church of the Nativity, south door to crypt, #258
Technique scratched
Condition poor
Content unidentified signs
Access DSa00a (photograph, M. Stone)

Inscription 4728
Site Church of the Nativity, pillar L, #259
Dating 991
Technique incised
Condition fair
Dimensions 11 x 12 cm.
Content Spanish inscription
Limitation *Tentative decipherment only*
Access DUb70 (photograph, M. Stone)

Inscription 4729
Site Church of the Nativity, pillar L, #259
Technique scratched
Condition poor
Dimensions 2.5 x 1 cm.
Content Arabic inscription
Access DUb70 (photograph, M. Stone)

Inscription 4730
Site Church of the Nativity, pillar L, #259
Technique incised
Condition excellent
Dimensions 14 x 6 cm.
Content crosses with inscription
Access DUb70 (photograph, M. Stone)

Inscription 4731
Site Church of the Nativity, pillar L, #259
Technique scratched
Condition poor
Content unidentified signs
Access DUb70 (photograph, M. Stone)

Inscription 4732
Site Church of the Nativity, pillar L, #259
Technique scratched
Condition excellent
Dimensions 4.5 x 4 cm.
Content crosses alone
Access DUb70 (photograph, M. Stone)

Inscription 4733
Site Church of the Nativity, north door to apse, #260
Technique incised
Condition fair
Dimensions 30 x 10 cm.
Content Latin inscription
Access DUb74 (photograph, M. Stone)

Inscription 4734
Site Church of the Nativity, pillar L, #259
Technique scratched
Condition poor
Dimensions 5 x 1 cm.
Content Georgian inscription
Access DUb72 (photograph, M. Stone)

Inscription 4735
Site Church of the Nativity, pillar L, #259
Technique scratched
Condition poor
Dimensions 4 x 4 cm.
Content Greek inscription
Limitation *Tentative decipherment only*
Access DUb72 (photograph, M. Stone)

Inscription 4736
Site Church of the Nativity, pillar L, #259
Technique scratched
Condition good
Content crosses alone
Access DUb72 (photograph, M. Stone)

Inscription 4737
Site Church of the Nativity, pillar B3, #268
Technique scratched
Condition poor
Content Latin inscription
Limitation *Tentative decipherment only*
Access DSa16 (photograph, M. Stone)

Inscription 4738
Site Church of the Nativity, pillar B2, #269
Technique scratched
Condition excellent
Dimensions 4 x 4 cm.
Content crosses alone
Access DSb17 (photograph, M. Stone)

Inscription 4739
Site Church of the Nativity, pillar B2, #269
Technique scratched
Condition good
Dimensions 7 x 7 cm.
Content crosses alone
Access DSb17 (photograph, M. Stone)

Inscription 4740
Site Church of the Nativity, pillar B2, #269
Technique scratched
Condition good
Dimensions 2 x 2 cm.
Content crosses alone
Access DSb17 (photograph, M. Stone)

Inscription 4741
Site Church of the Nativity, pillar B2, #269
Technique scratched
Condition good
Content crosses alone
Access DSb17 (photograph, M. Stone)

Inscription 4742
Site Church of the Nativity, north door to crypt, #262
Dating 1616
Technique scratched
Condition fair
Dimensions 12 x 10 cm.
Content Armenian inscription
Limitation *Study only*
Access DRa01 (photograph, M. Stone)

Inscription 4743
Site Church of the Nativity, north door to crypt, #262
Technique scratched
Condition poor
Content Arabic inscription
Access DRa01 (photograph, M. Stone)

Inscription 4744
Site Church of the Nativity, north door to crypt, #262
Technique scratched
Condition good
Content crosses alone
Access DRa01 (photograph, M. Stone)

Inscription 4745
Site Church of the Nativity, north door to crypt, #262
Technique scratched
Condition good
Dimensions 40 x 30 cm.
Content Armenian inscription
Limitation *Study only*
Access DRa03 (photograph, M. Stone)

Inscription 4746
Site Church of the Nativity, north door to crypt, #262
Technique scratched
Condition good
Content Armenian inscription
Limitation *Study only*
Access DRa03 (photograph, M. Stone)

Inscription 4747
Site Church of the Nativity, north door to crypt, #262
Technique scratched
Condition poor
Content Armenian inscription
Access DRa03 (photograph, M. Stone)

Inscription 4748
Site Church of the Nativity, north door to crypt, #262
Technique scratched
Condition good
Dimensions 24 x 3 cm.
Content Armenian inscription
Limitation *Study only*
Access DRa03 (photograph, M. Stone)

Inscription 4749
Site Church of the Nativity, north door to crypt, #262
Technique scratched
Condition good
Dimensions 9.5 x .5 cm.
Content Armenian inscription
Limitation *Study only*
Access DRa03 (photograph, M. Stone)

Inscription 4750
Site Church of the Nativity, north door to crypt, #262
Technique scratched
Condition good
Dimensions 1 x 1 cm.
Content crosses with inscription
Access DRa03 (photograph, M. Stone)

Inscription 4751
Site Church of the Nativity, north door to crypt, #262
Technique scratched
Condition good
Dimensions 1 x 2 cm.
Content crosses with inscription
Access DRa03 (photograph, M. Stone)

Inscription 4752
Site Church of the Nativity, north door to crypt, #262
Technique scratched
Condition poor
Content Armenian inscription
Limitation *Tentative decipherment only*
Access DRa03 (photograph, M. Stone)

Inscription 4753
Site Church of the Nativity, north door to crypt, #262
Technique scratched
Condition fair
Dimensions 4 x 1 cm.
Content Latin inscription
Limitation *Tentative decipherment only*
Access DRa03 (photograph, M. Stone)

Inscription 4754
Site Church of the Nativity, north door to crypt, #262
Technique scratched
Condition fair
Dimensions 1 x 1 cm.
Content crosses with inscription
Access DRa03 (photograph, M. Stone)

Inscription 4755
Site Church of the Nativity, north door to crypt, #262
Technique scratched
Condition poor
Content Armenian inscription
Access DRa03 (photograph, M. Stone)

Inscription 4756
Site Church of the Nativity, north door to crypt, #262
Technique scratched
Condition fair
Content Arabic inscription
Access DRa03 (photograph, M. Stone)

Inscription 4757
Site Church of the Nativity, north door to crypt, #262
Technique scratched
Condition poor
Content Greek inscription
Access DRa03 (photograph, M. Stone)

Inscription 4758
Site Church of the Nativity, north door to crypt, #262
Technique scratched
Condition poor
Content Armenian inscription
Limitation *Tentative decipherment only*
Access DRa03 (photograph, M. Stone)

Inscription 4759
Site Church of the Nativity, north door to crypt, #262
Technique scratched
Condition fair
Content crosses alone
Access DRa03 (photograph, M. Stone)

Inscription 4760
Site Church of the Nativity, north door to crypt, #262
Dating 1415
Technique scratched
Condition good
Dimensions 6 x 10 cm.
Content Armenian inscription
Limitation *Study only*
Access DRa03 (photograph, M. Stone)

Inscription 4761
Site Church of the Nativity, north door to crypt, #262
Technique scratched
Condition good
Dimensions 5 x 1 cm.
Content Latin inscription
Limitation *Tentative decipherment only*
Access DRa05 (photograph, M. Stone)

Inscription 4762
Site Church of the Nativity, north door to crypt, #262
Technique scratched
Condition poor
Content Arabic inscription
Limitation *Tentative decipherment only*
Access DRa05 (photograph, M. Stone)

Inscription 4763
Site Church of the Nativity, north door to crypt, #262
Technique scratched
Condition good
Dimensions 3 x 1 cm.
Content Latin inscription
Limitation *Tentative decipherment only*
Access DRa05 (photograph, M. Stone)

Inscription 4764
Site Church of the Nativity, north door to crypt, #262
Technique chiselled
Condition excellent
Dimensions 6.5 x 4.5 cm.
Content crosses alone
Access DRa05 (photograph, M. Stone)

Inscription 4765
Site Church of the Nativity, north door to crypt, #262
Technique scratched
Condition poor
Dimensions 6 x 1 cm.
Content unidentified inscription
Access DRa05 (photograph, M. Stone)

Inscription 4766
Site Church of the Nativity, north door to crypt, #262
Technique scratched
Condition poor
Content Greek inscription
Limitation *Tentative decipherment only*
Access DRa05 (photograph, M. Stone)

Inscription 4767
Site Church of the Nativity, north door to crypt, #262
Technique scratched
Condition good
Content crosses alone
Access DRa05 (photograph, M. Stone)

Inscription 4768
Site Church of the Nativity, north door to crypt, #262
Technique scratched
Condition excellent
Dimensions 8 x 11 cm.
Content crosses alone
Comment *group of crosses*
Access DRa09 (photograph, M. Stone)

Inscription 4769
Site Church of the Nativity, north door to crypt, #262
Technique scratched
Condition excellent
Content crosses alone
Access DRa09 (photograph, M. Stone)

Inscription 4770
Site Church of the Nativity, pillar D8, #274
Technique scratched
Condition excellent
Dimensions 15 x 3 cm.
Content Arabic inscription
Access DTb57-58 (photograph, M. Stone)

Inscription 4771
Site Church of the Nativity, pillar D8, #274
Technique scratched
Condition excellent
Content Arabic inscription
Access DTb57-58 (photograph, M. Stone)

Inscription 4772
Site Church of the Nativity, pillar D8, #274
Technique chiselled
Condition good
Content crosses alone
Access DTb57-58 (photograph, M. Stone)

Inscription 4773
Site Church of the Nativity, pillar B6, #264
Technique scratched
Condition poor
Dimensions 9 x 1 cm.
Content Armenian inscription
Access DRa17 (photograph, M. Stone)

Inscription 4774
Site Church of the Nativity, pillar B6, #264
Technique scratched
Condition fair
Content Armenian inscription
Limitation *Study only*
Access DRa17 (photograph, M. Stone)

Inscription 4775
Site Church of the Nativity, pillar B6, #264
Technique scratched
Condition poor
Content Greek inscription
Limitation *Tentative decipherment only*
Access DRa17 (photograph, M. Stone)

Inscription 4776
Site Church of the Nativity, pillar B6, #264
Technique scratched
Condition poor
Content Latin inscription
Limitation *Tentative decipherment only*
Access DRa17 (photograph, M. Stone)

Inscription 4777
Site Church of the Nativity, pillar B6, #264
Technique scratched
Condition poor
Content unidentified inscription
Access DRa17 (photograph, M. Stone)

Inscription 4778
Site Church of the Nativity, north door to crypt, #262
Technique scratched
Condition poor
Dimensions 7 x 4 cm.
Content unidentified inscription
Access DRa17 (photograph, M. Stone)

Inscription 4779
Site Church of the Nativity, north door to crypt, #262
Technique scratched
Condition poor
Content Arabic inscription
Access DRa17 (photograph, M. Stone)

Inscription 4780
Site Church of the Nativity, north door to crypt, #262
Technique scratched
Condition fair
Content crosses alone
Access DRa17 (photograph, M. Stone)

Inscription 4781
Site Church of the Nativity, north door to crypt, #262
Technique scratched
Condition poor
Content unidentified inscription
Access DRa17 (photograph, M. Stone)

Inscription 4782
Site Church of the Nativity, north door to crypt, #262
Technique scratched
Condition poor
Content unidentified inscription
Access DRa17 (photograph, M. Stone)

Inscription 4783
Site Church of the Nativity, north door to crypt, #262
Technique scratched
Condition poor
Content Latin inscription
Limitation *Tentative decipherment only*
Access DRa17 (photograph, M. Stone)

Inscription 4784
Site Church of the Nativity, north door to crypt, #262
Technique scratched
Condition poor
Content unidentified inscription
Access DRa17 (photograph, M. Stone)

Inscription 4785
Site Church of the Nativity, north door to crypt, #262
Technique scratched
Condition poor
Content Arabic inscription
Access DRa17 (photograph, M. Stone)

Inscription 4786
Site Church of the Nativity, north door to crypt, #262
Technique scratched
Condition fair
Content crosses alone
Access DRa17 (photograph, M. Stone)

Inscription 4787
Site Jebel Muneijat F, #63
Technique incised
Condition good
Content Nabatean inscription
Limitation *Tentative decipherment only*
Access BX24 (photograph, U. Avner)

Inscription 4788
Site Jebel Muneijat F, #63
Technique incised
Condition good
Content Nabatean inscription
Limitation *Tentative decipherment only*
Access BX04a (photograph, U. Avner)

Inscription 4789
Site Jebel Muneijat F, #63
Technique incised
Condition good
Content Nabatean inscription
Limitation *Tentative decipherment only*
Access BX05a (photograph, U. Avner)

Inscription 4790
Site Jebel Muneijat F, #63
Technique incised
Condition fair
Content Nabatean inscription
Limitation *Tentative decipherment only*
Access BX15 (photograph, U. Avner)

Inscription 4791
Site Jebel Muneijat F, #63
Technique incised
Condition fair
Content Nabatean inscription
Limitation *Tentative decipherment only*
Access BX28a (photograph, U. Avner)

Inscription 4792
Site Jebel Muneijat F, #63
Technique incised
Condition fair
Content Nabatean inscription
Limitation *Tentative decipherment only*
Access BX31a (photograph, U. Avner)

Inscription 4793
Site Jebel Muneijat F, #63
Technique incised
Condition fair
Content Nabatean inscription
Limitation *Tentative decipherment only*
Access BX19 (photograph, U. Avner)

Inscription **4794**
Site Jebel Muneijat F, #63
Technique incised
Condition poor
Content Nabatean inscription
Limitation *Tentative decipherment only*
Access BX20 (photograph, U. Avner)

Inscription **4795**
Site Jebel Muneijat F, #63
Technique incised
Condition fair
Content Nabatean inscription
Limitation *Tentative decipherment only*
Access BX28 (photograph, U. Avner)

Inscription **4796**
Site Jebel Muneijat F, #63
Technique incised
Condition poor
Content Nabatean inscription
Limitation *Tentative decipherment only*
Access BX28 (photograph, U. Avner)

Inscription **4797**
Site Jebel Muneijat F, #63
Technique incised
Condition fair
Content Nabatean inscription
Limitation *Tentative decipherment only*
Access BX32a (photograph, U. Avner)

Inscription **4798**
Site Jebel Muneijat F, #63
Technique incised
Condition poor
Content Nabatean inscription
Limitation *Tentative decipherment only*
Access BX23a (photograph, U. Avner)

Inscription **4799**
Site Jebel Muneijat F, #63
Technique incised
Condition poor
Content Nabatean inscription
Limitation *Tentative decipherment only*
Access BX33a (photograph, U. Avner)

Inscription **4800**
Site Jebel Muneijat F, #63
Technique incised
Condition poor
Content Nabatean inscription
Limitation *Tentative decipherment only*
Access BX04 (photograph, U. Avner)

Inscription **4801**
Site Jebel Muneijat F, #63
Technique incised
Condition poor
Content Nabatean inscription
Limitation *Tentative decipherment only*
Access BX02 (photograph, U. Avner)

Inscription **4802**
Site Jebel Muneijat F, #63
Technique incised
Condition fair
Content Nabatean inscription
Limitation *Tentative decipherment only*
Access BX09a (photograph, U. Avner)

Inscription **4803**
Site Jebel Muneijat F, #63
Technique incised
Condition poor
Content Nabatean inscription
Limitation *Tentative decipherment only*
Access BX17a (photograph, U. Avner)

Inscription **4804**
Site Jebel Muneijat F, #63
Technique incised
Condition poor
Content Nabatean inscription
Limitation *Tentative decipherment only*
Access BX15a (photograph, U. Avner); *see also* BX16

Inscription **4805**
Site Jebel Muneijat F, #63
Technique incised
Condition poor
Content Nabatean inscription
Limitation *Tentative decipherment only*
Access BX08a (photograph, U. Avner); *see also* BX10

Inscription **4806**
Site Jebel Muneijat F, #63
Technique incised
Condition poor
Content Nabatean inscription
Limitation *Tentative decipherment only*
Access BX27 (photograph, U. Avner)

Inscription **4807**
Site Jebel Muneijat F, #63
Technique incised
Condition poor
Content Nabatean inscription
Limitation *Tentative decipherment only*
Access BX07 (photograph, U. Avner); *see also* BX12

Inscription **4808**
Site Jebel Muneijat F, #63
Technique incised
Condition poor
Content Nabatean inscription
Limitation *Tentative decipherment only*
Access BX26 (photograph, U. Avner)

Inscription **4809**
Site Jebel Muneijat F, #63
Technique incised
Condition poor
Content Nabatean inscription
Limitation *Tentative decipherment only*
Access BX22 (photograph, U. Avner)

Inscription **4810**
Site Jebel Muneijat F, #63
Technique incised
Condition poor
Content rock drawing
Comment *bird?*
Access BX02a (photograph, U. Avner)

Inscription **4811**
Site Jebel Muneijat F, #63
Technique incised
Condition poor
Content rock drawing
Comment *fragments*
Access BX14 (photograph, U. Avner)

Inscription **4812**
Site Jebel Muneijat F, #63
Technique incised
Condition poor
Content Nabatean inscription
Limitation *Tentative decipherment only*
Access BX29 (photograph, U. Avner)

Inscription **4813**
Site Jebel Muneijat F, #63
Technique incised
Condition poor
Content Nabatean inscription
Limitation *Tentative decipherment only*
Access BX34a (photograph, U. Avner)

Inscription **4814**
Site Jebel Musa, Vale of Elijah, #29
Technique incised
Condition excellent
Content varied crosses
Access GL02 (photograph, Project)

Inscription **4815**
Site Church of the Nativity, pillar B6, #264
Technique scratched
Condition fair
Content Armenian inscription
Limitation *Study only*
Access DRb19 (photograph, M. Stone)

Inscription **4816**
Site Church of the Nativity, pillar B6, #264
Technique scratched
Condition poor
Content Armenian inscription
Limitation *Study only*
Access DRb19 (photograph, M. Stone)

Inscription **4817**
Site Church of the Nativity, pillar B6, #264
Technique scratched
Condition excellent
Content Armenian inscription
Limitation *Study only*
Access DRb19 (photograph, M. Stone)

Inscription **4818**
Site Church of the Nativity, pillar B6, #264
Technique scratched
Condition fair
Content Greek inscription
Limitation *Tentative decipherment only*
Access DRb19 (photograph, M. Stone)

Inscription **4819**
Site Church of the Nativity, pillar B6, #264
Technique scratched
Condition poor
Content Greek inscription
Limitation *Tentative decipherment only*
Access DRb19 (photograph, M. Stone)

Inscription **4820**
Site Church of the Nativity, pillar B6, #264
Technique scratched
Condition fair
Content Greek inscription
Limitation *Tentative decipherment only*
Access DRb19 (photograph, M. Stone)

Inscription **4821**
Site Wadi Haggag, #118
Technique incised
Condition excellent
Content rock drawing
Comment *camel*
Access EY14 (photograph, project)

Inscription **4822**
Site Church of the Nativity, pillar B6, #264
Technique scratched
Condition fair
Content Armenian inscription
Limitation *Study only*
Access DRb19 (photograph, M. Stone)

Inscription **4823**
Site Church of the Nativity, pillar B6, #264
Technique scratched
Condition fair
Content Armenian inscription
Limitation *Tentative decipherment only*
Access DRb19 (photograph, M. Stone)

Inscription **4824**
Site Church of the Nativity, pillar B6, #264
Technique scratched
Condition fair
Content Armenian inscription
Limitation *Tentative decipherment only*
Access DRb19 (photograph, M. Stone)

Inscription **4825**
Site Church of the Nativity, pillar B6, #264
Technique scratched
Condition fair
Content Greek inscription
Limitation *Tentative decipherment only*
Access DRb19 (photograph, M. Stone)

Inscription **4826**
Site Church of the Nativity, pillar B6, #264
Technique scratched
Condition poor
Content Arabic inscription
Access DRb19 (photograph, M. Stone)

Inscription **4827**
Site Church of the Nativity, pillar B6, #264
Technique scratched
Condition good
Content crosses alone
Access DRb19 (photograph, M. Stone)

Inscription **4828**
Site Church of the Nativity, pillar B6, #264
Technique punched
Condition fair
Content crosses alone
Access DRb19 (photograph, M. Stone)

Inscription **4829**
Site Church of the Nativity, pillar B6, #264
Technique scratched
Condition good
Content crosses alone
Access DRb19 (photograph, M. Stone)

Inscription **4830**
Site Wadi Umm Sidra, #174
Technique incised
Condition fair
Content rock drawing
Comment *animal*
Access FL35-35a (photograph, Project)

Inscription **4831**
Site Church of the Nativity, pillar B6, #264
Technique scratched
Condition excellent
Content crosses alone
Access DRb20 (photograph, M. Stone)

Inscription **4832**
Site Church of the Nativity, pillar B6, #264
Technique scratched
Condition good
Content Armenian inscription
Limitation *Study only*
Access DRb20 (photograph, M. Stone)

Inscription **4833**
Site Church of the Nativity, pillar B6, #264
Technique scratched
Condition fair
Content Armenian inscription
Limitation *Study only*
Access DRb20 (photograph, M. Stone)

Inscription **4834**
Site Church of the Nativity, pillar B6, #264
Technique scratched
Condition fair
Content Armenian inscription
Limitation *Study only*
Access DRb20 (photograph, M. Stone)

Inscription **4835**
Site Church of the Nativity, pillar B6, #264
Technique scratched
Condition excellent
Content crosses alone
Access DRb20 (photograph, M. Stone)

Inscription **4836**
Site Church of the Nativity, pillar B6, #264
Technique scratched
Condition fair
Content Armenian inscription
Limitation *Study only*
Access DRb20 (photograph, M. Stone)

Inscription **4837**
Site Church of the Nativity, pillar B6, #264
Technique scratched
Condition excellent
Content crosses alone
Access DRb20 (photograph, M. Stone)

Inscription **4838**
Site Church of the Nativity, pillar B6, #264
Technique scratched
Condition poor
Content unidentified inscription
Access DRb20 (photograph, M. Stone)

Inscription **4839**
Site Church of the Nativity, pillar B6, #264
Technique scratched
Condition poor
Content Armenian inscription
Comment *illegible*
Access DRb20 (photograph, M. Stone)

Inscription **4840**
Site Church of the Nativity, pillar B6, #264
Technique scratched
Condition good
Content crosses alone
Access DRb20 (photograph, M. Stone)

Inscription **4841**
Site Church of the Nativity, pillar B6, #264
Technique scratched
Condition poor
Content unidentified inscription
Access DRb20 (photograph, M. Stone)

Inscription **4842**
Site Church of the Nativity, pillar B6, #264
Technique scratched
Condition good
Content Armenian inscription
Limitation *Study only*
Access DRb21 (photograph, M. Stone); *see also* DRb22

Inscription **4843**
Site Church of the Nativity, pillar B6, #264
Technique scratched
Condition fair
Content Armenian inscription
Limitation *Study only*
Access DRb21 (photograph, M. Stone)

Inscription **4844**
Site Church of the Nativity, pillar B6, #264
Technique scratched
Condition good
Content Armenian inscription
Limitation *Study only*
Access DRb21 (photograph, M. Stone); *see also* DRb22

Inscription **4845**
Site Church of the Nativity, pillar B6, #264
Technique scratched
Condition poor
Content Armenian inscription
Limitation *Tentative decipherment only*
Access DRb21 (photograph, M. Stone)

Inscription **4846**
Site Church of the Nativity, pillar B6, #264
Technique scratched
Condition poor
Content Armenian inscription
Comment *illegible*
Access DRb21 (photograph, M. Stone)

Inscription **4847**
Site Church of the Nativity, pillar B6, #264
Technique scratched
Condition poor
Content Armenian inscription
Limitation *Tentative decipherment only*
Access DRb21 (photograph, M. Stone)

Inscription **4848**
Site Church of the Nativity, pillar B6, #264
Technique scratched
Condition poor
Content Armenian inscription
Comment *illegible*
Access DRb21 (photograph, M. Stone)

Inscription **4849**
Site Church of the Nativity, pillar B6, #264
Technique scratched
Condition good
Content Armenian inscription
Limitation *Tentative decipherment only*
Access DRb21 (photograph, M. Stone)

Inscription **4850**
Site Church of the Nativity, pillar B6, #264
Technique scratched
Condition poor
Content Armenian inscription
Comment *illegible*
Access DRb21 (photograph, M. Stone)

Inscription **4851**
Site Church of the Nativity, pillar B6, #264
Technique scratched
Condition fair
Content crosses with inscription
Access DRb21 (photograph, M. Stone)

Inscription **4852**
Site Church of the Nativity, pillar B6, #264
Technique scratched
Condition good
Content crosses alone
Access DRb21 (photograph, M. Stone)

Inscription **4853**
Site Church of the Nativity, pillar B6, #264
Technique scratched
Condition good
Content Armenian inscription
Limitation *Study only*
Access DRb22 (photograph, M. Stone)

Inscription **4854**
Site Church of the Nativity, pillar B6, #264
Technique scratched
Condition fair
Content Armenian inscription
Limitation *Tentative decipherment only*
Access DRb22 (photograph, M. Stone)

Inscription **4855**
Site Church of the Nativity, pillar B6, #264
Technique scratched
Condition fair
Content Georgian inscription
Access DRb22 (photograph, M. Stone)

Inscription **4856**
Site Church of the Nativity, pillar B6, #264
Technique scratched
Condition good
Content crosses alone
Access DRb22 (photograph, M. Stone)

Inscription **4857**
Site Church of the Nativity, pillar B6, #264
Technique scratched
Condition good
Content Armenian inscription
Limitation *Tentative decipherment only*
Access DRb22 (photograph, M. Stone)

Inscription **4858**
Site Church of the Nativity, pillar B6, #264
Technique scratched
Condition good
Content crosses alone
Access DRb22 (photograph, M. Stone)

Inscription **4859**
Site Church of the Nativity, pillar B6, #264
Technique scratched
Condition fair
Content Armenian inscription
Limitation *Study only*
Access DRb22 (photograph, M. Stone)

Inscription **4860**
Site Church of the Nativity, pillar B6, #264
Technique painted
Condition fair
Content Arabic inscription
Access DRb23 (photograph, M. Stone)

Inscription **4861**
Site Church of the Nativity, pillar B6, #264
Technique scratched
Condition fair
Content Armenian inscription
Limitation *Tentative decipherment only*
Access DRb23 (photograph, M. Stone)

Inscription **4862**
Site Church of the Nativity, pillar B6, #264
Technique painted
Condition good
Content English inscription
Limitation *Tentative decipherment only*
Access DRb23 (photograph, M. Stone)

Inscription **4863**
Site Church of the Nativity, pillar B6, #264
Technique scratched
Condition fair
Content Armenian inscription
Access DRb23 (photograph, M. Stone)

Inscription **4864**
Site Church of the Nativity, pillar B6, #264
Technique scratched
Condition poor
Content Greek inscription
Limitation *Tentative decipherment only*
Access DRb23 (photograph, M. Stone)

Inscription **4865**
Site Church of the Nativity, pillar B6, #264
Technique painted
Condition poor
Content Armenian inscription
Access DRb24 (photograph, M. Stone)

Inscription **4866**
Site Church of the Nativity, pillar B6, #264
Technique scratched
Condition poor
Content Arabic inscription
Access DRb24 (photograph, M. Stone)

Inscription **4867**
Site Church of the Nativity, pillar B6, #264
Technique scratched
Condition poor
Content Arabic inscription
Access DRb24 (photograph, M. Stone)

Inscription **4868**
Site Church of the Nativity, pillar B6, #264
Technique scratched
Condition poor
Content Latin inscription
Access DRb24 (photograph, M. Stone)

Inscription **4869**
Site Church of the Nativity, pillar B6, #264
Technique scratched
Condition poor
Content unidentified inscription
Access DRb24 (photograph, M. Stone)

Inscription **4870**
Site Church of the Nativity, pillar B6, #264
Technique scratched
Condition poor
Content Arabic inscription
Access DRb24 (photograph, M. Stone); *see also* DRb25

Inscription **4871**
Site Church of the Nativity, pillar B6, #264
Technique scratched
Condition poor
Content Latin inscription
Limitation *Tentative decipherment only*
Access DRb25 (photograph, M. Stone)

Inscription **4872**
Site Church of the Nativity, pillar B6, #264
Technique scratched
Condition poor
Content Latin inscription
Access DRb25 (photograph, M. Stone)

Inscription **4873**
Site Church of the Nativity, pillar B6, #264
Technique scratched
Condition poor
Content Latin inscription
Limitation *Tentative decipherment only*
Access DRb25 (photograph, M. Stone)

Inscription **4874**
Site Church of the Nativity, pillar B6, #264
Technique scratched
Condition poor
Content Arabic inscription
Access DRb25 (photograph, M. Stone)

Inscription **4875**
Site Church of the Nativity, pillar B6, #264
Technique scratched
Condition poor
Content Latin inscription
Limitation *Tentative decipherment only*
Access DRb25 (photograph, M. Stone)

Inscription **4876**
Site Church of the Nativity, pillar B6, #264
Technique scratched
Condition poor
Content Greek inscription
Limitation *Tentative decipherment only*
Access DRb25 (photograph, M. Stone); *see also* DRb24

Inscription **4877**
Site Church of the Nativity, pillar B6, #264
Technique scratched
Condition poor
Content unidentified signs
Access DRb25 (photograph, M. Stone)

Inscription **4878**
Site Church of the Nativity, pillar B6, #264
Technique scratched
Condition good
Content Armenian inscription
Limitation *Study only*
Access DRb26 (photograph, M. Stone)

Inscription **4879**
Site Church of the Nativity, pillar B6, #264
Technique scratched
Condition poor
Content Arabic inscription
Access DRb26 (photograph, M. Stone)

Inscription **4880**
Site Church of the Nativity, pillar B6, #264
Technique scratched
Condition poor
Content unidentified inscription
Access DRb26 (photograph, M. Stone)

Inscription **4881**
Site Church of the Nativity, pillar B6, #264
Technique scratched
Condition good
Content crosses alone
Access DRb26 (photograph, M. Stone)

Inscription **4882**
Site Church of the Nativity, pillar B6, #264
Technique scratched
Condition good
Content crosses alone
Access DRb26 (photograph, M. Stone)

Inscription **4883**
Site Church of the Nativity, pillar B6, #264
Technique scratched
Condition fair
Content unidentified signs
Access DRb26 (photograph, M. Stone)

Inscription **4884**
Site Church of the Nativity, pillar B6, #264
Technique scratched
Condition poor
Content unidentified inscription
Access DRb26 (photograph, M. Stone)

Inscription **4885**
Site Church of the Nativity, pillar B6, #264
Technique scratched
Condition poor
Content unidentified inscription
Access DRb26 (photograph, M. Stone)

Inscription **4886**
Site Church of the Nativity, pillar B6, #264
Technique scratched
Condition poor
Content unidentified signs
Access DRb26 (photograph, M. Stone)

Inscription **4887**
Site Church of the Nativity, pillar B6, #264
Technique scratched
Condition poor
Content Greek inscription
Access DRb26 (photograph, M. Stone)

Inscription **4888**
Site Church of the Nativity, pillar B6, #264
Technique scratched
Condition excellent
Content English inscription
Limitation *Tentative decipherment only*
Access DRb26 (photograph, M. Stone)

Inscription **4889**
Site Church of the Nativity, pillar B6, #264
Technique scratched
Condition poor
Content Greek inscription
Limitation *Tentative decipherment only*
Access DRb26 (photograph, M. Stone)

Inscription **4890**
Site Church of the Nativity, pillar B6, #264
Technique scratched
Condition fair
Content crosses with inscription
Access DRb26 (photograph, M. Stone)

Inscription **4891**
Site Church of the Nativity, pillar B5, #265
Technique scratched
Condition good
Content Armenian inscription
Limitation *Study only*
Access DRb27 (photograph, M. Stone)

Inscription **4892**
Site Church of the Nativity, pillar B5, #265
Technique scratched
Condition poor
Content Latin inscription
Limitation *Tentative decipherment only*
Access DRb28 (photograph, M. Stone)

Inscription **4893**
Site Church of the Nativity, pillar B5, #265
Technique scratched
Condition fair
Content Latin inscription
Limitation *Tentative decipherment only*
Access DRb30 (photograph, M. Stone); *see also* DRb32

Inscription **4894**
Site Church of the Nativity, pillar B5, #265
Technique scratched
Condition poor
Content Arabic inscription
Access DRb30 (photograph, M. Stone); *see also* DRb32, DRb33

Inscription **4895**
Site Church of the Holy Sepulchre, St. Helena Chapel 1, #292
Technique scratched
Condition good
Content Arabic inscription
Access FH07-08 (photograph, Project)

Inscription **4896**
Site Church of the Holy Sepulchre, St. Helena Chapel 1, #292
Technique scratched
Condition fair
Content Arabic inscription
Access FH07-08 (photograph, Project)

Inscription **4897**
Site Wadi Haggag, #118
Technique scratched
Condition fair
Content crosses alone
Access CQ74 (photograph, Z. Radovan)

Inscription **4898**
Site Wadi Mukatab, #64
Technique scratched
Condition good
Content rock drawing
Comment *animals*
Access CS59 (photograph, Z. Radovan)

Inscription **4899**
Site A-Tor, #101
Technique scratched
Condition fair
Content Greek inscription
Limitation *Tentative decipherment only*
Access CT08 (photograph, A. Goren)

Inscription **4900**
Site Wadi Sug, #205
Technique scratched
Condition poor
Content Arabic inscription
Access CT06 (photograph, A. Goren)

Inscription **4901**
Site Santa Katarina, #10
Technique chiselled
Condition good
Content crosses alone
Access AGd34-35 (photograph, M. Stone); *see also* FE20

Inscription **4902**
Site Qunteilat Ajrud, #211
Technique scratched
Condition poor
Content Greek inscription
Limitation *Tentative decipherment only*
Access DN29 (photograph, A. Goren)

Inscription **4903**
Site Wadi Baba, Baba 1, #190
Condition good
Content geology
Access DJ60-61 (photograph, A. Goren); *see also* DJ62-63

Inscription **4904**
Site Wadi Baba, Baba 1, #190
Condition good
Content geology
Access DJ58-59 (photograph, A. Goren); *see also* DJ56-57

Inscription **4905**
Site Ostrakine, #208
Technique painted
Condition poor
Content rock drawing
Comment *elaborately incised circles or round frames*
Access DG02-03 (photograph, Y. Tsafrir); *see also* DG06-07

Inscription **4906**
Site Sinai, #0
Technique scratched
Condition poor
Content Nabatean inscription
Limitation *Tentative decipherment only*
Access DM14a-15 (photograph, A. Goren)

Inscription **4907**
Site Sinai, #0
Technique painted
Condition poor
Content rock drawing
Comment *circle with line*
Access DM14a-15 (photograph, A. Goren)

Inscription **4908**
Site Sinai, #0
Technique scratched
Condition poor
Content unidentified signs
Access DM14a-15 (photograph, A. Goren)

Inscription **4909**
Site Jebel Muneijat F, #63
Technique scratched
Condition poor
Content rock drawing
Comment *animals*
Access BX21a (photograph, U. Avner)

Inscription **4910**
Site Jebel Muneijat F, #63
Technique scratched
Condition poor
Content Nabatean inscription
Access BX25 (photograph, U. Avner)

Inscription **4911**
Site Jebel Muneijat F, #63
Technique scratched
Condition poor
Content Nabatean inscription
Access BX30 (photograph, U. Avner)

Inscription **4912**
Site Sinai, #0
Technique scratched
Condition poor
Content Nabatean inscription
Limitation *Tentative decipherment only*
Access DM15a-16 (photograph, A. Goren)

Inscription **4913**
Site Sinai, #0
Technique scratched
Condition fair
Content Nabatean inscription
Limitation *Tentative decipherment only*
Access DM15a-16 (photograph, A. Goren)

Inscription **4914**
Site Sinai, #0
Technique scratched
Condition poor
Content Nabatean inscription
Access DM15a-16 (photograph, A. Goren)

Inscription **4915**
Site Sinai, #0
Technique scratched
Condition poor
Content Arabic inscription
Access DM16a-17 (photograph, A. Goren)

Inscription **4916**
Site Sinai, #0
Technique scratched
Condition poor
Content Arabic inscription
Access DM16a-17 (photograph, A. Goren)

Inscription **4917**
Site Sinai, #0
Technique scratched
Condition poor
Content Arabic inscription
Access DM17a-18 (photograph, A. Goren)

Inscription **4918**
Site Sinai, #0
Technique scratched
Condition poor
Content unidentified inscription
Access DM17a-18 (photograph, A. Goren)

Inscription **4919**
Site Sinai, #0
Technique scratched
Condition poor
Content unidentified signs
Access DM17a-18 (photograph, A. Goren)

Inscription **4920**
Site Sinai, #0
Technique scratched
Condition poor
Content Nabatean inscription
Limitation *Tentative decipherment only*
Access DL15 (photograph, A. Goren); *see also* DL19, DM18a-19

Inscription **4921**
Site Sinai, #0
Technique scratched
Condition poor
Content Nabatean inscription
Access DL15 (photograph, A. Goren); *see also* DL19, DM18a-19

Inscription **4922**
Site Sinai, #0
Technique scratched
Condition poor
Content Nabatean inscription
Access DL15 (photograph, A. Goren); *see also* DL19, DM18a-19

Inscription **4923**
Site Sinai, #0
Technique scratched
Condition poor
Content Nabatean inscription
Access DL15 (photograph, A. Goren); *see also* DL19, DM18a-19

Inscription **4924**
Site Church of the Holy Sepulchre, #375
Technique incised
Condition good
Dimensions 9 x 5 cm.
Content Armenian inscription
Limitation *Tentative decipherment only*
Access FG31-32 (photograph, Project)

Inscription **4925**
Site Church of the Holy Sepulchre, #375
Technique scratched
Condition poor
Dimensions 3 x 2 cm.
Content unidentified signs
Access FG31-32 (photograph, Project)

Inscription **4926**
Site Church of the Holy Sepulchre, #375
Technique scratched
Condition fair
Dimensions 5 x 1 cm.
Content Syriac inscription
Limitation *Tentative decipherment only*
Access FG31-32 (photograph, Project)

Inscription **4927**
Site Church of the Holy Sepulchre, #375
Technique incised
Condition poor
Dimensions 9 x 1.5 cm.
Content Armenian inscription
Limitation *Tentative decipherment only*
Access FG31-32 (photograph, Project)

Inscription **4928**
Site Church of the Holy Sepulchre, #375
Technique incised
Condition poor
Dimensions 4 x 1 cm.
Content unidentified inscription
Access FG31-32 (photograph, Project)

Inscription **4929**
Site Church of the Holy Sepulchre, #375
Technique incised
Condition good
Content crosses alone
Access FG31-32 (photograph, Project)

Inscription **4930**
Site Church of the Holy Sepulchre, #375
Technique scratched
Condition good
Dimensions 2 x 1 cm.
Content English inscription
Limitation *Tentative decipherment only*
Access FG31-32 (photograph, Project)

Inscription **4931**
Site Wadi Biraq, #79
Technique incised
Condition excellent
Content rock drawing
Comment *camel with rider*
Access EZ33 (photograph, Project)

Inscription **4932**
Site Wadi Biraq, #79
Technique scratched
Condition poor
Dimensions 70 x 40 cm.
Content rock drawing
Access EZ34 (photograph, Project); *see also* EX03, EZ35

Inscription **4933**
Site Wadi Biraq, #79
Technique scratched
Condition poor
Content unidentified signs
Comment *parallel lines*
Access EZ34 (photograph, Project); *see also* EX03, EZ35

Inscription **4934**
Site Qunteilat Ajrud, #211
Technique scratched
Condition excellent
Content Nabatean inscription
Limitation *Tentative decipherment only*
Access DN30 (photograph, A. Goren)

Inscription **4935**
Site Qunteilat Ajrud, #211
Technique scratched
Condition fair
Content Nabatean inscription
Limitation *Tentative decipherment only*
Access DN30 (photograph, A. Goren)

Inscription **4936**
Site Qunteilat Ajrud, #211
Technique scratched
Condition fair
Content Nabatean inscription
Limitation *Tentative decipherment only*
Access DN30 (photograph, A. Goren)

Inscription 4937
Site Qunteilat Ajrud, #211
Technique scratched
Condition fair
Content Nabatean inscription
Limitation *Tentative decipherment only*
Access DN30 (photograph, A. Goren)

Inscription 4938
Site Qunteilat Ajrud, #211
Technique scratched
Condition good
Content Nabatean inscription
Limitation *Tentative decipherment only*
Access DN30 (photograph, A. Goren)

Inscription 4939
Site Qunteilat Ajrud, #211
Technique scratched
Condition poor
Content Nabatean inscription
Access DN30 (photograph, A. Goren)

Inscription 4940
Site Qunteilat Ajrud, #211
Technique scratched
Condition excellent
Content rock drawing
Comment *hunters with bows and arrows pursuing animals*
Access DN30 (photograph, A. Goren)

Inscription 4941
Site Qunteilat Ajrud, #211
Technique scratched
Condition good
Content rock drawing
Comment *line drawing of a horse's head*
Access DN30 (photograph, A. Goren)

Inscription 4942
Site Qunteilat Ajrud, #211
Technique scratched
Condition excellent
Content rock drawing
Comment *human with bow and arrow*
Access DN30 (photograph, A. Goren)

Inscription 4943
Site Wadi Tueiba, #226
Technique scratched
Condition good
Content rock drawing
Comment *animal and human figures*
Access FE22 (photograph, Project)

Inscription 4944
Site Qunteilat Ajrud, #211
Technique scratched
Condition fair
Content Nabatean inscription
Limitation *Tentative decipherment only*
Access DN31 (photograph, A. Goren)

Inscription 4945
Site Qunteilat Ajrud, #211
Technique scratched
Condition poor
Content Nabatean inscription
Limitation *Tentative decipherment only*
Access DN31 (photograph, A. Goren)

Inscription 4946
Site Qunteilat Ajrud, #211
Technique scratched
Condition fair
Content Greek inscription
Limitation *Tentative decipherment only*
Access DN31 (photograph, A. Goren)

Inscription 4947
Site Qunteilat Ajrud, #211
Technique incised
Condition good
Content rock drawing
Comment *animal*
Access DN31 (photograph, A. Goren)

Inscription 4948
Site A-Tor, Bir Abu Sueira, #191
Technique scratched
Condition poor
Content Greek inscription
Limitation *Tentative decipherment only*
Access CT30 (photograph, A. Goren); *see also* CT38

Inscription 4949
Site A-Tor, Bir Abu Sueira, #191
Technique scratched
Condition poor
Content unidentified signs
Access CT30 (photograph, A. Goren); *see also* CT38

Inscription 4950
Site A-Tor, Bir Abu Sueira, #191
Technique scratched
Condition poor
Content unidentified signs
Access CT30 (photograph, A. Goren); *see also* CT38

Inscription 4951
Site Sinai, #0
Technique scratched
Condition fair
Content Arabic inscription
Access DC25-26 (photograph, A. Goren)

Inscription 4952
Site Sinai, #0
Technique scratched
Condition good
Content crosses with inscription
Access DC25-26 (photograph, A. Goren)

Inscription **4953**
Site Sinai, #0
Technique scratched
Condition good
Content unidentified signs
Access DC25-26 (photograph, A. Goren)

Inscription **4954**
Site Sinai, #0
Technique incised
Condition fair
Content rock drawing
Comment *straight lines*
Access DC25-26 (photograph, A. Goren)

Inscription **4955**
Site Sinai, #0
Technique scratched
Condition poor
Content rock drawing
Comment *cross?*
Access DC25-26 (photograph, A. Goren)

Inscription **4956**
Site Church of the Nativity, approach to St James, #271
Technique chiselled
Condition poor
Content Armenian inscription
Access DTa19-20 (photograph, M. Stone)

Inscription **4957**
Site Church of the Nativity, approach to St James, #271
Technique chiselled
Condition fair
Content crosses with inscription
Access DTa19-20 (photograph, M. Stone)

Inscription **4958**
Site Sinai, #0
Technique incised
Condition poor
Content Arabic inscription
Access DM12a-13 (photograph, A. Goren)

Inscription **4959**
Site Sinai, #0
Technique painted
Condition poor
Content Hebrew inscription
Comment *ostrakon*
Access DP44-45 (photograph, A. Goren)

Inscription **4960**
Site Ostrakine, #208
Technique incised
Condition poor
Content Greek inscription
Limitation *Tentative decipherment only*
Access DG24-25 (photograph, Y. Tsafrir)

Inscription **4961**
Site Ostrakine, #208
Technique scratched
Condition poor
Content unidentified inscription
Access DG24-25 (photograph, Y. Tsafrir)

Inscription **4962**
Site Ostrakine, #208
Technique scratched
Condition poor
Content Nabatean inscription
Limitation *Tentative decipherment only*
Access DL20 (photograph, A. Goren)

Inscription **4963**
Site Ostrakine, #208
Technique scratched
Condition poor
Content unidentified inscription
Access DL14 (photograph, A. Goren); *see also* DM21a-22

Inscription **4964**
Site Jebel Muneijat F, #63
Technique incised
Condition poor
Content unidentified inscription
Access BX20a (photograph, U. Avner)

Inscription **4965**
Site Ostrakine, #208
Technique scratched
Condition poor
Content crosses alone
Access DL17 (photograph, A. Goren); *see also* DM08a-09

Inscription **4966**
Site Ostrakine, #208
Technique scratched
Condition poor
Content unidentified signs
Access DL17 (photograph, A. Goren); *see also* DM08a-09

Inscription **4967**
Site Sinai, #0
Technique painted
Condition poor
Content Latin inscription
Access DP62-63 (photograph, A. Goren)

Inscription **4968**
Site Ostrakine, #208
Technique scratched
Condition poor
Content rock drawing
Comment *animals*
Access DL11 (photograph, A. Goren)

Inscription **4969**
Site Ostrakine, #208
Technique painted
Condition poor
Content rock drawing
Comment *obscure*
Access CX70-71 (photograph, A. Goren); *see also* DG04-05, DG08-09

Inscription **4970**
Site Sinai, #0
Technique scratched
Condition fair
Content Arabic inscription
Access CR10 (photograph, Z. Radovan)

Inscription **4971**
Site Wadi Haggag, Wadi Haggag, #125
Technique scratched
Condition poor
Content Nabatean inscription
Limitation *Tentative decipherment only*
Access CP62 (photograph, Z. Radovan)

Inscription **4972**
Site Wadi Haggag, Wadi Haggag, #125
Technique scratched
Condition poor
Content Nabatean inscription
Access CP62 (photograph, Z. Radovan)

Inscription **4973**
Site Wadi Haggag, Wadi Haggag, #125
Technique scratched
Condition poor
Content unidentified inscription
Access CP62 (photograph, Z. Radovan)

Inscription **4974**
Site Wadi Haggag, Wadi Haggag, #125
Technique scratched
Condition fair
Content encircled crosses
Access CP62 (photograph, Z. Radovan)

Inscription **4975**
Site Wadi Haggag, Wadi Haggag, #125
Technique scratched
Condition poor
Content rock drawing
Comment *lines*
Access CP62 (photograph, Z. Radovan)

Inscription **4976**
Site Wadi Haggag, Wadi Haggag, #125
Technique scratched
Condition poor
Content Nabatean inscription
Access CP62 (photograph, Z. Radovan)

Inscription **4977**
Site Church of the Nativity, pillar D9, #273
Technique scratched
Condition good
Content Latin inscription
Limitation *Tentative decipherment only*
Access DTb55-56 (photograph, M. Stone)

Inscription **4978**
Site Church of the Nativity, pillar D9, #273
Technique scratched
Condition good
Content unidentified signs
Access DTb55-56 (photograph, M. Stone)

Inscription **4979**
Site Church of the Nativity, pillar D9, #273
Technique scratched
Condition good
Content crosses alone
Access DTb55-56 (photograph, M. Stone)

Inscription **4980**
Site Church of the Nativity, pillar D9, #273
Technique scratched
Condition poor
Content unidentified inscription
Access DTb55-56 (photograph, M. Stone)

Inscription **4981**
Site Church of the Nativity, pillar D9, #273
Technique scratched
Condition poor
Content Arabic inscription
Access DTb55-56 (photograph, M. Stone)

Inscription **4982**
Site Church of the Nativity, pillar D9, #273
Technique scratched
Condition fair
Content crosses alone
Access DTb55-56 (photograph, M. Stone)

Inscription **4983**
Site Church of the Nativity, pillar D9, #273
Technique scratched
Condition poor
Content Arabic inscription
Access DTb55-56 (photograph, M. Stone)

Inscription **4984**
Site Church of the Nativity, pillar D9, #273
Technique scratched
Condition poor
Content unidentified inscription
Access DTb55-56 (photograph, M. Stone)

Inscription **4985**
Site Church of the Nativity, pillar D9, #273
Technique scratched
Condition poor
Content crosses alone
Access DTb55-56 (photograph, M. Stone)

Inscription **4986**
Site Wadi Tueiba, #226
Technique scratched
Condition fair
Content Arabic inscription
Access BV14 (photograph, U. Avner); *see also* CF22

Inscription **4987**
Site Wadi Tueiba, #226
Technique punched
Condition fair
Content Greek inscription
Limitation *Tentative decipherment only*
Access BV15 (photograph, U. Avner)

Inscription **4988**
Site Wadi Tueiba, #226
Technique scratched
Condition good
Content rock drawing
Comment *humans, animals*
Access CD05-06 (photograph, U. Avner); *see also* CE17

Inscription **4989**
Site Wadi Tueiba, #226
Technique scratched
Condition fair
Content Nabatean inscription
Limitation *Tentative decipherment only*
Access CE15 (photograph, U. Avner)

Inscription **4990**
Site Wadi Tueiba, #226
Technique scratched
Condition fair
Content Greek inscription
Limitation *Tentative decipherment only*
Access CE15 (photograph, U. Avner)

Inscription **4991**
Site Wadi Tueiba, #226
Technique scratched
Condition poor
Content Greek inscription
Limitation *Tentative decipherment only*
Access CE15 (photograph, U. Avner)

Inscription **4992**
Site Wadi Tueiba, #226
Technique scratched
Condition fair
Content rock drawing
Comment *ibexes*
Access CE16 (photograph, U. Avner)

Inscription **4993**
Site Wadi Tueiba, #226
Technique scratched
Condition poor
Content Greek inscription
Limitation *Tentative decipherment only*
Access CF09 (photograph, U. Avner); *see also* CF15, CU29a-30, CU30a-31

Inscription **4994**
Site Wadi Tueiba, #226
Technique punched
Condition poor
Content Greek inscription
Limitation *Tentative decipherment only*
Access CF15 (photograph, U. Avner); *see also* CF09, CU29a-30, CU30a-31

Inscription **4995**
Site Wadi Tueiba, #226
Technique scratched
Condition fair
Content Arabic inscription
Access CF16 (photograph, U. Avner)

Inscription **4996**
Site Wadi Tueiba, #226
Technique scratched
Condition poor
Content Arabic inscription
Access CF16 (photograph, U. Avner)

Inscription **4997**
Site Wadi Tueiba, #226
Technique painted
Condition poor
Content rock drawing
Comment *horse with rider*
Access CF16 (photograph, U. Avner)

Inscription **4998**
Site Ein Hudra, #117
Technique incised
Condition good
Dimensions 90 x 50 cm.
Content rock drawing
Comment *camel*
Access EX24 (photograph, Project)

Inscription **4999**
Site Wadi Tueiba, #226
Technique scratched
Condition fair
Content Arabic inscription
Access CF22 (photograph, U. Avner)

Inscription **5000**
Site Wadi Tueiba, #226
Technique incised
Condition excellent
Content rock drawing
Comment *human figure*
Access CF24 (photograph, U. Avner)

Inscription **5001**
Site Wadi Tueiba, #226
Technique incised
Condition excellent
Content rock drawing
Comment *wolf*
Access CF25 (photograph, U. Avner)

Inscription **5002**
Site Wadi Tueiba, #226
Technique incised
Condition good
Content rock drawing
Comment *two warriors, one on horseback raising a spear, the other on foot armed with a small round shield and a weapon*
Access CF29 (photograph, U. Avner); *see also* CJ08

Inscription **5003**
Site Wadi Tueiba, #226
Technique incised
Condition good
Content crosses alone
Access CF29 (photograph, U. Avner); *see also* CJ08

Inscription **5004**
Site Wadi Tueiba, #226
Technique incised
Condition poor
Content rock drawing
Comment *ship with mast*
Access CG01 (photograph, U. Avner)

Inscription **5005**
Site Wadi Tueiba, #226
Technique incised
Condition excellent
Content unidentified inscription
Access CG04 (photograph, U. Avner)

Inscription **5006**
Site Wadi Umm Sidra, #174
Technique punched
Condition poor
Content Arabic inscription
Access CG07a (photograph, U. Avner)

Inscription **5007**
Site Wadi Umm Sidra, #174
Technique incised
Condition fair
Content unidentified inscription
Access CG09a (photograph, U. Avner)

Inscription **5008**
Site Wadi Umm Sidra, #174
Technique incised
Condition poor
Content unidentified signs
Access CG09a (photograph, U. Avner)

Inscription **5009**
Site Wadi Umm Sidra, #174
Technique incised
Condition poor
Content Arabic inscription
Access CG09a (photograph, U. Avner)

Inscription **5010**
Site Wadi Biraq, #79
Technique incised
Condition excellent
Content rock drawing
Comment *camels*
Access EZ10 (photograph, Project); *see also* EZ11, EZ16, EZ17

Inscription **5011**
Site Wadi Biraq, #79
Technique incised
Condition good
Content rock drawing
Comment *camels*
Access EZ10 (photograph, Project); *see also* EZ11

Inscription **5012**
Site Wadi Biraq, #79
Technique incised
Condition poor
Content unidentified signs
Access EZ10 (photograph, Project); *see also* EZ11

Inscription **5013**
Site Wadi Biraq, #79
Technique incised
Condition poor
Content unidentified signs
Access EZ10 (photograph, Project); *see also* EZ11

Inscription **5014**
Site Wadi Biraq, #79
Technique incised
Condition poor
Content unidentified signs
Access EZ10 (photograph, Project); *see also* EZ11

Inscription **5015**
Site Wadi Tueiba, #226
Technique incised
Condition good
Content Nabatean inscription
Access CG14 (photograph, U. Avner)

Inscription **5016**
Site Wadi Tueiba, #226
Technique incised
Condition excellent
Content Arabic inscription
Access CG16 (photograph, U. Avner)

Inscription **5017**
Site Wadi Tueiba, #226
Technique incised
Condition good
Content rock drawing
Comment *animals*
Access CG16 (photograph, U. Avner)

Inscription 5018
Site Wadi Tueiba, #226
Technique incised
Condition excellent
Content Arabic inscription
Access CG16 (photograph, U. Avner)

Inscription 5019
Site Wadi Tueiba, #226
Technique incised
Condition good
Content Nabatean inscription
Limitation *Tentative decipherment only*
Access CG19 (photograph, U. Avner)

Inscription 5020
Site Ras el Jundi, Qalᶜat el Jundi, #212
Technique incised
Condition good
Content rock drawing
Comment *animals*
Access EO09 (photograph, Z. Meshel)

Inscription 5021
Site Wadi Tueiba, #226
Technique incised
Condition good
Content crosses alone
Access CG19 (photograph, U. Avner)

Inscription 5022
Site Ras el Jundi, Qalᶜat el Jundi, #212
Technique incised
Condition good
Content rock drawing
Comment *ibexes*
Access EO09 (photograph, Z. Meshel)

Inscription 5023
Site Wadi Tueiba, #226
Technique incised
Condition good
Content crosses alone
Access CG19 (photograph, U. Avner)

Inscription 5024
Site Wadi Tueiba, #226
Technique incised
Condition good
Content crosses alone
Access CG19 (photograph, U. Avner)

Inscription 5025
Site Wadi Tueiba, #226
Technique scratched
Condition poor
Content unidentified signs
Access CG19 (photograph, U. Avner)

Inscription 5026
Site Wadi Tueiba, #226
Technique incised
Condition good
Content Nabatean inscription
Limitation *Tentative decipherment only*
Access CG32 (photograph, U. Avner); *see also* CG38, CG39, CH15

Inscription 5027
Site Wadi Tueiba, #226
Technique incised
Condition good
Content crosses with inscription
Access CG32 (photograph, U. Avner); *see also* CG38, CG39, CH15

Inscription 5028
Site Wadi Tueiba, #226
Technique incised
Condition poor
Content unidentified signs
Access CG32 (photograph, U. Avner); *see also* CG38, CG39, CH15

Inscription 5029
Site Wadi Tueiba, #226
Technique incised
Condition fair
Content Arabic inscription
Access CG33 (photograph, U. Avner)

Inscription 5030
Site Wadi Tueiba, #226
Technique incised
Condition poor
Content Arabic inscription
Access CG33 (photograph, U. Avner)

Inscription 5031
Site Wadi Tueiba, #226
Technique incised
Condition fair
Content Arabic inscription
Access CG34 (photograph, U. Avner)

Inscription 5032
Site Wadi Tueiba, #226
Technique incised
Condition good
Content Arabic inscription
Access CG34 (photograph, U. Avner)

Inscription 5033
Site Wadi Tueiba, #226
Technique incised
Condition poor
Content unidentified signs
Access CG34 (photograph, U. Avner)

Inscription **5034**
Site Sinai, #0
Technique incised
Condition good
Dimensions 52 x 10 cm.
Content Arabic inscription
Access ECi/7 (photograph, U. Avner)

Inscription **5035**
Site Sinai, #0
Technique incised
Condition fair
Dimensions 32 x 12 cm.
Content Arabic inscription
Access ECi/7 (photograph, U. Avner)

Inscription **5036**
Site Sinai, #0
Technique incised
Condition poor
Dimensions 16 x 8 cm.
Content unidentified signs
Access ECi/7 (photograph, U. Avner)

Inscription **5037**
Site Sinai, #0
Technique incised
Condition poor
Dimensions 6 x 6 cm.
Content unidentified signs
Access ECi/7 (photograph, U. Avner)

Inscription **5038**
Site Wadi Umm Sidra, #174
Technique incised
Condition good
Content rock drawing
Comment *pair of scissors; squares, animals*
Access CG36 (photograph, U. Avner)

Inscription **5039**
Site Wadi Umm Sidra, #174
Technique incised
Condition excellent
Content Nabatean inscription
Limitation *Tentative decipherment only*
Access CG37 (photograph, U. Avner); *see also* FL32-32a

Inscription **5040**
Site Wadi Umm Sidra, #174
Technique incised
Condition excellent
Content Nabatean inscription
Limitation *Tentative decipherment only*
Access CG37 (photograph, U. Avner); *see also* FL32-32a

Inscription **5041**
Site Wadi Tueiba, #226
Technique incised
Condition fair
Content Nabatean inscription
Limitation *Tentative decipherment only*
Access CG40 (photograph, U. Avner); *see also* FR03

Inscription **5042**
Site Wadi Tueiba, #226
Technique punched
Condition poor
Content Latin inscription
Limitation *Tentative decipherment only*
Access CG40 (photograph, U. Avner); *see also* FR03

Inscription **5043**
Site Wadi Umm Sidra, #174
Technique incised
Condition excellent
Content Greek inscription
Limitation *Tentative decipherment only*
Access FK56-57 (photograph, Project); *see also* FK72-73, FL58-58a

---

Inscription **5044**
Site Wadi Umm Sidra, #174
Technique incised
Condition fair
Content English inscription
Limitation *Tentative decipherment only*
Access CI02 (photograph, U. Avner); *see also* FK58-59, FK72-73

Inscription **5045**
Site Wadi Umm Sidra, #174
Technique incised
Condition excellent
Content rock drawing
Comment *seven-branched candelabrum with curved branches*
Access CI02 (photograph, U. Avner); *see also* FK58, FK72-73

Inscription **5046**
Site Wadi Umm Sidra, #174
Technique incised
Condition good
Content rock drawing
Comment *horse with rider*
Access CH02 (photograph, U. Avner)

Inscription **5047**
Site Wadi Umm Sidra, #174
Technique incised
Condition poor
Content unidentified inscription
Access CI02 (photograph, U. Avner); *see also* FK72-73

Inscription **5048**
Site Wadi Umm Sidra, #174
Technique incised
Condition excellent
Content crosses alone
Access CI02 (photograph, U. Avner); *see also* FK72-73

Inscription **5049**
Site Wadi Umm Sidra, #174
Technique scratched
Condition poor
Content Nabatean inscription
Limitation *Tentative decipherment only*
Access CH02 (photograph, U. Avner)

Inscription **5050**
Site Wadi Umm Sidra, #174
Technique punched
Condition good
Content Nabatean inscription
Limitation *Tentative decipherment only*
Access CH03 (photograph, U. Avner); *see also* FK05, FL06-06a

---

Inscription **5051**
Site Umm Rashrash, #376
Technique incised
Condition poor
Content Arabic inscription
Access CH04 (photograph, U. Avner); *see also* FR01

Inscription **5052**
Site Wadi Tueiba, #226
Technique scratched
Condition good
Content Arabic inscription
Access CH12 (photograph, U. Avner)

Inscription **5053**
Site Wadi Tueiba, #226
Technique scratched
Condition fair
Content rock drawing
Comment *ibex*
Access CH12 (photograph, U. Avner); *see also* CH13a, FR02

Inscription **5054**
Site Wadi Tueiba, #226
Technique incised
Condition good
Content rock drawing
Comment *straight lines*
Access CH12 (photograph, U. Avner); *see also* CH13a, FR02

Inscription **5055**
Site Wadi Tueiba, #226
Technique incised
Condition good
Content rock drawing
Comment *animals*
Access CH12 (photograph, U. Avner); *see also* CH13a, FR02

Inscription **5056**
Site Wadi Tueiba, #226
Technique scratched
Condition excellent
Content Arabic inscription
Access CH13a (photograph, U. Avner); *see also* FR02

Inscription **5057**
Site Wadi Tueiba, #226
Technique incised
Condition poor
Content unidentified signs
Access CH13a (photograph, U. Avner); *see also* FR02

Inscription **5058**
Site Rud el Ir, Jebel Serabit, #109
Technique incised
Condition excellent
Content Arabic inscription
Access EO01 (photograph, Z. Meshel)

Inscription **5059**
Site Wadi Tueiba, #226
Technique scratched
Condition poor
Content crosses with inscription
Access AId60-61 (photograph, M. Stone)

Inscription **5060**
Site Wadi Tueiba, #226
Technique scratched
Condition poor
Content Greek inscription
Access AId60-61 (photograph, M. Stone)

Inscription **5061**
Site Wadi Mukatab, #64
Technique painted
Condition excellent
Content Greek inscription
Limitation *Tentative decipherment only*
Access CQ66 (photograph, Z. Radovan)

Inscription **5062**
Site Jebel Umm Shumer, Bir Ramhan, #5
Technique incised
Condition poor
Content Greek inscription
Limitation *Tentative decipherment only*
Access DQ02 (photograph, Project)

Inscription **5063**
Site Jebel Umm Shumer, Bir Ramhan, #5
Technique incised
Condition poor
Content Greek inscription
Limitation *Tentative decipherment only*
Access DQ02 (photograph, Project)

Inscription **5064**
Site Jebel Umm Shumer, Bir Ramhan, #5
Technique scratched
Condition poor
Content Greek inscription
Limitation *Tentative decipherment only*
Access DQ02 (photograph, Project)

Inscription **5065**
Site Sinai, #0
Technique scratched
Condition poor
Content rock drawing
Comment *animals*
Access CJ02 (photograph, U. Avner)

Inscription **5066**
Site Sinai, #0
Technique incised
Condition excellent
Content rock drawing
Comment *swastika and wavy lines*
Access CJ03 (photograph, U. Avner)

Inscription **5067**
Site Wadi Haggag, rock 5, #131
Technique scratched
Condition poor
Content unidentified signs
Access CJ04 (photograph, U. Avner); *see also* AAd24, ACa06, AP25, AP26, BG79, BH80

Inscription **5068**
Site Wadi Haggag, rock 5, #131
Technique scratched
Condition poor
Content Greek inscription
Limitation *Tentative decipherment only*
Access CJ04 (photograph, U. Avner); *see also* AAd24, ACa06, AP25, AP26, BG79, BH80

Inscription **5069**
Site Wadi Haggag, rock 5, #131
Technique scratched
Condition poor
Content unidentified inscription
Access CJ04 (photograph, U. Avner); *see also* AAd24, ACa06, AP25, AP26, BG79, BH80

Inscription **5070**
Site Sinai, #0
Technique incised
Condition excellent
Content rock drawing
Comment *group of camels, horses with riders*
Access CJ06 (photograph, U. Avner)

Inscription **5071**
Site Sinai, #0
Technique scratched
Condition poor
Content Arabic inscription
Access CJ06 (photograph, U. Avner)

Inscription **5072**
Site A-Tor, Bir Abu Sueira, #191
Technique incised
Condition poor
Content unidentified inscription
Access DY05 (photograph, Y. Tsafrir)

Inscription **5073**
Site A-Tor, Bir Abu Sueira, #191
Technique scratched
Condition poor
Content Arabic inscription
Access DY05 (photograph, Y. Tsafrir)

Inscription **5074**
Site Sinai, #0
Technique incised
Condition fair
Content Nabatean inscription
Limitation *Tentative decipherment only*
Access CJ09 (photograph, U. Avner)

Inscription **5075**
Site Sinai, #0
Technique incised
Condition good
Content Nabatean inscription
Limitation *Tentative decipherment only*
Access CJ11 (photograph, U. Avner)

Inscription **5076**
Site Sinai, #0
Technique incised
Condition excellent
Content rock drawing
Comment *camel*
Access CJ11 (photograph, U. Avner)

Inscription **5077**
Site Sinai, #0
Technique incised
Condition poor
Content unidentified signs
Access CJ11 (photograph, U. Avner)

Inscription **5078**
Site Sinai, #0
Technique incised
Condition good
Content Nabatean inscription
Limitation *Tentative decipherment only*
Access CJ12 (photograph, U. Avner)

Inscription **5079**
Site Sinai, #0
Technique incised
Condition poor
Content Nabatean inscription
Limitation *Tentative decipherment only*
Access CJ12 (photograph, U. Avner)

Inscription **5080**
Site Sinai, #0
Technique incised
Condition good
Content Nabatean inscription
Limitation *Tentative decipherment only*
Access CJ14 (photograph, U. Avner)

Inscription **5081**
Site Sinai, #0
Technique incised
Condition good
Content Greek inscription
Limitation *Tentative decipherment only*
Access CJ14 (photograph, U. Avner)

Inscription **5082**
Site Sinai, #0
Technique incised
Condition excellent
Content rock drawing
Comment *animal with rider*
Access CJ14 (photograph, U. Avner)

Inscription **5083**
Site Sinai, #0
Technique incised
Condition poor
Content Nabatean inscription
Access CJ14 (photograph, U. Avner)

Inscription **5084**
Site Sinai, #0
Technique incised
Condition poor
Content unidentified signs
Access CJ14 (photograph, U. Avner)

Inscription **5085**
Site Sinai, #0
Technique incised
Condition fair
Content Nabatean inscription
Limitation *Tentative decipherment only*
Access CJ19 (photograph, U. Avner)

Inscription **5086**
Site Sinai, #0
Technique incised
Condition fair
Content Nabatean inscription
Limitation *Tentative decipherment only*
Access CJ19 (photograph, U. Avner)

Inscription **5087**
Site Sinai, #0
Technique incised
Condition fair
Content Nabatean inscription
Limitation *Tentative decipherment only*
Access CJ19 (photograph, U. Avner)

Inscription **5088**
Site Umm Araq, #87
Technique incised
Condition excellent
Content Nabatean inscription
Limitation *Tentative decipherment only*
Access CK01 (photograph, U. Avner); *see also* AJ05

Inscription **5089**
Site Umm Araq, #87
Technique incised
Condition good
Content Nabatean inscription
Limitation *Tentative decipherment only*
Access CK01 (photograph, U. Avner); *see also* AJ05

Inscription **5090**
Site Umm Araq, #87
Technique incised
Condition fair
Content Nabatean inscription
Limitation *Tentative decipherment only*
Access CK01 (photograph, U. Avner); *see also* AJ05

Inscription **5091**
Site Umm Araq, #87
Technique incised
Condition fair
Content Nabatean inscription
Limitation *Tentative decipherment only*
Access CK01 (photograph, U. Avner); *see also* AJ05

Inscription **5092**
Site Umm Araq, #87
Technique scratched
Condition excellent
Content Nabatean inscription
Limitation *Tentative decipherment only*
Access CK01 (photograph, U. Avner); *see also* AJ05

Inscription 5093
Site Umm Araq, #87
Technique scratched
Condition poor
Content Nabatean inscription
Limitation *Tentative decipherment only*
Access CK01 (photograph, U. Avner); *see also* AJ05

Inscription 5094
Site Umm Araq, #87
Technique scratched
Condition fair
Content Nabatean inscription
Limitation *Tentative decipherment only*
Access CK01 (photograph, U. Avner); *see also* AJ05

Inscription 5095
Site Umm Araq, #87
Technique incised
Condition poor
Content Nabatean inscription
Limitation *Tentative decipherment only*
Access CK01 (photograph, U. Avner); *see also* AJ05

Inscription 5096
Site Umm Araq, #87
Technique incised
Condition excellent
Content Nabatean inscription
Limitation *Tentative decipherment only*
Access CK01 (photograph, U. Avner); *see also* AJ05

Inscription 5097
Site Umm Araq, #87
Technique incised
Condition poor
Content Nabatean inscription
Limitation *Tentative decipherment only*
Access CK01 (photograph, U. Avner); *see also* AJ05

Inscription 5098
Site Umm Araq, #87
Technique incised
Condition poor
Content Nabatean inscription
Limitation *Tentative decipherment only*
Access CK01 (photograph, U. Avner); *see also* AJ05

Inscription 5099
Site Umm Araq, #87
Technique incised
Condition excellent
Content Nabatean inscription
Limitation *Tentative decipherment only*
Access CK01 (photograph, U. Avner); *see also* AJ05

Inscription 5100
Site Umm Araq, #87
Technique scratched
Condition good
Content Nabatean inscription
Limitation *Tentative decipherment only*
Access CK01 (photograph, U. Avner); *see also* AJ05

Inscription 5101
Site Umm Araq, #87
Technique scratched
Condition poor
Content Nabatean inscription
Limitation *Tentative decipherment only*
Access CK01 (photograph, U. Avner); *see also* AJ05

Inscription 5102
Site Umm Araq, #87
Technique scratched
Condition fair
Content Nabatean inscription
Limitation *Tentative decipherment only*
Access CK01 (photograph, U. Avner); *see also* AJ05

Inscription 5103
Site Umm Araq, #87
Technique incised
Condition fair
Content Nabatean inscription
Access CK01 (photograph, U. Avner); *see also* AJ05

Inscription 5104
Site Umm Araq, #87
Technique scratched
Condition poor
Content Nabatean inscription
Access CK01 (photograph, U. Avner); *see also* AJ05

Inscription 5105
Site Umm Araq, #87
Technique scratched
Condition good
Content Nabatean inscription
Access CK01 (photograph, U. Avner); *see also* AJ05

Inscription 5106
Site Umm Araq, #87
Technique scratched
Condition poor
Content Nabatean inscription
Access CK01 (photograph, U. Avner); *see also* AJ05

Inscription 5107
Site Umm Araq, #87
Technique incised
Condition poor
Content Nabatean inscription
Access CK01 (photograph, U. Avner); *see also* AJ05

Inscription 5108
Site Umm Araq, #87
Technique incised
Condition excellent
Content rock drawing
Comment *ibex*
Access CK01 (photograph, U. Avner)

Inscription 5109
Site Sinai, #0
Technique incised
Condition excellent
Content crosses alone
Access CK02 (photograph, U. Avner)

Inscription 5110
Site Sinai, #0
Technique incised
Condition excellent
Content crosses alone
Access CK02 (photograph, U. Avner)

Inscription 5111
Site Sinai, #0
Technique incised
Condition poor
Content rock drawing
Comment *hunter and animal*
Access CK02 (photograph, U. Avner)

Inscription 5112
Site Sinai, #0
Technique scratched
Condition poor
Content Nabatean inscription
Access CK02 (photograph, U. Avner)

Inscription 5113
Site Sinai, #0
Technique scratched
Condition poor
Content Nabatean inscription
Access CK02 (photograph, U. Avner)

Inscription 5114
Site Sinai, #0
Technique scratched
Condition poor
Content Nabatean inscription
Access CK02 (photograph, U. Avner)

Inscription 5115
Site Sinai, #0
Technique scratched
Condition poor
Content Nabatean inscription
Access CK02 (photograph, U. Avner)

Inscription 5116
Site Sinai, #0
Technique incised
Condition excellent
Content rock drawing
Comment *gameboard? eighty-one circles arranged in a square*
Access CK10 (photograph, U. Avner)

Inscription 5117
Site Wadi Haggag, #118
Technique incised
Condition excellent
Content Greek inscription
Limitation *Tentative decipherment only*
Access CK03 (photograph, U. Avner)

Inscription 5118
Site Wadi Haggag, #118
Technique scratched
Condition excellent
Content crosses alone
Access CK03 (photograph, U. Avner)

Inscription 5119
Site Wadi Haggag, #118
Technique chiselled
Condition excellent
Content varied crosses
Access CK03 (photograph, U. Avner)

Inscription 5120
Site Wadi Haggag, #118
Technique scratched
Condition excellent
Content crosses alone
Access CK03 (photograph, U. Avner)

Inscription 5121
Site Wadi Haggag, #118
Technique incised
Condition poor
Content Greek inscription
Limitation *Tentative decipherment only*
Access CK03 (photograph, U. Avner)

Inscription 5122
Site Wadi Haggag, #118
Technique incised
Condition excellent
Content encircled crosses
Access CK06 (photograph, U. Avner)

Inscription 5123
Site Wadi Haggag, #118
Technique incised
Condition fair
Content Greek inscription
Access CK06 (photograph, U. Avner)

Inscription 5124
Site Wadi Haggag, #118
Technique incised
Condition excellent
Content footsteps
Access CK11 (photograph, U. Avner)

Inscription 5125
Site Wadi Haggag, #118
Technique incised
Condition excellent
Content footsteps
Access CK11 (photograph, U. Avner)

Inscription 5126
Site Wadi Haggag, #118
Technique incised
Condition fair
Content rock drawing
Comment *animal*
Access CK11 (photograph, U. Avner)

Inscription 5127
Site Wadi Haggag, #118
Technique incised
Condition excellent
Content rock drawing
Comment *camel*
Access CK11 (photograph, U. Avner)

Inscription 5128
Site Wadi Haggag, #118
Technique incised
Condition excellent
Content footsteps
Access CK11 (photograph, U. Avner)

Inscription 5129
Site Wadi Haggag, rock 3, #125
Technique incised
Condition poor
Content unidentified inscription
Access CK11 (photograph, U. Avner)

Inscription 5130
Site Wadi Haggag, rock 3, #125
Technique incised
Condition excellent
Content crosses alone
Access ABe28 (photograph, M. Stone); *see also* FU02, FU10

Inscription 5131
Site Wadi Haggag, rock 3, #125
Technique incised
Condition poor
Content unidentified signs
Access ABe28 (photograph, M. Stone); *see also* FU02, FU10

Inscription 5132
Site Wadi Haggag, rock 3, #125
Technique scratched
Condition poor
Content unidentified inscription
Access ABe28 (photograph, M. Stone); *see also* FU10

Inscription 5133
Site Wadi Haggag, rock 3, #125
Technique incised
Condition excellent
Content crosses alone
Access ABe28 (photograph, M. Stone); *see also* FU10

Inscription 5134
Site Wadi Haggag, rock 3, #125
Technique scratched
Condition good
Content crosses alone
Access ABe28 (photograph, M. Stone)

Inscription 5135
Site Wadi Haggag, rock 3, #125
Technique scratched
Condition excellent
Content crosses alone
Access ABe28 (photograph, M. Stone)

Inscription 5136
Site Wadi Umm Sidra, #174
Technique incised
Condition poor
Content Nabatean inscription
Limitation *Tentative decipherment only*
Access FL40-40a (photograph, Project)

Inscription 5137
Site Wadi Umm Sidra, #174
Technique incised
Condition poor
Content wasems and other Bedouin marks
Access FL40-40a (photograph, Project)

Inscription 5138
Site Wadi Shellal, Shellal 1, #91
Technique incised
Condition poor
Content Greek inscription
Access FE13 (photograph, Project)

Inscription 5139
Site Wadi Shellal, Shellal 1, #91
Technique incised
Condition poor
Content unidentified inscription
Access FE13 (photograph, Project)

Inscription **5140**
Site Wadi Umm Sidra, #174
Technique punched
Condition fair
Content Nabatean inscription
Limitation *Tentative decipherment only*
Access FL96-96a (photograph, Project)

Inscription **5141**
Site Wadi Umm Sidra, #174
Technique incised
Condition good
Content Nabatean inscription
Limitation *Tentative decipherment only*
Access FL96-96a (photograph, Project)

Inscription **5142**
Site Wadi Umm Sidra, #174
Technique incised
Condition poor
Content rock drawing
Comment *uncertain*
Access FL96-96a (photograph, Project)

Inscription **5143**
Site Jebel Musa, #19
Technique scratched
Condition poor
Content unidentified inscription
Access AHc21-22 (photograph, M. Stone)

Inscription **5144**
Site Jebel Musa, #19
Technique scratched
Condition poor
Content unidentified inscription
Access AHc21-22 (photograph, M. Stone)

Inscription **5145**
Site Jebel Musa, #19
Technique scratched
Condition poor
Content unidentified inscription
Access AHc21-22 (photograph, M. Stone)

Inscription **5146**
Site Jebel Musa, #19
Technique scratched
Condition poor
Content Arabic inscription
Access AHc21-22 (photograph, M. Stone)

Inscription **5147**
Site Jebel Musa, #19
Technique scratched
Condition poor
Content unidentified inscription
Access AHd27-28 (photograph, M. Stone); *see also* AHd37-38

Inscription **5148**
Site Wadi Umm Sidra, #174
Technique incised
Condition poor
Content Nabatean inscription
Limitation *Tentative decipherment only*
Access FK62-63 (photograph, Project)

Inscription **5149**
Site Wadi Umm Sidra, #174
Technique incised
Condition good
Content Nabatean inscription
Limitation *Tentative decipherment only*
Access FK62-63 (photograph, Project)

Inscription **5150**
Site Wadi Umm Sidra, #174
Technique scratched
Condition poor
Content unidentified signs
Access FK62-63 (photograph, Project)

Inscription **5151**
Site Wadi Haggag, rock 3, #125
Technique incised
Condition poor
Content Greek inscription
Limitation *Tentative decipherment only*
Access AN07 (photograph, Z. Radovan)

Inscription **5152**
Site Wadi Haggag, rock 3, #125
Technique incised
Condition poor
Content unidentified signs
Access AR31 (photograph, Z. Radovan)

Inscription **5153**
Site Wadi Haggag, rock 3, #125
Technique incised
Condition good
Content Old North Arabic inscription
Limitation *Tentative decipherment only*
Access AT59 (photograph, Z. Radovan); *see also* AT60

Inscription **5154**
Site Wadi Haggag, rock 3, #125
Technique incised
Condition excellent
Content crosses alone
Access AT59 (photograph, Z. Radovan); *see also* AT60

Inscription **5155**
Site Wadi Haggag, rock 3, #125
Technique incised
Condition poor
Content Greek inscription
Access AV77 (photograph, Z. Radovan); *see also* AV78

Inscription 5156
Site Wadi Haggag, rock 3, #125
Technique incised
Condition poor
Content unidentified inscription
Access AW80 (photograph, Z. Radovan); *see also* AV79

Inscription 5157
Site Wadi Haggag, rock 3, #125
Technique incised
Condition excellent
Content crosses with inscription
Access AW80 (photograph, Z. Radovan); *see also* AV79

Inscription 5158
Site Wadi Haggag, rock 3, #125
Technique incised
Condition good
Content crosses alone
Access AW80 (photograph, Z. Radovan); *see also* AV79

Inscription 5159
Site Sinai, #0
Technique incised
Condition poor
Content Greek inscription
Limitation *Tentative decipherment only*
Access AZ15 (photograph, Z. Radovan); *see also* AZ16, BA19, BB20

Inscription 5160
Site Sinai, #0
Technique scratched
Condition poor
Content Greek inscription
Limitation *Tentative decipherment only*
Access AZ15 (photograph, Z. Radovan); *see also* AZ16, BA19, BB20

Inscription 5161
Site Sinai, #0
Technique incised
Condition poor
Content Greek inscription
Access AZ15 (photograph, Z. Radovan); *see also* AZ16, BA19, BB20

Inscription 5162
Site Sinai, #0
Technique incised
Condition poor
Content crosses alone
Access AZ15 (photograph, Z. Radovan); *see also* AZ16, BA19, BB20

Inscription 5163
Site Sinai, #0
Technique scratched
Condition poor
Content unidentified inscription
Access AZ15 (photograph, Z. Radovan); *see also* AZ16, BA19, BB20

Inscription 5164
Site Sinai, #0
Technique incised
Condition poor
Content Greek inscription
Access AZ15 (photograph, Z. Radovan); *see also* AZ16, BA19, BB20

Inscription 5165
Site Wadi Haggag, rock 3 area 1, #126
Technique incised
Condition poor
Content Greek inscription
Limitation *Tentative decipherment only*
Access AX22 (photograph, Z. Radovan); *see also* ABd20, AY23, BG83, BG84, BJ05, BJ06

Inscription 5166
Site Wadi Haggag, rock 3 area 1, #126
Technique incised
Condition excellent
Content crosses with inscription
Access AX22 (photograph, Z. Radovan); *see also* ABd20, AY23, BG83, BG84, BJ05, BJ06

Inscription 5167
Site Wadi Haggag, rock 3 area 1, #126
Technique incised
Condition poor
Content unidentified inscription
Access AX22 (photograph, Z. Radovan); *see also* ABd20, AY23, BG83, BG84, BJ05, BJ06

Inscription 5168
Site Wadi Haggag, rock 3 area 1, #126
Technique incised
Condition poor
Content Greek inscription
Limitation *Tentative decipherment only*
Access AX22 (photograph, Z. Radovan); *see also* ABd20, AY23, BG83, BG84, BJ05, BJ06

Inscription 5169
Site Wadi Haggag, rock 5, #131
Technique incised
Condition poor
Content crosses alone
Access BC54 (photograph, Z. Radovan); *see also* AAd21, AO15, AO16, BD55

Inscription 5170
Site Wadi Haggag, rock 5, #131
Technique incised
Condition poor
Content Greek inscription
Limitation *Tentative decipherment only*
Access BC54 (photograph, Z. Radovan); *see also* AAd21, AO15, AO16, BD55

Inscription 5171
Site Wadi Haggag, rock 3, #125
Technique scratched
Condition excellent
Content crosses alone
Access ABc14 (photograph, M. Stone); *see also* AW87, AW88, BC67, BD68

Inscription 5172
Site Qunteilat Ajrud, #211
Technique incised
Condition poor
Content Nabatean inscription
Limitation *Tentative decipherment only*
Access ECi/1 (photograph, U. Avner); *see also* DN27

Inscription 5173
Site Qunteilat Ajrud, #211
Technique incised
Condition poor
Content Nabatean inscription
Limitation *Tentative decipherment only*
Access ECi/1 (photograph, U. Avner); *see also* DN27

Inscription 5174
Site Qunteilat Ajrud, #211
Technique incised
Condition good
Content Nabatean inscription
Limitation *Tentative decipherment only*
Access ECi/1 (photograph, U. Avner); *see also* DN27

Inscription 5175
Site Qunteilat Ajrud, #211
Technique incised
Condition excellent
Content Nabatean inscription
Limitation *Tentative decipherment only*
Access ECi/1 (photograph, U. Avner); *see also* DN27

Inscription 5176
Site Qunteilat Ajrud, #211
Technique incised
Condition good
Content Nabatean inscription
Limitation *Tentative decipherment only*
Access ECi/1 (photograph, U. Avner); *see also* DN27

Inscription 5177
Site Qunteilat Ajrud, #211
Technique incised
Condition poor
Content Nabatean inscription
Access ECi/1 (photograph, U. Avner); *see also* DN27

Inscription 5178
Site Qunteilat Ajrud, #211
Technique incised
Condition poor
Content Nabatean inscription
Limitation *Tentative decipherment only*
Access ECi/1 (photograph, U. Avner); *see also* DN27

Inscription 5179
Site Qunteilat Ajrud, #211
Technique incised
Condition good
Content Old North Arabic inscription
Limitation *Tentative decipherment only*
Access ECi/1 (photograph, U. Avner); *see also* DN27

Inscription 5180
Site Qunteilat Ajrud, #211
Technique incised
Condition poor
Content unidentified inscription
Access ECi/1 (photograph, U. Avner); *see also* DN27

Inscription 5181
Site Wadi Mukatab, #64
Technique incised
Condition fair
Content Greek inscription
Limitation *Tentative decipherment only*
Access FK10-11 (photograph, Project); *see also* FL39-39a

Inscription 5182
Site Sinai, #0
Technique incised
Condition poor
Content Nabatean inscription
Limitation *Tentative decipherment only*
Access ECi/2 (photograph, U. Avner)

Inscription 5183
Site Sinai, #0
Technique incised
Condition poor
Content Nabatean inscription
Access ECi/2 (photograph, U. Avner)

Inscription 5184
Site Sinai, #0
Technique incised
Condition excellent
Content Greek inscription
Limitation *Tentative decipherment only*
Access ECi/3 (photograph, U. Avner)

Inscription 5185
Site Sinai, #0
Technique incised
Condition excellent
Content crosses with inscription
Access ECi/3 (photograph, U. Avner)

Inscription 5186
Site Sinai, #0
Technique incised
Condition poor
Content Greek inscription
Limitation *Tentative decipherment only*
Access ECi/3 (photograph, U. Avner)

Inscription 5187
Site Sinai, #0
Technique incised
Condition good
Content crosses with inscription
Access ECi/3 (photograph, U. Avner)

Inscription 5188
Site Sinai, #0
Technique incised
Condition poor
Content unidentified inscription
Access ECi/3 (photograph, U. Avner)

Inscription 5189
Site Sinai, #0
Technique incised
Condition good
Content Arabic inscription
Access ECi/4 (photograph, U. Avner)

Inscription 5190
Site Sinai, #0
Technique chiselled
Condition excellent
Content Egyptian hieroglyphs
Access ECi/5 (photograph, U. Avner)

Inscription 5191
Site Sinai, #0
Technique incised
Condition good
Content Greek inscription
Limitation *Tentative decipherment only*
Access ECi/6 (photograph, U. Avner)

Inscription 5192
Site Sinai, #0
Technique scratched
Condition poor
Content Greek inscription
Access ECi/6 (photograph, U. Avner)

Inscription 5193
Site Sinai, #0
Technique scratched
Condition poor
Content unidentified signs
Access ECi/6 (photograph, U. Avner)

Inscription 5194
Site Church of the Holy Sepulchre, #375
Dating 1895
Technique incised
Condition fair
Content Russian inscription
Limitation *Tentative decipherment only*
Access FJ26 (photograph, Project)

Inscription 5195
Site A-Tor, Bir Abu Sueira, #191
Technique scratched
Condition poor
Content unidentified inscription
Access DY05 (photograph, Y. Tsafrir)

Inscription 5196
Site Church of the Holy Sepulchre, #375
Technique scratched
Condition poor
Content unidentified inscription
Access FJ26 (photograph, Project)

Inscription 5197
Site Church of the Holy Sepulchre, #375
Technique incised
Condition fair
Content Greek inscription
Limitation *Tentative decipherment only*
Access FJ26 (photograph, Project)

Inscription 5198
Site Sinai, #0
Technique incised
Condition fair
Content Arabic inscription
Access ECii/1 (photograph, U. Avner)

Inscription 5199
Site Sinai, #0
Technique incised
Condition excellent
Content crosses with inscription
Access ECii/1 (photograph, U. Avner)

Inscription 5200
Site Sinai, #0
Technique incised
Condition poor
Content Arabic inscription
Access ECii/1 (photograph, U. Avner)

Inscription 5201
Site Sinai, #0
Technique incised
Condition poor
Content Arabic inscription
Access ECii/1 (photograph, U. Avner)

Inscription 5202
Site Sinai, #0
Technique incised
Condition poor
Content unidentified signs
Access ECii/1 (photograph, U. Avner)

Inscription 5203
Site Sinai, #0
Technique scratched
Condition poor
Content Arabic inscription
Access ECii/2 (photograph, U. Avner)

Inscription 5204
Site Sinai, #0
Technique scratched
Condition poor
Content Arabic inscription
Access ECii/2 (photograph, U. Avner)

Inscription 5205
Site Sinai, #0
Technique scratched
Condition fair
Content Arabic inscription
Access ECii/2 (photograph, U. Avner)

Inscription 5206
Site Sinai, #0
Technique scratched
Condition fair
Content Arabic inscription
Access ECii/2 (photograph, U. Avner)

Inscription 5207
Site Sinai, #0
Technique incised
Condition excellent
Content rock drawing
Comment *camels, humans with bows and arrows*
Access ECii/3 (photograph, U. Avner)

Inscription 5208
Site Sinai, #0
Technique incised
Condition fair
Content Nabatean inscription
Limitation *Tentative decipherment only*
Access ECii/3 (photograph, U. Avner)

Inscription 5209
Site Sinai, #0
Technique incised
Condition poor
Content unidentified inscription
Access ECii/3 (photograph, U. Avner)

Inscription 5210
Site Sinai, #0
Technique incised
Condition poor
Content Nabatean inscription
Limitation *Tentative decipherment only*
Access ECii/4 (photograph, U. Avner)

Inscription 5211
Site Sinai, #0
Technique incised
Condition excellent
Dimensions 28 x 11 cm.
Content rock drawing
Comment *animals*
Access ECii/4 (photograph, U. Avner)

Inscription 5212
Site Sinai, #0
Technique incised
Condition fair
Content Arabic inscription
Access ECii/5 (photograph, U. Avner)

Inscription 5213
Site Sinai, #0
Technique incised
Condition excellent
Content Arabic inscription
Access ECii/6 (photograph, U. Avner)

Inscription 5214
Site Sinai, #0
Technique incised
Condition fair
Content Arabic inscription
Access FK34-35 (photograph, Project)

Inscription 5215
Site Sinai, #0
Technique scratched
Condition fair
Content Arabic inscription
Access ECii/7 (photograph, U. Avner)

Inscription 5216
Site Sinai, #0
Technique scratched
Condition fair
Content Arabic inscription
Access ECii/7 (photograph, U. Avner)

Inscription 5217
Site Sinai, #0
Technique scratched
Condition fair
Content unidentified signs
Access ECii/7 (photograph, U. Avner)

Inscription 5218
Site Sinai, #0
Dating 1879
Technique incised
Condition excellent
Content Greek inscription
Limitation *Tentative decipherment only*
Access ECiii/1 (photograph, U. Avner)

Inscription 5219
Site Sinai, #0
Technique scratched
Condition poor
Content Greek inscription
Access ECiii/1 (photograph, U. Avner)

Inscription 5220
Site Sinai, #0
Technique scratched
Condition poor
Content Greek inscription
Limitation *Tentative decipherment only*
Access ECiii/1 (photograph, U. Avner)

Inscription 5221
Site Sinai, #0
Technique scratched
Condition fair
Content Greek inscription
Limitation *Tentative decipherment only*
Access ECiii/1 (photograph, U. Avner)

Inscription 5222
Site Sinai, #0
Technique incised
Condition excellent
Content Arabic inscription
Access ECiii/2 (photograph, U. Avner)

Inscription 5223
Site Sinai, #0
Technique incised
Condition excellent
Content rock drawing
Comment *animals*
Access ECiii/2 (photograph, U. Avner)

Inscription 5224
Site Sinai, #0
Technique incised
Condition excellent
Content crosses alone
Access ECiii/2 (photograph, U. Avner)

Inscription 5225
Site Wadi Mukatab, #64
Technique incised
Condition poor
Content Nabatean inscription
Limitation *Tentative decipherment only*
Access DE23a-24 (photograph, A. Goren)

Inscription 5226
Site Wadi Haggag, rock 3, #125
Technique incised
Condition poor
Content Greek inscription
Limitation *Tentative decipherment only*
Access BG71 (photograph, Z. Radovan); *see also* BG72

Inscription 5227
Site Wadi Haggag, rock 3, #125
Technique incised
Condition poor
Content unidentified signs
Access BG71 (photograph, Z. Radovan); *see also* BG72

Inscription 5228
Site Wadi Haggag, rock 3, #125
Technique incised
Condition poor
Content unidentified signs
Access BG71 (photograph, Z. Radovan); *see also* ABd21, AT53, AT54, BH81, BH82, BK08

Inscription 5229
Site Sinai, #0
Technique incised
Condition good
Content Greek inscription
Limitation *Tentative decipherment only*
Access BI97 (photograph, Z. Radovan); *see also* BJ98

Inscription 5230
Site Sinai, #0
Technique scratched
Condition poor
Content unidentified inscription
Access BI97 (photograph, Z. Radovan); *see also* BJ98

Inscription 5231
Site Sinai, #0
Technique incised
Condition poor
Content Arabic inscription
Access BI97 (photograph, Z. Radovan); *see also* BJ98

Inscription 5232
Site Sinai, #0
Technique scratched
Condition poor
Content unidentified signs
Access BI97 (photograph, Z. Radovan); *see also* BJ98

Inscription 5233
Site Sinai, #0
Technique scratched
Condition poor
Content Greek inscription
Limitation *Tentative decipherment only*
Access BI97 (photograph, Z. Radovan); *see also* BJ98

Inscription 5234
Site Sinai, #0
Technique scratched
Condition poor
Content unidentified inscription
Access BI97 (photograph, Z. Radovan); *see also* BJ98

Inscription **5235**
Site Sinai, #0
Technique scratched
Condition poor
Content Greek inscription
Access BI97 (photograph, Z. Radovan); *see also* BJ98

Inscription **5236**
Site Church of the Nativity, pillar B6, #264
Technique scratched
Condition poor
Content Armenian inscription
Limitation *Tentative decipherment only*
Access DRa16 (photograph, M. Stone)

Inscription **5237**
Site Wadi Haggag, rock 3, #125
Technique incised
Condition poor
Content Latin inscription
Limitation *Tentative decipherment only*
Access AX22 (photograph, Z. Radovan); *see also* ABd20, AY23, BG83, BG84, BJ05, BJ06

Inscription **5238**
Site Wadi Haggag, rock 3, #125
Technique incised
Condition fair
Content unidentified signs
Access AX22 (photograph, Z. Radovan); *see also* ABd20, AY23, BG83, BG84, BJ05, BJ06

Inscription **5239**
Site Wadi Haggag, rock 3, #125
Technique incised
Condition poor
Content crosses alone
Access AX22 (photograph, Z. Radovan); *see also* ABd20, AY23, BG83, BG84, BJ05, BJ06

Inscription **5240**
Site Wadi Haggag, rock 3, #125
Technique incised
Condition poor
Content unidentified inscription
Access BK07 (photograph, Z. Radovan); *see also* ABd21, AT53, AT54, BH81, BH82, BK08

Inscription **5241**
Site Wadi Haggag, rock 3, #125
Technique incised
Condition poor
Content Greek inscription
Limitation *Tentative decipherment only*
Access BK51 (photograph, Z. Radovan); *see also* BK50

Inscription **5242**
Site Wadi Haggag, rock 3, #125
Technique incised
Condition poor
Content Greek inscription
Limitation *Tentative decipherment only*
Access BK51 (photograph, Z. Radovan); *see also* BK50

Inscription **5243**
Site Wadi Haggag, rock 3, #125
Technique incised
Condition poor
Content unidentified inscription
Access BL53 (photograph, Z. Radovan); *see also* BK52

Inscription **5244**
Site Wadi Haggag, rock 3, #125
Technique incised
Condition poor
Content crosses alone
Access BL53 (photograph, Z. Radovan); *see also* BK52

Inscription **5245**
Site Sinai, #0
Technique incised
Condition fair
Content Arabic inscription
Access BU06a (photograph, U. Avner)

Inscription **5246**
Site Sinai, #0
Technique incised
Condition fair
Dimensions 46 x 28 cm.
Content Arabic inscription
Access BU06b (photograph, U. Avner)

Inscription **5247**
Site Sinai, #0
Technique incised
Condition poor
Dimensions 37 x 5 cm.
Content Arabic inscription
Access BU07a (photograph, U. Avner)

Inscription **5248**
Site Sinai, #0
Technique incised
Condition poor
Dimensions 20 x 8 cm.
Content Arabic inscription
Access BU07a (photograph, U. Avner)

Inscription **5249**
Site Sinai, #0
Technique scratched
Condition poor
Dimensions 38 x 20 cm.
Content Arabic inscription
Access BU05b (photograph, U. Avner)

Inscription 5250
Site Sinai, #0
Technique incised
Condition poor
Dimensions 29 x 16 cm.
Content rock drawing
Comment *camels*
Access BU05b (photograph, U. Avner)

Inscription 5251
Site Sinai, #0
Technique incised
Condition poor
Dimensions 37 x 12 cm.
Content Arabic inscription
Access BU05a (photograph, U. Avner); *see also* BU04a, BU04b

Inscription 5252
Site Sinai, #0
Technique incised
Condition fair
Content Arabic inscription
Access BU05a (photograph, U. Avner); *see also* BU04b

Inscription 5253
Site Sinai, #0
Technique incised
Condition good
Dimensions 6 x 12 cm.
Content crosses alone
Access BU05a (photograph, U. Avner); *see also* BU04a, BU04b

Inscription 5254
Site Sinai, #0
Technique incised
Condition good
Dimensions 40 x 10 cm.
Content Arabic inscription
Access BU05a (photograph, U. Avner); *see also* BU04b

Inscription 5255
Site Sinai, #0
Technique incised
Condition poor
Dimensions 28 x 8 cm.
Content Arabic inscription
Access BU05a (photograph, U. Avner); *see also* BU04b

Inscription 5256
Site Sinai, #0
Technique incised
Condition poor
Dimensions 32 x 12 cm.
Content Arabic inscription
Access BU03b (photograph, U. Avner)

Inscription 5257
Site Sinai, #0
Technique incised
Condition poor
Dimensions 4 x 18 cm.
Content rock drawing
Comment *human figure*
Access BU03b (photograph, U. Avner)

Inscription 5258
Site Sinai, #0
Technique incised
Condition poor
Dimensions 12 x 6 cm.
Content Arabic inscription
Access BU02a (photograph, U. Avner); *see also* BU03a

Inscription 5259
Site Sinai, #0
Technique incised
Condition fair
Dimensions 57 x 21 cm.
Content Arabic inscription
Access BU02a (photograph, U. Avner); *see also* BU03a

Inscription 5260
Site Sinai, #0
Technique punched
Condition excellent
Dimensions 9 x 5 cm.
Content English inscription
Limitation *Tentative decipherment only*
Access BU02a (photograph, U. Avner); *see also* BU03a

Inscription 5261
Site Sinai, #0
Technique incised
Condition good
Dimensions 20 x 10 cm.
Content Arabic inscription
Access BU02b (photograph, U. Avner)

Inscription 5262
Site Church of the Holy Sepulchre, #375
Technique incised
Condition poor
Content Greek inscription
Limitation *Tentative decipherment only*
Access FJ31 (photograph, Project)

Inscription 5263
Site Church of the Holy Sepulchre, #375
Technique incised
Condition poor
Content crosses alone
Access FJ31 (photograph, Project)

Inscription 5264
Site Church of the Holy Sepulchre, #375
Technique incised
Condition good
Content encircled crosses
Access FJ31 (photograph, Project)

Inscription 5265
Site Church of the Holy Sepulchre, #375
Technique scratched
Condition poor
Content crosses alone
Access FJ31 (photograph, Project)

Inscription 5266
Site Jebel Sirbal, #189
Technique incised
Condition poor
Dimensions 10 x 10 cm.
Content unidentified signs
Access BW03 (photograph, U. Avner)

Inscription 5267
Site Jebel Sirbal, #189
Technique incised
Condition poor
Dimensions 120 x 18 cm.
Content Nabatean inscription
Limitation *Tentative decipherment only*
Access BW04 (photograph, U. Avner)

Inscription 5268
Site Jebel Sirbal, #189
Technique incised
Condition poor
Dimensions 40 x 10 cm.
Content Nabatean inscription
Access BW04 (photograph, U. Avner)

Inscription 5269
Site Jebel Sirbal, #189
Technique incised
Condition poor
Dimensions 35 x 10 cm.
Content Nabatean inscription
Access BW04 (photograph, U. Avner)

Inscription 5270
Site Jebel Sirbal, #189
Technique incised
Condition poor
Dimensions 25 x 5 cm.
Content unidentified signs
Access BW04 (photograph, U. Avner)

Inscription 5271
Site Jebel Sirbal, #189
Technique incised
Condition poor
Dimensions 70 x 15 cm.
Content unidentified inscription
Access BW06a (photograph, U. Avner)

Inscription 5272
Site Jebel Sirbal, #189
Technique incised
Condition poor
Dimensions 60 x 12 cm.
Content Nabatean inscription
Limitation *Tentative decipherment only*
Access BW08a (photograph, U. Avner)

Inscription 5273
Site Jebel Sirbal, #189
Technique incised
Condition poor
Dimensions 46 x 10 cm.
Content Nabatean inscription
Access BW11 (photograph, U. Avner)

Inscription 5274
Site Jebel Sirbal, #189
Technique incised
Condition poor
Dimensions 110 x 30 cm.
Content Nabatean inscription
Limitation *Tentative decipherment only*
Access BW11a (photograph, U. Avner)

Inscription 5275
Site Jebel Sirbal, #189
Technique scratched
Condition poor
Dimensions 30 x 10 cm.
Content Nabatean inscription
Access BW11a (photograph, U. Avner)

Inscription 5276
Site Jebel Sirbal, #189
Technique scratched
Condition poor
Dimensions 40 x 10 cm.
Content Nabatean inscription
Limitation *Tentative decipherment only*
Access BW11a (photograph, U. Avner)

Inscription 5277
Site Jebel Sirbal, #189
Technique scratched
Condition poor
Dimensions 40 x 10 cm.
Content Nabatean inscription
Limitation *Tentative decipherment only*
Access BW11a (photograph, U. Avner)

Inscription 5278
Site Jebel Sirbal, #189
Technique scratched
Condition poor
Dimensions 60 x 10 cm.
Content Nabatean inscription
Access BW11a (photograph, U. Avner)

Inscription **5279**
Site Jebel Sirbal, #189
Technique incised
Condition poor
Dimensions 25 x 10 cm.
Content Nabatean inscription
Access BW11a (photograph, U. Avner)

Inscription **5280**
Site Jebel Sirbal, #189
Technique scratched
Condition poor
Dimensions 110 x 15 cm.
Content Nabatean inscription
Access BW11a (photograph, U. Avner)

Inscription **5281**
Site Jebel Sirbal, #189
Technique incised
Condition poor
Dimensions 150 x 50 cm.
Content Nabatean inscription
Limitation *Tentative decipherment only*
Access BW12a (photograph, U. Avner); *see also* BW13

Inscription **5282**
Site Jebel Sirbal, #189
Technique incised
Condition fair
Dimensions 50 x 10 cm.
Content Nabatean inscription
Limitation *Tentative decipherment only*
Access BW12a (photograph, U. Avner); *see also* BW13

Inscription **5283**
Site Jebel Sirbal, #189
Technique scratched
Condition good
Content Nabatean inscription
Limitation *Tentative decipherment only*
Access BW13a (photograph, U. Avner); *see also* BW14

Inscription **5284**
Site Jebel Sirbal, #189
Technique scratched
Condition poor
Content Nabatean inscription
Limitation *Tentative decipherment only*
Access BW13a (photograph, U. Avner); *see also* BW14

Inscription **5285**
Site Jebel Sirbal, #189
Technique scratched
Condition poor
Content Nabatean inscription
Access BW13a (photograph, U. Avner); *see also* BW14

Inscription **5286**
Site Jebel Sirbal, #189
Technique scratched
Condition fair
Content Nabatean inscription
Limitation *Tentative decipherment only*
Access BW13a (photograph, U. Avner); *see also* BW14

Inscription **5287**
Site Jebel Sirbal, #189
Technique scratched
Condition poor
Content Nabatean inscription
Limitation *Tentative decipherment only*
Access BW13a (photograph, U. Avner); *see also* BW14

Inscription **5288**
Site Jebel Sirbal, #189
Technique scratched
Condition poor
Content Nabatean inscription
Limitation *Tentative decipherment only*
Access BW13a (photograph, U. Avner); *see also* BW14

Inscription **5289**
Site Jebel Sirbal, #189
Technique scratched
Condition poor
Content Nabatean inscription
Access BW13a (photograph, U. Avner); *see also* BW14

Inscription **5290**
Site Jebel Sirbal, #189
Technique scratched
Condition poor
Content Nabatean inscription
Access BW13a (photograph, U. Avner)

Inscription **5291**
Site Jebel Sirbal, #189
Technique scratched
Condition poor
Content Nabatean inscription
Limitation *Tentative decipherment only*
Access BW13a (photograph, U. Avner)

Inscription **5292**
Site Jebel Sirbal, #189
Technique scratched
Condition poor
Content Nabatean inscription
Limitation *Tentative decipherment only*
Access BW13a (photograph, U. Avner)

Inscription **5293**
Site Jebel Sirbal, #189
Technique scratched
Condition poor
Content Nabatean inscription
Access BW13a (photograph, U. Avner)

Inscription 5294
Site Jebel Sirbal, #189
Technique scratched
Condition poor
Content Nabatean inscription
Limitation *Tentative decipherment only*
Access BW13a (photograph, U. Avner)

Inscription 5295
Site Jebel Sirbal, #189
Technique scratched
Condition fair
Content Nabatean inscription
Limitation *Tentative decipherment only*
Access BW14 (photograph, U. Avner)

Inscription 5296
Site Jebel Sirbal, #189
Technique scratched
Condition poor
Content Nabatean inscription
Limitation *Tentative decipherment only*
Access BW14 (photograph, U. Avner)

Inscription 5297
Site Jebel Sirbal, #189
Technique incised
Condition fair
Content Nabatean inscription
Limitation *Tentative decipherment only*
Access BW14 (photograph, U. Avner)

Inscription 5298
Site Jebel Sirbal, #189
Technique scratched
Condition fair
Content Nabatean inscription
Limitation *Tentative decipherment only*
Access BW14 (photograph, U. Avner)

Inscription 5299
Site Jebel Sirbal, #189
Technique scratched
Condition fair
Content Nabatean inscription
Limitation *Tentative decipherment only*
Access BW14 (photograph, U. Avner)

Inscription 5300
Site Jebel Sirbal, #189
Technique scratched
Condition fair
Content Nabatean inscription
Limitation *Tentative decipherment only*
Access BW14 (photograph, U. Avner)

Inscription 5301
Site Jebel Sirbal, #189
Technique incised
Condition poor
Content Nabatean inscription
Limitation *Tentative decipherment only*
Access BW15a (photograph, U. Avner)

Inscription 5302
Site Jebel Sirbal, #189
Technique incised
Condition poor
Content Nabatean inscription
Limitation *Tentative decipherment only*
Access BW15a (photograph, U. Avner)

Inscription 5303
Site Jebel Sirbal, #189
Technique incised
Condition poor
Content Nabatean inscription
Limitation *Tentative decipherment only*
Access BW15a (photograph, U. Avner)

Inscription 5304
Site Jebel Sirbal, #189
Technique incised
Condition poor
Content Nabatean inscription
Limitation *Tentative decipherment only*
Access BW15a (photograph, U. Avner)

Inscription 5305
Site Jebel Sirbal, #189
Technique incised
Condition fair
Content Nabatean inscription
Limitation *Tentative decipherment only*
Access BW15a (photograph, U. Avner)

Inscription 5306
Site Jebel Sirbal, #189
Technique incised
Condition poor
Content Nabatean inscription
Limitation *Tentative decipherment only*
Access BW15a (photograph, U. Avner)

Inscription 5307
Site Jebel Sirbal, #189
Technique incised
Condition poor
Content Nabatean inscription
Access BW15a (photograph, U. Avner)

Inscription 5308
Site Jebel Sirbal, #189
Technique incised
Condition poor
Content Nabatean inscription
Access BW15a (photograph, U. Avner)

Inscription 5309
Site Jebel Sirbal, #189
Technique incised
Condition poor
Dimensions 2 x 5 cm.
Content Nabatean inscription
Access BW03a (photograph, U. Avner)

Inscription 5310
Site Jebel Sirbal, #189
Technique scratched
Condition poor
Dimensions 5 x 5 cm.
Content unidentified signs
Access BW03a (photograph, U. Avner)

Inscription 5311
Site Jebel Sirbal, #189
Technique scratched
Condition poor
Dimensions 5 x 8 cm.
Content unidentified signs
Access BW03a (photograph, U. Avner)

Inscription 5312
Site Jebel Sirbal, #189
Technique scratched
Condition poor
Content unidentified signs
Access BW10a (photograph, U. Avner)

Inscription 5313
Site Jebel Sirbal, #189
Technique scratched
Condition poor
Content unidentified inscription
Access BW10a (photograph, U. Avner)

Inscription 5314
Site Jebel Sirbal, #189
Technique incised
Condition poor
Dimensions 45 x 20 cm.
Content Nabatean inscription
Access BW10 (photograph, U. Avner)

Inscription 5315
Site Jebel Sirbal, #189
Technique incised
Condition poor
Content unidentified inscription
Access BW07a (photograph, U. Avner)

Inscription 5316
Site Jebel Sirbal, #189
Technique incised
Condition poor
Content unidentified signs
Access BW07a (photograph, U. Avner)

Inscription 5317
Site Jebel Sirbal, #189
Technique incised
Condition poor
Dimensions 80 x 30 cm.
Content unidentified signs
Access BW08 (photograph, U. Avner)

Inscription 5318
Site Jebel Sirbal, #189
Technique scratched
Condition poor
Dimensions 8 x 10 cm.
Content Nabatean inscription
Limitation *Tentative decipherment only*
Access BW07 (photograph, U. Avner)

Inscription 5319
Site Jebel Sirbal, #189
Technique scratched
Condition poor
Content Nabatean inscription
Limitation *Tentative decipherment only*
Access BW12 (photograph, U. Avner)

Inscription 5320
Site Jebel Sirbal, #189
Technique scratched
Condition poor
Content Nabatean inscription
Limitation *Tentative decipherment only*
Access BW04a (photograph, U. Avner)

Inscription 5321
Site Jebel Sirbal, #189
Technique incised
Condition poor
Content unidentified signs
Access BW09a (photograph, U. Avner)

Inscription 5322
Site Sinai, #0
Technique painted
Condition excellent
Content Arabic inscription
Access CH31 (photograph, U. Avner); *see also* CH30a, CH31a, CH32

Inscription 5323
Site Sinai, #0
Technique incised
Condition excellent
Content Arabic inscription
Access CH17a (photograph, U. Avner); *see also* CH18, CH18a

Inscription 5324
Site Sinai, #0
Technique incised
Condition fair
Content Arabic inscription
Access CH17a (photograph, U. Avner); *see also* CH18, CH18a

Inscription 5325
Site Sinai, #0
Technique incised
Condition good
Content Arabic inscription
Access CH26 (photograph, U. Avner); *see also* CH25a

Inscription **5326**
Site Sinai, #0
Technique incised
Condition excellent
Content Latin inscription
Limitation *Tentative decipherment only*
Access CH26 (photograph, U. Avner); *see also* CH25a

Inscription **5327**
Site Wadi Umm Sidra, #174
Technique incised
Condition fair
Content Arabic inscription
Access FL51-51a (photograph, Project)

Inscription **5328**
Site Sinai, #0
Technique scratched
Condition fair
Content Arabic inscription
Access CH26 (photograph, U. Avner); *see also* CH25a

Inscription **5329**
Site Sinai, #0
Technique incised
Condition excellent
Content rock drawing
Comment *two human figures*
Access CI01 (photograph, U. Avner)

Inscription **5330**
Site Sinai, #0
Technique incised
Condition poor
Content unidentified signs
Access CI09 (photograph, U. Avner)

Inscription **5331**
Site Wadi Umm Sidra, #174
Technique scratched
Condition poor
Content Greek inscription
Limitation *Tentative decipherment only*
Access CI02 (photograph, U. Avner)

Inscription **5332**
Site Wadi Umm Sidra, #174
Technique incised
Condition poor
Content Arabic inscription
Access FL48-48a (photograph, Project)

Inscription **5333**
Site Wadi Umm Sidra, #174
Technique incised
Condition poor
Content unidentified inscription
Access CI02 (photograph, U. Avner)

Inscription **5334**
Site Wadi Mukatab, #64
Technique incised
Condition poor
Content Greek inscription
Limitation *Tentative decipherment only*
Access FK44-45 (photograph, Project)

Inscription **5335**
Site Wadi Mukatab, #64
Technique scratched
Condition poor
Content rock drawing
Comment *straight lines*
Access FK44-45 (photograph, Project)

Inscription **5336**
Site Wadi Mukatab, #64
Technique scratched
Condition poor
Content unidentified signs
Access FK44-45 (photograph, Project)

Inscription **5337**
Site Sinai, #0
Technique incised
Condition excellent
Content rock drawing
Comment *seven-branched candelabrum with straight branches*
Access CI03 (photograph, U. Avner); *see also* FE14

Inscription **5338**
Site Sinai, #0
Technique incised
Condition poor
Content Hebrew inscription
Limitation *Tentative decipherment only*
Access CI03 (photograph, U. Avner); *see also* FE14

Inscription **5339**
Site Sinai, #0
Technique incised
Condition fair
Content unidentified signs
Access CI03 (photograph, U. Avner); *see also* FE14

Inscription **5340**
Site Sinai, #0
Technique incised
Condition poor
Content rock drawing
Comment *line drawings*
Access CI04 (photograph, U. Avner)

Inscription **5341**
Site A-Tor, Bir Abu Sueira, #191
Technique scratched
Condition poor
Content unidentified inscription
Access DY05 (photograph, Y. Tsafrir)

Inscription 5342
Site Wadi Arade, Arade 5, #111
Technique incised
Condition good
Content rock drawing
Comment *three humans on horseback carrying spears*
Access CI06 (photograph, U. Avner)

Inscription 5343
Site Wadi Arade, Arade 5, #111
Technique incised
Condition excellent
Content rock drawing
Comment *ibexes*
Access CI07 (photograph, U. Avner)

Inscription 5344
Site Wadi Umm Sidra, #174
Technique painted
Condition good
Content Nabatean inscription
Limitation *Tentative decipherment only*
Access FL07-07a (photograph, Project)

Inscription 5345
Site Ein Hudra, #117
Technique incised
Condition excellent
Content rock drawing
Comment *animals*
Access CI09 (photograph, U. Avner)

Inscription 5346
Site Ein Hudra, #117
Technique incised
Condition excellent
Content rock drawing
Comment *two seven-branched candelabra with straight branches*
Access CI09 (photograph, U. Avner)

Inscription 5347
Site Ein Hudra, #117
Technique scratched
Condition poor
Content rock drawing
Comment *animals*
Access CI09 (photograph, U. Avner)

Inscription 5348
Site A-Tor, Bir Abu Sueira, #191
Technique scratched
Condition poor
Content unidentified inscription
Access DY05 (photograph, Y. Tsafrir)

Inscription 5349
Site Sinai, #0
Technique incised
Condition poor
Content Greek inscription
Access CI10 (photograph, U. Avner)

Inscription 5350
Site Sinai, #0
Technique incised
Condition fair
Content Greek inscription
Limitation *Tentative decipherment only*
Access CI11 (photograph, U. Avner)

Inscription 5351
Site Sinai, #0
Technique incised
Condition good
Content Greek inscription
Limitation *Tentative decipherment only*
Access CI11 (photograph, U. Avner)

Inscription 5352
Site Sinai, #0
Technique incised
Condition fair
Content rock drawing
Comment *schematic drawing of a human figure*
Access CI11 (photograph, U. Avner)

Inscription 5353
Site Wadi Tueiba, #226
Technique incised
Condition poor
Content Nabatean inscription
Limitation *Tentative decipherment only*
Access CI12 (photograph, U. Avner)

Inscription 5354
Site Wadi Tueiba, #226
Technique incised
Condition good
Content unidentified signs
Access CI12 (photograph, U. Avner)

Inscription 5355
Site Wadi Tueiba, #226
Technique incised
Condition poor
Content Nabatean inscription
Limitation *Tentative decipherment only*
Access CI12 (photograph, U. Avner)

Inscription 5356
Site Wadi Tueiba, #226
Technique incised
Condition fair
Content unidentified signs
Access CI12 (photograph, U. Avner)

Inscription 5357
Site Wadi Tueiba, #226
Technique scratched
Condition poor
Content Nabatean inscription
Access CI12 (photograph, U. Avner)

Inscription 5358
Site Wadi Tueiba, #226
Technique incised
Condition poor
Content Nabatean inscription
Limitation *Tentative decipherment only*
Access CI12 (photograph, U. Avner)

Inscription 5359
Site Wadi Tueiba, #226
Technique scratched
Condition poor
Content unidentified inscription
Access CI12 (photograph, U. Avner)

Inscription 5360
Site Wadi Tueiba, #226
Technique scratched
Condition poor
Content Greek inscription
Limitation *Tentative decipherment only*
Access CI12 (photograph, U. Avner)

Inscription 5361
Site Wadi Tueiba, #226
Technique scratched
Condition fair
Content Greek inscription
Limitation *Tentative decipherment only*
Access CI12 (photograph, U. Avner)

Inscription 5362
Site Wadi Arade, Arade 5, #111
Technique incised
Condition excellent
Content Nabatean inscription
Limitation *Tentative decipherment only*
Access CI13 (photograph, U. Avner); *see also* ER09a, ER10a

Inscription 5363
Site Wadi Arade, Arade 5, #111
Technique incised
Condition excellent
Content rock drawing
Comment *camels with riders*
Access CI13 (photograph, U. Avner); *see also* ER09a, ER10a

Inscription 5364
Site Wadi Arade, Arade 5, #111
Technique scratched
Condition fair
Content unidentified signs
Access CI13 (photograph, U. Avner); *see also* ER09a, ER10a

Inscription 5365
Site Wadi Biraq, #79
Technique incised
Condition excellent
Dimensions 110 x 80 cm.
Content rock drawing
Comment *camel with rider*
Access EZ34 (photograph, Project); *see also* EZ04

Inscription 5366
Site Wadi Tueiba, #226
Technique incised
Condition excellent
Content rock drawing
Comment *ibexes and hunters mounted on camels and horses*
Access CI15 (photograph, U. Avner)

Inscription 5367
Site Wadi Biraq, #79
Technique incised
Condition excellent
Dimensions 210 x 80 cm.
Content rock drawing
Comment *human figure pursuing three ibexes*
Access EZ05 (photograph, Project); *see also* EZ06, EZ07

Inscription 5368
Site Sinai, #0
Technique punched
Condition poor
Content Old North Arabic inscription
Limitation *Tentative decipherment only*
Access CI16 (photograph, U. Avner)

Inscription 5369
Site Sinai, #0
Technique incised
Condition poor
Content Greek inscription
Limitation *Tentative decipherment only*
Access CI17 (photograph, U. Avner)

Inscription 5370
Site Sinai, #0
Technique incised
Condition poor
Content crosses with inscription
Access CI17 (photograph, U. Avner)

Inscription 5371
Site Ras el Kalb, #235
Technique incised
Condition poor
Content Greek inscription
Limitation *Tentative decipherment only*
Access CJ17 (photograph, U. Avner)

Inscription 5372
Site Ras el Kalb, #235
Technique incised
Condition poor
Content crosses with inscription
Access CJ17 (photograph, U. Avner)

Inscription 5373
Site Sinai, #0
Technique incised
Condition good
Content wasems and other Bedouin marks
Access CJ10 (photograph, U. Avner)

Inscription 5374
Site Sinai, #0
Technique incised
Condition poor
Content Greek inscription
Limitation *Tentative decipherment only*
Access CJ13 (photograph, U. Avner)

Inscription 5375
Site Sinai, #0
Technique incised
Condition poor
Content crosses with inscription
Access CJ13 (photograph, U. Avner)

Inscription 5376
Site Sinai, #0
Technique incised
Condition fair
Content Greek inscription
Limitation *Tentative decipherment only*
Access CJ13 (photograph, U. Avner)

Inscription 5377
Site Sinai, #0
Technique incised
Condition poor
Content Greek inscription
Limitation *Tentative decipherment only*
Access CJ13 (photograph, U. Avner)

Inscription 5378
Site Sinai, #0
Technique incised
Condition poor
Content crosses alone
Access CJ13 (photograph, U. Avner)

Inscription 5379
Site Sinai, #0
Technique incised
Condition fair
Content Greek inscription
Limitation *Tentative decipherment only*
Access CJ15 (photograph, U. Avner)

Inscription 5380
Site Sinai, #0
Technique incised
Condition poor
Content Nabatean inscription
Limitation *Tentative decipherment only*
Access CJ15 (photograph, U. Avner)

Inscription 5381
Site Sinai, #0
Technique incised
Condition good
Content Nabatean inscription
Limitation *Tentative decipherment only*
Access CJ15 (photograph, U. Avner)

Inscription 5382
Site Sinai, #0
Technique incised
Condition poor
Content Nabatean inscription
Limitation *Tentative decipherment only*
Access CJ15 (photograph, U. Avner)

Inscription 5383
Site Sinai, #0
Technique incised
Condition fair
Content Nabatean inscription
Limitation *Tentative decipherment only*
Access CJ15 (photograph, U. Avner)

Inscription 5384
Site Wadi Tueiba, #226
Technique scratched
Condition good
Content Greek inscription
Limitation *Tentative decipherment only*
Access CJ16 (photograph, U. Avner)

Inscription 5385
Site Wadi Tueiba, #226
Technique scratched
Condition poor
Content Greek inscription
Limitation *Tentative decipherment only*
Access CJ16 (photograph, U. Avner)

Inscription 5386
Site Wadi Tueiba, #226
Technique scratched
Condition poor
Content rock drawing
Comment *line drawing of a human*
Access CJ16 (photograph, U. Avner)

Inscription 5387
Site Wadi Tueiba, #226
Technique scratched
Condition poor
Content crosses alone
Access CJ16 (photograph, U. Avner)

Inscription 5388
Site Wadi Tueiba, #226
Technique scratched
Condition good
Content rock drawing
Comment *row of squares*
Access CJ16 (photograph, U. Avner)

Inscription 5389
Site Wadi Tueiba, #226
Technique scratched
Condition fair
Content unidentified signs
Access CJ16 (photograph, U. Avner)

Inscription **5390**
Site Wadi Tueiba, #226
Technique incised
Condition good
Content unidentified signs
Access CJ16 (photograph, U. Avner)

Inscription **5391**
Site Sinai, #0
Technique incised
Condition good
Content Nabatean inscription
Limitation *Tentative decipherment only*
Access CJ18 (photograph, U. Avner)

Inscription **5392**
Site Sinai, #0
Technique incised
Condition poor
Content Greek inscription
Limitation *Tentative decipherment only*
Access CJ18 (photograph, U. Avner)

Inscription **5393**
Site Sinai, #0
Technique incised
Condition poor
Content Greek inscription
Limitation *Tentative decipherment only*
Access CJ18 (photograph, U. Avner)

Inscription **5394**
Site Sinai, #0
Technique incised
Condition poor
Content unidentified signs
Access CJ18 (photograph, U. Avner)

Inscription **5395**
Site Sinai, #0
Technique incised
Condition good
Content Nabatean inscription
Limitation *Tentative decipherment only*
Access CK12 (photograph, U. Avner)

Inscription **5396**
Site Sinai, #0
Technique punched
Condition good
Content English inscription
Limitation *Tentative decipherment only*
Access CK12 (photograph, U. Avner)

Inscription **5397**
Site Sinai, #0
Technique incised
Condition good
Content rock drawing
Comment *animals*
Access CK12 (photograph, U. Avner)

Inscription **5398**
Site Sinai, #0
Technique incised
Condition poor
Content rock drawing
Comment *camels*
Access CK13 (photograph, U. Avner)

Inscription **5399**
Site Sinai, #0
Technique incised
Condition fair
Content rock drawing
Comment *enigmatic; straight lines and concentric circles*
Access CK14 (photograph, U. Avner)

Inscription **5400**
Site Sinai, #0
Technique incised
Condition fair
Content rock drawing
Comment *animals and humans*
Access CK15 (photograph, U. Avner)

Inscription **5401**
Site Sinai, #0
Technique incised
Condition poor
Content rock drawing
Comment *animal*
Access CK16 (photograph, U. Avner)

Inscription **5402**
Site Sinai, #0
Technique incised
Condition excellent
Content rock drawing
Comment *wolf*
Access CK17 (photograph, U. Avner)

Inscription **5403**
Site Sinai, #0
Technique incised
Condition excellent
Content Greek inscription
Limitation *Tentative decipherment only*
Access CK18 (photograph, U. Avner)

Inscription **5404**
Site Sinai, #0
Technique incised
Condition excellent
Content Nabatean inscription
Limitation *Tentative decipherment only*
Access CK18 (photograph, U. Avner)

Inscription **5405**
Site Sinai, #0
Technique incised
Condition good
Content Nabatean inscription
Limitation *Tentative decipherment only*
Access CP58 (photograph, Z. Radovan)

Inscription 5406
Site Sinai, #0
Technique incised
Condition poor
Content Greek inscription
Limitation *Tentative decipherment only*
Access CP58 (photograph, Z. Radovan)

Inscription 5407
Site Sinai, #0
Technique incised
Condition poor
Content Nabatean inscription
Limitation *Tentative decipherment only*
Access CP58 (photograph, Z. Radovan)

Inscription 5408
Site Sinai, #0
Technique incised
Condition poor
Content Nabatean inscription
Limitation *Tentative decipherment only*
Access CP58 (photograph, Z. Radovan)

Inscription 5409
Site Sinai, #0
Technique chiselled
Condition good
Content Egyptian hieroglyphs
Access CX34-35 (photograph, A. Goren)

Inscription 5410
Site Sinai, #0
Technique chiselled
Condition good
Content Egyptian hieroglyphs
Access CX36-37 (photograph, A. Goren)

Inscription 5411
Site Sinai, #0
Technique chiselled
Condition poor
Content Egyptian hieroglyphs
Access CX38-39 (photograph, A. Goren)

Inscription 5412
Site Sinai, #0
Technique chiselled
Condition poor
Content Egyptian hieroglyphs
Comment *fragments*
Access CX44-45 (photograph, A. Goren)

Inscription 5413
Site Sinai, #0
Technique chiselled
Condition poor
Content Egyptian hieroglyphs
Comment *fragments*
Access CX44-45 (photograph, A. Goren); *see also* CX40-41, CX42-43, CX54-55, CX56-57

Inscription 5414
Site Sinai, #0
Technique chiselled
Condition poor
Content Egyptian hieroglyphs
Comment *fragments*
Access CX46-47 (photograph, A. Goren); *see also* CX40-41, CX42-43, CX54-55, CX56-57

Inscription 5415
Site Sinai, #0
Technique chiselled
Condition poor
Content Egyptian hieroglyphs
Comment *fragments*
Access CX50-51 (photograph, A. Goren); *see also* CX48-49

Inscription 5416
Site Sinai, #0
Technique chiselled
Condition poor
Content Egyptian hieroglyphs
Comment *fragments*
Access CX52-53 (photograph, A. Goren); *see also* CX48-49

Inscription 5417
Site Church of the Nativity, north door to crypt, #262
Technique scratched
Condition fair
Content Arabic inscription
Access DRa11 (photograph, M. Stone)

Inscription 5418
Site Church of the Nativity, north door to crypt, #262
Technique scratched
Condition fair
Content crosses with inscription
Access DRa11 (photograph, M. Stone)

Inscription 5419
Site Church of the Nativity, north door to crypt, #262
Technique scratched
Condition good
Content Arabic inscription
Access DRa11 (photograph, M. Stone)

Inscription 5420
Site Church of the Nativity, north door to crypt, #262
Technique scratched
Condition good
Content crosses with inscription
Access DRa11 (photograph, M. Stone)

Inscription **5421**
Site Church of the Nativity, north door to crypt, #262
Technique scratched
Condition fair
Content encircled crosses
Access DRa11 (photograph, M. Stone)

Inscription **5422**
Site Church of the Nativity, north door to crypt, #262
Technique incised
Condition fair
Content Syriac inscription
Limitation *Tentative decipherment only*
Access DRa11 (photograph, M. Stone)

Inscription **5423**
Site Church of the Nativity, pillar B5, #265
Technique scratched
Condition poor
Dimensions 19 x 6 cm.
Content Arabic inscription
Access DRb31 (photograph, M. Stone)

Inscription **5424**
Site Church of the Nativity, pillar B5, #265
Technique scratched
Condition poor
Content Latin inscription
Access DRb31 (photograph, M. Stone)

Inscription **5425**
Site Church of the Nativity, pillar B5, #265
Technique scratched
Condition poor
Dimensions 8 x 10 cm.
Content unidentified signs
Access DRb31 (photograph, M. Stone)

Inscription **5426**
Site Church of the Nativity, pillar B5, #265
Technique scratched
Condition poor
Content Arabic inscription
Access DRb32 (photograph, M. Stone)

Inscription **5427**
Site Church of the Nativity, pillar B5, #265
Technique scratched
Condition poor
Content Latin inscription
Access DRb32 (photograph, M. Stone)

Inscription **5428**
Site Church of the Nativity, pillar B5, #265
Technique scratched
Condition poor
Content Arabic inscription
Access DRb32 (photograph, M. Stone)

Inscription **5429**
Site Church of the Nativity, pillar B5, #265
Technique scratched
Condition poor
Content Arabic inscription
Access DRb32 (photograph, M. Stone)

Inscription **5430**
Site Church of the Nativity, pillar B5, #265
Technique scratched
Condition poor
Content Latin inscription
Access DRb35 (photograph, M. Stone)

Inscription **5431**
Site Church of the Nativity, pillar B5, #265
Technique punched
Condition poor
Content Arabic inscription
Access DRb36 (photograph, M. Stone)

Inscription **5432**
Site A-Tor, Bir Abu Sueira, #191
Technique painted
Condition poor
Content rock drawing
Comment *sketch of person clothed in tunic and mantle, holding a spoked wheel (St. Catharine?); face and right hand have been erased*
Access DY03 (photograph, Y. Tsafrir)

Inscription **5433**
Site A-Tor, Bir Abu Sueira, #191
Technique scratched
Condition poor
Content unidentified inscription
Access DY03 (photograph, Y. Tsafrir)

Inscription **5434**
Site A-Tor, Bir Abu Sueira, #191
Technique painted
Condition poor
Content rock drawing
Comment *boat with mast*
Access DY04 (photograph, Y. Tsafrir); *see also* DY02

Inscription **5435**
Site A-Tor, Bir Abu Sueira, #191
Technique scratched
Condition poor
Content crosses alone
Access DY02 (photograph, Y. Tsafrir)

Inscription **5436**
Site A-Tor, Bir Abu Sueira, #191
Technique scratched
Condition poor
Content unidentified inscription
Access DY02 (photograph, Y. Tsafrir)

Inscription 5437
Site A-Tor, Bir Abu Sueira, #191
Technique scratched
Condition good
Content varied crosses
Access DY23 (photograph, Y. Tsafrir)

Inscription 5438
Site A-Tor, Bir Abu Sueira, #191
Technique scratched
Condition good
Content Greek inscription
Limitation *Tentative decipherment only*
Access DY23 (photograph, Y. Tsafrir)

Inscription 5439
Site A-Tor, Bir Abu Sueira, #191
Technique scratched
Condition poor
Content crosses alone
Access DY23 (photograph, Y. Tsafrir)

Inscription 5440
Site Sinai, #0
Technique punched
Condition good
Content rock drawing
Comment *animal with young*
Access ED18-18a (photograph, A. Goren); *see also* ED24-24a, ED29-29a, ED30-30a, ED34-34a, ED36-36a

---

Inscription 5441
Site Sinai, #0
Technique punched
Condition fair
Content unidentified signs
Access ED18-18a (photograph, A. Goren); *see also* ED24-24a, ED29-29a, ED30-30a, ED34-34a, ED36-36a

---

Inscription 5442
Site Sinai, #0
Technique incised
Condition excellent
Content rock drawing
Comment *ibexes*
Access ED20-20a (photograph, A. Goren)

Inscription 5443
Site Sinai, #0
Technique incised
Condition poor
Content unidentified signs
Access ED20-20a (photograph, A. Goren)

Inscription 5444
Site Sinai, #0
Technique punched
Condition poor
Content rock drawing
Comment *squares linked into a chain*
Access ED20-20a (photograph, A. Goren)

Inscription 5445
Site Sinai, #0
Technique incised
Condition excellent
Content rock drawing
Comment *humans and animals*
Access ED23-23a (photograph, A. Goren); *see also* ED25-25a, ED27-27a, ED28-28a, ED29-29a, ED35-35a

---

Inscription 5446
Site Sinai, #0
Technique punched
Condition poor
Content varied crosses
Access ED26-26a (photograph, A. Goren)

Inscription 5447
Site Sinai, #0
Technique punched
Condition poor
Content rock drawing
Comment *animals*
Access ED33-33a (photograph, A. Goren); *see also* ED27-27a

Inscription 5448
Site Sinai, #0
Technique incised
Condition poor
Content unidentified inscription
Access ED37-37a (photograph, A. Goren)

Inscription 5449
Site Sinai, #0
Technique chiselled
Condition poor
Dimensions 7.5 x 3 cm.
Content Egyptian hieroglyphs
Access EE29a-30 (photograph, A. Goren)

Inscription 5450
Site Sinai, #0
Technique chiselled
Condition poor
Dimensions 7.5 x 8 cm.
Content Egyptian hieroglyphs
Access EE29a-30 (photograph, A. Goren)

Inscription 5451
Site Sinai, #0
Technique chiselled
Condition poor
Dimensions 1 x 1 cm.
Content Egyptian hieroglyphs
Access EE29a-30 (photograph, A. Goren)

Inscription 5452
Site Sinai, #0
Technique incised
Condition fair
Content Arabic inscription
Access EF26a-27 (photograph, A. Goren)

Inscription **5453**
Site Sinai, #0
Technique incised
Condition poor
Content Arabic inscription
Access EF26a-27 (photograph, A. Goren)

Inscription **5454**
Site Sinai, #0
Technique incised
Condition fair
Content rock drawing
Comment *palm branches*
Access EF26a-27 (photograph, A. Goren)

Inscription **5455**
Site Sinai, #0
Technique incised
Condition poor
Content Arabic inscription
Access EF26a-27 (photograph, A. Goren)

Inscription **5456**
Site Sinai, #0
Technique incised
Condition poor
Content Arabic inscription
Access EF26a-27 (photograph, A. Goren)

Inscription **5457**
Site Sinai, #0
Technique incised
Condition poor
Content unidentified inscription
Access EF26a-27 (photograph, A. Goren)

Inscription **5458**
Site Sinai, #0
Technique scratched
Condition poor
Content unidentified inscription
Access EF26a-27 (photograph, A. Goren)

Inscription **5459**
Site Sinai, #0
Technique incised
Condition excellent
Content Nabatean inscription
Limitation *Tentative decipherment only*
Access EG20-21 (photograph, A. Goren); *see also* EG22-23

Inscription **5460**
Site Sinai, #0
Technique incised
Condition excellent
Content Nabatean inscription
Limitation *Tentative decipherment only*
Access EG20-21 (photograph, A. Goren); *see also* EG22-23

Inscription **5461**
Site Sinai, #0
Technique incised
Condition good
Content Nabatean inscription
Limitation *Tentative decipherment only*
Access EG20-21 (photograph, A. Goren); *see also* EG22-23

Inscription **5462**
Site Sinai, #0
Technique incised
Condition poor
Content Nabatean inscription
Access EG20-21 (photograph, A. Goren); *see also* EG22-23

Inscription **5463**
Site Sinai, #0
Technique incised
Condition good
Content Nabatean inscription
Limitation *Tentative decipherment only*
Access EG20-21 (photograph, A. Goren); *see also* EG22-23

Inscription **5464**
Site Sinai, #0
Technique incised
Condition fair
Content Nabatean inscription
Limitation *Tentative decipherment only*
Access EG20-21 (photograph, A. Goren); *see also* EG22-23

Inscription **5465**
Site Sinai, #0
Technique incised
Condition poor
Content unidentified inscription
Access EG20-21 (photograph, A. Goren); *see also* EG22-23

Inscription **5466**
Site Sinai, #0
Technique incised
Condition poor
Content rock drawing
Comment *animals*
Access EG22-23 (photograph, A. Goren)

Inscription **5467**
Site Sinai, #0
Technique incised
Condition poor
Content Nabatean inscription
Limitation *Tentative decipherment only*
Access EG22-23 (photograph, A. Goren)

Inscription 5468
Site Sinai, #0
Technique incised
Condition fair
Content Nabatean inscription
Limitation *Tentative decipherment only*
Access EG34-35 (photograph, A. Goren); *see also* EG32-33

Inscription 5469
Site Sinai, #0
Technique incised
Condition poor
Content Nabatean inscription
Limitation *Tentative decipherment only*
Access EG34-35 (photograph, A. Goren); *see also* EG32-33

Inscription 5470
Site Sinai, #0
Technique incised
Condition fair
Content Nabatean inscription
Limitation *Tentative decipherment only*
Access EG26-27 (photograph, A. Goren)

Inscription 5471
Site Sinai, #0
Technique incised
Condition poor
Content Nabatean inscription
Access EG26-27 (photograph, A. Goren)

Inscription 5472
Site Church of the Holy Sepulchre, #375
Technique painted
Condition poor
Content Greek inscription
Limitation *Tentative decipherment only*
Access EL01 (photograph, M. Stone); *see also* EL02-03

Inscription 5473
Site Church of the Holy Sepulchre, #375
Technique scratched
Condition poor
Content Arabic inscription
Access EL01 (photograph, M. Stone); *see also* EL02-03

Inscription 5474
Site Church of the Holy Sepulchre, #375
Technique scratched
Condition poor
Content Arabic inscription
Access EL01 (photograph, M. Stone); *see also* EL02-03

Inscription 5475
Site Church of the Holy Sepulchre, #375
Technique painted
Condition poor
Content Arabic inscription
Access EL01 (photograph, M. Stone); *see also* EL02-03

Inscription 5476
Site Church of the Holy Sepulchre, #375
Technique painted
Condition poor
Content Arabic inscription
Access EL01 (photograph, M. Stone); *see also* EL02-03

Inscription 5477
Site Church of the Holy Sepulchre, #375
Technique painted
Condition poor
Content Arabic inscription
Access EL01 (photograph, M. Stone); *see also* EL02-03

Inscription 5478
Site Church of the Holy Sepulchre, #375
Technique painted
Condition poor
Content Arabic inscription
Access EL01 (photograph, M. Stone); *see also* EL02-03

Inscription 5479
Site Church of the Holy Sepulchre, #375
Technique painted
Condition poor
Content Arabic inscription
Access EL01 (photograph, M. Stone); *see also* EL02-03

Inscription 5480
Site Church of the Holy Sepulchre, #375
Technique scratched
Condition poor
Content Arabic inscription
Access EL01 (photograph, M. Stone); *see also* EL02-03

Inscription 5481
Site Church of the Holy Sepulchre, #375
Technique scratched
Condition poor
Content Armenian inscription
Limitation *Tentative decipherment only*
Access EL01 (photograph, M. Stone); *see also* EL02-03

Inscription 5482
Site Church of the Holy Sepulchre, #375
Technique painted
Condition poor
Content unidentified inscription
Access EL04-05 (photograph, M. Stone); *see also* EL06-07

Inscription 5483
Site Church of the Holy Sepulchre, #375
Technique scratched
Condition poor
Content Arabic inscription
Access EL04-05 (photograph, M. Stone); *see also* EL06-07

Inscription 5484
Site Church of the Holy Sepulchre, #375
Technique painted
Condition poor
Content Arabic inscription
Access EL04-05 (photograph, M. Stone); *see also* EL06-07

Inscription 5485
Site Church of the Holy Sepulchre, #375
Technique painted
Condition poor
Content Arabic inscription
Access EL04-05 (photograph, M. Stone); *see also* EL06-07

Inscription 5486
Site Church of the Holy Sepulchre, #375
Technique painted
Condition poor
Content Arabic inscription
Access EL04-05 (photograph, M. Stone); *see also* EL06-07

Inscription 5487
Site Church of the Holy Sepulchre, #375
Technique painted
Condition poor
Content Arabic inscription
Access EL04-05 (photograph, M. Stone); *see also* EL06-07

Inscription 5488
Site Church of the Holy Sepulchre, #375
Technique scratched
Condition poor
Content unidentified inscription
Access EL08-09 (photograph, M. Stone)

Inscription 5489
Site Church of the Holy Sepulchre, #375
Technique scratched
Condition poor
Content unidentified inscription
Access EL08-09 (photograph, M. Stone)

Inscription 5490
Site Church of the Holy Sepulchre, #375
Technique scratched
Condition poor
Content unidentified inscription
Access EL08-09 (photograph, M. Stone)

Inscription 5491
Site Church of the Holy Sepulchre, #375
Technique scratched
Condition good
Content crosses alone
Access EL08-09 (photograph, M. Stone)

Inscription 5492
Site Church of the Holy Sepulchre, #375
Technique scratched
Condition good
Content encircled crosses
Access EL08-09 (photograph, M. Stone)

Inscription 5493
Site Church of the Holy Sepulchre, #375
Technique scratched
Condition good
Content unidentified signs
Access EL08-09 (photograph, M. Stone)

Inscription 5494
Site Church of the Holy Sepulchre, #375
Technique scratched
Condition fair
Content Armenian inscription
Limitation *Tentative decipherment only*
Access EL10-11 (photograph, M. Stone); *see also* EL12-13

Inscription 5495
Site Church of the Holy Sepulchre, #375
Technique painted
Condition poor
Content unidentified inscription
Access EL10-11 (photograph, M. Stone); *see also* EL12-13

Inscription 5496
Site Church of the Holy Sepulchre, #375
Technique punched
Condition poor
Content Arabic inscription
Access EL10-11 (photograph, M. Stone); *see also* EL12-13

Inscription 5497
Site Church of the Holy Sepulchre, #375
Technique scratched
Condition poor
Content unidentified inscription
Access EL10-11 (photograph, M. Stone); *see also* EL12-13

Inscription 5498
Site A-Tor, Bir Abu Sueira, #191
Technique incised
Condition fair
Content Arabic inscription
Access EN06 (photograph, Project); *see also* EN01

Inscription 5499
Site A-Tor, Bir Abu Sueira, #191
Technique incised
Condition fair
Content Arabic inscription
Access EN06 (photograph, Project); *see also* EN01

Inscription 5500
Site A-Tor, Bir Abu Sueira, #191
Technique incised
Condition excellent
Content Arabic inscription
Access EN06 (photograph, Project); *see also* EN01

Inscription 5501
Site A-Tor, Bir Abu Sueira, #191
Technique incised
Condition good
Content Arabic inscription
Access EN06 (photograph, Project); *see also* EN01

Inscription 5502
Site A-Tor, Bir Abu Sueira, #191
Technique painted
Condition excellent
Content Italian inscription
Limitation *Tentative decipherment only*
Access EN06 (photograph, Project); *see also* EN01

Inscription 5503
Site A-Tor, Bir Abu Sueira, #191
Technique painted
Condition fair
Content Russian inscription
Limitation *Tentative decipherment only*
Access EN06 (photograph, Project); *see also* EN01

Inscription 5504
Site A-Tor, Bir Abu Sueira, #191
Dating 18?3
Technique painted
Condition fair
Content English inscription
Limitation *Tentative decipherment only*
Access EN06 (photograph, Project); *see also* EN01

Inscription 5505
Site A-Tor, Bir Abu Sueira, #191
Dating 1875
Technique incised
Condition poor
Content Latin inscription
Limitation *Tentative decipherment only*
Access EN06 (photograph, Project); *see also* EN01

Inscription 5506
Site A-Tor, Bir Abu Sueira, #191
Technique painted
Condition good
Content Russian inscription
Access EN06 (photograph, Project); *see also* EN01

Inscription 5507
Site A-Tor, Bir Abu Sueira, #191
Technique incised
Condition poor
Content unidentified inscription
Access EN06 (photograph, Project); *see also* EN01

Inscription 5508
Site A-Tor, Bir Abu Sueira, #191
Technique incised
Condition poor
Content Arabic inscription
Access EN06 (photograph, Project); *see also* EN01

Inscription 5509
Site A-Tor, Bir Abu Sueira, #191
Dating 18?7
Technique painted
Condition poor
Content Latin inscription
Limitation *Tentative decipherment only*
Access EN06 (photograph, Project); *see also* EN01

Inscription 5510
Site A-Tor, Bir Abu Sueira, #191
Technique incised
Condition fair
Content unidentified inscription
Access EN06 (photograph, Project); *see also* EN01

Inscription 5511
Site A-Tor, Bir Abu Sueira, #191
Dating 1?85
Technique painted
Condition poor
Content Russian inscription
Access EN06 (photograph, Project); *see also* EN01

Inscription 5512
Site A-Tor, Bir Abu Sueira, #191
Technique painted
Condition poor
Content unidentified inscription
Access EN06 (photograph, Project); *see also* EN01

Inscription 5513
Site A-Tor, Bir Abu Sueira, #191
Technique scratched
Condition poor
Content unidentified inscription
Access EN06 (photograph, Project); *see also* EN01

Inscription **5514**
Site A-Tor, Bir Abu Sueira, #191
Technique scratched
Condition poor
Content unidentified inscription
Access EN06 (photograph, Project); *see also* EN01

Inscription **5515**
Site A-Tor, Bir Abu Sueira, #191
Technique painted
Condition poor
Content Latin inscription
Access EN06 (photograph, Project); *see also* EN01

Inscription **5516**
Site A-Tor, Bir Abu Sueira, #191
Dating 1852
Technique incised
Condition good
Content English inscription
Limitation *Tentative decipherment only*
Access EN05 (photograph, Project); *see also* EN02

Inscription **5517**
Site A-Tor, Bir Abu Sueira, #191
Technique incised
Condition fair
Content varied crosses
Access EN05 (photograph, Project); *see also* EN02

Inscription **5518**
Site A-Tor, Bir Abu Sueira, #191
Technique incised
Condition poor
Content unidentified inscription
Access EN05 (photograph, Project); *see also* EN02

Inscription **5519**
Site A-Tor, Bir Abu Sueira, #191
Technique incised
Condition poor
Content unidentified signs
Access EN05 (photograph, Project); *see also* EN02

Inscription **5520**
Site Jebel Ṣafṣafa, Vale of John, ascent to, #380
Technique incised
Condition excellent
Content Greek inscription
Limitation *Tentative decipherment only*
Comment *abbreviation or monogram?*
Access GL27 (photograph, Project)

Inscription **5521**
Site A-Tor, Bir Abu Sueira, #191
Technique incised
Condition fair
Content Arabic inscription
Access EN04 (photograph, Project); *see also* EN03

Inscription **5522**
Site A-Tor, Bir Abu Sueira, #191
Technique painted
Condition poor
Content Arabic inscription
Access EN04 (photograph, Project); *see also* EN03

Inscription **5523**
Site A-Tor, Bir Abu Sueira, #191
Technique scratched
Condition poor
Content unidentified inscription
Access EN04 (photograph, Project); *see also* EN03

Inscription **5524**
Site Jebel Musa, #19
Technique scratched
Condition poor
Content Greek inscription
Limitation *Tentative decipherment only*
Access EM01 (photograph, Project)

Inscription **5525**
Site A-Tor, Bir Abu Sueira, #191
Technique painted
Condition good
Content rock drawing
Comment *square with geometric decoration*
Access EN08 (photograph, Project)

Inscription **5526**
Site A-Tor, Bir Abu Sueira, #191
Technique painted
Condition poor
Content Greek inscription
Limitation *Tentative decipherment only*
Access EN08 (photograph, Project)

Inscription **5527**
Site A-Tor, Bir Abu Sueira, #191
Technique scratched
Condition poor
Content Greek inscription
Limitation *Tentative decipherment only*
Access EN09 (photograph, Project)

Inscription **5528**
Site A-Tor, Bir Abu Sueira, #191
Technique scratched
Condition poor
Content Greek inscription
Limitation *Tentative decipherment only*
Access EN09 (photograph, Project)

Inscription 5529
Site A-Tor, Bir Abu Sueira, #191
Technique scratched
Condition poor
Content Greek inscription
Access EN09 (photograph, Project)

Inscription 5530
Site A-Tor, Bir Abu Sueira, #191
Technique scratched
Condition poor
Content Greek inscription
Limitation *Tentative decipherment only*
Access EN09 (photograph, Project)

Inscription 5531
Site A-Tor, Bir Abu Sueira, #191
Technique scratched
Condition poor
Content Greek inscription
Limitation *Tentative decipherment only*
Access EN09 (photograph, Project)

Inscription 5532
Site A-Tor, Bir Abu Sueira, #191
Technique scratched
Condition poor
Content unidentified inscription
Access EN09 (photograph, Project)

Inscription 5533
Site Sinai, #0
Technique incised
Condition poor
Content Greek inscription
Limitation *Tentative decipherment only*
Access EK21 (photograph, Project)

Inscription 5534
Site Sinai, #0
Technique incised
Condition fair
Content unidentified signs
Access EK21 (photograph, Project)

Inscription 5535
Site Sinai, #0
Technique incised
Condition good
Content rock drawing
Comment *camels*
Access EK21 (photograph, Project)

Inscription 5536
Site Nahal Avdat, Nahal Avdat 2, #158
Technique incised
Condition good
Content rock drawing
Comment *perhaps an inscription*
Access GE13 (photograph, Project)

Inscription 5537
Site Nahal Avdat, Nahal Avdat 2, #158
Technique scratched
Condition fair
Dimensions 35 x 10 cm.
Content rock drawing
Comment *ibex, human figure, dog*
Access GE13 (photograph, Project)

Inscription 5538
Site Nahal Avdat, Nahal Avdat 2, #158
Technique scratched
Condition good
Content wasems & other Bedouin marks
Comment *identification uncertain*
Access GE13 (photograph, Project)

Inscription 5539
Site Nahal Avdat, Nahal Avdat 2, #158
Technique incised
Condition good
Dimensions 50 x 9 cm.
Content Old North Arabic inscription
Access GE19 (photograph, Project)

Inscription 5540
Site Nahal Avdat, Nahal Avdat 2, #158
Technique incised
Condition poor
Content rock drawing
Comment *animals*
Access GE19 (photograph, Project)

Inscription 5541
Site Nahal Avdat, Nahal Avdat 2, #158
Technique incised
Condition good
Content rock drawing
Comment *human figures, ibex, other animals*
Access GE20 (photograph, Project)

Inscription 5542
Site Nahal Avdat, Nahal Avdat 2, #158
Technique incised
Condition fair
Content unidentified signs
Access GE22 (photograph, Project)

Inscription 5543
Site Nahal Avdat, Nahal Avdat 2, #158
Technique incised
Condition fair
Dimensions 30 x 11 cm.
Content rock drawing
Comment *two ibexes*
Access GE23 (photograph, Project)

Inscription 5544
Site Mt. Karkom, Nahal Karkom 2, #224
Technique incised
Condition excellent
Content rock drawing
Comment *humans, ibexes*
Access GF06 (photograph, Project)

Inscription 5545
Site Mt. Karkom, Nahal Karkom 2, #224
Technique incised
Condition good
Content crosses alone
Comment *cross or swastika*
Access GF06 (photograph, Project)

Inscription 5546
Site Mt. Karkom, Nahal Karkom 2, #224
Technique incised
Condition excellent
Content rock drawing
Comment *human adult and child, many ibexes, animals, scorpion*
Access GF01 (photograph, Project)

Inscription 5547
Site Mt. Karkom, Nahal Karkom 2, #224
Technique incised
Condition excellent
Content unidentified signs
Comment *circles*
Access GF01 (photograph, Project)

Inscription 5548
Site Mt. Karkom, Nahal Karkom 2, #224
Technique incised
Condition good
Content rock drawing
Comment *scorpion and unclear signs*
Access GF03 (photograph, Project)

Inscription 5549
Site Mt. Karkom, Nahal Karkom 2, #224
Technique incised
Condition good
Content rock drawing
Comment *centipede and animal*
Access GF03 (photograph, Project)

Inscription 5550
Site Mt. Karkom, Nahal Karkom 2, #224
Technique incised
Condition poor
Content Old North Arabic inscription
Comment *identification uncertain*
Access GF03 (photograph, Project)

Inscription 5551
Site Mt. Karkom, Nahal Karkom 2, #224
Technique incised
Condition good
Dimensions 20 x 9 cm.
Content rock drawing
Comment *ibex and wolf*
Access GF04 (photograph, Project)

Inscription 5552
Site Mt. Karkom, Nahal Karkom 2, #224
Technique incised
Condition good
Dimensions 8 x 8 cm.
Content rock drawing
Comment *ibex*
Access GF04 (photograph, Project)

Inscription 5553
Site Mt. Karkom, Nahal Karkom 2, #224
Technique incised
Condition good
Content rock drawing
Comment *scorpion*
Access GF04 (photograph, Project)

Inscription 5554
Site Mt. Karkom, Nahal Karkom 2, #224
Technique incised
Condition good
Content rock drawing
Comment *ibex, wolf, horizontal line*
Access GF05 (photograph, Project)

Inscription 5555
Site Mt. Karkom, Nahal Karkom 2, #224
Technique incised
Condition good
Dimensions 10 x 8 cm.
Content Old North Arabic inscription
Access GF10 (photograph, Project)

Inscription 5556
Site Mt. Karkom, Nahal Karkom 2, #224
Technique incised
Condition good
Content rock drawing
Comment *ibexes*
Access GF11 (photograph, Project)

Inscription 5557
Site Mt. Karkom, Nahal Karkom 2, #224
Technique incised
Condition poor
Content Arabic inscription
Access GF12 (photograph, Project)

Inscription 5558
Site Mt. Karkom, Nahal Karkom 2, #224
Technique incised
Condition poor
Content unidentified signs
Access GF12 (photograph, Project)

Inscription 5559
Site Mt. Karkom, Nahal Karkom 2, #224
Technique incised
Condition good
Content rock drawing
Comment *serpentine shape*
Access GF13 (photograph, Project)

Inscription 5560
Site Mt. Karkom, Nahal Karkom 2, #224
Technique incised
Condition poor
Dimensions 9 x 7.5 cm.
Content Old North Arabic inscription
Access GF15 (photograph, Project)

Inscription 5561
Site Jebel Himayyir, #82
Technique incised
Condition good
Content Nabatean inscription
Limitation *Tentative decipherment only*
Access AJ01 (photograph, M. Stone)

Inscription 5562
Site Jebel Himayyir, #82
Technique scratched
Condition fair
Content Nabatean inscription
Limitation *Tentative decipherment only*
Access AJ01 (photograph, M. Stone)

Inscription 5563
Site Jebel Himayyir, #82
Technique scratched
Condition good
Content Nabatean inscription
Limitation *Tentative decipherment only*
Access AJ01 (photograph, M. Stone)

Inscription 5564
Site Jebel Himayyir, #82
Technique scratched
Condition fair
Content Nabatean inscription
Limitation *Tentative decipherment only*
Access AJ01 (photograph, M. Stone)

Inscription 5565
Site Jebel Himayyir, #82
Technique scratched
Condition good
Content Nabatean inscription
Limitation *Tentative decipherment only*
Access AJ01 (photograph, M. Stone)

Inscription 5566
Site Jebel Himayyir, #82
Technique scratched
Condition poor
Content Nabatean inscription
Limitation *Tentative decipherment only*
Access AJ01 (photograph, M. Stone)

Inscription 5567
Site Jebel Himayyir, #82
Technique scratched
Condition fair
Content Nabatean inscription
Limitation *Tentative decipherment only*
Access AJ01 (photograph, M. Stone)

Inscription 5568
Site Jebel Himayyir, #82
Technique scratched
Condition poor
Content Nabatean inscription
Limitation *Tentative decipherment only*
Access AJ01 (photograph, M. Stone)

Inscription 5569
Site Jebel Himayyir, #82
Technique scratched
Condition good
Content Nabatean inscription
Limitation *Tentative decipherment only*
Access AJ01 (photograph, M. Stone)

Inscription 5570
Site Jebel Himayyir, #82
Technique scratched
Condition poor
Content Nabatean inscription
Limitation *Tentative decipherment only*
Access AJ01 (photograph, M. Stone)

Inscription 5571
Site Jebel Himayyir, #82
Technique scratched
Condition poor
Content Nabatean inscription
Access AJ01 (photograph, M. Stone)

Inscription 5572
Site Jebel Himayyir, #82
Technique scratched
Condition poor
Content Nabatean inscription
Limitation *Tentative decipherment only*
Access AJ01 (photograph, M. Stone)

Inscription 5573
Site Jebel Himayyir, #82
Technique scratched
Condition fair
Content Nabatean inscription
Limitation *Tentative decipherment only*
Access AJ01 (photograph, M. Stone)

Inscription 5574
Site Jebel Himayyir, #82
Technique scratched
Condition poor
Content Nabatean inscription
Limitation *Tentative decipherment only*
Access AJ01 (photograph, M. Stone)

Inscription 5575
Site Jebel Himayyir, #82
Technique scratched
Condition poor
Content Nabatean inscription
Access AJ01 (photograph, M. Stone)

Inscription **5576**
Site Jebel Himayyir, #82
Technique scratched
Condition poor
Content Nabatean inscription
Access AJ01 (photograph, M. Stone)

Inscription **5577**
Site Jebel Himayyir, #82
Technique scratched
Condition poor
Content Nabatean inscription
Access AJ01 (photograph, M. Stone)

Inscription **5578**
Site Jebel Himayyir, #82
Technique scratched
Condition poor
Content Nabatean inscription
Access AJ01 (photograph, M. Stone)

Inscription **5579**
Site Jebel Himayyir, #82
Technique incised
Condition good
Content rock drawing
Comment *animals*
Access AJ01 (photograph, M. Stone)

Inscription **5580**
Site Jebel Himayyir, #82
Technique incised
Condition good
Content unidentified signs
Access AJ01 (photograph, M. Stone)

Inscription **5581**
Site Jebel Himayyir, #82
Technique incised
Condition good
Content unidentified signs
Access AJ01 (photograph, M. Stone)

Inscription **5582**
Site Jebel Himayyir, #82
Technique scratched
Condition poor
Content unidentified inscription
Access AJ01 (photograph, M. Stone)

Inscription **5583**
Site Jebel Himayyir, #82
Technique incised
Condition excellent
Content Nabatean inscription
Limitation *Tentative decipherment only*
Access AJ03 (photograph, M. Stone)

Inscription **5584**
Site Jebel Himayyir, #82
Technique incised
Condition excellent
Content Nabatean inscription
Limitation *Tentative decipherment only*
Access AJ03 (photograph, M. Stone)

Inscription **5585**
Site Jebel Himayyir, #82
Technique incised
Condition excellent
Content Nabatean inscription
Limitation *Tentative decipherment only*
Access AJ03 (photograph, M. Stone)

Inscription **5586**
Site Jebel Himayyir, #82
Technique incised
Condition poor
Content unidentified signs
Access AJ03 (photograph, M. Stone)

Inscription **5587**
Site Jebel Himayyir, #82
Technique incised
Condition good
Content rock drawing
Comment *ibex*
Access AJ03 (photograph, M. Stone)

Inscription **5588**
Site Ras el Jundi, Qalʿat el Jundi, #212
Technique scratched
Condition good
Content rock drawing
Comment *six-pointed star*
Access EO02 (photograph, Z. Meshel)

Inscription **5589**
Site Ras el Jundi, Qalʿat el Jundi, #212
Technique chiselled
Condition fair
Content Arabic inscription
Access EO02 (photograph, Z. Meshel)

Inscription **5590**
Site Church of the Holy Sepulchre, #375
Technique scratched
Condition poor
Content unidentified inscription
Access FG43-44 (photograph, Project)

Inscription **5591**
Site Church of the Holy Sepulchre, #375
Technique scratched
Condition poor
Content Greek inscription
Access FG43-44 (photograph, Project)

Inscription **5592**
Site Church of the Holy Sepulchre, #375
Technique incised
Condition poor
Content unidentified inscription
Access FG43-44 (photograph, Project)

Inscription **5593**
Site Church of the Holy Sepulchre, #375
Technique scratched
Condition poor
Content unidentified inscription
Access FG43-44 (photograph, Project)

Inscription	**5594**
Site	Church of the Holy Sepulchre, #375
Technique	scratched
Condition	poor
Content	unidentified inscription
Access	FG43-44 (photograph, Project)

Inscription	**5595**
Site	Church of the Holy Sepulchre, #375
Technique	scratched
Condition	poor
Content	unidentified inscription
Access	FG43-44 (photograph, Project)

Inscription	**5596**
Site	Church of the Holy Sepulchre, #375
Technique	scratched
Condition	poor
Content	unidentified inscription
Access	FG51-52 (photograph, Project)

Inscription	**5597**
Site	Church of the Holy Sepulchre, #375
Technique	scratched
Condition	good
Content	crosses with inscription
Access	FG51-52 (photograph, Project)

Inscription	**5598**
Site	Church of the Holy Sepulchre, #375
Technique	scratched
Condition	poor
Content	unidentified inscription
Access	FG51-52 (photograph, Project)

Inscription	**5599**
Site	Church of the Holy Sepulchre, #375
Technique	scratched
Condition	excellent
Content	crosses with inscription
Access	FG51-52 (photograph, Project)

Inscription	**5600**
Site	Church of the Holy Sepulchre, #375
Technique	scratched
Condition	good
Content	crosses alone
Access	FG51-52 (photograph, Project)

Inscription	**5601**
Site	Church of the Holy Sepulchre, #375
Technique	scratched
Condition	excellent
Content	crosses alone
Access	FG51-52 (photograph, Project)

Inscription	**5602**
Site	Church of the Holy Sepulchre, #375
Technique	scratched
Condition	good
Content	crosses alone
Access	FG51-52 (photograph, Project)

Inscription	**5603**
Site	Church of the Holy Sepulchre, #375
Technique	scratched
Condition	fair
Content	crosses alone
Access	FG51-52 (photograph, Project)

Inscription	**5604**
Site	Church of the Holy Sepulchre, #375
Technique	scratched
Condition	poor
Content	Arabic inscription
Access	FG51-52 (photograph, Project)

Inscription	**5605**
Site	Church of the Holy Sepulchre, #375
Technique	scratched
Condition	poor
Content	Arabic inscription
Access	FG51-52 (photograph, Project)

Inscription	**5606**
Site	Church of the Holy Sepulchre, #375
Technique	scratched
Condition	good
Content	Greek inscription
Limitation	*Tentative decipherment only*
Access	FG51-52 (photograph, Project)

Inscription	**5607**
Site	Umm Araq, #87
Technique	incised
Condition	fair
Content	Nabatean inscription
Limitation	*Tentative decipherment only*
Access	AJ07 (photograph, M. Stone)

Inscription	**5608**
Site	Umm Araq, #87
Technique	incised
Condition	fair
Content	Nabatean inscription
Limitation	*Tentative decipherment only*
Access	AJ07 (photograph, M. Stone)

Inscription	**5609**
Site	Umm Araq, #87
Technique	incised
Condition	good
Content	Nabatean inscription
Limitation	*Tentative decipherment only*
Access	AJ07 (photograph, M. Stone)

Inscription	**5610**
Site	Umm Araq, #87
Technique	incised
Condition	poor
Content	Nabatean inscription
Limitation	*Tentative decipherment only*
Access	AJ07 (photograph, M. Stone)

Inscription	**5611**
Site	Umm Araq, #87
Technique	incised
Condition	fair
Content	Nabatean inscription
Limitation	*Tentative decipherment only*
Access	AJ07 (photograph, M. Stone)

Inscription	**5612**
Site	Umm Araq, #87
Technique	incised
Condition	poor
Content	Nabatean inscription
Access	AJ07 (photograph, M. Stone)

Inscription	**5613**
Site	Umm Araq, #87
Technique	incised
Condition	fair
Content	Nabatean inscription
Limitation	*Tentative decipherment only*
Access	AJ09 (photograph, M. Stone)

Inscription	**5614**
Site	Umm Araq, #87
Technique	incised
Condition	poor
Content	Nabatean inscription
Access	AJ09 (photograph, M. Stone)

Inscription	**5615**
Site	Umm Araq, #87
Technique	incised
Condition	poor
Content	Nabatean inscription
Limitation	*Tentative decipherment only*
Access	AJ09 (photograph, M. Stone)

Inscription	**5616**
Site	Umm Araq, #87
Technique	incised
Condition	poor
Content	Nabatean inscription
Limitation	*Tentative decipherment only*
Access	AJ09 (photograph, M. Stone)

Inscription	**5617**
Site	Umm Araq, #87
Technique	incised
Condition	poor
Content	unidentified signs
Access	AJ09 (photograph, M. Stone)

Inscription	**5618**
Site	Wadi Shellal, #90
Technique	incised
Condition	good
Content	Nabatean inscription
Limitation	*Tentative decipherment only*
Access	AJ11 (photograph, M. Stone)

Inscription	**5619**
Site	Wadi Shellal, #90
Technique	incised
Condition	fair
Content	Nabatean inscription
Limitation	*Tentative decipherment only*
Access	AJ11 (photograph, M. Stone)

Inscription	**5620**
Site	Wadi Shellal, #90
Technique	incised
Condition	fair
Content	Nabatean inscription
Limitation	*Tentative decipherment only*
Access	AJ11 (photograph, M. Stone)

Inscription	**5621**
Site	Wadi Shellal, #90
Technique	incised
Condition	good
Content	Nabatean inscription
Limitation	*Tentative decipherment only*
Access	AJ11 (photograph, M. Stone)

Inscription	**5622**
Site	Wadi Shellal, #90
Technique	incised
Condition	good
Content	rock drawing
Comment	*hunters on horseback*
Access	AJ11 (photograph, M. Stone)

Inscription	**5623**
Site	Wadi Shellal, #90
Technique	incised
Condition	poor
Content	Nabatean inscription
Limitation	*Tentative decipherment only*
Access	AJ13 (photograph, M. Stone)

Inscription	**5624**
Site	Wadi Shellal, #90
Technique	incised
Condition	poor
Content	Nabatean inscription
Limitation	*Tentative decipherment only*
Access	AJ13 (photograph, M. Stone)

Inscription	**5625**
Site	Wadi Shellal, #90
Technique	incised
Condition	poor
Content	Nabatean inscription
Limitation	*Tentative decipherment only*
Access	AJ13 (photograph, M. Stone)

Inscription	**5626**
Site	Wadi Shellal, #90
Technique	incised
Condition	good
Content	Nabatean inscription
Limitation	*Tentative decipherment only*
Access	AJ15 (photograph, M. Stone)

Inscription **5627**
Site Wadi Shellal, #90
Technique incised
Condition poor
Content Nabatean inscription
Limitation *Tentative decipherment only*
Access AJ15 (photograph, M. Stone)

Inscription **5628**
Site Wadi Shellal, #90
Technique incised
Condition poor
Content Nabatean inscription
Limitation *Tentative decipherment only*
Access AJ15 (photograph, M. Stone)

Inscription **5629**
Site Wadi Shellal, #90
Technique incised
Condition poor
Content Nabatean inscription
Limitation *Tentative decipherment only*
Access AJ15 (photograph, M. Stone)

Inscription **5630**
Site Wadi Shellal, #90
Technique incised
Condition poor
Content Nabatean inscription
Limitation *Tentative decipherment only*
Access AJ15 (photograph, M. Stone)

Inscription **5631**
Site Wadi Shellal, #90
Technique incised
Condition fair
Content Greek inscription
Limitation *Tentative decipherment only*
Access AJ15 (photograph, M. Stone)

Inscription **5632**
Site Wadi Shellal, #90
Technique incised
Condition poor
Content Nabatean inscription
Access AJ15 (photograph, M. Stone)

Inscription **5633**
Site Wadi Shellal, #90
Technique incised
Condition poor
Content Nabatean inscription
Access AJ15 (photograph, M. Stone)

Inscription **5634**
Site Wadi Shellal, #90
Technique incised
Condition poor
Content rock drawing
Comment *animals*
Access AJ15 (photograph, M. Stone)

Inscription **5635**
Site Wadi Shellal, #90
Technique incised
Condition poor
Content Nabatean inscription
Access AJ15 (photograph, M. Stone)

Inscription **5636**
Site Wadi Shellal, #90
Technique incised
Condition poor
Content Nabatean inscription
Access AJ15 (photograph, M. Stone)

Inscription **5637**
Site Wadi Shellal, #90
Technique incised
Condition poor
Content rock drawing
Comment *animals*
Access AJ15 (photograph, M. Stone)

Inscription **5638**
Site Wadi Shellal, #90
Technique incised
Condition good
Content rock drawing
Comment *four straight parallel lines; square*
Access AJ25 (photograph, M. Stone)

Inscription **5639**
Site Wadi Shellal, #90
Technique incised
Condition poor
Content rock drawing
Comment *footsteps?*
Access AJ27 (photograph, M. Stone)

Inscription **5640**
Site Wadi Shellal, #90
Technique incised
Condition fair
Content rock drawing
Comment *human figures*
Access AJ29 (photograph, M. Stone)

Inscription **5641**
Site Wadi Shellal, #90
Technique incised
Condition poor
Content rock drawing
Comment *four parallel lines and three-sided square; very similar to insc. 5638*
Access AJ31 (photograph, M. Stone)

Inscription **5642**
Site Wadi Shellal, #90
Technique incised
Condition poor
Content rock drawing
Comment *rough ovals*
Access AJ33 (photograph, M. Stone)

Inscription	**5643**
Site	Wadi Shellal, #90
Technique	incised
Condition	good
Content	footsteps
Access	AJ35 (photograph, M. Stone)

Inscription	**5644**
Site	Wadi Shellal, #90
Technique	incised
Condition	poor
Content	unidentified signs
Access	AJ35 (photograph, M. Stone)

Inscription	**5645**
Site	Wadi Shellal, #90
Technique	incised
Condition	fair
Content	rock drawing
Comment	*five-pointed star*
Access	AJ35 (photograph, M. Stone)

Inscription	**5646**
Site	Wadi Shellal, #90
Technique	incised
Condition	poor
Content	unidentified inscription
Access	AJ35 (photograph, M. Stone)

Inscription	**5647**
Site	Wadi Shellal, #90
Technique	incised
Condition	fair
Content	rock drawing
Comment	*ibexes*
Access	AJ37 (photograph, M. Stone)

Inscription	**5648**
Site	Wadi Shellal, #90
Technique	incised
Condition	fair
Content	rock drawing
Comment	*human with bow and arrow*
Access	AJ39 (photograph, M. Stone)

Inscription	**5649**
Site	Wadi Shellal, #90
Technique	incised
Condition	poor
Content	rock drawing
Comment	*stylized animals*
Access	AJ41 (photograph, M. Stone)

Inscription	**5650**
Site	Wadi Shellal, #90
Technique	incised
Condition	good
Content	rock drawing
Comment	*ibex*
Access	AJ43 (photograph, M. Stone)

Inscription	**5651**
Site	Wadi Shellal, #90
Technique	incised
Condition	fair
Content	rock drawing
Comment	*handprint*
Access	AJ45 (photograph, M. Stone)

Inscription	**5652**
Site	Wadi Shellal, #90
Technique	incised
Condition	fair
Content	Nabatean inscription
Limitation	*Tentative decipherment only*
Access	AJ47 (photograph, M. Stone); *see also* AJ53

Inscription	**5653**
Site	Wadi Shellal, #90
Technique	incised
Condition	fair
Content	footsteps
Access	AJ49 (photograph, M. Stone)

Inscription	**5654**
Site	Wadi Shellal, #90
Technique	incised
Condition	poor
Content	Nabatean inscription
Limitation	*Tentative decipherment only*
Access	AJ49 (photograph, M. Stone)

Inscription	**5655**
Site	Wadi Shellal, #90
Technique	incised
Condition	poor
Content	unidentified signs
Access	AJ49 (photograph, M. Stone)

Inscription	**5656**
Site	Wadi Shellal, #90
Technique	incised
Condition	poor
Content	unidentified signs
Access	AJ49 (photograph, M. Stone)

Inscription	**5657**
Site	Wadi Shellal, #90
Technique	incised
Condition	poor
Content	Nabatean inscription
Limitation	*Tentative decipherment only*
Access	AJ51 (photograph, M. Stone)

Inscription	**5658**
Site	Wadi Shellal, #90
Technique	incised
Condition	poor
Content	unidentified signs
Access	AJ51 (photograph, M. Stone)

Inscription **5659**
Site Wadi Shellal, #90
Technique incised
Condition fair
Content footsteps
Access AJ53 (photograph, M. Stone)

Inscription **5660**
Site Wadi Shellal, #90
Technique incised
Condition poor
Content Nabatean inscription
Limitation *Tentative decipherment only*
Access AJ53 (photograph, M. Stone)

Inscription **5661**
Site Wadi Shellal, #90
Technique incised
Condition fair
Content rock drawing
Comment *circle with eight projecting lines*
Access AJ53 (photograph, M. Stone)

Inscription **5662**
Site Wadi Shellal, #90
Technique incised
Condition poor
Content unidentified signs
Access AJ53 (photograph, M. Stone)

Inscription **5663**
Site Wadi Shellal, #90
Technique incised
Condition good
Content Nabatean inscription
Limitation *Tentative decipherment only*
Access AJ55 (photograph, M. Stone)

Inscription **5664**
Site Wadi Shellal, #90
Technique incised
Condition poor
Content Nabatean inscription
Limitation *Tentative decipherment only*
Access AJ55 (photograph, M. Stone)

Inscription **5665**
Site Wadi Shellal, #90
Technique incised
Condition fair
Content rock drawing
Comment *animals*
Access AJ57 (photograph, M. Stone)

Inscription **5666**
Site Wadi Shellal, #90
Technique incised
Condition good
Content rock drawing
Comment *circle with line inside and line below*
Access AJ59 (photograph, M. Stone)

Inscription **5667**
Site Wadi Shellal, #90
Technique incised
Condition excellent
Content rock drawing
Comment *animals and humans*
Access AJ61 (photograph, M. Stone)

Inscription **5668**
Site Wadi Shellal, #90
Technique incised
Condition excellent
Content rock drawing
Comment *circle with many projecting lines*
Access AJ63 (photograph, M. Stone)

Inscription **5669**
Site Wadi Shellal, #90
Technique incised
Condition poor
Content Nabatean inscription
Limitation *Tentative decipherment only*
Access AJ65 (photograph, M. Stone)

Inscription **5670**
Site Wadi Shellal, #90
Technique incised
Condition poor
Content Nabatean inscription
Limitation *Tentative decipherment only*
Access AJ65 (photograph, M. Stone)

Inscription **5671**
Site Wadi Shellal, #90
Technique incised
Condition poor
Content Nabatean inscription
Access AJ65 (photograph, M. Stone)

Inscription **5672**
Site Wadi Shellal, #90
Technique incised
Condition fair
Content rock drawing
Comment *animals*
Access AJ67 (photograph, M. Stone)

Inscription **5673**
Site Wadi Shellal, #90
Technique incised
Condition fair
Content rock drawing
Comment *animals*
Access AJ69 (photograph, M. Stone)

Inscription **5674**
Site Wadi Shellal, #90
Technique incised
Condition fair
Content rock drawing
Comment *animals*
Access AJ71 (photograph, M. Stone)

Inscription **5675**
Site Wadi Shellal, #90
Technique incised
Condition good
Content rock drawing
Comment *animals*
Access AJ73 (photograph, M. Stone)

Inscription **5676**
Site Wadi Shellal, #90
Technique incised
Condition good
Content Nabatean inscription
Limitation *Tentative decipherment only*
Access AK01 (photograph, M. Stone)

Inscription **5677**
Site Wadi Shellal, #90
Technique incised
Condition fair
Content varied crosses
Access AK01 (photograph, M. Stone)

Inscription **5678**
Site Wadi Shellal, #90
Technique incised
Condition fair
Content crosses alone
Access AK01 (photograph, M. Stone)

Inscription **5679**
Site Wadi Shellal, #90
Technique incised
Condition fair
Content Nabatean inscription
Limitation *Tentative decipherment only*
Access AK03 (photograph, M. Stone)

Inscription **5680**
Site Wadi Shellal, #90
Technique incised
Condition poor
Content Nabatean inscription
Limitation *Tentative decipherment only*
Access AK03 (photograph, M. Stone)

Inscription **5681**
Site Wadi Shellal, #90
Technique incised
Condition fair
Content Nabatean inscription
Limitation *Tentative decipherment only*
Access AK03 (photograph, M. Stone)

Inscription **5682**
Site Wadi Shellal, #90
Technique incised
Condition fair
Content Nabatean inscription
Limitation *Tentative decipherment only*
Access AK03 (photograph, M. Stone)

Inscription **5683**
Site Wadi Shellal, #90
Technique incised
Condition poor
Content Nabatean inscription
Limitation *Tentative decipherment only*
Access AK03 (photograph, M. Stone)

Inscription **5684**
Site Wadi Shellal, #90
Technique incised
Condition good
Content crosses alone
Access AK03 (photograph, M. Stone)

Inscription **5685**
Site Wadi Shellal, #90
Technique incised
Condition poor
Content Nabatean inscription
Access AK03 (photograph, M. Stone)

Inscription **5686**
Site Wadi Shellal, #90
Technique incised
Condition poor
Content Nabatean inscription
Access AK03 (photograph, M. Stone)

Inscription **5687**
Site Wadi Shellal, #90
Technique incised
Condition poor
Content Nabatean inscription
Access AK03 (photograph, M. Stone)

Inscription **5688**
Site Wadi Shellal, #90
Technique incised
Condition poor
Content unidentified signs
Access AK03 (photograph, M. Stone)

Inscription **5689**
Site Wadi Shellal, #90
Technique incised
Condition fair
Content crosses alone
Access AK03 (photograph, M. Stone)

Inscription **5690**
Site Wadi Shellal, #90
Technique incised
Condition excellent
Content Nabatean inscription
Limitation *Tentative decipherment only*
Access AK05 (photograph, M. Stone)

Inscription **5691**
Site Wadi Shellal, #90
Technique incised
Condition fair
Content rock drawing
Comment *ibex*
Access AK05 (photograph, M. Stone)

Inscription 5692
Site Wadi Shellal, #90
Technique incised
Condition poor
Content Nabatean inscription
Limitation *Tentative decipherment only*
Access AK05 (photograph, M. Stone)

Inscription 5693
Site Wadi Shellal, #90
Technique incised
Condition poor
Content Nabatean inscription
Limitation *Tentative decipherment only*
Access AK05 (photograph, M. Stone)

Inscription 5694
Site Wadi Shellal, #90
Technique incised
Condition poor
Content Nabatean inscription
Limitation *Tentative decipherment only*
Access AK05 (photograph, M. Stone)

Inscription 5695
Site Wadi Shellal, #90
Technique scratched
Condition fair
Content Arabic inscription
Access AK05 (photograph, M. Stone)

Inscription 5696
Site Wadi Shellal, #90
Technique scratched
Condition good
Content rock drawing
Comment *schematic drawing of human*
Access AK05 (photograph, M. Stone)

Inscription 5697
Site Wadi Shellal, #90
Technique incised
Condition poor
Content Nabatean inscription
Limitation *Tentative decipherment only*
Access AK05 (photograph, M. Stone)

Inscription 5698
Site Wadi Shellal, #90
Technique scratched
Condition poor
Content unidentified signs
Access AK05 (photograph, M. Stone)

Inscription 5699
Site Wadi Shellal, #90
Technique incised
Condition poor
Content Nabatean inscription
Limitation *Tentative decipherment only*
Access AK07 (photograph, M. Stone)

Inscription 5700
Site Wadi Shellal, #90
Technique incised
Condition fair
Content Nabatean inscription
Limitation *Tentative decipherment only*
Access AK07 (photograph, M. Stone)

Inscription 5701
Site Wadi Shellal, #90
Technique incised
Condition poor
Content Nabatean inscription
Access AK07 (photograph, M. Stone)

Inscription 5702
Site Wadi Shellal, #90
Technique incised
Condition fair
Content rock drawing
Comment *camels and ibexes*
Access AK07 (photograph, M. Stone)

Inscription 5703
Site Wadi Shellal, #90
Technique incised
Condition poor
Content Nabatean inscription
Limitation *Tentative decipherment only*
Access AK09 (photograph, M. Stone)

Inscription 5704
Site Wadi Shellal, #90
Technique incised
Condition poor
Content Nabatean inscription
Limitation *Tentative decipherment only*
Access AK09 (photograph, M. Stone)

Inscription 5705
Site Wadi Shellal, #90
Technique incised
Condition poor
Content Nabatean inscription
Access AK09 (photograph, M. Stone)

Inscription 5706
Site Wadi Shellal, #90
Technique incised
Condition poor
Content Nabatean inscription
Access AK09 (photograph, M. Stone)

Inscription 5707
Site Wadi Shellal, #90
Technique incised
Condition poor
Content unidentified inscription
Access AK09 (photograph, M. Stone)

Inscription	**5708**
Site	Wadi Shellal, #90
Technique	incised
Condition	fair
Content	rock drawing
Comment	*circle enclosing straight lines*
Access	AK09 (photograph, M. Stone)

Inscription	**5709**
Site	Wadi Shellal, #90
Technique	incised
Condition	fair
Content	rock drawing
Comment	*camel and human figure*
Access	AK09 (photograph, M. Stone)

Inscription	**5710**
Site	Wadi Shellal, #90
Technique	scratched
Condition	poor
Content	Arabic inscription
Access	AK09 (photograph, M. Stone)

Inscription	**5711**
Site	Wadi Shellal, #90
Technique	incised
Condition	good
Content	Nabatean inscription
Limitation	*Tentative decipherment only*
Access	AK11 (photograph, M. Stone)

Inscription	**5712**
Site	Wadi Shellal, #90
Technique	incised
Condition	poor
Content	Nabatean inscription
Limitation	*Tentative decipherment only*
Access	AK11 (photograph, M. Stone)

Inscription	**5713**
Site	Wadi Shellal, #90
Technique	incised
Condition	poor
Content	Nabatean inscription
Limitation	*Tentative decipherment only*
Access	AK11 (photograph, M. Stone)

Inscription	**5714**
Site	Wadi Shellal, #90
Technique	incised
Condition	poor
Content	Nabatean inscription
Access	AK11 (photograph, M. Stone)

Inscription	**5715**
Site	Wadi Shellal, #90
Technique	incised
Condition	poor
Content	Nabatean inscription
Limitation	*Tentative decipherment only*
Access	AK11 (photograph, M. Stone)

Inscription	**5716**
Site	Wadi Shellal, #90
Technique	incised
Condition	poor
Content	Nabatean inscription
Limitation	*Tentative decipherment only*
Access	AK11 (photograph, M. Stone)

Inscription	**5717**
Site	Wadi Shellal, #90
Technique	incised
Condition	poor
Content	Nabatean inscription
Limitation	*Tentative decipherment only*
Access	AK11 (photograph, M. Stone)

Inscription	**5718**
Site	Wadi Shellal, #90
Technique	incised
Condition	poor
Content	Nabatean inscription
Access	AK11 (photograph, M. Stone)

Inscription	**5719**
Site	Wadi Shellal, #90
Technique	incised
Condition	poor
Content	Nabatean inscription
Access	AK11 (photograph, M. Stone)

Inscription	**5720**
Site	Wadi Shellal, #90
Technique	incised
Condition	poor
Content	Nabatean inscription
Access	AK11 (photograph, M. Stone)

Inscription	**5721**
Site	Wadi Shellal, #90
Technique	incised
Condition	excellent
Content	Nabatean inscription
Limitation	*Tentative decipherment only*
Access	AK13 (photograph, M. Stone)

Inscription	**5722**
Site	Wadi Shellal, #90
Technique	incised
Condition	excellent
Content	Nabatean inscription
Limitation	*Tentative decipherment only*
Access	AK13 (photograph, M. Stone)

Inscription	**5723**
Site	Wadi Shellal, #90
Technique	incised
Condition	poor
Content	Nabatean inscription
Limitation	*Tentative decipherment only*
Access	AK13 (photograph, M. Stone)

Inscription 5724
Site Wadi Shellal, #90
Technique incised
Condition poor
Content Nabatean inscription
Limitation *Tentative decipherment only*
Access AK13 (photograph, M. Stone)

Inscription 5725
Site Wadi Shellal, #90
Technique incised
Condition poor
Content Nabatean inscription
Limitation *Tentative decipherment only*
Access AK13 (photograph, M. Stone)

Inscription 5726
Site Wadi Shellal, #90
Technique incised
Condition poor
Content Nabatean inscription
Limitation *Tentative decipherment only*
Access AK13 (photograph, M. Stone)

Inscription 5727
Site Wadi Shellal, #90
Technique incised
Condition poor
Content Nabatean inscription
Access AK13 (photograph, M. Stone)

Inscription 5728
Site Wadi Shellal, #90
Technique incised
Condition poor
Content Nabatean inscription
Access AK13 (photograph, M. Stone)

Inscription 5729
Site Wadi Shellal, #90
Technique incised
Condition fair
Content rock drawing
Comment *animals*
Access AK13 (photograph, M. Stone)

Inscription 5730
Site Wadi Shellal, #90
Technique incised
Condition poor
Content Nabatean inscription
Access AK13 (photograph, M. Stone)

Inscription 5731
Site Wadi Shellal, #90
Technique incised
Condition poor
Content unidentified signs
Access AK13 (photograph, M. Stone)

Inscription 5732
Site Wadi Shellal, #90
Technique incised
Condition poor
Content Nabatean inscription
Limitation *Tentative decipherment only*
Access AK15 (photograph, M. Stone)

Inscription 5733
Site Wadi Shellal, #90
Technique incised
Condition poor
Content Nabatean inscription
Access AK15 (photograph, M. Stone)

Inscription 5734
Site Wadi Shellal, #90
Technique incised
Condition poor
Content Nabatean inscription
Access AK15 (photograph, M. Stone)

Inscription 5735
Site Wadi Shellal, #90
Technique incised
Condition poor
Content Nabatean inscription
Access AK15 (photograph, M. Stone)

Inscription 5736
Site Wadi Shellal, #90
Technique incised
Condition poor
Content unidentified signs
Access AK15 (photograph, M. Stone)

Inscription 5737
Site Wadi Shellal, #90
Technique incised
Condition fair
Content Nabatean inscription
Limitation *Tentative decipherment only*
Access AK17 (photograph, M. Stone)

Inscription 5738
Site Wadi Shellal, #90
Technique incised
Condition fair
Content Nabatean inscription
Limitation *Tentative decipherment only*
Access AK17 (photograph, M. Stone)

Inscription 5739
Site Wadi Shellal, #90
Technique incised
Condition poor
Content Nabatean inscription
Access AK17 (photograph, M. Stone)

Inscription 5740
Site Wadi Shellal, #90
Technique incised
Condition poor
Content Nabatean inscription
Limitation *Tentative decipherment only*
Access AK19 (photograph, M. Stone)

Inscription 5741
Site Wadi Shellal, #90
Technique incised
Condition poor
Content Nabatean inscription
Limitation *Tentative decipherment only*
Access AK19 (photograph, M. Stone)

Inscription 5742
Site Wadi Shellal, #90
Technique incised
Condition poor
Content Nabatean inscription
Access AK19 (photograph, M. Stone)

Inscription 5743
Site Wadi Shellal, #90
Technique incised
Condition poor
Content Nabatean inscription
Access AK19 (photograph, M. Stone)

Inscription 5744
Site Wadi Shellal, #90
Technique incised
Condition fair
Content Nabatean inscription
Limitation *Tentative decipherment only*
Access AK21 (photograph, M. Stone)

Inscription 5745
Site Wadi Shellal, #90
Technique incised
Condition poor
Content Nabatean inscription
Limitation *Tentative decipherment only*
Access AK21 (photograph, M. Stone)

Inscription 5746
Site Wadi Shellal, #90
Technique incised
Condition poor
Content Nabatean inscription
Limitation *Tentative decipherment only*
Access AK21 (photograph, M. Stone)

Inscription 5747
Site Wadi Shellal, #90
Technique incised
Condition fair
Content Nabatean inscription
Limitation *Tentative decipherment only*
Access AK21 (photograph, M. Stone)

Inscription 5748
Site Wadi Shellal, #90
Technique incised
Condition poor
Content Nabatean inscription
Limitation *Tentative decipherment only*
Access AK21 (photograph, M. Stone)

Inscription 5749
Site Wadi Shellal, #90
Technique painted
Condition fair
Content Arabic inscription
Access AK23 (photograph, M. Stone)

Inscription 5750
Site Wadi Shellal, #90
Technique incised
Condition poor
Content Nabatean inscription
Access AK23 (photograph, M. Stone)

Inscription 5751
Site Wadi Shellal, #90
Technique incised
Condition poor
Content Nabatean inscription
Access AK23 (photograph, M. Stone)

Inscription 5752
Site Wadi Shellal, #90
Technique incised
Condition poor
Content Nabatean inscription
Limitation *Tentative decipherment only*
Access AK23 (photograph, M. Stone)

Inscription 5753
Site Wadi Shellal, #90
Technique incised
Condition poor
Content Nabatean inscription
Limitation *Tentative decipherment only*
Access AK23 (photograph, M. Stone)

Inscription 5754
Site Wadi Shellal, #90
Technique incised
Condition poor
Content Nabatean inscription
Limitation *Tentative decipherment only*
Access AK23 (photograph, M. Stone); *see also* AK25

Inscription 5755
Site Wadi Shellal, #90
Technique incised
Condition poor
Content Nabatean inscription
Limitation *Tentative decipherment only*
Access AK25 (photograph, M. Stone); *see also* AK27

Inscription **5756**
Site Wadi Shellal, #90
Technique incised
Condition poor
Content Nabatean inscription
Limitation *Tentative decipherment only*
Access AK25 (photograph, M. Stone); *see also* AK27

Inscription **5757**
Site Wadi Shellal, #90
Technique incised
Condition poor
Content Nabatean inscription
Limitation *Tentative decipherment only*
Access AK25 (photograph, M. Stone); *see also* AK27

Inscription **5758**
Site Wadi Shellal, #90
Technique incised
Condition poor
Content Nabatean inscription
Access AK25 (photograph, M. Stone)

Inscription **5759**
Site Wadi Shellal, #90
Technique incised
Condition poor
Content Nabatean inscription
Limitation *Tentative decipherment only*
Access AK25 (photograph, M. Stone)

Inscription **5760**
Site Wadi Shellal, #90
Technique incised
Condition fair
Content Nabatean inscription
Limitation *Tentative decipherment only*
Access AK25 (photograph, M. Stone)

Inscription **5761**
Site Wadi Shellal, #90
Technique incised
Condition poor
Content Nabatean inscription
Access AK25 (photograph, M. Stone); *see also* AK27

Inscription **5762**
Site Wadi Shellal, #90
Technique incised
Condition good
Content Nabatean inscription
Limitation *Tentative decipherment only*
Access AK25 (photograph, M. Stone); *see also* AK27

Inscription **5763**
Site Wadi Shellal, #90
Technique incised
Condition poor
Content Nabatean inscription
Access AK25 (photograph, M. Stone)

Inscription **5764**
Site Wadi Shellal, #90
Technique incised
Condition poor
Content Nabatean inscription
Access AK25 (photograph, M. Stone)

Inscription **5765**
Site Wadi Shellal, #90
Technique incised
Condition poor
Content unidentified signs
Access AK25 (photograph, M. Stone)

Inscription **5766**
Site Wadi Shellal, #90
Technique incised
Condition poor
Content rock drawing
Comment *animals*
Access AK25 (photograph, M. Stone)

Inscription **5767**
Site Wadi Shellal, #90
Technique incised
Condition poor
Content Nabatean inscription
Access AK27 (photograph, M. Stone)

Inscription **5768**
Site Wadi Shellal, #90
Technique incised
Condition poor
Content Nabatean inscription
Limitation *Tentative decipherment only*
Access AK27 (photograph, M. Stone)

Inscription **5769**
Site Wadi Shellal, #90
Technique scratched
Condition poor
Content Nabatean inscription
Limitation *Tentative decipherment only*
Access AK27 (photograph, M. Stone)

Inscription **5770**
Site Wadi Shellal, #90
Technique incised
Condition poor
Content Nabatean inscription
Limitation *Tentative decipherment only*
Access AK27 (photograph, M. Stone)

Inscription **5771**
Site Wadi Shellal, #90
Technique incised
Condition fair
Content Nabatean inscription
Limitation *Tentative decipherment only*
Access AK27 (photograph, M. Stone)

Inscription **5772**
Site Wadi Shellal, #90
Technique incised
Condition poor
Content Nabatean inscription
Limitation *Tentative decipherment only*
Access AK27 (photograph, M. Stone)

Inscription **5773**
Site Wadi Shellal, #90
Technique incised
Condition poor
Content Nabatean inscription
Limitation *Tentative decipherment only*
Access AK27 (photograph, M. Stone)

Inscription **5774**
Site Wadi Shellal, #90
Technique incised
Condition poor
Content Nabatean inscription
Access AK27 (photograph, M. Stone)

Inscription **5775**
Site Wadi Shellal, #90
Technique incised
Condition poor
Content Nabatean inscription
Limitation *Tentative decipherment only*
Access AK27 (photograph, M. Stone)

Inscription **5776**
Site Wadi Shellal, #90
Technique incised
Condition poor
Content Nabatean inscription
Access AK27 (photograph, M. Stone)

Inscription **5777**
Site Wadi Shellal, #90
Technique incised
Condition poor
Content Nabatean inscription
Access AK27 (photograph, M. Stone)

Inscription **5778**
Site Wadi Shellal, #90
Technique incised
Condition poor
Content Nabatean inscription
Access AK27 (photograph, M. Stone)

Inscription **5779**
Site Wadi Shellal, #90
Technique incised
Condition poor
Content Nabatean inscription
Limitation *Tentative decipherment only*
Access AK29 (photograph, M. Stone)

Inscription **5780**
Site Wadi Shellal, #90
Technique incised
Condition poor
Content Nabatean inscription
Limitation *Tentative decipherment only*
Access AK29 (photograph, M. Stone)

Inscription **5781**
Site Wadi Shellal, #90
Technique incised
Condition excellent
Content Nabatean inscription
Limitation *Tentative decipherment only*
Access AK29 (photograph, M. Stone)

Inscription **5782**
Site Wadi Shellal, #90
Technique punched
Condition poor
Content Nabatean inscription
Access AK29 (photograph, M. Stone)

Inscription **5783**
Site Wadi Shellal, #90
Technique punched
Condition poor
Content Nabatean inscription
Limitation *Tentative decipherment only*
Access AK29 (photograph, M. Stone)

Inscription **5784**
Site Wadi Shellal, #90
Technique incised
Condition fair
Content Nabatean inscription
Limitation *Tentative decipherment only*
Access AK29 (photograph, M. Stone)

Inscription **5785**
Site Wadi Shellal, #90
Technique scratched
Condition poor
Content Nabatean inscription
Access AK29 (photograph, M. Stone)

Inscription **5786**
Site Wadi Shellal, #90
Technique incised
Condition excellent
Content Nabatean inscription
Limitation *Tentative decipherment only*
Access AK31 (photograph, M. Stone)

Inscription **5787**
Site Wadi Shellal, #90
Technique incised
Condition poor
Content Nabatean inscription
Limitation *Tentative decipherment only*
Access AK31 (photograph, M. Stone)

Inscription 5788
Site Wadi Shellal, #90
Technique incised
Condition poor
Content Nabatean inscription
Limitation *Tentative decipherment only*
Access AK31 (photograph, M. Stone)

Inscription 5789
Site Wadi Shellal, #90
Technique incised
Condition poor
Content Nabatean inscription
Limitation *Tentative decipherment only*
Access AK31 (photograph, M. Stone)

Inscription 5790
Site Wadi Shellal, #90
Technique incised
Condition poor
Content Nabatean inscription
Limitation *Tentative decipherment only*
Access AK31 (photograph, M. Stone)

Inscription 5791
Site Wadi Shellal, #90
Technique incised
Condition poor
Content Nabatean inscription
Limitation *Tentative decipherment only*
Access AK31 (photograph, M. Stone)

Inscription 5792
Site Wadi Shellal, #90
Technique incised
Condition poor
Content Nabatean inscription
Limitation *Tentative decipherment only*
Access AK31 (photograph, M. Stone)

Inscription 5793
Site Wadi Shellal, #90
Technique incised
Condition good
Content crosses alone
Access AK31 (photograph, M. Stone)

Inscription 5794
Site Wadi Shellal, #90
Technique incised
Condition excellent
Content Nabatean inscription
Limitation *Tentative decipherment only*
Access AK33 (photograph, M. Stone)

Inscription 5795
Site Wadi Shellal, #90
Technique incised
Condition good
Content Nabatean inscription
Limitation *Tentative decipherment only*
Access AK33 (photograph, M. Stone)

Inscription 5796
Site Wadi Shellal, #90
Technique incised
Condition fair
Content Nabatean inscription
Limitation *Tentative decipherment only*
Access AK33 (photograph, M. Stone)

Inscription 5797
Site Wadi Shellal, #90
Technique incised
Condition fair
Content Nabatean inscription
Limitation *Tentative decipherment only*
Access AK33 (photograph, M. Stone)

Inscription 5798
Site Wadi Shellal, #90
Technique incised
Condition poor
Content Nabatean inscription
Limitation *Tentative decipherment only*
Access AK33 (photograph, M. Stone)

Inscription 5799
Site Wadi Shellal, #90
Technique incised
Condition poor
Content Nabatean inscription
Limitation *Tentative decipherment only*
Access AK33 (photograph, M. Stone)

Inscription 5800
Site Wadi Shellal, #90
Technique incised
Condition poor
Content Nabatean inscription
Limitation *Tentative decipherment only*
Access AK33 (photograph, M. Stone)

Inscription 5801
Site Wadi Shellal, #90
Technique incised
Condition poor
Content Nabatean inscription
Limitation *Tentative decipherment only*
Access AK33 (photograph, M. Stone)

Inscription 5802
Site Wadi Shellal, #90
Technique incised
Condition excellent
Content Nabatean inscription
Limitation *Tentative decipherment only*
Access AK35 (photograph, M. Stone)

Inscription 5803
Site Wadi Shellal, #90
Technique incised
Condition good
Content Nabatean inscription
Limitation *Tentative decipherment only*
Access AK35 (photograph, M. Stone)

Inscription	**5804**
Site	Wadi Shellal, #90
Technique	incised
Condition	excellent
Content	Nabatean inscription
Limitation	*Tentative decipherment only*
Access	AK37 (photograph, M. Stone)

Inscription	**5805**
Site	Wadi Shellal, #90
Technique	incised
Condition	fair
Content	Nabatean inscription
Limitation	*Tentative decipherment only*
Access	AK37 (photograph, M. Stone)

Inscription	**5806**
Site	Wadi Shellal, #90
Technique	incised
Condition	good
Content	Nabatean inscription
Limitation	*Tentative decipherment only*
Access	AK39 (photograph, M. Stone)

Inscription	**5807**
Site	Wadi Shellal, #90
Technique	incised
Condition	good
Content	rock drawing
Comment	*animals*
Access	AK39 (photograph, M. Stone)

Inscription	**5808**
Site	Wadi Shellal, #90
Technique	incised
Condition	fair
Content	rock drawing
Comment	*two ships with masts*
Access	AK43 (photograph, M. Stone)

Inscription	**5809**
Site	Wadi Shellal, #90
Technique	incised
Condition	fair
Content	rock drawing
Comment	*animals*
Access	AK43 (photograph, M. Stone)

Inscription	**5810**
Site	Wadi Shellal, #90
Technique	incised
Condition	poor
Content	Nabatean inscription
Limitation	*Tentative decipherment only*
Access	AK45 (photograph, M. Stone)

Inscription	**5811**
Site	Wadi Shellal, #90
Technique	incised
Condition	poor
Content	Nabatean inscription
Limitation	*Tentative decipherment only*
Access	AK45 (photograph, M. Stone)

Inscription	**5812**
Site	Wadi Shellal, #90
Technique	incised
Condition	poor
Content	Nabatean inscription
Limitation	*Tentative decipherment only*
Access	AK45 (photograph, M. Stone)

Inscription	**5813**
Site	Wadi Shellal, #90
Technique	incised
Condition	poor
Content	Nabatean inscription
Limitation	*Tentative decipherment only*
Access	AK45 (photograph, M. Stone)

Inscription	**5814**
Site	Serabit el Khadem, #86
Technique	chiselled
Condition	excellent
Content	Egyptian hieroglyphs
Access	EO07 (photograph, Z. Meshel)

Inscription	**5815**
Site	Wadi Shellal, #90
Technique	scratched
Condition	poor
Content	Nabatean inscription
Limitation	*Tentative decipherment only*
Access	AK45 (photograph, M. Stone)

Inscription	**5816**
Site	Wadi Shellal, #90
Technique	scratched
Condition	poor
Content	Nabatean inscription
Limitation	*Tentative decipherment only*
Access	AK45 (photograph, M. Stone)

Inscription	**5817**
Site	Wadi Shellal, #90
Technique	incised
Condition	poor
Content	Nabatean inscription
Limitation	*Tentative decipherment only*
Access	AK45 (photograph, M. Stone)

Inscription	**5818**
Site	Wadi Shellal, #90
Technique	incised
Condition	poor
Content	Nabatean inscription
Limitation	*Tentative decipherment only*
Access	AK45 (photograph, M. Stone)

Inscription	**5819**
Site	Wadi Shellal, #90
Technique	incised
Condition	poor
Content	unidentified inscription
Access	AK45 (photograph, M. Stone)

Inscription 5820
Site Wadi Shellal, #90
Technique incised
Condition poor
Content Nabatean inscription
Limitation *Tentative decipherment only*
Access AK47 (photograph, M. Stone)

Inscription 5821
Site Wadi Shellal, #90
Technique incised
Condition poor
Content Nabatean inscription
Limitation *Tentative decipherment only*
Access AK47 (photograph, M. Stone)

Inscription 5822
Site Wadi Shellal, #90
Technique incised
Condition poor
Content Nabatean inscription
Access AK47 (photograph, M. Stone)

Inscription 5823
Site Wadi Shellal, #90
Technique incised
Condition poor
Content Nabatean inscription
Access AK47 (photograph, M. Stone)

Inscription 5824
Site Wadi Shellal, #90
Technique incised
Condition poor
Content Nabatean inscription
Limitation *Tentative decipherment only*
Access AK47 (photograph, M. Stone)

Inscription 5825
Site Wadi Shellal, #90
Technique incised
Condition poor
Content Nabatean inscription
Access AK47 (photograph, M. Stone)

Inscription 5826
Site Wadi Shellal, #90
Technique incised
Condition good
Content Nabatean inscription
Limitation *Tentative decipherment only*
Access AK49 (photograph, M. Stone)

Inscription 5827
Site Wadi Shellal, #90
Technique punched
Condition good
Content Nabatean inscription
Limitation *Tentative decipherment only*
Access AK49 (photograph, M. Stone)

Inscription 5828
Site Wadi Shellal, #90
Technique incised
Condition good
Content Nabatean inscription
Limitation *Tentative decipherment only*
Access AK49 (photograph, M. Stone)

Inscription 5829
Site Wadi Shellal, #90
Technique incised
Condition fair
Content Nabatean inscription
Limitation *Tentative decipherment only*
Access AK49 (photograph, M. Stone)

Inscription 5830
Site Wadi Shellal, #90
Technique incised
Condition poor
Content Nabatean inscription
Limitation *Tentative decipherment only*
Access AK49 (photograph, M. Stone)

Inscription 5831
Site Wadi Shellal, #90
Technique punched
Condition poor
Content Nabatean inscription
Limitation *Tentative decipherment only*
Access AK49 (photograph, M. Stone)

Inscription 5832
Site Wadi Shellal, #90
Technique incised
Condition poor
Content Arabic inscription
Access AK49 (photograph, M. Stone)

Inscription 5833
Site Wadi Shellal, #90
Technique incised
Condition poor
Content Nabatean inscription
Limitation *Tentative decipherment only*
Access AK51 (photograph, M. Stone)

Inscription 5834
Site Wadi Shellal, #90
Technique incised
Condition poor
Content Nabatean inscription
Limitation *Tentative decipherment only*
Access AK51 (photograph, M. Stone)

Inscription 5835
Site Wadi Shellal, #90
Technique incised
Condition poor
Content Nabatean inscription
Limitation *Tentative decipherment only*
Access AK53 (photograph, M. Stone)

Inscription **5836**
Site Wadi Shellal, #90
Technique incised
Condition poor
Content Nabatean inscription
Limitation *Tentative decipherment only*
Access AK53 (photograph, M. Stone)

Inscription **5837**
Site Wadi Shellal, #90
Technique incised
Condition poor
Content unidentified inscription
Access AK53 (photograph, M. Stone)

Inscription **5838**
Site Wadi Shellal, #90
Technique incised
Condition poor
Content Nabatean inscription
Limitation *Tentative decipherment only*
Access AK55 (photograph, M. Stone)

Inscription **5839**
Site Wadi Shellal, #90
Technique incised
Condition poor
Content Nabatean inscription
Access AK55 (photograph, M. Stone)

Inscription **5840**
Site Wadi Shellal, #90
Technique incised
Condition poor
Content Nabatean inscription
Access AK55 (photograph, M. Stone)

Inscription **5841**
Site Wadi Shellal, #90
Technique incised
Condition poor
Content Nabatean inscription
Limitation *Tentative decipherment only*
Access AK57 (photograph, M. Stone)

Inscription **5842**
Site Wadi Shellal, #90
Technique incised
Condition poor
Content Nabatean inscription
Limitation *Tentative decipherment only*
Access AK57 (photograph, M. Stone)

Inscription **5843**
Site Wadi Shellal, #90
Technique incised
Condition poor
Content Nabatean inscription
Limitation *Tentative decipherment only*
Access AK57 (photograph, M. Stone)

Inscription **5844**
Site Wadi Shellal, #90
Technique incised
Condition poor
Content Nabatean inscription
Limitation *Tentative decipherment only*
Access AK57 (photograph, M. Stone)

Inscription **5845**
Site Wadi Shellal, #90
Technique incised
Condition poor
Content Nabatean inscription
Access AK57 (photograph, M. Stone)

Inscription **5846**
Site Wadi Shellal, #90
Technique incised
Condition poor
Content Nabatean inscription
Limitation *Tentative decipherment only*
Access AK59 (photograph, M. Stone); *see also* AK61

Inscription **5847**
Site Wadi Shellal, #90
Technique incised
Condition fair
Content Nabatean inscription
Limitation *Tentative decipherment only*
Access AK59 (photograph, M. Stone); *see also* AK61

Inscription **5848**
Site Wadi Shellal, #90
Technique incised
Condition poor
Content Nabatean inscription
Limitation *Tentative decipherment only*
Access AK59 (photograph, M. Stone); *see also* AK61

Inscription **5849**
Site Wadi Shellal, #90
Technique incised
Condition poor
Content Nabatean inscription
Access AK59 (photograph, M. Stone); *see also* AK61

Inscription **5850**
Site Wadi Shellal, #90
Technique incised
Condition poor
Content Nabatean inscription
Limitation *Tentative decipherment only*
Access AK59 (photograph, M. Stone); *see also* AK61

Inscription 5851
Site Wadi Shellal, #90
Technique punched
Condition poor
Content rock drawing
Comment *circle*
Access AK59 (photograph, M. Stone)

Inscription 5852
Site Wadi Shellal, #90
Technique punched
Condition good
Content Nabatean inscription
Limitation *Tentative decipherment only*
Access AK63 (photograph, M. Stone)

Inscription 5853
Site Wadi Shellal, #90
Technique incised
Condition fair
Content Nabatean inscription
Limitation *Tentative decipherment only*
Access AK65 (photograph, M. Stone)

Inscription 5854
Site Wadi Shellal, #90
Technique punched
Condition good
Content Nabatean inscription
Limitation *Tentative decipherment only*
Access AK67 (photograph, M. Stone)

Inscription 5855
Site Wadi Shellal, #90
Technique punched
Condition good
Content rock drawing
Comment *curved lines*
Access AK67 (photograph, M. Stone)

Inscription 5856
Site Wadi Shellal, #90
Technique punched
Condition excellent
Content Nabatean inscription
Limitation *Tentative decipherment only*
Access AK69 (photograph, M. Stone)

Inscription 5857
Site Wadi Shellal, #90
Technique punched
Condition poor
Content Nabatean inscription
Limitation *Tentative decipherment only*
Access AK69 (photograph, M. Stone)

Inscription 5858
Site Wadi Shellal, #90
Technique punched
Condition poor
Content unidentified signs
Access AK69 (photograph, M. Stone)

Inscription 5859
Site Wadi Haggag, #118
Technique incised
Condition good
Content rock drawing
Comment *ibexes, horses and human figures*
Access AL26-27 (photograph, M. Stone)

Inscription 5860
Site Sinai, #0
Technique incised
Condition poor
Content rock drawing
Comment *animal*
Access ECiii/3 (photograph, U. Avner)

Inscription 5861
Site Sinai, #0
Technique incised
Condition good
Content rock drawing
Comment *animals*
Access ECiii/4 (photograph, U. Avner)

Inscription 5862
Site Sinai, #0
Technique incised
Condition fair
Content rock drawing
Comment *human figure and animal*
Access ECiii/5 (photograph, U. Avner)

Inscription 5863
Site Sinai, #0
Technique incised
Condition fair
Content rock drawing
Comment *line drawing of bird*
Access ECiii/6 (photograph, U. Avner)

Inscription 5864
Site Sinai, #0
Technique incised
Condition poor
Content varied crosses
Access ECiii/7 (photograph, U. Avner)

Inscription 5865
Site Sinai, #0
Technique incised
Condition poor
Content unidentified signs
Access ECiii/7 (photograph, U. Avner)

Inscription 5866
Site Sinai, #0
Technique incised
Condition poor
Content unidentified signs
Access ECiii/7 (photograph, U. Avner)

Inscription **5867**
Site Sinai, #0
Technique incised
Condition fair
Content Egyptian hieroglyphs
Access ECiv/1 (photograph, U. Avner)

Inscription **5868**
Site Sinai, #0
Technique incised
Condition poor
Content Egyptian hieroglyphs
Access ECiv/1 (photograph, U. Avner)

Inscription **5869**
Site Sinai, #0
Technique incised
Condition poor
Content Arabic inscription
Access ECiv/2 (photograph, U. Avner)

Inscription **5870**
Site Sinai, #0
Technique incised
Condition good
Content crosses alone
Access ECiv/2 (photograph, U. Avner)

Inscription **5871**
Site Sinai, #0
Technique incised
Condition good
Content rock drawing
Comment *ibexes, horse with rider, curved lines*
Access ECiv/3 (photograph, U. Avner)

Inscription **5872**
Site Sinai, #0
Technique incised
Condition good
Content rock drawing
Comment *human figures and animals*
Access ECiv/4 (photograph, U. Avner)

Inscription **5873**
Site Sinai, #0
Technique incised
Condition poor
Content Arabic inscription
Access ECiv/5 (photograph, U. Avner)

Inscription **5874**
Site Sinai, #0
Technique incised
Condition poor
Content Arabic inscription
Access ECiv/6 (photograph, U. Avner); *see also* ECiv/7

Inscription **5875**
Site Sinai, #0
Technique incised
Condition poor
Content Arabic inscription
Access ECiv/6 (photograph, U. Avner); *see also* ECiv/7

Inscription **5876**
Site Sinai, #0
Technique incised
Condition poor
Content Arabic inscription
Access ECiv/6 (photograph, U. Avner); *see also* ECiv/7

Inscription **5877**
Site Sinai, #0
Technique scratched
Condition poor
Content Latin inscription
Limitation *Tentative decipherment only*
Access ECiv/6 (photograph, U. Avner); *see also* ECiv/7

Inscription **5878**
Site Sinai, #0
Technique incised
Condition fair
Content crosses with inscription
Access ECiv/6 (photograph, U. Avner); *see also* ECiv/7

Inscription **5879**
Site Sinai, #0
Technique incised
Condition good
Content crosses alone
Access ECiv/7 (photograph, U. Avner)

Inscription **5880**
Site Sinai, #0
Technique incised
Condition poor
Content unidentified signs
Access ECiv/7 (photograph, U. Avner)

Inscription **5881**
Site Sinai, #0
Technique incised
Condition poor
Content Arabic inscription
Access ECiv/7 (photograph, U. Avner)

Inscription **5882**
Site Sinai, #0
Technique incised
Condition poor
Content unidentified signs
Access ECiv/7 (photograph, U. Avner)

Inscription 5883
Site Sinai, #0
Technique incised
Condition poor
Content rock drawing
Comment *five-branched candelabrum, similar to insc. 1828*
Access ECiv/8 (photograph, U. Avner)

Inscription 5884
Site Wadi Wata, #225
Technique incised
Condition poor
Content Nabatean inscription
Limitation *Tentative decipherment only*
Access ER02a (photograph, Project); *see also* ER01a

Inscription 5885
Site Wadi Wata, #225
Technique incised
Condition poor
Content Nabatean inscription
Access ER02a (photograph, Project); *see also* ER01a

Inscription 5886
Site Wadi Wata, #225
Technique incised
Condition excellent
Content Nabatean inscription
Limitation *Tentative decipherment only*
Access ER04a (photograph, Project); *see also* ER05a

Inscription 5887
Site Wadi Wata, #225
Technique incised
Condition fair
Content Nabatean inscription
Limitation *Tentative decipherment only*
Access ER04a (photograph, Project); *see also* ER05a, ER06a

Inscription 5888
Site Wadi Wata, #225
Technique incised
Condition poor
Content Nabatean inscription
Access ER04a (photograph, Project); *see also* ER05a

Inscription 5889
Site Wadi Wata, #225
Technique incised
Condition excellent
Content Nabatean inscription
Limitation *Tentative decipherment only*
Access ER04a (photograph, Project); *see also* ER06a

Inscription 5890
Site Wadi Wata, #225
Technique incised
Condition good
Content Russian inscription
Limitation *Tentative decipherment only*
Access ER04a (photograph, Project); *see also* ER08a

Inscription 5891
Site Wadi Wata, #225
Technique incised
Condition excellent
Content Russian inscription
Limitation *Tentative decipherment only*
Access ER04a (photograph, Project); *see also* ER08a

Inscription 5892
Site Wadi Wata, #225
Technique incised
Condition good
Content Russian inscription
Limitation *Tentative decipherment only*
Access ER04a (photograph, Project); *see also* ER08a

Inscription 5893
Site Wadi Wata, #225
Technique incised
Condition excellent
Content Russian inscription
Limitation *Tentative decipherment only*
Access ER04a (photograph, Project); *see also* ER07a

Inscription 5894
Site Wadi Wata, #225
Technique punched
Condition good
Content rock drawing
Comment *animals*
Access ER04a (photograph, Project); *see also* ER05a, ER06a, ER07a

---

Inscription 5895
Site Wadi Wata, #225
Technique incised
Condition good
Content unidentified signs
Access ER04a (photograph, Project)

Inscription 5896
Site Wadi Wata, #225
Technique punched
Condition poor
Content unidentified signs
Access ER05a (photograph, Project); *see also* ER04a

Inscription **5897**
Site Wadi Wata, #225
Technique incised
Condition good
Content Old North Arabic inscription
Access ER07a (photograph, Project); *see also* ER04a

Inscription **5898**
Site Wadi Sreij, Wadi Sreij, #381
Technique incised
Condition excellent
Content Greek inscription
Limitation *Tentative decipherment only*
Access GL23 (photograph, Project)

Inscription **5899**
Site Wadi Sreij, Wadi Sreij, #381
Technique incised
Condition excellent
Content crosses with inscription
Access GL23 (photograph, Project)

Inscription **5900**
Site Wadi Wata, #225
Technique incised
Condition excellent
Content Greek inscription
Limitation *Tentative decipherment only*
Access ER12a (photograph, Project); *see also* ER11a, ER13a, ER30a, ER31a

---

Inscription **5901**
Site Wadi Wata, #225
Technique incised
Condition fair
Content Nabatean inscription
Limitation *Tentative decipherment only*
Access ER12a (photograph, Project); *see also* ER11a, ER30a, ER31a

---

Inscription **5902**
Site Wadi Wata, #225
Technique incised
Condition fair
Content Nabatean inscription
Limitation *Tentative decipherment only*
Access ER14a (photograph, Project)

Inscription **5903**
Site Wadi Wata, #225
Technique incised
Condition good
Content Greek inscription
Limitation *Tentative decipherment only*
Access ER15a (photograph, Project); *see also* ER16a

Inscription **5904**
Site Wadi Wata, #225
Technique incised
Condition good
Content rock drawing
Comment *camel*
Access ER15a (photograph, Project); *see also* ER16a

Inscription **5905**
Site Santa Katarina, Justinian doors rt, #9
Technique incised
Condition excellent
Content Greek inscription
Limitation *Tentative decipherment only*
Access CL03 (photograph, Ann Arbor); *see also* CL08

Inscription **5906**
Site Santa Katarina, Justinian doors rt, #9
Technique scratched
Condition poor
Content unidentified inscription
Access CL03 (photograph, Ann Arbor); *see also* CL08

Inscription **5907**
Site Santa Katarina, Justinian doors rt, #9
Technique incised
Condition excellent
Content crosses with inscription
Access CL03 (photograph, Ann Arbor); *see also* CL08

Inscription **5908**
Site Santa Katarina, Justinian doors rt, #9
Technique scratched
Condition good
Content Greek inscription
Limitation *Tentative decipherment only*
Access CL03 (photograph, Ann Arbor); *see also* CL08

Inscription **5909**
Site Santa Katarina, Justinian doors rt, #9
Technique scratched
Condition poor
Content unidentified inscription
Access CL03 (photograph, Ann Arbor); *see also* CL08

Inscription **5910**
Site Santa Katarina, Justinian doors rt, #9
Technique scratched
Condition poor
Content Greek inscription
Limitation *Tentative decipherment only*
Access CL03 (photograph, Ann Arbor); *see also* CL07

Inscription **5911**
Site Santa Katarina, Justinian doors rt, #9
Technique scratched
Condition poor
Content Greek inscription
Access CL03 (photograph, Ann Arbor); *see also* CL07

Inscription **5912**
Site Santa Katarina, Justinian doors rt, #9
Technique scratched
Condition poor
Content Greek inscription
Limitation *Tentative decipherment only*
Access CL03 (photograph, Ann Arbor); *see also* CL07

Inscription **5913**
Site Santa Katarina, Justinian doors rt, #9
Technique scratched
Condition poor
Content Greek inscription
Access CL03 (photograph, Ann Arbor); *see also* CL08

Inscription **5914**
Site Santa Katarina, Justinian doors rt, #9
Technique scratched
Condition poor
Content Greek inscription
Limitation *Tentative decipherment only*
Comment *monogram*
Access CL03 (photograph, Ann Arbor); *see also* CL03

Inscription **5915**
Site Santa Katarina, Justinian doors rt, #9
Technique scratched
Condition poor
Content Greek inscription
Limitation *Tentative decipherment only*
Access CL03 (photograph, Ann Arbor); *see also* CL08

Inscription **5916**
Site Santa Katarina, Justinian doors rt, #9
Technique scratched
Condition poor
Content crosses with inscription
Comment *following insc. 5915*
Access CL03 (photograph, Ann Arbor); *see also* CL08

Inscription **5917**
Site Santa Katarina, Justinian doors rt, #9
Technique scratched
Condition poor
Content Greek inscription
Limitation *Tentative decipherment only*
Access CL03 (photograph, Ann Arbor); *see also* CL08

Inscription **5918**
Site Santa Katarina, Justinian doors rt, #9
Technique scratched
Condition poor
Content Greek inscription
Access CL03 (photograph, Ann Arbor); *see also* CL08

Inscription **5919**
Site Santa Katarina, Justinian doors rt, #9
Technique scratched
Condition poor
Content Latin inscription
Access CL03 (photograph, Ann Arbor); *see also* CL07

Inscription **5920**
Site Santa Katarina, Justinian doors rt, #9
Technique scratched
Condition poor
Content Arabic inscription
Access CL03 (photograph, Ann Arbor); *see also* CL07

Inscription **5921**
Site Wadi Wata, #225
Technique incised
Condition fair
Content Greek inscription
Limitation *Tentative decipherment only*
Access ER26a (photograph, Project); *see also* ER27a

Inscription **5922**
Site Wadi Wata, #225
Technique incised
Condition poor
Content unidentified signs
Access ER26a (photograph, Project); *see also* ER27a

Inscription **5923**
Site Wadi Wata, #225
Technique incised
Condition good
Content Nabatean inscription
Limitation *Tentative decipherment only*
Access ER28a (photograph, Project)

Inscription **5924**
Site Wadi Wata, #225
Technique incised
Condition poor
Content unidentified signs
Access ER28a (photograph, Project)

Inscription **5925**
Site Wadi Wata, #225
Technique incised
Condition poor
Content Nabatean inscription
Limitation *Tentative decipherment only*
Access ER29a (photograph, Project)

Inscription **5926**
Site Wadi Wata, #225
Technique incised
Condition poor
Content crosses alone
Access ER29a (photograph, Project)

Inscription **5927**
Site Wadi Wata, #225
Technique scratched
Condition poor
Content unidentified signs
Access ER29a (photograph, Project)

Inscription **5928**
Site Wadi Wata, #225
Technique incised
Condition good
Content Nabatean inscription
Limitation *Tentative decipherment only*
Access ER32a (photograph, Project); *see also* ER33a

Inscription **5929**
Site Wadi Wata, #225
Technique incised
Condition poor
Content Nabatean inscription
Limitation *Tentative decipherment only*
Access ER32a (photograph, Project); *see also* ER33a

Inscription **5930**
Site Wadi Wata, #225
Technique incised
Condition good
Content Nabatean inscription
Limitation *Tentative decipherment only*
Access ER32a (photograph, Project); *see also* ER33a

Inscription **5931**
Site Wadi Wata, #225
Technique incised
Condition good
Content Nabatean inscription
Limitation *Tentative decipherment only*
Access ER34a (photograph, Project)

Inscription **5932**
Site Wadi Wata, #225
Technique incised
Condition excellent
Content rock drawing
Comment *camel*
Access ER34a (photograph, Project)

Inscription **5933**
Site Sinai, #0
Technique incised
Condition excellent
Content Arabic inscription
Access ES01 (photograph, Project)

Inscription **5934**
Site Sinai, #0
Technique incised
Condition good
Dimensions 20 x 20 cm.
Content unidentified signs
Access ES04 (photograph, Project); *see also* ES05

Inscription **5935**
Site Sinai, #0
Technique incised
Condition fair
Dimensions 120 x 150 cm.
Content rock drawing
Comment *two human figures, perhaps playing a game*
Access ES04 (photograph, Project); *see also* ES05

Inscription **5936**
Site Sinai, #0
Technique incised
Condition excellent
Dimensions 70 x 135 cm.
Content rock drawing
Comment *outline drawing of ibex*
Access ES04 (photograph, Project); *see also* ES06

Inscription **5937**
Site Sinai, #0
Technique incised
Condition poor
Content Arabic inscription
Access ES09 (photograph, Project)

Inscription **5938**
Site Sinai, #0
Technique incised
Condition fair
Dimensions 150 x 55 cm.
Content rock drawing
Comment *animal*
Access ES10 (photograph, Project)

Inscription **5939**
Site Sinai, #0
Technique incised
Condition poor
Content rock drawing
Comment *humans*
Access ES11 (photograph, Project); *see also* ES12

Inscription **5940**
Site Sinai, #0
Technique incised
Condition good
Content Nabatean inscription
Limitation *Tentative decipherment only*
Access ES14 (photograph, Project); *see also* ES13

Inscription **5941**
Site Sinai, #0
Technique incised
Condition excellent
Content Nabatean inscription
Limitation *Tentative decipherment only*
Access ES15 (photograph, Project); *see also* ES16

Inscription **5942**
Site Sinai, #0
Technique incised
Condition excellent
Content Nabatean inscription
Limitation *Tentative decipherment only*
Access ES15 (photograph, Project); *see also* ES16

Inscription **5943**
Site Sinai, #0
Technique incised
Condition good
Content unidentified signs
Access ES15 (photograph, Project); *see also* ES16

Inscription **5944**
Site Sinai, #0
Technique incised
Condition excellent
Content Nabatean inscription
Limitation *Tentative decipherment only*
Access ES18 (photograph, Project); *see also* ES17

Inscription **5945**
Site Sinai, #0
Technique incised
Condition excellent
Content rock drawing
Comment *camels and ibexes*
Access ES18 (photograph, Project); *see also* ES17

Inscription **5946**
Site Sinai, #0
Technique incised
Condition poor
Content unidentified inscription
Access ES19 (photograph, Project)

Inscription **5947**
Site Sinai, #0
Technique incised
Condition poor
Content unidentified signs
Access ES19 (photograph, Project)

Inscription **5948**
Site Sinai, #0
Technique incised
Condition poor
Content Nabatean inscription
Limitation *Tentative decipherment only*
Access ES20 (photograph, Project); *see also* ES21

Inscription **5949**
Site Sinai, #0
Technique incised
Condition fair
Content rock drawing
Comment *animals*
Access ES20 (photograph, Project); *see also* ES21

Inscription **5950**
Site Sinai, #0
Technique incised
Condition fair
Content Nabatean inscription
Limitation *Tentative decipherment only*
Access ES25 (photograph, Project); *see also* ES26, ES27, ES28, ES29, ET02, ET03

Inscription **5951**
Site Sinai, #0
Technique incised
Condition good
Content Nabatean inscription
Limitation *Tentative decipherment only*
Access ES25 (photograph, Project); *see also* ES26, ES27, ES28, ES29, ET02, ET03

Inscription **5952**
Site Sinai, #0
Technique incised
Condition poor
Content Nabatean inscription
Limitation *Tentative decipherment only*
Access ES25 (photograph, Project); *see also* ES26, ES27, ES28, ES29, ET02, ET03

Inscription **5953**
Site Sinai, #0
Technique incised
Condition poor
Content rock drawing
Comment *animals and human figures*
Access ES25 (photograph, Project); *see also* ES26, ET02

Inscription **5954**
Site Sinai, #0
Technique incised
Condition good
Content Nabatean inscription
Limitation *Tentative decipherment only*
Access ES31 (photograph, Project); *see also* ES30, ES32, ES33, ET01, ET02

Inscription **5955**
Site Sinai, #0
Technique incised
Condition fair
Content Nabatean inscription
Limitation *Tentative decipherment only*
Access ES35 (photograph, Project); *see also* ES34

Inscription **5956**
Site Sinai, #0
Technique incised
Condition poor
Content unidentified signs
Access ES35 (photograph, Project); *see also* ES34

Inscription **5957**
Site Sinai, #0
Technique incised
Condition good
Content rock drawing
Comment *human figures*
Access ET08 (photograph, Project); *see also* ET09

Inscription **5958**
Site Sinai, #0
Technique incised
Condition good
Content rock drawing
Comment *camels*
Access ET10 (photograph, Project); *see also* ET11, ET12

Inscription **5959**
Site Sinai, #0
Technique incised
Condition good
Content Nabatean inscription
Limitation *Tentative decipherment only*
Access ET13 (photograph, Project); *see also* ET14

Inscription **5960**
Site Sinai, #0
Technique incised
Condition poor
Content unidentified signs
Access ET13 (photograph, Project); *see also* ET14

Inscription **5961**
Site Sinai, #0
Technique incised
Condition good
Content rock drawing
Comment *animals*
Access ET13 (photograph, Project); *see also* ET14

Inscription **5962**
Site Sinai, #0
Technique incised
Condition poor
Content Nabatean inscription
Access ET16 (photograph, Project); *see also* ET17

Inscription **5963**
Site Sinai, #0
Technique incised
Condition excellent
Content Old North Arabic inscription
Limitation *Tentative decipherment only*
Access ET18 (photograph, Project)

Inscription **5964**
Site Sinai, #0
Technique incised
Condition good
Content unidentified signs
Access ET18 (photograph, Project)

Inscription **5965**
Site Sinai, #0
Technique incised
Condition good
Content rock drawing
Comment *human figures hunting animals with bow and arrow*
Access ET20 (photograph, Project)

Inscription **5966**
Site Sinai, #0
Technique incised
Condition good
Content Arabic inscription
Access EV01 (photograph, Project); *see also* EV02, EV03, EV04

Inscription **5967**
Site Sinai, #0
Technique scratched
Condition fair
Content Nabatean inscription
Limitation *Tentative decipherment only*
Access EU11 (photograph, Project)

Inscription **5968**
Site Sinai, #0
Technique incised
Condition good
Content Nabatean inscription
Limitation *Tentative decipherment only*
Access EU11 (photograph, Project)

Inscription **5969**
Site Sinai, #0
Technique scratched
Condition poor
Content Nabatean inscription
Limitation *Tentative decipherment only*
Access EU11 (photograph, Project)

Inscription **5970**
Site Sinai, #0
Technique incised
Condition poor
Content Nabatean inscription
Access EU11 (photograph, Project)

Inscription **5971**
Site Sinai, #0
Technique incised
Condition fair
Content rock drawing
Comment *animals*
Access EU11 (photograph, Project)

Inscription **5972**
Site Sinai, #0
Technique incised
Condition good
Content Nabatean inscription
Limitation *Tentative decipherment only*
Access EU12 (photograph, Project); *see also* EU13

Inscription **5973**
Site Sinai, #0
Technique scratched
Condition good
Content Nabatean inscription
Limitation *Tentative decipherment only*
Access EU12 (photograph, Project); *see also* EU13

Inscription **5974**
Site Sinai, #0
Technique incised
Condition fair
Content Nabatean inscription
Limitation *Tentative decipherment only*
Access EU12 (photograph, Project); *see also* EU13

Inscription **5975**
Site Sinai, #0
Technique incised
Condition fair
Content Nabatean inscription
Limitation *Tentative decipherment only*
Access EU14 (photograph, Project)

Inscription **5976**
Site Wadi Biraq, #79
Technique incised
Condition excellent
Dimensions 110 x 25 cm.
Content rock drawing
Comment *horse with riders*
Access EZ01 (photograph, Project); *see also* EZ02

Inscription **5977**
Site Sinai, #0
Technique incised
Condition fair
Content Nabatean inscription
Limitation *Tentative decipherment only*
Access EU17 (photograph, Project)

Inscription **5978**
Site Sinai, #0
Technique incised
Condition excellent
Content Nabatean inscription
Limitation *Tentative decipherment only*
Access EU18 (photograph, Project)

Inscription **5979**
Site Sinai, #0
Technique incised
Condition excellent
Content crosses with inscription
Access EU18 (photograph, Project)

Inscription **5980**
Site Sinai, #0
Technique incised
Condition good
Content Nabatean inscription
Limitation *Tentative decipherment only*
Access EV06 (photograph, Project); *see also* EV05

Inscription **5981**
Site Sinai, #0
Technique incised
Condition good
Content Nabatean inscription
Limitation *Tentative decipherment only*
Access EV06 (photograph, Project); *see also* EV05

Inscription **5982**
Site Sinai, #0
Technique incised
Condition fair
Content rock drawing
Comment *ibex*
Access EV09 (photograph, Project)

Inscription **5983**
Site Sinai, #0
Technique incised
Condition fair
Content Arabic inscription
Access EV10 (photograph, Project)

Inscription **5984**
Site Sinai, #0
Technique incised
Condition poor
Content Old North Arabic inscription
Limitation *Tentative decipherment only*
Access EV12 (photograph, Project); *see also* EV11

Inscription **5985**
Site Sinai, #0
Technique incised
Condition good
Content rock drawing
Comment *three ibexes with fringed horns*
Access EV14 (photograph, Project); *see also* EV13

Inscription **5986**
Site Sinai, #0
Technique incised
Condition fair
Content Greek inscription
Limitation *Tentative decipherment only*
Access EV15 (photograph, Project); *see also* EV16

Inscription **5987**
Site Sinai, #0
Technique incised
Condition fair
Content crosses with inscription
Access EV15 (photograph, Project); *see also* EV16

Inscription **5988**
Site Sinai, #0
Technique incised
Condition poor
Content Greek inscription
Limitation *Tentative decipherment only*
Access EV17 (photograph, Project)

Inscription **5989**
Site Sinai, #0
Technique incised
Condition excellent
Content Latin inscription
Limitation *Tentative decipherment only*
Access EV18 (photograph, Project)

Inscription **5990**
Site Sinai, #0
Technique incised
Condition poor
Content Greek inscription
Limitation *Tentative decipherment only*
Access EV18 (photograph, Project)

Inscription **5991**
Site Sinai, #0
Technique incised
Condition good
Content Nabatean inscription
Limitation *Tentative decipherment only*
Access EV19 (photograph, Project)

Inscription **5992**
Site Sinai, #0
Technique incised
Condition good
Content Nabatean inscription
Limitation *Tentative decipherment only*
Access EV19 (photograph, Project)

Inscription **5993**
Site Sinai, #0
Technique incised
Condition poor
Content Nabatean inscription
Limitation *Tentative decipherment only*
Access EV19 (photograph, Project)

Inscription **5994**
Site Sinai, #0
Technique scratched
Condition fair
Content Nabatean inscription
Limitation *Tentative decipherment only*
Access EV19 (photograph, Project)

Inscription **5995**
Site Sinai, #0
Technique incised
Condition good
Content crosses alone
Access EV19 (photograph, Project)

Inscription **5996**
Site Sinai, #0
Technique incised
Condition poor
Content Nabatean inscription
Limitation *Tentative decipherment only*
Access EV19 (photograph, Project)

Inscription **5997**
Site Sinai, #0
Technique incised
Condition poor
Content Greek inscription
Limitation *Tentative decipherment only*
Access EV23 (photograph, Project); *see also* EV24

Inscription **5998**
Site Sinai, #0
Technique incised
Condition fair
Content Greek inscription
Limitation *Tentative decipherment only*
Access EV23 (photograph, Project); *see also* EV24

Inscription **5999**
Site Sinai, #0
Technique incised
Condition good
Content crosses with inscription
Access EV23 (photograph, Project); *see also* EV24

Inscription **6000**
Site Sinai, #0
Technique incised
Condition poor
Content Greek inscription
Limitation *Tentative decipherment only*
Access EV23 (photograph, Project)

CATALOGUE OF SITES

Key to Location

LOCATION	SITE	NUMBER
A-Tor	A-Tor	101
	Bir Abu Sueira	191
Bir Sueir	Bir Sueir	172
Church of the Holy Sepulchre		375
	St. Helena Chapel 1	292
Church of the Nativity		
	approach to St James	271
	iron door in narthex	251
	left stairs to podium	249
	north door to apse	260
	north door to crypt	262
	pier P	263
	pillar B11	254
	pillar B11(B10)	255
	pillar B2	269
	pillar B3	268
	pillar B4	266
	pillar B5	265
	pillar B6	264
	pillar B7	257
	pillar B9	256
	pillar C10	252
	pillar C2	241
	pillar C3	242
	pillar C4	243
	pillar C5	244
	pillar C7	246
	pillar C8	247
	pillar C9	248
	pillar D8	274
	pillar D9	273
	pillar L	259
	south door to crypt	258
	St. James	270
	well inside	267
Ein Hudra	Ein Hudra	117
Jebel Himayyir	Jebel Himayyir	82
Jebel Maharun	Jebel Maharun	317
Jebel Muneijat F	Jebel Muneijat F	63
Jebel Musa	Jebel Musa	19
	Vale of Elijah	29
	Wadi el Deir	35
Jebel Naqus	Jebel Naqus	103
Jebel Ṣafṣafa	Vale of John, ascent to	380
Jebel Serabit	Rud el Ir	109
	Wadi Suwiq	280
	Wadi Thmareh	282
Mt. Karkom	Nahal Karkom 2	224

LOCATION	SITE	NUMBER
Nahal Avdat	Nahal Avdat 2	158
Ras el Jundi	Qalʿat el Jundi	212
Santa Katarina	Justinian doors rt	9
	Santa Katarina	10
Serabit el Khadem	Serabit el Khadem	86
Sinai	unknown	0
Timna	Timna 1	279
Umm Araq	Umm Araq	87
Jebel Sirbal	Hajjer Ulumbardi	194
	Jebel Sirbal	189
	Wadi Ajaleh	188
	Wadi Alayat	187
	Wadi Nakhleh	221
	Wadi Qseib	222
Jebel Tarbush	Jebel Tarbush	315
Jebel Umm Shumer	Bir Ramhan	5
Naqb el Hawa	Naqb el Hawa	44
Ostrakine	Ostrakine	208
Qunteilat Ajrud	Qunteilat Ajrud	211
Umm Rashrash	Umm Rashrash	376
Wadi Abu Ghadhayyat	Ghadhayyat 1	36
Wadi Arade	Arade 5	111
Wadi Baba	Baba 1	190
Wadi Biraq	Wadi Biraq	79
Wadi el Ahdar	Wadi el Ahdar	52
Wadi el Ein	Ras el Kalb	235
Wadi Firan	Jebel Tahuneh	325
	Wadi Firan	53
	Wadi Khabar	328
Wadi Haggag	rock 3	125
	rock 3 area 1	126
	rock 5	131
	Wadi Haggag	118
Wadi Hamileh	Wadi Hamileh	218
Wadi Hibran	Wadi Hibran	51
Wadi Leja	Wadi Leja	27
Wadi Lethi	Wadi Lethi 1	150
Wadi Mukatab	Wadi Mukatab	64
Wadi Shellal	Shellal 1	91
	Wadi Shellal	90
Wadi Sidri	Wadi Sidri	77
Wadi Sreij	Wadi Sreij, ascent	381
Wadi Sug	Wadi Sug	205
Wadi Sulaf	Wadi Sulaf	48
Wadi Tueiba	Wadi Tueiba	226
Wadi Umm Sidra	Wadi Umm Sidra	174
Wadi Wata	Wadi Wata	225

Site Number 0
Site Name unknown
Location Sinai
Comment *General site designator, used as a convention for inscriptions whose exact location is unknown.*

Site Number 5
Site Name Bir Ramhan
Location Jebel Umm Shumer
Area Code J
UTM 59351379
ITM 04707537
Geology granite
Comment *Greek inscriptions and crosses en route to Santa Katarina via Wadi Rahba. Access to Wadi Rahba is gained from A-Tur via Wadi Isla or via Wadi Thanan.*

Site Number 9
Site Name Justinian doors rt
Location Santa Katarina
Area Code A
UTM 59561592
ITM 04937752
Geology wooden doors
Comment *Inscriptions incised on borders of panels of right valve of Justinian doors of the church of Santa Katarina. The wood is badly cracked. There are inscriptions on both valves, inside and outside. See Stone, Armenian Inscriptions, illustration 11.*

Site Number 10
Site Name Santa Katarina
Location Santa Katarina
Area Code A
UTM 59561592
ITM 04937752
Geology granite
Comment *General site designator.*

Site Number 19
Site Name Jebel Musa
Location Jebel Musa
Area Code A
UTM 59551574
ITM 04927732
Geology granite
Comment *General site designator.*

Site Number 27
Site Name Wadi Leja
Location Wadi Leja
Area Code A
UTM 59421573
ITM 04807732
Geology granite
Comment *General site designator. Byzantine paving and footsteps throughout the wadi (Stone, Sinai Diary 93). See Stone, Armenian Inscriptions, illustration 8.*

Site Number 29
Site Name Vale of Elijah
Location Jebel Musa
Area Code A
UTM 59541580
ITM 05927737
Geology granite

Site Number 35
Site Name Wadi el Deir
Location Jebel Musa
Area Code A
UTM 59631583
ITM 05047740
Geology granite
Comment *General site designator of the wadi containing the Monastery of Santa Katarina. Inscriptions noted include Nabatean and one incomplete Russian inscription on boulders both inside and outside the perimeter wall of the monastery. This site does not include inscriptions found inside the walls of the monastery itself.*

Site Number 36
Site Name Ghadhayyat 1
Location Wadi Abu Ghadhayyat
Area Code L
UTM 63931952
ITM 09378102
Geology sandstone
Comment *Bifurcated hadbe; Greek inscription, drawings, Arabic inscription, wasems (Stone, Notebook, I 88; Sinai Diary, 172). Also a group of crosses, including five large ones. See photograph in Stone, Armenian Inscriptions, illustration 45.*

Site Number 44
Site Name Naqb el Hawa
Location Naqb el Hawa
Area Code A
UTM 59041614
ITM 04437800
Geology granite
Comment *General site designator.*

Site Number 48
Site Name Wadi Sulaf
Location Wadi Sulaf
Area Code B
UTM 57501670
ITM 02887830
Geology granite
Comment *General site designator.*

Site Number 51
Site Name Wadi Hibran
Location Wadi Hibran
Area Code B
UTM 57201590
ITM 02587752
Geology granite
Comment *General site designator.*

Site Number 52
Site Name Wadi el Ahdar
Location Wadi el Ahdar
Area Code B
UTM 58701880
ITM 04138040
Geology granite
Comment *General site designator.*

Site Number 53
Site Name Wadi Firan
Location Wadi Firan
Area Code C
UTM 55401810
ITM 00807975
Geology granite
Comment *General site designator.*

Site Number 63
Site Name Jebel Muneijat F
Location Jebel Muneijat
Area Code C
UTM 56421740
ITM 01787906
Geology granite
Comment *Mountain near Wadi Firan.*

Site Number 64
Site Name Wadi Mukatab
Location Wadi Mukatab
Area Code D
UTM 54201901
ITM 99628068
Geology sandstone
Comment *General site designator. The wadi contains many inscriptions in Nabatean, a few in Greek and Arabic. The sides of the wadi are of low sandstone. The southwest and northeast sides are covered with inscriptions.*

Site Number 77
Site Name Wadi Sidri
Location Wadi Sidri
Area Code E
UTM 53001940
ITM 98458110
Geology granite, sandstone
Comment *General site designator.*

Site Number 79
Site Name Wadi Biraq
Location Wadi Biraq
Area Code E
UTM 55901980
ITM 01358146
Geology sandstone
Comment *General site designator.*

Site Number 82
Site Name Jebel Himayyir
Location Jebel Himayyir
Area Code E
UTM 55322127
ITM 00808293
Geology sandstone
Comment *Drawing of twelve ostriches in a row, Nabatean inscriptions (M. Fakash, Mountainous Mining Area, 143).*

Site Number 86
Site Name Serabit el Khadem
Location Serabit el Khadem
Area Code F
UTM 55462123
ITM 99938291
Geology sandstone
Comment *General site designator.*

Site Number 87
Site Name Umm Araq
Location Umm Araq
Area Code F
UTM 54792169
ITM 00258336
Geology sandstone
Comment *Very large sandstone rock. Nabatean inscriptions and drawings on east side; northeast corner contains many Nabatean inscriptions; Nabatean inscriptions also on fallen rocks; adjacent rock face with numerous Nabatean inscriptions. Some Arabic inscriptions on this rock. Southwest corner contains Nabatean inscriptions, rock drawings and an Old North Arabic inscription, as well as unidentified signs (Stone, Sinai Diary, 80-81; Notebook III, 13).*

Site Number 90
Site Name Wadi Shellal
Location Wadi Shellal
Area Code F
UTM 53002020
ITM 98458180
Geology sandstone
Comment *General site designator. The following sites in this area are designated as sites Shellal 1-7: nos. 91, 92, 93, 94, 95, 96, 97.*

Site Number 91
Site Name Shellal 1
Location Wadi Shellal
Area Code F
UTM 53092023
ITM 98558195
Geology sandstone
Comment *Site with Greek and Nabatean inscriptions and drawings (Stone, Notebook III, 27).*

Site Number 101
Site Name A-Tor
Location A-Tor
Area Code G
UTM 56101230
ITM 01417396
Geology limestone
Comment *General site designator. Christian inscriptions in the plaster of monastic cells: see E. H. Palmer, Desert of Sinai, 1.222.*

Site Number **103**
Site Name Jebel Naqus
Location Jebel Naqus
Area Code G
UTM 55461333
ITM 00607498
Geology limestone
Comment *General site designator.*

Site Number **109**
Site Name Rud el Ir
Location Jebel Serabit
Area Code E
UTM 53922125
ITM 99388219
Geology sandstone

Site Number **111**
Site Name Arade 5
Location Wadi Arade
Area Code H
UTM 62501900
ITM 07948055
Geology sandstone
Comment *General site designator.*

Site Number **117**
Site Name Ein Hudra
Location Ein Hudra
Area Code L
UTM 63881963
ITM 09358126
Geology sandstone
Comment *General site designator.*

Site Number **118**
Site Name Wadi Haggag
Location Wadi Haggag
Area Code L
UTM 63701950
ITM 09148098
Geology sandstone
Comment *General site designator. See also Wadi Rum, Jebel Rum.*

Site Number **125**
Site Name rock 3
Location Wadi Haggag
Area Code L
UTM 63761959
ITM 09208106
Geology sandstone
Comment *See Stone, Armenian Inscriptions, plan VI, p. 100.*

Site Number **126**
Site Name rock 3 area 1
Location Wadi Haggag
Area Code L
UTM 63761956
ITM 09208106
Geology sandstone
Comment *Face at southern corner of Rock 3. See Stone, Armenian Inscriptions, plan VI, p. 100.*

Site Number **131**
Site Name rock 5
Location Wadi Haggag
Area Code L
UTM 63891955
ITM 09368106
Geology sandstone
Comment *See Stone, Armenian Inscriptions, illustration 3.*

Site Number **150**
Site Name Wadi Lethi 1
Location Wadi Lethi
Area Code N
UTM 64482188
ITM 09968337
Geology sandstone
Comment *Eastern of two wadis by this name. Tumuli on the eastern side. Extensive chalcolithic sites (Stone, Notebook VI, 11).*

Site Number **158**
Site Name Nahal Avdat 2
Location Nahal Avdat
Area Code I
ITM 02521277
Geology limestone
Comment *Further from Ein Avdat than Nahal Avdat 1; group of rocks on side of wadi.*

Site Number **172**
Site Name Bir Sueir
Location Bir Sueir
Area Code P
UTM 12358518
ITM 66832373
Geology sandstone
Comment *Drawings, over, 50 crosses, Greek inscriptions (Stone, Sinai Diary 147). Arabic, including square script, and Nabatean (Stone, Notebook V). Map of finds in Stone, Notebook VI, 11, and text of Greek inscription in Stone, Notebook VI, 11.*

Site Number **174**
Site Name Wadi Umm Sidra
Location Wadi Umm Sidra
Area Code W
UTM 67702730
ITM 13358875
Geology sandstone
Comment *General site designator. Also called Canyon of Inscriptions. Special file assembled by B. Shulman of Eilat has been incorporated into the Project records.*

Site Number **187**
Site Name Wadi Alayat
Location Jebel Sirbal
Area Code C
UTM 56351738
ITM 01757898
Geology granite

Site Number 188
Site Name Wadi Ajaleh
Location Jebel Sirbal
Area Code C
UTM 56051735
ITM 01457898
Geology granite

Site Number 189
Site Name Jebel Sirbal
Location Jebel Sirbal
Area Code C
UTM 56311696
ITM 01757858
Geology granite
Comment *General site designator. Numerous Nabatean inscriptions (Dahari in Rabinovitz, Sirbal, 29).*

Site Number 190
Site Name Baba 1
Location Wadi Baba
Area Code F
UTM 52852046
ITM 98338218
Geology granite
Comment *Directly south of Bir Rakis, entrance to canyon of Wadi Baba, on east wall, on isolated rock.*

Site Number 191
Site Name Bir Abu Sueira
Location A-Tor
Area Code G
UTM 55491305
ITM 00897472
Geology limestone
Comment *Site of monastery of Raithou near A-Tor.*

Site Number 194
Site Name Hajjer Ulumbardi
Location Jebel Sirbal
Area Code C
UTM 56381674
ITM 01797838
Geology granite
Comment *Negev, Ketovot Drom Sinai, 335 (Jebel Umm Barid). U. Dahari in Rabinovitz, Sirbal 29, 38.*

Site Number 205
Site Name Wadi Sug
Location Wadi Sug
Area Code E
UTM 54702129
ITM 00168296
Geology sandstone
Comment *A. Negev, Ketovot Drom Sinai, 335.*

Site Number 208
Site Name Ostrakine
Location Ostrakine
Area Code U
ITM 00030598
Geology sandstone
Comment *See El Filusat (site code 207).*

Site Number 211
Site Name Qunteilat Ajrud
Location Qunteilat Ajrud
Area Code V
ITM 09049506
Geology limestone
Comment *General site designator.*

Site Number 212
Site Name Qalʿat el Jundi
Location Ras el Jundi
Area Code Q
UTM 51253024
ITM 96099202
Geology limestone
Comment *General site designator.*

Site Number 218
Site Name Wadi Hamileh
Location Wadi Hamileh
Area Code E
UTM 55322067
ITM 00788234
Geology sandstone
Comment *General site designator. North of Wadi el Sheikh. Drawings and Nabatean inscriptions (M. Farkash, Mountainous Mining Area, 139).*

Site Number 221
Site Name Wadi Nakhleh
Location Jebel Sirbal
Area Code C
UTM 56171738
ITM 01597889
Geology granite
Comment *A. Negev, Ketovot Drom Sinai, 335*

Site Number 222
Site Name Wadi Qseib
Location Jebel Sirbal
Area Code C
UTM 55761697
ITM 01157860
Geology granite
Comment *A. Negev, Ketovot Drom Sinai, 335.*

Site Number 223
Site Name Wadi Teibeh
Location Jebel Tarbush
Area Code B
UTM 58121620
ITM 03487782
Geology granite
Comment *Z. Meshel, Qadmoniot Sinai.*

Site Number 224
Site Name Nahal Karkom 2
Location Mt. Karkom
Area Code I
ITM *12499676, 12489678, 12489679*
Geology limestone
Comment *Branch of Nahal Karkom. A low, elongated hill to the northwest of Nahal Karkom. Numerous North Arabic inscriptions, drawings, and symbols.*

Site Number **225**
Site Name Wadi Wata
Location Wadi Wata
Area Code F
UTM 53502297
ITM 99018465
Geology sandstone
Comment *At the foot of the escarpment of the Tih.*

Site Number **226**
Site Name Wadi Tueiba
Location Wadi Tueiba
Area Code W
UTM 68112641
ITM 13688782
Geology sandstone
Comment *South of Eilat. General site designator.*

Site Number **235**
Site Name Ras el Kalb
Location Wadi el Ein
Area Code M
UTM 63822172
ITM 09308320
Geology sandstone

Site Number **241**
Site Name pillar C2
Location Church of the Nativity
Area Code IB
Comment *An Arabic inscription.*

Site Number **242**
Site Name pillar C3
Location Church of the Nativity
Area Code IB
Comment *On the west side, Latin and Arabic inscriptions. On the south side, the letter 'P'.*

Site Number **243**
Site Name pillar C4
Location Church of the Nativity
Area Code IB
Comment *On the west side. an Arabic inscription. On the southwest, Armenian and Latin inscriptions.*

Site Number **244**
Site Name pillar C5
Location Church of the Nativity
Area Code IB
Comment *On the south side: Latin, Greek, unidentified; on the east: English, Arabic; on the north: Arabic and very faint, unidentified.*

Site Number **246**
Site Name pillar C7
Location Church of the Nativity
Area Code IB
Comment *On the west side, an Arabic inscription. On the south, a Greek inscription. On the southeast, two Greek inscriptions.*

Site Number **247**
Site Name pillar C8
Location Church of the Nativity
Area Code IB
Comment *On the south and east sides, Arabic inscriptions. On the south, a Latin inscription.*

Site Number **248**
Site Name pillar C9
Location Church of the Nativity
Area Code IB
Comment *On the west side, three Arabic, one Greek inscription. On the south, Greek inscriptions, painting and cross. On the east, an Arabic inscription.*

Site Number **249**
Site Name left stairs to podium
Location Church of the Nativity
Area Code IB
Comment *Before the lower step, a Greek inscription. Two Arabic inscriptions on the top stair.*

Site Number **251**
Site Name iron door in narthex
Location Church of the Nativity
Area Code IB
Comment *Russian inscription on iron door. Armenian inscription on the north side.*

Site Number **252**
Site Name pillar C10
Location Church of the Nativity
Area Code IB
Comment *On west side, Armenian and Greek inscriptions. On the south, an Arabic inscription.*

Site Number **254**
Site Name pillar B11
Location Church of the Nativity
Area Code IB
Comment *On the west side a Greek inscription and on the southwest, an Arabic inscription.*

Site Number **255**
Site Name pillar B11(B10)
Location Church of the Nativity
Area Code IB
Comment *On the west side, a Russian inscription.*

Site Number **256**
Site Name pillar B9
Location Church of the Nativity
Area Code IB
Comment *On the west and northwest sides, Armenian inscriptions. On the southwest, Arabic and Armenian inscriptions.*

Site Number **257**
Site Name pillar B7
Location Church of the Nativity
Area Code IB
Comment *On the north side, Armenian and Arabic inscriptions and cross. On the west, Arabic, Armenian, Greek inscriptions and cross. On the east, an Armenian inscription.*

Site Number 258
Site Name south door to crypt
Location Church of the Nativity
Area Code IB
Comment *On the west side, Arabic and unidentified inscriptions. On the east, crosses, Armenian, Italian and Spanish inscriptions.*

Site Number 259
Site Name pillar L
Location Church of the Nativity
Area Code IB
Comment *On the northwest side, a Spanish inscription. On the north, a Georgian inscription.*

Site Number 260
Site Name north door to apse
Location Church of the Nativity
Area Code IB
Comment *Above the stairs, a Latin Gothic inscription. On the northwest side, an Arabic inscription.*

Site Number 262
Site Name north door to crypt
Location Church of the Nativity
Area Code IB
Comment *On the west side, Armenian and Arabic inscriptions and crosses. On the east side, Armenian, Syriac, Arabic and Franciscan inscriptions and crosses.*

Site Number 263
Site Name pier P
Location Church of the Nativity
Area Code IB
Comment *An Armenian inscription.*

Site Number 264
Site Name pillar B6
Location Church of the Nativity
Area Code IB
Comment *On the north side, Armenian, Latin and Greek inscriptions. On the west, Latin, Armenian, Arabic inscriptions and crosses.*

Site Number 265
Site Name pillar B5
Location Church of the Nativity
Area Code IB
Comment *On the west side, Armenian, Greek, Syriac and Arabic inscriptions. On the north, Latin and Arabic inscriptions.*

Site Number 266
Site Name pillar B4
Location Church of the Nativity
Area Code IB
Comment *On the north side, a Latin inscription. On the northeast, an Arabic inscription. On the northwest, an Armenian inscription and an Arabic inscription. On the west side, a Latin inscription.*

Site Number 267
Site Name well inside
Location Church of the Nativity
Area Code IB
Comment *Greek inscription.*

Site Number 268
Site Name pillar B3
Location Church of the Nativity
Area Code IB
Comment *On the east side, an Arabic inscription.*

Site Number 269
Site Name pillar B2
Location Church of the Nativity
Area Code IB
Comment *On the north side, a cross.*

Site Number 270
Site Name St. James
Location Church of the Nativity
Area Code IB
Comment *On the north side, an Armenian inscription. On the east, an inscription. Around the cross, an Armenian inscription, crosses, Greek inscription. On the west, crosses. On the south, an Armenian inscription.*

Site Number 271
Site Name approach to St James
Location Church of the Nativity
Area Code IB

Site Number 273
Site Name pillar D9
Location Church of the Nativity
Area Code IB
Comment *On the west side, a Coptic inscription.*

Site Number 274
Site Name pillar D8
Location Church of the Nativity
Area Code IB

Site Number 279
Site Name Timna 1
Location Timna
Area Code I
UTM 68782950
ITM 14459088
Geology granite
Comment *Temple of the Goddess Hathor.*

Site Number 280
Site Name Wadi Suwiq
Location Jebel Serabit
Area Code E
UTM 54532137
ITM 99988304
Geology granite

Site Number 282
Site Name Wadi Thmareh
Location Jebel Serabit
Area Code E
UTM 53232100
ITM 98698271
Geology granite

Site Number **292**
Site Name St. Helena Chapel 1
Location Church of the Holy Sepulchre
Area Code IB
Comment *Downstairs one flight, opposite Armenian altar, between stairs and caretaker's chamber, to left of steps (facing up).*

Site Number **317**
Site Name Jebel Maharun
Location Jebel Maharun
Area Code H
Comment *Between Ein Hudra and Santa Katarina area, does not exist on the map.*

Site Number **325**
Site Name Jebel Tahuneh
Location Wadi Firan
Area Code C
UTM 56321761
ITM 01747925
Geology sandstone

Site Number **328**
Site Name Wadi Khabar
Location Wadi Firan
Area Code C
UTM 56581780
ITM 01997942
Geology sandstone

Site Number **375**
Site Name Church of the Holy Sepulchre
Location Church of the Holy Sepulchre
Area Code IB
Comment *General site designator.*

Site Number **376**
Site Name Umm Rashrash
Location Umm Rashrash
Area Code W
Comment *Near Eilat. General site designator*

Site Number **380**
Site Name Vale of John, ascent to
Location Jebel Ṣafṣafa
Area Code A
Comment *Ascent to Vale of John from direction of Ras Ṣafṣafa.*

Site Number **381**
Site Name Wadi Sreij, ascent
Location Wadi Sreij
Area Code A
Comment *Ascent from Wadi Sreij to Ras Ṣafṣafa.*

INDEXES

Index by Date

Index by Content

3097 3098 3099 3100 3101 3102 3103 3104 3105 3106 3107 3108 3109 3110 3111 3112
3113 3114 3115 3116 3117 3118 3119 3120 3121 3122 3123 3124 3125 3126 3127 3128
3129 3130 3131 3132 3133 3134 3135 3136 3137 3138 3139 3140 3141 3142 3143 3144
3145 3146 3147 3148 3149 3150 3151 3152 3153 3154 3155 3156 3157 3158 3159 3160
3161 3162 3163 3164 3165 3166 3167 3168 3169 3170 3171 3172 3173 3174 3175 3176
3177 3178 3179 3180 3181 3182 3183 3184 3185 3186 3187 3188 3189 3190 3191 3192
3193 3194 3195 3196 3197 3198 3199 3200 3201 3202 3203 3204 3205 3206 3207 3208
3209 3210 3211 3212 3213 3214 3215 3216 3217 3218 3219 3220 3221 3222 3223 3224
3225 3226 3227 3228 3229 3230 3231 3232 3233 3234 3235 3236 3237 3238 3239 3240
3241 3242 3243 3244 3245 3246 3247 3248 3249 3250 3251 3252 3253 3254 3255 3256
3257 3258 3259 3260 3261 3262 3263 3264 3265 3266 3267 3268 3269 3270 3271 3272
3273 3274 3275 3276 3277 3278 3279 3280 3281 3282 3283 3284 3285 3286 3287 3288
3289 3290 3291 3292 3293 3294 3295 3296 3297 3298 3299 3300 3301 3302 3303 3304
3305 3306 3307 3308 3309 3310 3311 3312 3313 3314 3315 3316 3317 3318 3319 3320
3321 3322 3323 3324 3325 3326 3327 3328 3329 3330 3331 3332 3333 3334 3335 3336
3337 3338 3339 3340 3341 3342 3343 3344 3345 3346 3347 3348 3349 3350 3351 3352
3353 3354 3355 3356 3357 3358 3359 3360 3361 3362 3363 3364 3365 3366 3367 3368
3369 3370 3371 3372 3373 3374 3375 3376 3377 3378 3379 3380 3381 3382 3383 3384
3385 3386 3387 3388 3389 3390 3391 3392 3393 3394 3395 3396 3397 3398 3399 3400
3401 3402 3403 3404 3405 3406 3407 3408 3409 3410 3411 3412 3413 3414 3415 3416
3417 3418 3419 3420 3421 3422 3423 3424 3425 3426 3427 3428 3429 3430 3431 3432
3433 3434 3435 3436 3437 3438 3439 3440 3441 3442 3443 3444 3445 3446 3447 3448
3449 3450 3451 3452 3453 3454 3455 3456 3457 3458 3459 3460 3461 3462 3463 3464
3465 3466 3467 3468 3469 3470 3471 3472 3473 3474 3475 3476 3477 3478 3479 3480
3481 3482 3483 3484 3485 3486 3487 3488 3489 3490 3491 3492 3493 3494 3495 3496
3497 3498 3499 3500 3501 3502 3503 3504 3505 3506 3507 3508 3509 3510 3511 3512
3513 3514 3515 3516 3517 3518 3519 3520 3521 3522 3523 3524 3534 3535 3536 3537
3538 3539 3540 3541 3542 3543 3544 3545 3546 3547 3581 3582 3583 3584 3585 3586
3587 3588 3589 3590 3591 3592 3593 3594 3595 3596 3597 3598 3599 3601 3602 3603
3604 3605 3606 3607 3608 3609 3610 3611 3612 3613 3614 3615 3616 3617 3618 3619
3620 3621 3622 3623 3624 3625 3626 3627 3628 3629 3630 3631 3632 3633 3634 3635
3636 3637 3638 3639 3640 3641 3642 3643 3644 3645 3646 3647 3648 3649 3650 3651
3652 3653 3654 3655 3656 3657 3658 3659 3660 3661 3662 3663 3664 3665 3666 3667
3668 3669 3670 3671 3672 3673 3674 3675 3676 3677 3678 3679 3680 3681 3682 3683
3684 3685 3686 3687 3688 3689 3690 3691 3692 3693 3694 3695 3696 3697 3698 3699
3700 3701 3702 3703 3704 3705 3706 3707 3708 3709 3710 3711 3712 3713 3714 3715
3716 3717 3718 3719 3720 3721 3722 3723 3724 3725 3726 3727 3728 3729 3730 3731
3732 3733 3734 3735 3736 3737 3738 3739 3740 3741 3742 3743 3744 3745 3746 3747
3748 3749 3750 3751 3752 3753 3754 3755 3756 3757 3758 3759 3760 3761 3762 3763
3764 3765 3766 3767 3768 3769 3770 3771 3772 3773 3774 3775 3776 3777 3778 3779
3780 3781 3782 3783 3784 3785 3786 3787 3788 3789 3790 3791 3792 3793 3794 3795
3796 3797 3798 3799 3800 3801 3802 3803 3804 3805 3806 3807 3808 3809 3810 3811
3812 3813 3814 3815 3816 3817 3818 3819 3820 3821 3822 3823 3824 3825 3826 3827
3828 3829 3830 3831 3832 3833 3834 3835 3836 3837 3838 3839 3840 3841 3842 3843
3844 3845 3846 3847 3848 3849 3850 3851 3852 3853 3854 3855 3856 3857 3858 3859
3860 3861 3862 3863 3864 3865 3866 3867 3868 3869 3870 3871 3872 3873 3874 3875
3876 3877 3878 3879 3880 3881 3882 3883 3884 3885 3886 3887 3888 3889 3890 3891
3892 3893 3894 3895 3896 3897 3898 3899 3900 3901 3902 3903 3904 3905 3906 3907
3908 3909 3910 3911 3912 3913 3914 3915 3916 3917 3918 3919 3920 3921 3922 3923
3924 3925 3926 3927 3928 3929 3930 3931 3932 3933 3934 3935 3936 3937 3938 3939
3940 3941 3942 3943 3944 3945 3946 3947 3948 3949 3950 3951 3952 3953 3954 3955
3956 3957 3958 3959 3960 3961 3962 3963 3964 3965 3966 3967 3968 3969 3970 3971
3972 3973 3974 3975 3976 3977 3978 3979 3980 3981 3982 3983 3984 3985 3986 3987
3988 3989 3990 3991 3992 3993 3994 3995 3996 3997 3998 3999 4000 4001 4002 4003
4004 4005 4006 4007 4008 4009 4010 4011 4012 4013 4014 4015 4016 4017 4018 4019
4020 4021 4022 4023 4024 4025 4026 4027 4028 4029 4030 4031 4032 4033 4034 4035
4036 4037 4038 4039 4040 4041 4042 4043 4044 4045 4046 4047 4048 4049 4050 4051
4053 4054 4055 4056 4057 4058 4059 4060 4061 4062 4063 4064 4065 4066 4067 4068
4069 4070 4071 4072 4073 4074 4075 4076 4077 4078 4079 4080 4081 4082 4083 4084
4085 4086 4087 4088 4089 4090 4091 4092 4093 4094 4095 4096 4097 4098 4099 4100
4101 4102 4103 4104 4105 4106 4107 4108 4109 4110 4111 4112 4113 4114 4115 4116
4117 4118 4119 4120 4121 4122 4123 4124 4125 4126 4127 4128 4129 4130 4131 4132
4133 4134 4135 4136 4137 4138 4139 4140 4141 4142 4143 4144 4145 4146 4147 4148
4149 4150 4151 4152 4153 4154 4155 4156 4157 4158 4159 4160 4161 4162 4163 4164
4165 4166 4167 4168 4169 4170 4171 4172 4173 4174 4175 4176 4177 4178 4179 4180
4181 4182 4183 4184 4185 4186 4187 4188 4189 4190 4191 4192 4193 4194 4195 4196
4197 4198 4199 4200 4201 4202 4203 4204 4205 4206 4207 4208 4209 4210 4211 4212
4213 4214 4215 4216 4217 4218 4219 4220 4221 4222 4223 4224 4225 4226 4227 4228
4229 4230 4231 4232 4233 4234 4235 4236 4237 4238 4239 4240 4241 4242 4243 4244

4249 4584 4814 5119 5437 5446 5517 5677 5864

OTHER ROCK MARKINGS
footsteps
5124 5125 5128 5643 5653 5659
geology
4904 4903
ornaments
4306 4280
rock drawings
3526 3575 3578 4294 4295 4298 4301 4309 4310 4414 4436 4442 4528 4534 4568 4573 4580 4594 4599 4604 4605 4614 4618 4621 4627 4680 4688 4703 4810 4811 4821 4830 4898 4905 4907 4909 4931 4932 4940 4941 4942 4943 4947 4954 4955 4968 4969 4975 4988 4992 4997 4998 5000 5001 5002 5004 5010 5011 5017 5020 5022 5038 5045 5046 5053 5054 5055 5065 5066 5070 5076 5082 5108 5111 5116 5126 5127 5142 5207 5211 5223 5250 5257 5329 5335 5337 5340 5342 5343 5345 5346 5347 5352 5363 5365 5366 5367 5386 5388 5397 5398 5399 5400 5401 5402 5432 5434 5440 5442 5444 5445 5447 5454 5466 5525 5535 5536 5537 5540 5541 5543 5544 5546 5548 5549 5551 5552 5553 5554 5556 5559 5579 5587 5588 5622 5634 5637 5638 5639 5640 5641 5642 5645 5647 5648 5649 5650 5651 5661 5665 5666 5667 5668 5672 5673 5674 5675 5691 5696 5702 5708 5709 5729 5766 5807 5808 5809 5851 5855 5859 5860 5861 5862 5863 5871 5872 5883 5894 5904 5932 5935 5936 5938 5939 5945 5949 5953 5957 5958 5961 5965 5971 5976 5982 5985
unidentified signs
4290 4302 4327 4477 4561 4562 4577 4579 4586 4603 4634 4655 4656 4672 4727 4731 4877 4883 4886 4908 4919 4925 4933 4949 4950 4953 4966 4978 5008 5012 5013 5014 5025 5028 5033 5036 5037 5057 5067 5077 5084 5131 5150 5152 5193 5202 5217 5227 5228 5232 5238 5266 5270 5310 5311 5312 5316 5317 5321 5330 5336 5339 5354 5356 5364 5389 5390 5394 5425 5441 5443 5493 5519 5534 5542 5547 5558 5580 5581 5586 5617 5644 5655 5656 5658 5662 5688 5698 5731 5736 5765 5858 5865 5866 5880 5882 5895 5896 5922 5924 5927 5934 5943 5947 5956 5960 5964
wasems and other Bedouin marks
5137 5373 5538

INDEX BY LOCATION

3834 3835 3836 3837 3838 3839 3840 3841 3842 3843 3844 3845 3846 3847 3848 3849
3850 3851 3852 3853 3854 3855 3856 3857 3858 3859 3860 3861 3862 3863 3864 3865
3866 3867 3868 3869 3870 3871 3872 3873 3874 3875 3876 3877 3878 3879 3880 3881
3882 3883 3884 3885 3886 3887 3888 3889 3890
Wadi Haggag
4300 4301 4302 4309 4310 4580 4594 4821 4897 4971 4972 4973 4974 4975 4976 5067
5068 5069 5117 5118 5119 5120 5121 5122 5123 5124 5125 5126 5127 5128 5129 5130
5131 5132 5133 5134 5135 5151 5152 5153 5154 5155 5156 5157 5158 5165 5166 5167
5168 5169 5170 5171 5226 5227 5228 5237 5238 5239 5240 5241 5242 5243 5244 5859
Wadi Hamileh
4219 4220 4221 4222 4223 4224 4225 4226 4227 4228
Wadi Hibran
3964 3965 3966 3967 3968 3969 3970 3971 3972 3973 3974 3975 3976 3977 3978 3979
3980 3981 3982 3983 3984 3985 3986 3987 3988 3989 3990 3991 3992 3993 3994 3995
3996 3997 3998 3999 4000 4001 4002 4003 4004 4005 4006 4007 4008 4009 4010 4011
4012
Wadi Leja
3531 3532 3533 3548 3550 3551 3552 3553 3554 3555 3556 3557 3558 4294
Wadi Lethi
4298
Wadi Mukatab
3574 3575 3576 3577 3578 3579 3580 4898 5061 5181 5225 5334 5335 5336
Wadi Shellal
4428 5138 5139 5618 5619 5620 5621 5622 5623 5624 5625 5626 5627 5628 5629 5630
5631 5632 5633 5634 5635 5636 5637 5638 5639 5640 5641 5642 5643 5644 5645 5646
5647 5648 5649 5650 5651 5652 5653 5654 5655 5656 5657 5658 5659 5660 5661 5662
5663 5664 5665 5666 5667 5668 5669 5670 5671 5672 5673 5674 5675 5676 5677 5678
5679 5680 5681 5682 5683 5684 5685 5686 5687 5688 5689 5690 5691 5692 5693 5694
5695 5696 5697 5698 5699 5700 5701 5702 5703 5704 5705 5706 5707 5708 5709 5710
5711 5712 5713 5714 5715 5716 5717 5718 5719 5720 5721 5722 5723 5724 5725 5726
5727 5728 5729 5730 5731 5732 5733 5734 5735 5736 5737 5738 5739 5740 5741 5742
5743 5744 5745 5746 5747 5748 5749 5750 5751 5752 5753 5754 5755 5756 5757 5758
5759 5760 5761 5762 5763 5764 5765 5766 5767 5768 5769 5770 5771 5772 5773 5774
5775 5776 5777 5778 5779 5780 5781 5782 5783 5784 5785 5786 5787 5788 5789 5790
5791 5792 5793 5794 5795 5796 5797 5798 5799 5800 5801 5802 5803 5804 5805 5806
5807 5808 5809 5810 5811 5812 5813 5815 5816 5817 5818 5819 5820 5821 5822 5823
5824 5825 5826 5827 5828 5829 5830 5831 5832 5833 5834 5835 5836 5837 5838 5839
5840 5841 5842 5843 5844 5845 5846 5847 5848 5849 5850 5851 5852 5853 5854 5855
5856 5857 5858
Wadi Sidri
4599 4600 4601
Wadi Sreij
5898 5899
Wadi Sug
4900
Wadi Sulaf
3947 3948 3949 3950 3951 3952 3953 3954 3955 3956 3957 3958 3959 3960 3961 3962
3963
Wadi Tueiba
4433 4434 4435 4436 4573 4604 4614 4618 4623 4624 4625 4626 4627 4661 4662 4703
4704 4943 4986 4987 4988 4989 4990 4991 4992 4993 4994 4995 4996 4997 4999 5000
5001 5002 5003 5004 5005 5015 5016 5017 5018 5019 5021 5023 5024 5025 5026 5027
5028 5029 5030 5031 5032 5033 5041 5042 5052 5053 5054 5055 5056 5057 5059 5060
5353 5354 5355 5356 5357 5358 5359 5360 5361 5366 5384 5385 5386 5387 5388 5389
5390
Wadi Umm Sidra
4052 4830 5006 5007 5008 5009 5038 5039 5040 5043 5044 5045 5046 5047 5048 5049
5050 5136 5137 5140 5141 5142 5148 5149 5150 5327 5331 5332 5333 5344
Wadi Wata
5884 5885 5886 5887 5888 5889 5890 5891 5892 5893 5894 5895 5896 5897 5900 5901
5902 5903 5904 5921 5922 5923 5924 5925 5926 5927 5928 5929 5930 5931 5932

Index by Content, Place and Date

Jebel Himayyir

unavailable 5561 5562 5563 5564 5565 5566 5567 5568 5569 5570 5571 5572 5573 5574 5575 5576 5577 5578 5583 5584 5585

Jebel Muneijat F

253 3932

unavailable 3925 3926 3927 3928 3929 3930 3931 3933 3934 3935 3936 3937 3938 3939 3940 3941 3942 3943 3944 3945 3946 4787 4788 4789 4790 4791 4792 4793 4794 4795 4796 4797 4798 4799 4800 4801 4802 4803 4804 4805 4806 4807 4808 4809 4812 4813 4910 4911

Jebel Musa

unavailable 4024 4025 4026 4027 4028 4029 4030 4031 4032 4033 4034 4035 4036 4037 4038 4039 4040 4041 4042 4043 4044 4045 4046 4047 4048 4049 4050 4051 4053 4054 4055 4056 4057 4058 4059 4060 4061 4062 4063 4064 4065 4066 4067 4068 4069 4070 4071 4072 4073 4074 4075 4076 4077 4078 4079 4080 4081 4082 4083 4084 4085 4086 4087 4088 4089 4090 4091 4092 4093 4094 4095 4096 4097 4098 4099 4100 4101 4102 4103 4104 4105 4106 4107 4108 4109 4110 4111 4112 4113 4114 4115 4116 4117 4118 4119 4120 4121 4122 4123 4124 4125 4126 4127 4128 4129 4130 4131 4132 4133 4134 4135 4136 4137 4138 4139 4140 4141 4142 4143 4144 4145 4146 4147 4148 4149 4150 4151 4152 4153 4154 4155 4156 4157 4158 4159 4160 4161 4162 4163 4164 4165 4166 4167 4168 4169 4170 4171 4172 4173 4174 4175 4176 4177 4178 4179 4180 4181 4182 4183 4184 4185 4186 4202

Jebel Serabit

unavailable 3621 3622 3623 3624 3625 3626 3627 3628 3629 3630 3631 3632 3633 3634 3635 3636 3637 3638 3639 3640 3641 3642 3643 3644 3645 3646 3647 3648 3649 3650 3651 3652 3653 3654 3655 3656 3657 3658 3659 3660 3661 3662 3663 3664 3665 3666 3667 3668 3669 3670 3671 3672 3673 3674 3675 3676 3677 3678 3679 3680 3681 3682 3683 3684 3685 3686 3687 3688 3689 3690 3691 3692 3693 3694 3695 3696 3697 3698 3699 3700 3701 3702 3703 3704 3705 3706 3707 3708 3709 3710 3711 3712 3713 3714 3715 3716 3717 3718 3719 3720 3721 3722 3723 3724 3725 3726 3727 3728 3729 3730 3731 3780 3891 3892 3893 3894 3895 3896 3897 3898 3899 3900 3901 3902 3903 3904 3905 3906 3907 3908 3909 3910 3911 3912 3913 3914 3915 3916 3917 3918 3919 3920 3921 3922 3923 3924 4229 4230 4231 4232 4233 4234 4235 4236 4237 4238 4239 4240 4241 4242 4243 4244 4245 4246 4247 4248

Jebel Sirbal

unavailable 3001 3002 3003 3004 3005 3006 3007 3008 3009 3010 3011 3012 3013 3014 3015 3016 3017 3018 3019 3020 3021 3022 3023 3024 3025 3026 3027 3028 3029 3030 3031 3032 3033 3034 3035 3036 3037 3038 3039 3040 3041 3042 3043 3044 3045 3046 3047 3048 3049 3050 3051 3052 3053 3054 3055 3056 3057 3058 3059 3060 3061 3062 3063 3064 3065 3066 3067 3068 3069 3070 3071 3072 3073 3074 3075 3076 3077 3078 3079 3080 3081 3082 3083 3084 3085 3086 3087 3088 3089 3090 3091 3092 3093 3094 3095 3096 3097 3098 3099 3100 3101 3102 3103 3104 3105 3106 3107 3108 3109 3110 3111 3112 3113 3114 3115 3116 3117 3118 3119 3120 3121 3122 3123 3124 3125 3126 3127 3128 3129 3130 3131 3132 3133 3134 3135 3136 3137 3138 3139 3140 3141 3142 3143 3144 3145 3146 3147 3148 3149 3150 3151 3152 3153 3154 3155 3156 3157 3158 3159 3160 3161 3162 3163 3164 3165 3166 3167 3168 3169 3170 3171 3172 3173 3174 3175 3176 3177 3178 3179 3180 3181 3182 3183 3184 3185 3186 3187 3188 3189 3190 3191 3192 3193 3194 3195 3196 3197 3198 3199 3200 3201 3202 3203 3204 3205 3206 3207 3208 3209 3210 3211 3212 3213 3214 3215 3216 3217 3218 3219 3220 3221 3222 3223 3224 3225 3226 3227 3228 3229 3230 3231 3232 3233 3234 3235 3236 3237 3238 3239 3240 3241 3242 3243 3244 3245 3246 3247 3248 3249 3250 3251 3252 3253 3254 3255 3256 3257 3258 3259 3260 3261 3262 3263 3264 3265 3266 3267 3268 3269 3270 3271 3272 3273 3274 3275 3276 3277 3278 3279 3280 3281 3282 3283 3284 3285 3286 3287 3288 3289 3290 3291 3292 3293 3294 3295 3296 3297 3298 3299 3300 3301 3302 3303 3304 3305 3306 3307 3308 3309 3310 3311 3312 3313 3314 3315 3316 3317 3318 3319 3320 3321 3322 3323 3324 3325 3326 3327 3328 3329 3330 3331 3332 3333 3334 3335 3336 3337 3338 3339 3340 3341 3342 3343 3344 3345 3346 3347 3348 3349 3350 3351 3352 3353 3354 3355 3356 3357 3358 3359 3360 3361 3362 3363 3364 3365 3366 3367 3368 3369 3370 3371 3372 3373 3374 3375 3376 3377 3378 3379 3380 3381 3382 3383 3384 3385 3386 3387 3388 3389 3390 3391 3392 3393 3394 3395 3396 3397 3398 3399 3400 3401 3402 3403

Wadi Shellal
unavailable 5618 5619 5620 5621 5623 5624 5625 5626 5627 5628 5629 5630 5632 5633 5635 5636 5652 5654 5657 5660 5663 5664 5669 5670 5671 5676 5679 5680 5681 5682 5683 5685 5686 5687 5690 5692 5693 5694 5697 5699 5700 5701 5703 5704 5705 5706 5711 5712 5713 5714 5715 5716 5717 5718 5719 5720 5721 5722 5723 5724 5725 5726 5727 5728 5730 5732 5733 5734 5735 5737 5738 5739 5740 5741 5742 5743 5744 5745 5746 5747 5748 5750 5751 5752 5753 5754 5755 5756 5757 5758 5759 5760 5761 5762 5763 5764 5767 5768 5769 5770 5771 5772 5773 5774 5775 5776 5777 5778 5779 5780 5781 5782 5783 5784 5785 5786 5787 5788 5789 5790 5791 5792 5794 5795 5796 5797 5798 5799 5800 5801 5802 5803 5804 5805 5806 5810 5811 5812 5813 5815 5816 5817 5818 5820 5821 5822 5823 5824 5825 5826 5827 5828 5829 5830 5831 5833 5834 5835 5836 5838 5839 5840 5841 5842 5843 5844 5845 5846 5847 5848 5849 5850 5852 5853 5854 5856 5857

Wadi Sulaf
unavailable 3947 3948 3949 3950 3951 3952 3953 3954 3955 3956 3957 3958 3959 3960 3961 3962 3963

Wadi Tueiba
unavailable 4623 4989 5015 5019 5026 5041 5353 5355 5357 5358

Wadi Umm Sidra
unavailable 5039 5040 5049 5050 5136 5140 5141 5148 5149 5344

Wadi Wata
unavailable 5884 5885 5886 5887 5888 5889 5901 5902 5923 5925 5928 5929 5930 5931

Old North Arabic inscriptions

Mt. Karkom
unavailable 5550 5555 5560

Nahal Avdat
unavailable 3549 5539

Qunteilat Ajrud
unavailable 5179

Sinai
unavailable 5368 5963 5984

Wadi Haggag
unavailable 5153

Wadi Mukatab
unavailable 3574 3579

Wadi Wata
unavailable 5897

Polish inscription

A-Tor
unavailable 4643

Russian inscriptions

A-Tor
1?85 5511
unavailable 4657 5503 5506

Church of the Holy Sepulchre
1895 5194

Church of the Nativity
unavailable 4273 4631 4635

Wadi Wata
unavailable 5890 5891 5892 5893

Spanish inscription

Church of the Nativity
991 4728

Syriac inscriptions

Church of the Holy Sepulchre
unavailable 4926

Church of the Nativity
unavailable 5422

unidentified inscriptions

A-Tor
unavailable 4651 4659 4682 5072 5195 5341 5348 5433 5436 5507 5510 5512 5513 5514 5518 5523 5532

Church of the Holy Sepulchre
unavailable 4928 5196 5482 5488 5489 5490 5495 5497 5590 5592 5593 5594 5595 5596 5598

Church of the Nativity

unavailable 4908 4919 4953 5036 5037 5077 5084 5193 5202 5217 5232 5330 5339 5394 5441 5443 5534 5865 5866 5880 5882 5934 5943 5947 5956 5960 5964
Umm Araq
unavailable 5617
Wadi Arade
unavailable 5364
Wadi Biraq
unavailable 4933 5012 5013 5014
Wadi Haggag
unavailable 4302 5067 5131 5152 5227 5228 5238
Wadi Mukatab
unavailable 5336
Wadi Shellal
unavailable 5644 5655 5656 5658 5662 5688 5698 5731 5736 5765 5858
Wadi Tueiba
unavailable 5025 5028 5033 5057 5354 5356 5389 5390
Wadi Umm Sidra
unavailable 5008 5150
Wadi Wata
unavailable 5895 5896 5922 5924 5927
wasems and other Bedouin marks
Nahal Avdat
unavailable 5538
Sinai
unavailable 5373
Wadi Umm Sidra
unavailable 5137

DATE DUE
